TALL TALES

The Glory Years of the NBA,
in the Words of the Men Who Played,
Coached, and Built Pro Basketball

TERRY PLUTO

A Fireside Book
Published by SIMON & SCHUSTER
New York   London   Toronto   Sydney   Tokyo   Singapore

FIRESIDE
Rockefeller Center
1230 Avenue of the Americas
New York, New York 10020

Copyright © 1992 by Terry Pluto

First Fireside Edition 1994

FIRESIDE and colophon are registered
trademarks of Simon & Schuster Inc.

Designed by Irving Perkins Associates, Inc.
Manufactured in the United States of America

10 9 8 7 6 5 4 3 2 1

Library of Congress Cataloging-in-Publication Data
Pluto, Terry, date.
    Tall tales/Terry Pluto.
        p.   cm.
    Includes index.
    1. National Basketball Association—History.   2. Basketball
players—United States.   I. Title.
GV885.515.N37P58 1992
796.323'64'0973—dc20   92–27476
                                                            CIP
ISBN: 0-671-74279-5
        0-671-89937-6 (Pbk.)

PHOTO CREDITS

AP/Wide World Photos, 22, 26; Courtesy of Gene Conley, 29, 30; Courtesy of Norm
Drucker, 16; Naismith Memorial Basketball Hall of Fame, 1, 3, 4, 5, 6, 7, 8, 12, 22, 23,
32; UPI/Bettmann, 2, 9, 10, 11, 13, 14, 15, 17, 18, 19, 20, 21, 24, 25, 28, 31, 33, 34.

The poems by Tom Meschery quoted herein are from the collection *Over the Rim*,
published by *McCall*, copyright © 1968, 1969, 1970 by Tom Meschery. Used by permission of the author.

To Roberta . . . who listened to all their stories.

CONTENTS

CAST OF CHARACTERS

MARV ALBERT: A former ballboy for the New York Knicks, he now broadcasts Knicks games for MSG Television and NBA games for NBC.

AL ATTLES: The former hard-nosed Warriors guard is now vice president of the Golden State Warriors.

RED AUERBACH: The Hall of Fame Celtics coach is now the team's president.

DON BARKSDALE: One of the NBA's first black players, he is in business in the Bay Area.

RICK BARRY: The Hall of Fame forward is now in broadcasting.

ELGIN BAYLOR: The Hall of Fame forward is the general manager of the L.A. Clippers.

ZELMO BEATY: The former star Hawks center is a financial consultant in Seattle.

AL BIANCHI: The former guard is a scout for the Miami Heat.

DANNY BIASONE: The former owner of the Syracuse Nats and father of the 24-second clock. He died in May of 1992.

MARTY BLAKE: The former Hawks GM is the NBA's director of scouting.

SID BORGIA: The former official is retired and lives in New York.

CARL BRAUN: The former Knicks guard had a highly successful career on Wall Street and now lives in Florida.

WILT CHAMBERLAIN: The Hall of Fame center owns Wilt Chamberlain's Restaurant in Boca Raton, Florida, and his latest book is *A View from Above.*

BARRY CLEMENS: The former forward is a stockbroker in Cleveland.

HASKELL COHEN: The former NBA public relations man still lives and works in New York.

GENE CONLEY: The former pitcher and Celtics center owns a small business and lives in Foxboro, Massachusetts.

LARRY COSTELLO: The former Syracuse guard is retired and lives in Florida.

BOB COUSY: The Hall of Fame guard does broadcasting work for the Celtics.

BILLY CUNNINGHAM: The Hall of Fame forward is president of the Miami Heat.

PETE D'AMBROSIO: The former official lives in Philadelphia.

NORM DRUCKER: The former official is retired and lives in Florida.

CHARLEY ECKMAN: The former official and Fort Wayne coach lives in Baltimore.

WAYNE EMBRY: The former center is general manager of the Cleveland Cavaliers.

BOB FERRY: The former center does broadcasting for NBC and still plays pickup basketball at the Naval Academy.

TOM GOLA: The Hall of Fame guard is a Philadelphia businessman.

RON GRINKER: A former mascot when Oscar Robertson played at the University of Cincinnati, he is a sports attorney based in Cincinnati.

JERRY GROSS: Former Hawks broadcaster is now a freelance broadcaster in San Diego.

RICHIE GUERIN: The former Knicks and Hawks guard is a New York businessman.

MATT GUOKAS: The former Sixers guard is coach of the Orlando Magic.

JOE GUSHUE: The former official lives in Philadelphia.

CLIFF HAGAN: The Hall of Fame forward lives in Lexington, Kentucky.

ALEX HANNUM: The veteran coach is in the construction business in northern California.

LESTER HARRISON: The former owner of the Rochester Royals is retired and still lives in Rochester.

JOHN HAVLICEK: The Hall of Famer lives in Weston, Massachusetts, and owns many businesses, including several Wendy's restaurants.

CHICK HEARN: Still does play-by-play for the Lakers.

TOM HEINSOHN: The Hall of Fame forward does broadcasting work for the Celtics.

KENNY HUDSON: The NBA's first black official does broadcasting work for the Celtics.

HOT ROD HUNDLEY: The former Lakers guard is a broadcaster for the Utah Jazz.

SAM JONES: The Hall of Fame guard lives in Washington, D.C.

BEN KERNER: The former owner of the St. Louis Hawks is retired and lives in St. Louis.

JOHNNY KERR: The former center is now a broacaster with the Chicago Bulls.

LEONARD KOPPETT: Veteran NBA sportswriter and author.

RUDY LaRUSSO: The former forward is a sports agent in L.A.

SLICK LEONARD: The former guard is a broadcaster for the Indiana Pacers.

EARL LLOYD: One of the early black players, he works for the Detroit Board of Education.

JIM LOSCUTOFF: The former Celtics forward lives in Andover, Massachusetts.

KEVIN LOUGHERY: The former guard is coach of the Miami Heat.

JERRY LUCAS: The Hall of Fame forward is in business in Middletown, Ohio.

ED MACAULEY: The Hall of Fame forward lives in St. Louis.

SLATER MARTIN: The Hall of Fame guard lives in Houston.

FRANK McGUIRE: The Hall of Fame coach lives in Columbia, South Carolina.

TOM MESCHERY: The forward turned poet lives in Truckee, California and teaches high school.

VINCE MILLER: Wilt Chamberlain's childhood friend lives in Philadelphia.

LEIGH MONTVILLE: Covered the 1969 playoffs for *The Boston Globe*. Now with *Sports Illustrated*.

DON NELSON: Former Boston forward, now coaches the Golden State Warriors.

PETE NEWELL: The Hall of Fame coach scouts for the Cleveland Cavs and lives in Palos Verdes, California.

BOB PETTIT: The Hall of Fame forward lives in New Orleans.

HARVEY POLLACK: The longtime Sixers PR man still produces the team's media guide.

FRANK RAMSEY: The Hall of Famer lives in Madisonville, Kentucky, where he owns a bank.

OSCAR ROBERTSON: The Hall of Fame guard is in business in Cincinnati.

BOB RYAN: Still a sportswriter with *The Boston Globe*.

SATCH SANDERS: The former forward works for the NBA as director of player relations.

FRED SCHAUS: The former Lakers coach is retired and lives in Morgantown, West Virginia.

DOLPH SCHAYES: The Hall of Fame forward is a businessman in Syracuse, New York.

CHARLIE SHARE: The former center is retired in St. Louis after a very successful business career.

BILL SHARMAN: The Hall of Fame guard is an advisor to the L.A. Lakers.

GENE SHUE: The ex-star guard is Player Personnel Director of the Philadelphia 76ers.

LARRY SIEGFRIED: Former Celtics guard, now lives in Toledo, Ohio.

LARRY STAVERMAN: The former forward is director of operations for the Cleveland Stadium.

EARL STROM: The former official is retired, and lives in Pottstown, Pennsylvania.

ROD THORN: The former guard is the NBA director of operations.

NATE THURMOND: The Hall of Fame center owns Big Nate's Barbeque in San Francisco.

JACK TWYMAN: The Hall of Fame forward owns the Super Foods grocery stores in Cincinnati.

JOHN VANAK: The former official is a private investigator in Lansford, Pennsylvania.

BUTCH VAN BREDA KOLFF: Former Lakers coach, now the coach at Hofstra University.

JERRY WEST: The Hall of Fame guard is general manager of the Los Angeles Lakers.

LENNY WILKENS: The Hall of Fame guard is coach of the Cleveland Cavs.

PAT WILLIAMS: The longtime NBA executive is president of the Orlando Magic.

GEORGE YARDLEY: The former forward is a successful businessman in Newport Beach, California.

I'm a baseball fan and history is an important part of baseball. Fans know about great players such as Ruth and Gehrig. They know about DiMaggio's 56-game hitting streak and Roger Maris's 61 home runs. But when it comes to basketball, fans act as if the game started with Larry Bird and Magic Johnson. They might remember Julius Erving, but they have no sense of history. Jerry West, Oscar Robertson, Elgin Baylor, Bill Russell and Wilt Chamberlain made the game great, but are almost forgotten. No one remembers that Boston won 11 titles in 13 years. No one remembers that Wilt Chamberlain was the most dominant player the game has ever seen. I tell people that Wilt once scored 100 points in a game and they say, "He did what?" People should know what Wilt and all these great players accomplished.

—Billy Cunningham

1

BEGINNINGS

Why Pro Basketball?

What we now know as the National Basketball Association came into existence in 1946 for three reasons:

1. Several young men on the make such as Ned Irish in New York and Walter Brown in Boston owned arenas and were making money from pro hockey. But hockey couldn't fill every open date in their buildings, so they needed another product to sell.

2. College basketball was popular and a good draw.

3. World War Two was over and the men were home, many of them with money in their pockets and the love of sports in their hearts. While the fans weren't demanding pro basketball, the men who owned the arenas would give it to them, whether they wanted it or not.

To play pro basketball in the late 1940s and early 1950s, you had to be tough. It didn't hurt if you had a couple of tattoos. The players were old GIs, and many of them had more eyes than teeth. They liked basketball, but they'd rather drink beer than play ball. And they'd rather fight than drink. Pro basketball merged all these interests: they played some ball, fought on the court, then went out for beer. If enough of the suds flowed, they got to fight again.

There was an infamous game between New York and Baltimore on March 26, 1949. The Knicks won in overtime, 103–99, to win the first round of the playoffs. Sound exciting? A close game, plenty at stake, and all of it played out at Madison Square Garden.

Well, all that was true—as far as it went.

But the crowd of about 10,000 saw a lot more than basketball. How about 100—yes, exactly 100—personal fouls? How about three full-blown fistfights? How about blood on the court and a three-hour game?

Back then, pro basketball wasn't exactly Fan-tas-tic.

But when they did get around to playing, the game wasn't all bad.

It was primitive, of course, unless your name was Joe Fulks, the Philadelphia star who made the jump shot famous. If you played basketball in the late 1940s and early 1950s, you probably shot a two-handed set shot.

And unless your name was Bobby Davies or Bob Cousy, you didn't dribble the ball behind your back or your coach would cut off both of your arms with a meat cleaver.

If you were a big man, you probably took a one-handed sweeping hook, from as far out as the top of the key. The hook is a terrific shot, nearly an impossible shot to block—at least until Bill Russell showed up in 1956. But taking this great shot from so far out is hard to explain since at this stage of the NBA, the lane was only six feet wide. (It became known as the "key" because with the wide foul circle on top of this narrow lane it resembled one.) A six-foot lane means just three feet of restricted space on either side of the basket; a big guy with an even bigger butt could station himself within four feet of the hoop and stand there all night—legally. How's that for getting inside position? Just ask George Mikan, who spent enough time in the lane to qualify to vote there. Still, most centers played 20 feet from the rim.

As for dunking—it was for doughnuts only. Even if a guy could dunk—and some of the early players could—it was only done during warmups to impress the crowd. Management liked that, but not the trick pulled by a Boston Celtic named Chuck Connors—yes, the same Chuck Connors who traded his shorts and sneakers for Hollywood cowboy boots and a rifle—who slammed on November 5, 1946. It was at Boston Garden and the Celtics had just installed a spanking-new basketball invention known as the glass backboard, only to learn it wasn't strong enough to take the beating Connors gave it. The 6-foot-7 forward from Seton Hall became the first man in basketball history to shatter a backboard with a dunk—even if it did happen in warmups. After that, players were still allowed to dunk in warmups, but only with care because glass backboards cost money. That is what the players—who earned about $3,000—always heard from the owners: "Hey, we can't do that, it costs money."

As for dunking in games, if you were of sane mind you just didn't do it. "Not unless you wanted to risk having someone tear your head off and hand it to you on the next play. Today, it's showtime. Back then, it was showing a guy up," said Alex Hannum, who started his long pro career in 1948.

So this was an elbows-out, feet-on-the-floor game. Nearly all of the rebounds were snared under the rim.

What the game did have in its favor were two crucial factors of basketball of any era and any level—ball movement and player movement.

The NBA of today often bogged down in "isolation" plays, where a player gets the ball on one side of the court and his four teammates head to the other side and watch him work 1-on-1. The early players would be appalled at this strategy, considering it selfish and self-destructive.

They believed in spreading out on the court and running. Often, the ball was thrown to a big man at the top of the key, and he would pass to cutters en route to the basket. If the cutter was covered, he simply threw the ball back out—remember, there was no 24-second clock—and the offense started all over again.

And these guys set picks. It was pick after pick after pick to free a shooter, the kind of picks that are a religious experience for most coaches to watch. While most of the final scores were in the 60s–70s and the shooting was usually under 40 percent, most of the shots taken were good ones, open ones and often very long ones. Some players would rather shoot from 30 feet—yes, 30 feet!—than three feet, even though no one had yet dreamed of a three-point shot. But the fear of set shooters with a soft touch was why nearly every coach preferred to play man-to-man defense, rather than a zone, which would allow the long-range gunners time to adjust their sights on the rim.

"I like the early pro game in its purest form," said veteran sportswriter Leonard Koppett. "It was much like the game we see in the women's NCAA tournament today. They can't jump three feet over the rim. They have to pass the ball, move, and they have great spacing. You didn't see all the players standing next to each other on the same part of the court."

In the early 1950s, the game changed—for the better.

"It was the influx of college stars," said Koppett. "They played a better, cleaner, more skilled brand of basketball as opposed to the guys who learned the game when they were in the service."

The names are at least vaguely familiar: Dolph Schayes, Bob Cousy, George Mikan, Carl Braun, Harry Gallatin, Ed Macauley, Slater Martin, Joe Fulks. Fulks was especially advanced, taking fallaway turnaround jumpers from 20 feet that were shot high enough to appear on radar screens. He was pro basketball's first 20-point scorer—when most guys couldn't score 10 if left alone in the gym for an hour. The very athletic Fulks also was 6-foot-5, the size of most early centers, who were more like clumsy cows than pivotmen.

The level of basketball these guys played was far ahead of their bosses, who had no idea how to run a pro league.

In the late 1940s, there were two pro leagues—the Basketball Association of America (BAA) and the National Basketball League (NBL). Games were being played in cities ranging from New York to Boston to Oshkosh to Anderson, Indiana. The NBA traces its roots to the BAA. And the BAA had its problems.

Consider its first playoffs in 1947. The league had two divisions, and the deep thinkers in the league office decided to have a playoff—with the first-place teams in each division meeting in the first round. The second-place teams also squared off, as did the third-place teams and the fourth-place teams. Talk about making the 60-game regular season meaningless; this setup insured that one of the division winners would not survive the first round.

The hockey influence was another problem. The arena operators would simply slap the wooden floor over ice. No insulation.

Some games were literally fogged out.

Other games were "rained out," as the ice melted and puddles appeared on the floor.

Some were nearly frozen out, since the arena operators would not turn on the heat in order to avoid melting the ice. Fans watched the games wrapped in blankets and players wore gloves on the bench.

After a few years, most of the ice-related ills were cured, but the average attendance was only about 3,000, about the same as the average salary. While the skill level improved every year, the games often were boorish and brutal, as a lot of players would still rather fight than swish a shot.

The owners had several brainstorms.

They originally went with a 48-minute game, eight minutes longer than the colleges to give the fans more buckets for the buck. Serious discussion was given to making it a 60-minute game—even more buckets for the buck—but someone realized that these games would probably last longer than some of their weak franchises, so the idea was scrapped.

They discussed "innings," with one team having the ball for two minutes, then the other team getting the ball for two minutes.

Another thought was to wait until the end of the quarter to shoot all the free throws to prevent the stoppages of action that came from all the fouls. They also would only shoot after fouls committed within 25 feet of the basket.

Mercifully, those ideas were rejected.

In 1949, a merger of the BAA and NBL was worked out and the

result was a wildly impractical 17-team league called the National Basketball Association. It included franchises in Waterloo, Iowa; Sheboygan, Wisconsin; and the Tri-Cities of Moline and Rock Island, Illinois, and Davenport, Iowa. The 17 teams were separated into three divisions, and scheduling was downright scary. Three of the teams played 62 games, four played 64 games and the rest played 68. The playoffs were an incomprehensible round-robin system.

Order finally began to come to the court in 1950, when the NBA was cut down to 11 teams with most of the tank towns eliminated. The shakedown continued, and by 1954 it was an eight-team league— Syracuse, New York, Boston and Philadelphia in the East; Fort Wayne, Minneapolis, Rochester and Milwaukee (soon to be St. Louis) in the West. Averaging over 5,000 fans, Syracuse was the top gate attraction in the early 1950s.

The NBA also made some other important moves. They integrated the league in 1950. They widened the lane from six to 12 feet in 1951 to prevent big men from clogging the middle.

But what may have saved the NBA was a scandal in college basketball and a decision that what the NBA needed was 24 seconds to shoot.

Fixing the NBA

When the NBA was being organized in 1950, college basketball was king. During the 1950–51 season, Knicks owner Ned Irish had only 18 home dates for his own NBA team; the rest of the time, Irish's Madison Square Garden was booked with top college games—a far better gate attraction than the struggling pro league. But in January of 1951, Manhattan College player Junius Kellogg told the Bronx District Attorney that he was approached by gamblers to shave points. This would be a major story, regardless of where it happened, but the fact that Kellogg spilled his guts in New York made it sound as if the foundation of the entire country was about to collapse, especially after the 10 New York dailies—yes, there were 10 newspapers—got through with the story. By the time the investigation was finished, it was revealed that 90 college games between 1947 and 1951 were fixed, with 33 players from six different colleges implicated. Several New York University and City College of New York players were also implicated, which kept the

New York papers busy for months. Two others were former Kentucky stars Ralph Beard and Alex Groza, who were with Indianapolis of the NBA when the scandal broke. They were banned from the NBA.

Meanwhile, the NBA came out of this looking relatively clean. The best publicity came from the fact that the Knicks had a strong team; they never won the NBA title, but they reached three straight Finals from 1951–53, George Mikan and Minneapolis beating them the last two times. The Knicks' weakness was a lack of a center to handle the 6-foot-10 Mikan. But that made their defeats almost noble—David vs. Goliath in the New York papers. Since the Knicks were New York's team, and since they were successful with such popular players as Dick McGuire, Carl Braun, Ernie Vandeweghe and Sweetwater Clifton, they received reams of positive press. Positive press in New York tends to mean positive press everywhere; that enhanced the image of the young NBA just as college basketball was engaged in serious damage control and praying the scandals would finally end. But the NBA remained on perilous ground. The league could not afford a scandal of its own.

LEONARD KOPPETT: For the NBA, the college basketball scandals could not have come at a better time. The scandals knocked the dominance of college basketball out of Madison Square Garden and other arenas, opening up more dates for the pros. The scandals forced Ned Irish to say, "Hey, the NBA is going to be the heart of my business." As the investigation went on and names were named, the NBA basically came through unscathed.

GEORGE YARDLEY: The only NBA player who was caught fixing games was Jack Molinas, who was my teammate in 1953 in Fort Wayne. We both were rookies, but I never knew that he was dealing with bookmakers. Neither did the guys who lived with him. They said Jack was on the phone a lot, but that was the only clue. I did hear that a couple of our other players may have been involved, but I never knew that for a fact. I know that no one approached me. I did hear that whatever fixing was done on the defensive end of the court. You just let your man score. Was it bad defense or did you simply let your man drive by you? How would anyone know the difference?

[The league got wind of Molinas's activity 29 games into his rookie season and the 6-foot-6 forward was suspended. He was also playing well, averaging 12 points and 8.2 rebounds in 32 minutes per game. Molinas later was involved in a college point-shaving scandal in the 1960s.]

CHARLEY ECKMAN: When I was hired to coach Fort Wayne in 1954, our owner [Fred Zollner] was convinced that a couple of our other players were on the take because they had been friends with Molinas. We had detectives follow them at home and on the road and we checked their phone records. Molinas was an out-and-out bad guy, and Zollner was worried that his influence had rubbed off on the other players. Finally, Zollner forced me to trade Mel Hutchins and Monk Meineke because they had been friends with Molinas. The detectives had nothing on those guys, but Zollner said, "I don't care, I want them out." This shows how sensitive and on guard the NBA was to gambling.

ALEX HANNUM: After seeing what had happened to all the college players who were caught in the scandals, the NBA guys were scared of gamblers. The owners told us, "You hang around with gamblers, you're through. No questions asked." The Molinas case proved their point. Other than Molinas, I don't believe that any pro player bet on games.

[In 24 Seconds to Shoot, *Leonard Koppett reported that an official named Sol Levy was fired during the 1952–53 season when it was learned that he had accepted $3,000 in bribes to fix three NBA games in 1950. The Molinas and Levy cases are the only two reported cases of fixing games in NBA history.]*

GEORGE YARDLEY: When it came to gambling, the fans were a different story. Especially the fans in New York. The biggest cheer would come when someone broke the point spread on the last shot of the game. When you played the Knicks at Madison Square Garden, about half the fans would cheer at the strangest times because they were more concerned about the point spread than the final score.

ALEX HANNUM: In my first game at Madison Square Garden, we were up by eight points over the Knicks and the fans yelled like hell. Then the score was tied, and the place was quiet. We later learned the point spread was eight. We also sensed that our salaries were being paid indirectly by the gamblers because a lot of the fans buying tickets were there to bet on the games.

JOHNNY KERR: Between games of the doubleheaders, the fans would meet under the Garden stands and they'd come out and yell, "Hey, we doubled our bets on you schmucks, so you better beat the spread." But no one came to us to fix a game or anything like that.

LEONARD KOPPETT: With the college scandals, the NBA saw an opportunity to capture the basketball fans, and one of the first attempts to do so was the 1951 All-Star Game. The league could show that while the college game was in turmoil, they were able to get the greatest players in the world on one court.

HASKELL COHEN: In the early 1950s, the NBA was considered such a small sport, probably fifth behind baseball, football, college basketball and boxing. I was hired as the NBA's public relations director in 1951 by Commissioner Maurice Podoloff. Maurice and I were the league office. We had no staff, just a few secretaries.

One day, Podoloff, [Boston owner] Walter Brown and I were sitting in the office, trying to come up with an idea to get some attention.

I said, "Why not an All-Star Game? Baseball does it and people like it."

Brown said, "I really like that idea. I'll host the game in Boston and make sure things are done right."

This was important, because no one knew if fans would buy tickets for an All-Star Game. So Walter Brown was giving us some security. In fact, the first two All-Star Games were in Boston because Walter Brown was the one owner who really wanted them.

LEONARD KOPPETT: The fans were somewhat intrigued by the game. *[The first two All-Star Games drew slightly over 10,000 at Boston Garden.]* But within the basketball community, there was tremendous excitement. What would happen when all these great players were on the court at the same time? Now, that's so commonplace that fans are almost tired of all-star games. Back then, it was a dazzling spectacle, especially since these players were able to blend their talents quickly and play some great basketball.

HASKELL COHEN: When we were organizing the first game, I told Maurice Podoloff that we should give the players gifts.

Podoloff said, "What do you have in mind?"

I said, "Maybe a pin or a ring."

He said, "Whatever it is, don't spend more than $2.25 each."

We later were able to cut a deal with a local store and each of the players received a television set.

CHARLEY ECKMAN: Podoloff was a small, round man who was a great administrator but knew nothing about basketball. He loved the sound of his own voice and had a million-dollar vocabulary. We called him Poodles Podoloff.

LESTER HARRISON: The NBA was so small and operated on such a short shoestring that we won the title in Rochester and the league couldn't afford to buy a championship trophy.

The league also didn't understand the power of television. Our first television contract [in the 1952–53 season] was with DuMont, an independent network. We didn't sell our stars like they do today. In fact, we put our worst games on because we feared that if we broadcast the best games, no one would buy a ticket. They'd all stay home and watch it for free. So what the public saw was the worst of pro basketball.

HASKELL COHEN: That contract with DuMont was 13 games for $39,000—or $3,000 per game. The next year, we moved to NBC and the deal was worth over $100,000—which was divided equally among the teams.

LEONARD KOPPETT: The NBA never had a significant revenue-producing TV contract in the 1950s. As the league got out of the small towns—Rochester to Cincinnati; Fort Wayne to Detroit; Syracuse to Philadelphia; and Minneapolis to L.A.—the interest of television networks grew. But there were arguments. The networks wanted the games on Saturday afternoons, but Saturday nights drew better. So some teams didn't want to be on national television because it hurt their gate. There was a lot of shortsighted thinking.

The Ultimate Slowdown

The best basketball team on the earth in the early 1950s was the Minneapolis Lakers. They had 6-foot-10 George Mikan in the middle, the man who set the standard for centers in the first half of this century. While Mikan wore glasses and had all the grace of a bison in rutting season, he also was a fierce competitor and had a surprisingly soft hook shot. When he did miss, he had the tenacity and strength to pursue his own rebound, and no one could keep him off the boards. But the Lakers were more than Mikan. They had a Hall of Fame point guard in Slater Martin, who lived to get the ball to big men. Jim Pollard may have been the most athletic of any forward in the early 1950s. In practice, he put on dazzling dunking displays. Vern Mikkelsen was the consummate power forward. The Lakers were loaded, winning titles in 1949, 1950, 1952, 1953 and 1954. Teams were willing to try anything to offset their talent, but no one went to such an extreme as Fort Wayne. Not every game before the 24-second clock was like Fort Wayne's 19–18 victory over the Minneapolis Lakers on November 22, 1950. Most final scores were in the 70s and 80s, with a 100-point outburst not that rare. But the fact that a 19–18 game could happen—that two NBA teams could play 48 minutes and combine for only 31 shots—was frightening. There were only eight field goals; Mikan had all four field goals for Minneapolis and 15 of their 18 points as no other Laker attempted more than two shots. The fourth-quarter score was Fort Wayne 3, Lakers 1.

The second game that indicated the NBA had major rule problems came only two weeks after the 19–18 game. It was a five-overtime clash between Rochester and Indianapolis in which the team that got the opening jump ball in each of the five overtime periods held on to the ball for the last shot. Everyone just stood around until the final seconds of the five-minute period.

The league's biggest problems were stalling and fouling in the fourth quarter. The team that was ahead would hold the ball and not shoot it, and the team that was behind would foul because that was the only way to get possession of the ball. Because of the constant fouling, officials were told by the league to ignore contact and keep the game moving. Since many of the NBA teams were also owned by hockey people, some powers in the league office insisted that a brawl was good for both the heart and the gate. This became a license to mug, and basketball was starting to look dangerously like hockey.

Things came to a head on March 20, 1954, in a nationally televised game between New York and Boston. The final score was 79–78 in favor of the Celtics, and the game lasted three hours and five minutes. The television audience never saw the last minute of play. After broadcasting three hours—including 45 foul-marred minutes of the fourth quarter—the TV people had had enough and cut away before the issue was settled, their point being, "Who wants to watch a bunch of guys shoot free throws?"

LEONARD KOPPETT: All you had to do was watch an NBA game before the 24-second clock and you realize that playing basketball for high stakes without a clock is impossible. People just assume that the pro game has always been the way it is today. Everything fell into place after the 24-second clock, but before the 1954–55 season and the clock, there were major changes in the rules every year to try and correct the basic fact that once you were ahead in the game, you could legally hold on to the ball as long as you wanted. The 19–18 game was the classic example.

SLATER MARTIN: The night before the 19–18 game, we had played Fort Wayne on their court and beat the devil out of them. The next night, the game moved to our home court in Minneapolis. We had a great team with George Mikan, Jim Pollard and Vern Mikkelsen. Playing a normal game, Fort Wayne knew it had no chance.

FRED SCHAUS: Murray Mendenhall was our coach and Minneapolis had beaten us a lot. Mikan was such a dominant force, we were at a loss when it came to stopping him. So Murray said, "Let's try something different. We have good guards, so let's see if we can pull their big people away from the basket. Let's spread the floor and see what happens."

We did not go into the game figuring the final score would be something like 19–18. We just thought we'd open in a stall for a few minutes, slow down the tempo and then it would be a regular game. But we got in front by a few points, we pulled our offense out and they just stood under the basket, refusing to come out and guard us. Since we were ahead, we just held the ball and tried to shorten the game by taking fewer shots.

SLATER MARTIN: We were ahead [13–11] at halftime, but Fort Wayne still wouldn't play normal basketball. We tried to press them a couple of times, but their guards would break our press and then they'd still hold the ball instead of taking a layup.

FRED SCHAUS: I played the whole game and took only one shot. John Oldham took most of our shots—five—and we called him the Gunner.

SLATER MARTIN: The fans hated it. They booed for a while. Then they gave up and started reading newspapers.

FRED SCHAUS: After a while, they started throwing the newspapers and other garbage on the floor. They really bombarded our coach.

SLATER MARTIN: After the game, the fans wanted their money back and I didn't blame them.

FRED SCHAUS: We won the game when Larry Foust hit a shot at the final gun. Even though we won, we never played another game like that. Everyone knew that kind of basketball would kill the league.

DANNY BIASONE: A more common problem was like a game in 1951 between us [Syracuse] and Boston. Auerbach's team got ahead by four points with about eight minutes left. Cousy was trying to dribble out the clock and we fouled him. The Celtics didn't attempt one field goal in the final eight minutes and we didn't make any of our shots.

ALEX HANNUM: If you saw a game before the 24-second clock, it was like a good college women's game today. The floor was spread, the ball moved around and the main shot was a set shot or a hook. But it was very physical, especially in the last quarter when the stalling began. Then we'd just clobber guys. I was as guilty as anyone of that because when I played, I was correctly labeled a hatchet man.

GENE SHUE: The set shots were taken from incredible range, well beyond the NBA three-point line of today. The game progressed from the two-handed set shot, to the one-handed set shot along with sweeping hook shots that were taken from 15–18 feet. Guards took what I call a "flying hook shot," where you'd be at the top of the key, take one or two dribbles toward the basket, but slightly angling to the side, and then take the hook off the run and bank it in. Cousy loved this shot. Joe Fulks was the first pro to take what we now consider a jump shot, and it took a while but other players started using it. So the game was developing nicely on one level, but the stalling and fouling had everyone worried.

FRED SCHAUS: It was a classic case of the coaches being ahead of the rules. Possession—not scoring—became the most important part of the game down the stretch. The owners got together and came up with new rules limiting fouls per period, jump balls after foul shots and things like that, but the coaches just found ways to beat them.

NORM DRUCKER: As an official, the pressure was on you at the end of the game not to call fouls. But when a team was behind, they'd nearly decapitate a guy to get a whistle. If you didn't call something, you'd have a riot. I remember one year, they would let the team with the ball keep possession instead of taking a foul shot. All that did was lead to more stalling and more fouling. Once, we had a center jump after each foul in the final three minutes—you had to jump against the defender who usually guarded you, not the one who fouled you. This led to a lot of arguments about who was supposed to be guarding whom.

SLATER MARTIN: The owners were so concerned about the state of the game that we even had an exhibition game on a 12-foot basket [ordinarily 10-foot]. This was supposed to stop the big man, specifically Mikan, from taking over the game. I'm 5-foot-10 and with me shooting at a 12-foot basket, I couldn't get the ball up that high. There were no such things as layups or tip-ins. A higher basket makes it even harder for a little man to score and a 12-foot basket would have sent the game back to the stone age. It also didn't address the trouble we were having with fouling at the end of the game.

[Rule changes in the early 1950s:
   1950–51: A jump ball after each foul shot in the last three minutes of the game.
   1951–52: A jump ball after each foul shot in the last two minutes, and the lane was widened from six to 12 feet. In the jump ball, the player who committed the foul jumped against the man who was fouled. This led to big guys trying to foul little guys.
   1952–53: The jump ball in the final two minutes was between the players who were normally matched up, which put a burden on the officials to decide who was supposed to be guarding whom.
   1953–54: Players were allowed only two fouls per quarter. If the player committed a third foul in the quarter, he was disqualified from the game.]

DANNY BIASONE: For a year, no one would listen to me. I said forget all these different rules about fouling, what we need is a time limit. Make them shoot the ball and we'd be all right. After they tried about everything else, they were willing to look at my idea.

Twenty-four Seconds That Saved the Game

The NBA played without a shot clock for its first nine seasons before Danny Biasone's idea of 24 seconds to shoot was adopted at the NBA's summer meetings in 1954. Other key rule changes were six fouls per team per quarter—after that, every foul meant two free throws. If the player was fouled in the act of shooting, he would receive three opportunities to make two free throws. If a player was "intentionally fouled in the backcourt," he would receive two free throws. In the last season before the clock, teams averaged 79 points per game. In the first year with the 24-second clock, the average was 93 points. After four years with the clock, it was 107 points. By 1959–60, the average was 115 points, with Boston scoring 124 per game.

DOLPH SCHAYES: Most people forget that Danny Biasone was the Wilbur Wright of basketball. Because he invented the 24-second clock, the game took off. Yet, he was a man who never played the game.

JOHNNY KERR: Danny was a small Italian guy. He wore long, double-breasted coats, Borsalino hats and smoked filter cigarettes. As he talked, he left the cigarette in his mouth and bit down on the filter. He made his money not in basketball, but at his bowling alley—Eastwood Recreation Center in Syracuse. He sat on the bench during games, usually next to the coach, with that cigarette clenched between his teeth. He'd yell at the officials, but seldom said anything to his coach during the games.

DANNY BIASONE: I had been in the bowling buiness since 1941—I had 10 lanes upstairs and a restaurant downstairs. I owned a semipro football team before World War Two. After the war, I didn't have enough guys to play football on my team. But I did for basketball, even though I didn't know a thing about the game. Lester Harrison had a good basketball team in Rochester. There's a natural rivalry between Rochester and Syracuse, so I wanted to play Rochester. They were in the National Basketball League—they wouldn't play us. I said I'd pay them $500 for a game. They still wouldn't do it. I raised my offer to $1,000. No soap. So I called the National Basketball League and told

them about it. They said for $1,000, I could be in their league and then
Harrison would have to play me. I sent them $1,000 and I owned a pro
basketball team for the 1946–47 season. So I got into the game by
accident. But I found I loved it. I studied it, and I hated seeing how
the fouling was destroying it.

I started talking about a time limit on possessions around 1951, after
the 19–18 game. I said baseball has three outs an inning, football has
four downs, every game has a limit on possessions except basketball.
Finally, I sold the idea to Maurice Podoloff. I said, let's have the 1954
summer meetings in Syracuse and I'll put on a game with a clock so
we can see how it works.

CHICK HEARN: The amazing thing about the 24-second clock is that
it started at 24 seconds and still is 24 seconds today. No one has seriously
considered changing it.

DANNY BIASONE: Now that I had this idea for a clock, I had to decide,
"How much time?" I looked at the box scores from the games I enjoyed,
games where they didn't screw around and stall. I noticed each team
took about 60 shots. That meant 120 shots per game.

So I took 48 minutes—2,880 seconds—and divided that by 120 shots.
The result was 24 seconds per shot.

That was it—24 seconds.

But I said it didn't have to be 24 seconds. It could be 30, 20, whatever—just something. But everyone said, "Danny, it's your idea, you
want 24, let's try 24."

DOLPH SCHAYES: Danny got together some of us pros who lived in
Syracuse and some local college and high school players for an exhibition game. It was held at a local high school.

HASKELL COHEN: We were going to have a game with a 24-second
clock, but no one had a clock. I always had a good wristwatch, so I
said I'd keep the time with my second hand. When the 24 seconds were
up, I'd just yell "Time." There were very few violations.

DOLPH SCHAYES: When the game started, we thought we had to take
quick shots—a pass and a shot was it—maybe 8–10 seconds. That made
for a bad game with a lot of dumb shots and turnovers. But as the game
went on, we saw the inherent genius in Danny's 24 seconds—you could
work the ball around for a good shot. During the game, Danny would

tell us, "Twenty-four seconds is a long time, take your time out there." He had complete confidence in his formula.

DANNY BIASONE: A month after that exhibition game, Podoloff polled every owner by phone and they all voted in favor of the 24-second clock. But they weren't positive it would work until we tried it out in the exhibition season. Since no one wanted to spend money for shot clocks that you might not need a month later, the time was kept by someone with a stopwatch sitting at press row during the exhibition games. Once the regular season started, the league bought shot clocks.

HASKELL COHEN: There were few—if any—complaints about the 24-second clock. It was immediately accepted and it gave us the kind of game we wanted for years—no endless stalling and fouling.

DOLPH SCHAYES: There weren't any real problems for the players. We liked it and there is something about 24 seconds that is just right for pro basketball.

NORM DRUCKER: I don't want to take anything away from Danny Biasone because the clock was a brilliant idea, but I think the players are such remarkable athletes that they could adjust to almost any time frame—20 seconds, 30 seconds, maybe even 16 seconds.

BILL SHARMAN: Once the idea of a 24-second clock was mentioned, I favored a 30-second clock, which we later used in both the American Basketball League and the American Basketball Association. I thought that gave the offense time for a couple more passes and more strategy. But as a player during that era, I was just grateful that they came up with some kind of clock.

GENE SHUE: Once the shot clock came in, the game was speeded up and it played into the hands of teams with good athletes. Within a few years, you had the clock, the use of the jump shot and the emergence of the black player in the league. All of this put the emphasis on the running game. The pieces of what we now see as the NBA were falling into place. Red Auerbach was the first to recognize this trend and he built a running team around Bill Russell. The great Celtics teams took advantage of Danny Biasone's 24-second clock.

EARL STROM: A number of years ago, I officiated a game in Syracuse.

I got together with Paul Seymour, Dolph Schayes and Larry Costello and we went to see Danny Biasone, who still owned the bowling alley then. I asked about the original 24-second clock and Danny said he still had it. We went into his office at the bowling alley and there it was.

I said, "Danny, this thing should be in the Hall of Fame."

He said, "It goes into the Hall of Fame when I go in."

Danny has a great point—he should be in.

DANNY BIASONE: Ah, I decided I won't live forever and the Hall of Fame wanted the clock, so a few years ago I gave it to them. Why the hell not? At least part of me is there.

2
WHEN SMALL TOWNS STOOD TALL

SYRACUSE

Syracuse brings back memories
of the NBA in its middleweight years.
It was a city with a bloody nose
and a swollen eye.
It had taken too many left hooks.
I remember the apprehension
as I stepped into its arena
and for the first time
the blows came from all angles—
a left of Kerr, a right of Costello,
an uppercut of Greer or Bianchi,
and the midsection with Walker and Gambee.
Eight, nine, ten—the best
middleweight around.

—TOM MESCHERY

While the New York newspapers—and the NBA office—wanted the New York Knicks to be the center of the basketball universe, the small towns were taking over the league in the middle 1950s. After the Knicks lost to Minneapolis in the 1953 Finals, they would not return to the Finals until 1970. And no franchise took more delight in the demise of the Knicks than the Syracuse Nationals.

People in New York viewed Syracuse as nothing more than an overgrown truck stop somewhere near the Arctic Circle. As Knicks owner Ned Irish said, "Do you know how bad it is to see the Knicks vs. Syracuse on the marquee at Madison Square Garden?" The 250,000 folks in Syracuse knew that the snobs of New York felt that way, which turned the Nats-Knicks games into holy wars.

New York had its theater, television and every conceivable pro franchise. Syracuse had one thing that made it special: the Nats. The town embraced the Nats the way it does the Syracuse University Orangemen today. Passions run deep when you're the only show in town.

In 1954, Syracuse nearly won the NBA title, losing to Minneapolis in seven games. The lack of a 24-second clock and the incessant fouling and stalling continued to plague the game. During the 1953–54 regular season, the Nats averaged 83.5 points. In the Finals, they were down to 70 points a night. Sure, the Lakers' defense had something to do with that, but as the games grew in importance, coaches became more conservative. That meant fewer shots and a willingness to take a small lead and try to dribble out the clock.

Then two things happened that led to Syracuse becoming the 1955 champions. First, Mikan retired. In the Lakers' 87–80 victory over Syracuse in Game 7 of the 1954 Finals, Mikan scored only 11, and was a dismal 2-of-11 from the field against a team that was searching for a center. Minneapolis pulled the game out because forward Jim Pollard did his Kangaroo Kid act for 21 points, Slater Martin was a steady influence at the point and scored 12, and a rookie named Clyde Lovellette came off the bench to toss in a dozen points. Mikan was 32, and even through his horn-rimmed glasses he could see that the Lakers' center of the future was the 6-foot-9 Lovellette. So after winning five titles in six years, Mikan stepped aside.

That was factor No. 1 that favored Syracuse.

Then came the summer of 1954, and the adoption of Syracuse owner Danny Biasone's 24-second clock. Biasone also drafted a mobile big man from Illinois named Johnny Kerr, who would fit in perfectly with the new up-tempo game that resulted from 24 seconds to shoot.

With the clock fueling the action, Boston averaged 101.4 points in the regular season. But the Celtics—one year away from Bill Russell—gave up 101.5. The Nats had the tightest defense in the league, but still gave up 89.7.

Syracuse had a terrific team. Dolph Schayes was a Larry Bird forerunner at forward. Paul Seymour and George King were shrewd, gritty guards. Kerr brought a sweeping hook shot and a remarkable knack for high-post passing to the center position. Earl Lloyd and Red Rocha were fierce, physical power forwards.

But another small town was rising—Fort Wayne, of all places. The Zollner Pistons were coached by a former official; with cigar-chomping

Charley Eckman rolling out the basketballs and patting his players on the butt, Fort Wayne won the Western Division with a 43-29 record. Syracuse was the elite of the East, also 43-29.

These two teams collided in the Finals. Yes, they were basketball's best, but that still didn't stop a lot of people—especially those powerful snobs in New York City—from asking, "How can the NBA be a big-league sport when Fort Wayne and Syracuse are in the Finals?"

Of course, the answer was that they beat out the Knicks, but the truth hurt.

Adding to the NBA's Little League national image was that Fort Wayne could not get into its own building for the Finals; it had been taken over by a pro bowling tournament. The New York wise guys had fun with that.

So Fort Wayne set up shop in Indianapolis. The Pistons were an impressive team. In the middle was Larry Foust, 6-foot-9 and listed at 250 pounds. Let's just say he wore the biggest pants in the league and he was a throwback to the huge, plodding dinosaur centers of the early Mikan Era. Surrounding the stationary Foust were two runner-and-jumper forwards in George Yardley and Mel Hutchins. The backcourt was experienced with a three-guard rotation of Max Zaslofsky, Andy Phillip and Frank Brian.

The series opened with Fort Wayne never having won a game in Syracuse in NBA history. The Pistons' record was 0-24, and after the first two games of the series it was 0-26. With the clock and Mikan's exit working in their favor, the Nats fans were convinced the 1955 title would be theirs. How could they miss? Surely former Nats guard Al Cervi would outcoach the novice Eckman in a seven-game series.

But when the series moved to Fort Wayne's "homecourt" in Indianapolis, the Pistons won all three games. Suddenly the Nats needed to win both games in Syracuse. It became a gunfight between Schayes and Yardley, Yardley prevailing 31–28 but the Nats winning the game, 109–108. That set up Game 7 in Syracuse. Consider that both teams led the league with 43 regular-season victories. They were 3-3 in the playoff Finals, so they couldn't be any closer. Often, a seventh game under these circumstances doesn't live up to expectations, but this one did. With a minute left, the score was 91–91. It stayed that way until 12 seconds remained, when the Nats' George King made a free throw. Then King stole the ball from the Pistons and Syracuse had a 92–91 win and its first—and last—NBA title. King led the Nats with 15 points and was the only member of his team to make half his field goal attempts. The Nats shot 33 percent from the field, including 4-of-18 by Schayes, *but prevailed because they scored 15 more points at the foul line. They also had a 55–44 rebounding advantage, with Kerr and Schayes snaring 11 each.*

DOLPH SCHAYES: Syracuse had a wonderful small-town feel to it. When you played for the Nats, the whole town embraced you, like Green Bay does with the Packers or Portland with the Blazers. We thought of ourselves as the underdog, the little guy taking on the big city. Our arena had only 6,400 seats and the fans were right on top of you.

AL BIANCHI: The best thing we had going for us was the weather. Visiting teams would get off the plane and be up to their asses in snow. The temperature would be 10 below.They'd walk into our building and our fans would get all over them. We beat many teams before the opening tip.

DOLPH SCHAYES: The weather was a factor. Syracuse winters are cold. Our fans were rabid and we had a very good team and a very physical team. At times, our homecourt advantage was overwhelming.

JOE GUSHUE: It would start snowing in Syracuse in October and you wouldn't see the pavement again until May.

NORM DRUCKER: You'd go to Syracuse and the fans knew you were there—and I'm speaking as an official. You'd be having bacon and eggs in the hotel coffee shop and some guy would stop by and say, "You're Drucker, right? You screwed us last time, don't do it again."

Then you'd step on the court and look at the Syracuse bench and there was Danny Biasone. Young officials would point to him and say, "Who's that guy?"

I'd say, "He owns the team."

Then I could see a lump in the official's throat. He was thinking, "I better not mess up or this guy will be on the phone to my boss."

EARL STROM: Danny was bald. He didn't say a lot to you during a game, but he'd glare when you made a call he didn't like. If he thought you really blew one, he'd snicker and that could make you feel stupid. But for years, Danny was on the bench, right next to his coach, be it Paul Seymour, Al Cervi or Alex Hannum.

JOHNNY KERR: Danny knew he didn't have to talk to the officials. Just his presence, that cigarette hanging from his mouth and the fact that everyone knew he invented the 24-second clock made him someone to be respected, even feared by officials.

DANNY BIASONE: One day [Knicks owner] Ned Irish told me that it looked bad for a team owner to be on the bench. He pushed through a rule that only coaches could sit on the bench, so I said no problem, I appointed myself assistant coach. The only reason I wanted to be on the bench was that I used to have some player-coaches. When they were on the court, I could keep track of the fouls and time-outs and make sure that the guys on the bench watched the game instead of messing around.

DOLPH SCHAYES: Danny never tried to coach the team. He left the Xs and Os to Cervi or Hannum or whoever. He didn't talk to the players during time-outs or make substitutions. The thing about Danny was that the team was his life. He owned a bowling alley and he made a little money there, but this was when the NBA was in its infancy, and there was little money for anyone. While he was around all the time, he didn't get in the way. We trusted him and we sensed his love of the game, his dedication to making basketball work in Syracuse. In the middle 1950s, there was a season when I averaged over 20 points and made the All-Star team. Danny called me in and said, "I know it's not fair, but I have to cut your salary $1,000. I have to cut everybody or else we can't operate." I took the cut, and at the end of that season he gave me a check for that thousand dollars.

SID BORGIA: It is true that Danny had the reputation among players and officials as being one of the most honest and understanding of all the NBA owners. People tell me that he was good because he didn't say much on the bench. In that building, he didn't have to. Officials deserved combat pay for working in Syracuse. Those fans were so crazy and they never believed their team did anything wrong.

JOHNNY KERR: Another reason that Danny didn't have to say anything was that [coach] Al Cervi could work the crowd. When a call went against us, he'd turn his back to the court, face the fans, raise his hands to the heavens as if to say, "Why is God punishing us with these officials?" Then the crowd would take over and shower the court with popcorn boxes and orange juice cartons.

EARL STROM: Their public address announcer was the worst. I'd work a Syracuse-Philly game. I'm from Pottstown, Pennsylvania, which is not a suburb of Philadelphia. But in Syracuse, they'd introduce me as "Earl Strom from Philadelphia." Right away, the crowd is on my butt. "What's a guy from Philly calling this game for?" Syracuse would commit their sixth foul of the period and the guy would say, "For Syracuse, that's six team fouls. Philadelphia has only one." Again, the house would come down on you. Sid Borgia would get so upset, he'd rush to the press table and scream at the PA guy to cut that crap out. It would stop them, but only for a while.

JOHN VANAK: Syracuse knew that it was tough to call fouls on them at home. They had guys like Al Bianchi, who just loved to flatten people. Al would knock a player on his ass and almost dare you to call a foul on him and take the heat from the crowd. Back then, there were no flagrant fouls. A guy could drive the lane, Al could hammer him, they would have to call an ambulance and it would still be only two shots.

AL BIANCHI: Against the good teams, our games were wars. Boston . . . boy, we always had great fights with them.

JOHN VANAK: There was a game where Jim Loscutoff grabbed Dolph Schayes by the throat with about two minutes left. They both fell down, and the next thing I knew fans were spilling out of the stands. We had a riot on our hands and it took a good half hour before we got the floor cleared and finished the game.

FRANK RAMSEY: The Syracuse fans were out of control. They'd throw cups full of Coke, programs, even batteries at you. That place was a hockey arena with sideboards. On the night of the big fight between Dolph and Loscutoff, the fans knocked over those hockey boards to get on the court and some of the fans were hurt when they ended up under the boards. It was like a stampede.

AL BIANCHI: There was a night when the Syracuse fans tried to storm the Boston dressing room. The players slammed the doors on a few hands, breaking their fingers. Another time, the Celtics were walking off the court after a game with a police escort. A fan dumped a beer on a Boston player.

The Celtic said to the cop, "Did you see that?"

The cop said, "Yeah, and you deserved it."

JOHN VANAK: The same kind of thing happened to Joe Gushue. He was leaving the court and a fan whacked him over the head with a rolled-up newspaper.

Joe told the cop, "Did you see that?"

The cop said, "The way you called the game, no one saw anything."

GENE CONLEY: Oh, their fans . . . you'd stand at the foul line and they'd throw candy bars at you. The guys on the bench got bombarded the most.

FRANK RAMSEY: There was a night the stuff being thrown at us was so bad that the officials told all of our subs to leave the bench and stay in the dressing room—for our own safety. The coach was out there alone. When Red Auerbach wanted to make a substitution, he had to stop the game. He'd send the player who was coming out into the dressing room with the message of who Red wanted as a replacement.

GENE CONLEY: Poor Frank Ramsey. To get off the court, you had to walk through a tunnel that went through the stands. The fans were all over us and one of them grabbed Frank around the neck and was strangling him. I punched the guy or Frank would have choked.

NORM DRUCKER: They had a fan called the Strangler. He was about 5-foot-6, maybe 220 pounds with a tremendous chest and arms. He'd run up and down the sidelines during the game and stand next to a player, screaming, "You SOB, you stink."

EARL STROM: If I had to guess, it probably was the Strangler who grabbed Ramsey. That fan got his name when he picked up Charley Eckman at halftime and had poor Charley hanging by the neck. Gene Conley hated that guy. One night, we were walking off the court and Gene saw the Strangler. Gene said, "When we get near that guy, duck." We got close. The Strangler reached down from the stands to grab me, I ducked and Conley drilled the guy, knocking his lights out with one punch.

NORM DRUCKER: The Strangler loved to run up to the Celtics' huddle and yell things. One night, I saw him there. Then I saw the huddle open, he disappeared inside and the huddle closed around him. When he came out, his mouth was bleeding. The Celtics worked him over.

AL BIANCHI: The Strangler had a black eye and a bloody nose and lip. But he came over to us and said, "Ah, those Boston guys don't even know how to punch."

EARL STROM: They had another fan who was a butcher. He was a big, heavyset guy and he would get all over Sid Borgia. During time-outs, Sid would walk in circles shaking his arms and legs to keep loose. The Butcher was all over him and Sid was screaming back at him. Sid's circles were getting wider and wider and he was getting closer and closer to the Butcher.

The Butcher yelled, "You don't have any guts."

Sid yelled, "Maybe you'd like to try my guts."

The Butcher said, "Yeah, right now."

Then the Butcher took off his coat, walked onto the court and Sid popped the guy, knocking him down. The Butcher started to get up and Sid punched him again. Then the cops came and hauled the Butcher away.

SID BORGIA: Some of my scariest moments were in Syracuse. There was a game where Syracuse was down by three points with 15 seconds left. Dolph Schayes drove the lane, dipped his shoulder, ran smack into Sweetwater Clifton, and in the same motion, he threw in a shot. All the fans thought the basket was good and Schayes would be going to the foul line for a three-point play. John Nucatola was working the game with me, and he called a charge—no basket, New York ball.

Al Cervi was coaching Syracuse and he went nuts. The guy called five straight time-outs to bitch at us and let the fans throw things.

Al McGuire was with the Knicks and he came up to me, put an arm around my shoulder and said, "Way to go, Sid."

All that did was incite the fans even more.

When the game ended, we couldn't get into the officials' dressing room. The fans had blocked the door and were waiting for us. We went into the Knicks' dressing room. We had a friend on the police force and after a couple of hours he got us out of the arena and back to our hotel. But before we could get more than a step into the lobby, the hotel manager said, "You can't stay here tonight. People are looking for you guys and I won't be responsible if something happens."

The manager sent someone to our rooms to gather up our stuff and we caught the 1 A.M. train out of town.

Life in Fort Wayne

The Fort Wayne Zollner Pistons had the first player to score 2,000 points in a season and the first and last NBA official to become a coach. The player was George Yardley, who scored 2,001 points in 1957–58 for a 27.8 average, the best the NBA had ever seen until that point. The coach was Charley Eckman, who had been an official for seven years before he was hired at the age of 33 in 1955. He lasted three and a half seasons, coaching the Pistons to the NBA Finals in 1955 and again in 1956. His final record was 123-118 and the Pistons never came that close to a title until 32 years after he left. Why were they called the Zollner Pistons? Because they were owned by Fred Zollner, who made his money in the piston business. In fact, one of the main reasons Zollner moved his Pistons to Detroit in 1957 was to be in the center of the automobile industry, which bought his products.

JOHNNY KERR: Fort Wayne was the typical NBA team of the middle 1950s. Every player from that era has memories of traveling to Fort Wayne. We'd take an all-night train and then stop in Waterloo, Indiana, which was as close as the train came to Fort Wayne. It would be five in the morning and that town looked like a set from *Bad Day at Black Rock*. There was a greasy spoon called the Green Parrot where there were always a couple of James Dean leather jacket type guys sipping coffee and smoking unfiltered cigarettes. They had been up all night and the players would have a couple of them give us a ride from Waterloo to the Van Ormond Hotel in Fort Wayne. These kids knew the train schedule and the basketball schedule; they knew the train didn't go into Fort Wayne and they would wait for us so they could give us the ride and make five bucks. The real contradiction to all this was that Fort Wayne was owned by one of the richest guys in the league.

CHARLEY ECKMAN: Fred Zollner may have been the wealthiest of the NBA owners in the 1950s. We never rode trains because he owned his own plane. I know for a fact that in the early days of the league when cash was short, the NBA came to Zollner for a loan, and his capital carried the league for a few months until things got squared away. He was a true sportsman owner. He never played basketball or any other sport that I know of. He started in sports by sponsoring a high-powered softball team, then gravitated into the NBA.

GEORGE YARDLEY: Zollner was around the team, he went to the games and we traveled with him on his plane, but he wasn't one to say much to the guys. His father had started the piston business and he took it over and kept it going. It was worth at least $10 million, which was a ton of money in those days. But I don't think that was where his heart was. He was not a promoter. In fact, he was so quiet we felt that he had the personality of a fence post. He didn't want people to get close to him.

CHARLEY ECKMAN: At the end of the 1953–54 season, I got a call from Fred Zollner. I lived in Baltimore and Fred wanted me to catch a flight to Miami the next morning to meet with him. I told him that I had only $18 in my pocket. He said all my expenses were paid for. I wasn't sure what he wanted, but I didn't think he wanted me to go from Baltimore to Miami just for a friendly lunch. Fort Wayne had a so-so year and bombed in the playoffs. I knew that some of the players didn't like [coach] Paul Birch. Anyway, Fred lived at the old Kenilworth Hotel, which was once owned by Arthur Godfrey. I got there in the afternoon. The bellman took my bags and led me to the biggest suite that I had ever seen. He told me that I had a driver and a Cadillac at my disposal and to order dinner when I wished. So I ate a great meal, called my driver and had him take me down Collins Avenue to look at those great hotels on Miami Beach. This was a side of life I had never seen. Then I told the driver to stop in front of a hot dog stand, and I walked up and had a couple of dogs just so I could remember who I was. I knew that Fred liked me. We used to talk a lot before and after games. I once mentioned that I thought I could coach, even though I had always been an official. He had fired Paul Birch, and he was giving me the big-shot treatment in Miami Beach, so it wasn't hard to figure what was on his mind.

SID BORGIA: It was hard for us officials to imagine Charley as a coach. He was a guy who wore gray pants all day and then wore them on the court at night when he officiated. He got by with a smile and a batch of jokes, and he kibitzed his way through the whole game.

SLICK LEONARD: Cigar-chomping Charley Eckman, his greatest asset was that he could talk his way into the Inaugural Ball.

CHARLEY ECKMAN: I met with Fred the next morning. He said, "Do you think you can coach my team?"

I said, "Absolutely."

He said, "Why?"

I said, "I think I can win a title with your team. It's that good. I don't care what happened last year."

Fred said, "That's a big order, but I happen to agree with you. I'll give you a two-year contract at $10,000 a year."

Fred turned out to be even more generous than that. He gave me a $4,000 bonus for getting the team to the finals in my first year, then he raised my second-year salary to $12,500.

NORM DRUCKER: Charley Eckman as an NBA coach? I think every official who worked with Charley was astounded when that happened.

SID BORGIA: Before Charley got the coaching job, Zollner used to sit on the end of the bench. Once I saw him sitting there with his girlfriend.

CHARLEY ECKMAN: Most of the time, Fred used to sit right next to Paul Birch during the games. I told Fred that I didn't think an owner on the bench was a good idea, and he agreed. But I had to report to Fred and he wanted to know everything that was going on and why I did what I did. We played Sunday afternoon games, and that night I'd fly from Fort Wayne to Miami with Fred on his private plane. He always had fried chicken on the plane and he would question me. Those sessions could be very tough. We'd get to Miami Sunday night, check into the Kenilworth Hotel, then fly back to Fort Wayne the next morning.

GENE SHUE: Zollner's plane was something else, an old DC-3. Every time we flew from Fort Wayne to the East Coast, we had to stop in Erie, Pennsylvania, to gas up or we'd run out of gas over the Great Lakes. We spent so much time in Erie, a couple of us were going to buy houses there. The plane also wasn't pressurized, and that meant the pilot had to try and fly between the clouds and the headwinds to keep out of the weather. So we were always going up and down, up and down. The players were in the back and Eckman and Zollner were in a private compartment up front.

GEORGE YARDLEY: Charley Eckman was exactly what we needed. Paul Birch was a drill sergeant. He kicked things, he broke things, he put people down. I played under him as a rookie and he didn't like me at all. I went a stretch of 15 games without playing. Birch liked guys who got into fights. Well, I got into a lot of fights, but lost them all. Birch was probably a nice guy if you met him in the right situation, but I have no idea what situation that would have been.

CHARLEY ECKMAN: Birch's reputation was that of a wild man. I know he had no use for Yardley, and I thought Yardley was the most talented guy they had. I came in and said I wasn't going to yell and scream. I had no set plays. Guys at the pro level don't need plays; they did better when left on their own. Sure, I had an out-of-bounds play, and during a time-out I might set up something. But all that X-and-O crap is for the birds. These guys were great players. What was I going to tell them? I tried to keep them happy and root like hell for them. Most of all, I was determined to play Yardley. Guys didn't dunk in games, but I officiated an exhibition game and Yardley dunked with ease. The best thing I did in my four years as coach was use George. Right after I got the job, I went to his home in California, took him to dinner and said, "You're my starting forward."

GEORGE YARDLEY: Charley's greatest attribute was that he treated us like human beings. He rolled the ball out and let us play. Remember, this was before Russell came to the Celtics, so I don't think I'm out of line by saying that we probably had the best talent in the league—Larry Foust, Mel Hutchins, Andy Phillip, Max Zaslofsky and myself. Charley decided he had a good job and went along for the ride. We probably should have won the title in 1955, but we lost to Syracuse in seven games. If Charley had a little more skill in the tactical area, it might have made a difference. What I remember most is that we had a great time.

NORM DRUCKER: Charley really was a pretty decent coach. I know that working for Fred Zollner couldn't have been easy. Charley told me that the day he was fired, Zollner called him in and said, "Charley, I'm going to make a change in your department." Charley looked around and thought, "Wait a minute, I'm the only guy in my department."

GEORGE YARDLEY: We got to the finals two years in a row, then Fred started trading everyone—Mel Hutchins, Larry Foust, myself—almost as if he didn't want to share the spotlight with his players. By the end, Charley had nothing to work with.

CHARLEY ECKMAN: The one thing I am the most proud of as coach is playing Yardley. He became the first player to score 2,000 points in a

season, and he was such a skinny, chalky-white bastard that you thought
he was dying from malnutrition.

TOM GOLA: Yardley may have been the best athlete in the league in
the middle 1950s. He was 6-foot-6 and could run and jump all day
long.

FRANK RAMSEY: George had a turnaround jumper—he took it right
in your face. He just jumped over you and shot like the guys do today.

EARL LLOYD: George wasn't a Clyde Drexler Phi Slamma Jamma type,
but if you saw him play today you'd still figure he was a good athlete,
a guy with a lot of moves. He's one of those great players who was
completely forgotten once Wilt, West, Oscar and all those superstars
came into the game—but he played their style.

JOHNNY KERR: Yardley's nickname was the Bird and it was perfect.

GEORGE YARDLEY: When I started, probably only 25 percent of the
guys used a jump shot. Guys with set shots—it was so hard for them
to pump-fake and then drive to the basket because it took forever to
make any kind of move. I think it's ludicrous to compare guys from my
era to the guys now, but a guy whose style is somewhat similar to mine
is Reggie Miller. He has that long-range jump shot but also a great first
step to the basket. I did those things, but not as well as him. Most guys
had vertical leaps of about a foot. I had 32 inches, which would make
me an average jumper today but that was the best in the NBA at that
time. Paul Arizin and I played the same style, and what made us different from the other guys with jump shots was that they shot on the
way *up,* to help them get strength behind their shots. Paul and I shot
at the peak of our jumps—almost on the way *down*—and that made
our shots much harder to block.

*[The Pistons moved to Detroit in the summer of 1957, and Yardley
scored 2,001 points and averaged 27.8 in 1957–58.]*

GEORGE YARDLEY: I broke George Mikan's record [1,932 in 1950–
51] for points in a season. I went into the last game of the season
needing 27 points to get 2,000. My teammates wanted me to do it and
they kept feeding me the ball—I scored 14 in the first quarter. Syracuse

did not want me to do it—they used Al Bianchi on me at first, then started double-teaming me, which was seldom done back then. Paul Seymour was coaching Syracuse and he later told me that one of the things he wanted out of life was for me not to get 2,000 points against him. I went about 10 minutes in the fourth quarter without scoring— they swarmed me whenever I got the ball. Finally, I knew I had to do something, so I cherry-picked. I didn't bother to go back on defense. I caught a long pass, I was out ahead of everyone and I dunked it for the 2,000th and 2,001th points. We weren't much for ceremony back then. The game wasn't stopped nor was anything said about the 2,000 points. I was able to keep the ball just because I scored at the end of the game. It was my one moment in the sun and it didn't last long.

[Bob Pettit scored 2,105 points the next season.]

And two years later, Wilt Chamberlain came along and he would have 2,000 points by midseason. The game was really changing.

Meanwhile, Back in Syracuse

The 1955 Nats were the first NBA championship team with black players—Earl Lloyd and Jim Tucker. Danny Biasone had by then drafted Johnny Kerr, and that added up to Syracuse's only championship team. A 6-foot-9 center who averaged 14 points and 11 rebounds in his 12-year career, Kerr has the second-longest ironman streak in NBA history with 844 consecutive games.

DANNY BIASONE: The first time I saw Johnny Kerr, I knew I was going to draft him. It was at the 1954 East-West All-Star Game at Madison Square Garden. This was before any team really scouted, we just went to the East-West game to look over the best talent. I needed a center. I saw Kerr taking his hook shot in warmups and I told the guy I was with, "He's my first-round pick."

JOHNNY KERR: Danny was sitting with Jack Andrews, a reporter for the *Syracuse Post-Standard*. Jack told me the conversation went like this:

Biasone said, "I know who we're going to draft."

Andrews asked, "Who?"

Biasone said, "The big redheaded kid down there shooting those hooks."

Andrews said, "You mean Kerr? Danny, how can you know that? All you've done is watch him warm up."

Biasone said, "I don't care. I like his hook shot. I need a center and he's a center."

So Andrews wrote that Biasone planned to make me the Nats' No. 1 pick. He said that he knew that for a fact because Biasone told him so. Imagine a general manager telling a sportswriter that today.

DOLPH SCHAYES: We thought we were a legitimate center away from being a championship team. Al Cervi was our coach and he was out of the New York school of players, which meant we ran a lot of motion—no set plays. We needed a center who could play the high post and pass, and that was Johnny's specialty.

JOHNNY KERR: I had never run into a coach like Cervi. His nickname was Digger and he made being scrappy an art form.

DOLPH SCHAYES: To be honest, everyone on the team despised Cervi. He wasn't a coach who would stroke some guys and give the others a pat on the back. He screamed at everybody. He was a street fighter and the team took on his mantle. We won a lot of games simply because of the toughness he instilled in us. Yet, we hated him for his pettiness. He would do things to intentionally annoy you like shorting you on the meal money.

JOHNNY KERR: Cervi wanted you to know who was boss. After practice, he would challenge you to a 1-on-1 game. If he lost, he wanted to play again, and again, and again, until he beat you. The veterans would tell me, "Listen, Johnny, just let Cervi win the first game, then you can take a shower and get out of here."

My real problem was that Cervi wouldn't leave me on the court for long. In the first 15 games of the season, he rotated Earl Lloyd and me at center, and he never gave either one of us enough time to get settled out there. It was like tag-team wrestling, with one guy touching the other's hand every two minutes while going in and out of the ring. Finally, I went to Cervi and said, "You have Earl and me shuffling in and out, it's killing us both. Earl's 6-foot-6, he's a natural forward. I can play center. Give us both a chance." Cervi played me that night and I got 23 points and 19 rebounds against Rochester. Earl was the power forward next to Dolph and we were on our way to the finals.

EARL LLOYD: What Johnny did for our team was give us an athlete in the middle, a guy who could run and jump along with his great passing.

JOHNNY KERR: We won the regular-season title and faced Fort Wayne in the championship. It was a 2-3-2 setup, with the first two games played at Syracuse, where we won them both.

CHARLEY ECKMAN: When it came time for our three home games, we couldn't get into our building in Fort Wayne. They had rented the arena to the American Bowling Congress for a PBA tournament. They figured with a ref as the coach, they didn't have to worry about Fort Wayne in the finals. Instead of the bowling tournament moving, they made us go down to Indianapolis and play. We won all three games there. Then Syracuse beat us in the sixth game at their place to set up the final.

JOHNNY KERR: After Fort Wayne got tossed out for the bowling tournament, all I could think was, "Thank God Danny Biasone owns his own bowling alley so we don't have to worry about the bowlers kicking us out in Syracuse."

I'll tell you something that pissed all of us off. When we walked into our building for the sixth game, we saw that they had champagne sitting in the Fort Wayne dressing room. They had planned a celebration in our backyard. There was no way we were going to lose that night. We knew there would be a seventh game.

EARL LLOYD: By the seventh game, we were really racked up. Three of our starters were playing with broken bones—George King had a broken wrist, Dolph had a broken wrist and I had a broken hand.

DOLPH SCHAYES: Fort Wayne had a 16-point lead at the half. If it were a year earlier, the game would have been over. If there were no 24-second clock, they could have dribbled out the second half and shot free throws.

JOHNNY KERR: For years, we kidded Danny Biasone that he invented the clock so he could win a title, but the clock did make the difference. In the first half, George Yardley and those guys were killing us. But we came back and had a 92–91 lead with about 10 seconds left.

CHARLEY ECKMAN: A couple of my guys blew their cool, yelled at the officials and got technical fouls in the second half. We let them right back in the game, but we still had the last shot.

JOHNNY KERR: I was guarding Larry Foust, 6-10, 250 pounds. He was the second-best center behind George Mikan in the early days of the league and he was pushing me all over. I was convinced that they were going to pass the ball to him and take advantage of the rookie. The roar of the Syracuse crowd was deafening. I didn't hear a thing Cervi said during the time-out. I kept thinking, "Foust is coming right at me, what am I going to do about it?" I was thinking about all the games, all the guys playing hurt, and I was going to blow the whole thing by letting Foust score.

CHARLEY ECKMAN: We had a couple of options. Foust was one. But so was Yardley. I just wanted a good shot, or at least some kind of shot.

JOHNNY KERR: Andy Phillip had the ball for Fort Wayne and he dribbled into the corner against Paul Seymour. When he did, George King left his man and then he and Seymour double-teamed Phillip, King stealing the ball. That was the ballgame.

CHARLEY ECKMAN: Kerr can say all the nice things he wants about Foust, but Kerr was a young colt back then and he just ran Big Larry off the court.

GEORGE YARDLEY: That game cost me a $500 watch, which was what Fred Zollner promised to buy us if we won. For most of the guys on the team, a $500 watch would have been 10 percent of their salary.

DANNY BIASONE: I have never been happier than that day. I recall seeing Michael Jordan hug the [1991] championship trophy and cry. That brought tears to my eyes because I did the same thing. Only it was long after everyone had left the dressing room. There was just the trophy and me. I held it, thought about being an Italian immigrant, a little guy who owned a bowling alley . . . For much of my life, I was a nobody, a broken-down bartender. I bawled like a baby. And can you believe it? A couple of years later, someone stole that trophy out of my office at the bowling alley?

JOHNNY KERR: We had a party with champagne. A two-day party. We got $1,400 a man for winning the title, but no championship ring.

DOLPH SCHAYES: The league didn't have a standard ring, but Danny bought us a little gold ring with a basketball on it.

JOHNNY KERR: That may be, but the only thing I ever got was a plaque from the Syracuse Optimist Club that said, "Congratulations, World Champions."

3
A CLOSE-KNIT LEAGUE

THE BULL SESSION

We talked about
a ballplayer this
a ballplayer that.
Into the night
our conversation
rose and fell:

> *a pick and roll*
> *a lousy call*
> *a stolen ball*

The three of us
would commiserate
until the light of dawn
crept stealthily through
the drawn hotel curtains.

pro basketball players
live in bat caves
upside down
hotel rooms
minds pointing
to darkness. . . .

—TOM MESCHERY

BILLY CUNNINGHAM: The biggest difference between modern basketball and the NBA of the 1950s and most of the 1960s was that we had togetherness. With only eight teams and 10 guys on a team, you're talking about 80 players in the entire league. There was no such thing as having your own room—you always had a roommate. Guys got to be friends. After games, guys from both teams would get together in a bar and have a few beers. I know we didn't make the money that these kids do today, but I'm sure we had more fun.

ALEX HANNUM: In New York, they had doubleheaders at Madison Square Garden, which meant that four teams—or half of the NBA— was in the same building on the same night. In the 1950s a lot of the guys were military veterans like myself. And to be honest, we drank beer—a lot of beer. If it wasn't for a hot shower and a cold beer, we never would have played pro ball. When I coached in St. Louis, they'd bring a case of beer into the dressing room after the game so the guys could help themselves.

But my fondest memories were of those New York doubleheaders. After the game, most of us would gather at a bar on Eighth Avenue called the Everglades. You had to carry your own equipment bag from the hotel to the Garden, so guys would dump their bags at the front of the bar. You'd see a pile of bags from four NBA teams and about 20–30 players.

When I was with Rochester, we had a rookie named Norm Swanson and he showed up at the Everglades one night with a black eye. Some thugs had beaten him up at another bar on Eighth Avenue. We had been drinking and we decided we'd get revenge for Norm. So guys from four teams went down to the bar, found the thugs that hit Norm and we cleaned that place out. We literally threw those guys into the street. The cops came, they recognized some of us and let us go with a warning.

TOM MESCHERY: All those stories about tremendous beer-drinking bouts are pretty accurate. There were no drugs. Very few guys drank hard liquor. But the beer—man, if guys today drank as much beer as we did, they'd probably have an investigation and put out a white paper on it.

One night Johnny Kerr and I stayed out until 7 A.M. That same night, we played and I scored 30. Another night, I saw Richie Guerin asleep at 4 A.M. in a bar on 1st Street in Greenwich Village. I figured he wouldn't hurt us that night, but Richie went for 42 points.

LENNY WILKENS: When I was a young player, several of the Hawks veterans took me out. They said they planned to sit in the bar until they filled this huge table with empty beer bottles. I had never seen anyone drink like those guys.

HOT ROD HUNDLEY: First of all, Lenny Wilkens was a good player. Secondly, he didn't drink and most of us were hung over, so that made him a great player.

LENNY WILKENS: I could kick Hot Rod's ass drunk or sober, but guys hardly ever drink today. Back then, nearly everyone did.

JIM LOSCUTOFF: It was a routine. You went out after a game, had 4–5 beers, then sweated it out the next day at practice. When we played in St. Louis and Detroit where they brought the free beer into the dressing room—it was like we'd died and gone to heaven.

JOHNNY KERR: What surprised me when I turned pro was Al Cervi asking me for a cigarette. In college, we didn't drink, we didn't smoke, they didn't even want us to date. But about half the players smoked. We'd light up at halftime. I drank a lot of beer. Once, we had a coach who said no more than one can of beer was allowed on a train ride, so we went out and bought these 40-ounce cans of Foster's. I don't know if I ever was in shape when I played. We did everything wrong—smoked, drank, ate red meat and crummy food. But Lord, we had a great time.

BARRY CLEMENS: In the middle 1960s, we were still getting seven bucks a day meal money. One of Oscar Robertson's favorite pregame meals was a couple of hot dogs. No one ever said what you should or shouldn't eat.

ALEX HANNUM: We loved all-night diners where the food was greasy, hot, a lot and cheap. It was everything they tell you not to eat today.

BARRY CLEMENS: The other thing players loved was poker. On airplanes, we'd take a blanket and either spread it over our laps or in the aisle and we'd toss our cards onto the blanket. The games went on for hours.

ALEX HANNUM: Hours? Some of the card games went on for days. Poker was a part of our lives. We'd play a game, stay up all night playing poker, sleep a few hours, play another basketball game and then come back to the hotel and continue the poker game. In St. Louis, Bob Pettit, Red Holzman and myself had some marathon games.

HOT ROD HUNDLEY: If we had an hour to kill in an airport, we'd take one of the equipment bags into the men's room, turn it over and use it for a small table and then break out the cards. Our coach never wanted us to play cards out on the concourse. We played poker on buses, planes, in hotels, you name it. The irony is that we had no money and all we wanted to do was gamble. Now, the players are loaded and they won't spend a cent. They don't drink, they don't go to bars. They don't play cards. They make millions, but they have no fun.

GEORGE YARDLEY: I didn't play poker because I was never comfortable taking money from a guy who was my teammate. I didn't want there to be any animosity building up because of a card game. But a group of us who didn't like to gamble used to play Monopoly and went to a lot of movies.

AL BIANCHI: Money was something we didn't talk about and we didn't have agents to talk about it with us. I roomed with Johnny Kerr for 10 years and never knew what he made. I came into the league making $5,200 and left making $15,000—that's after 10 years. I was afraid to hold out or ask for a real raise. I told Kerr, "If I ask for too much, they just might tell me to stay home."

RON GRINKER: Back then, money was a sacred subject. It was never mentioned. Now, all the guys talk about is who makes what.

AL BIANCHI: Nearly all of us had summer jobs to supplement our income. I worked construction, carrying hod, running the jackhammers and digging ditches. I also sold Buicks and did things that made me appreciate being paid to play pro ball.

GENE SHUE: I was an insurance man in the summer. I wanted to learn the business because I knew I'd need something after basketball. No one played in the NBA believing that they would make enough to be set for life.

JACK TWYMAN: The payroll for the 1958 Royals team was only $180,000.

JIM LOSCUTOFF: Now and then, I realize that Larry Bird makes more money for one game than I did in three years. But I believe that I made a lot more friends. The lack of money forced us to get closer.

FRANK RAMSEY: Instead of having nannies like these wives do today, when one of the wives or children were sick, the other wives came over with food to help out. Since none of us made any real money, there was nothing to be jealous about.

ROD THORN: I was a rookie in 1963 and I shared an apartment with Don Kojis, Barney Cable and Kevin Loughery. We each paid $30 a month for a two-bedroom place. There were only three beds, so we took turns sleeping on a couch in the living room.

LARRY STAVERMAN: When I was with the Royals, we trained at an air force base and slept on bunk beds in an old wooden barracks. We ate in the mess hall, we taped our own ankles and carried our own soap and towels. It was military life, and no one said a word.

BARRY CLEMENS: Things weren't as rigid. When I was with Chicago in 1966–67, we were on a West Coast trip and I wasn't playing much. I used to go out and find a gym or a playground to shoot around by myself, to try to stay sharp. Once, I went down to the beach in L.A. and was in a pickup game with some former college players. They didn't know who I was. One guy said, "Our recreation team has a game tonight. Want to play? One of our other guys can't make it."

I just wanted to play anywhere, so I went to their game that night and scored 51 points. After the game, one of the league officers said, "Nice game. You still owe us the $15 entry fee."

I said, "I'll catch you next game," and then I left.

The next morning I looked in the *Los Angeles Times* and saw they had a short story about the Rec. League games from that night and it mentioned that the guy whose name I used scored 51. I still have the clipping in my scrapbook.

CARL BRAUN: During the summer, on Saturdays at playgrounds near Rockaway Beach you'd see pickup games with Cousy, Dick McGuire, myself and other pros playing with the college kids or whoever was around.

OSCAR ROBERTSON: The players had a better sense of family because we came from stronger families than the players of today. We had people telling us what was right and what was wrong, and no one was giving us a handout. We had real summer jobs—mine was in construction. We knew that the only way we could survive was to pull together. We couldn't say, "Screw that guy, I've got my two million."

Twenty-five Bucks for a Punch

ROD THORN: I'm now the NBA's director of operations and one of my jobs is to police the league in terms of handing out fines and suspensions for fights. No one had that job in the 1950s and 1960s. There were fights all the time, and usually the refs let you fight it out for a while before they broke things up. Later, a guy might get fined 25 bucks for starting a fight, but it was no big deal.

I recall a night where Bob Ferry punched Walt Hazzard, knocking a tooth into the side of Hazzard's mouth. He had to miss 5–6 games and if Ferry was fined at all, it was $25.

There was another game where Al Bianchi was coaching and he came running onto the floor during a fight. Gus Johnson saw Al, decked him with a punch, and the imprint of Al's glasses stayed on Al's face for several days. Then our team's business manager came running out of the stands to defend Bianchi, and Johnson punched him, too.

DON BARKSDALE: When I came to the NBA, they had these little boxes in the dressing room. I wondered what they were for, then I saw the players put their false teeth in the boxes before they went out to play. I'd say that half of the players in the middle 1950s had their front teeth knocked out, and a lot of them lost their teeth because it was legal to get a rebound and then swing your elbow. Elbows knocked out far more teeth than punches.

GEORGE YARDLEY: I must have had about 80 stitches in my face, all from things that happened on the court. Guys would hit you with a clenched fist, just cutting your skull open. Over the years, I played with at least 40 different guys and I can't name one who had all of his own teeth.

AL BIANCHI: Sure we fought more than the players do today, but you didn't see the cheap shots like the Pistons' Bad Boys crap, where they cut your legs out from under you or throw you to the floor from behind. We had hard fouls, then the action would stop and two guys would just square off and have at it.

NORM DRUCKER: The hockey influence definitely was there in the early days. Many of the teams had a policeman, a guy you had to watch every moment when he stepped on the court. We had serious discussions about using a penalty box, like they have in hockey. That way, if a certain guy kept starting fights, we'd put him in the box for a couple of minutes and make his team play 4-on-5.

RUDY LARUSSO: Before my first exhibition game as a pro, Slick Leonard told me, "You're playing the Celtics. These guys will test you."

He meant Jim Loscutoff. Loscutoff got a rebound and fired an elbow at me, whacking me upside the head. On the next play, he tried to block me out and—Boom!—I knocked him into the third row. He came out swinging and I ended up in a brawl during my first game.

JOE GUSHUE: We called Loscutoff the Traffic Cop. You had to watch him every second.

RED AUERBACH: Loscutoff had two jobs: he was there to rebound and to make sure that nothing happened to Cousy.

BOB PETTIT: Loscutoff broke my arm. I went up for a layup, flipped over him, hit the floor and ended up with a fracture. Jim insisted he didn't do it on purpose. I believed him. Jim was hard as nails. He was Red Auerbach's enforcer, but I never knew him to try and injure somebody.

BOB COUSY: Auerbach's first policeman was Bob Brannum, then came Loscutoff. Loscutoff had far more basketball skills than Brannum. But Loscutoff also was there to fill Brannum's role.

Off the court, Brannum was one of the most gentle, compassionate men. But on the court, he knew that he had to do what Arnold [Auerbach] wanted. He literally fought to keep his job. In the early 1950s, we had a player come to training camp from Brown University. Frank Mahoney was his name, and he had far more basketball ability than Brannum. He had just spent two years in the trenches during the Korean War, so we knew he had to be tough.

After 10 days of double sessions, Mahoney came up to me and said, "Bob, what's going on here? Doesn't Brannum understand? I mean, we're on the same team here."

What Mahoney meant was that every time he drove to the basket, Brannum would deck him, and while Mahoney was on the floor Brannum would stand over him, glaring down and daring Mahoney to get up and fight. Arnold would never stop a scrimmage unless there was blood, so Mahoney got no help there. Finally, he just stopped driving and settled for outside shots. He got cut, and Brannum survived.

EARL LLOYD: If a player kept driving the lane against your team, you had no choice—you just knocked the guy down. Sometimes a player would drive to the basket and one of us would call out, "I've got him." Then we'd flatten the guy.

CARL BRAUN: Basketball was rougher when we played, but it is dirtier today. They've allowed the pivot play to be a wrestling match. If Dennis Rodman had shoved Richie Guerin from behind like Rodman did to Scottie Pippen in the 1991 playoffs, Rodman's teeth would have ended up in his nose. In our day, there were a lot more fights, but the unwritten rule was that you didn't do something to a guy that might take away his livelihood.

TOM MESCHERY: There are exceptions to everything, and Clyde Lovellette was the single dirtiest player in NBA history. He was downright mean. He seldom hit you with a fist; usually it was an elbow, a hip or a knee to a very vulnerable spot. He'd knock you down, then give you a hand up and say, "Sorry, kid." Then he'd do it again. I always felt Clyde was trying to hurt you.

WAYNE EMBRY: I hated playing Clyde. He'd elbow you in the Adam's apple, hit you in the face after you took a shot. If you ran past him, he threw his knee out. He was just a dirty player.

CLIFF HAGAN: People forget that Clyde was a good basketball player. He couldn't move up and down the court very well and he certainly couldn't jump. But he got a lot of rebounds and he had great range on his shot, especially for a center. He meant a lot to my game because his shooting brought the opposing center away from the basket and opened the middle for me.

MARTY BLAKE: Clyde fancied himself as a cowboy. He owned a cowboy hat and clothes. He had about 65 different guns. We were playing an exhibition tour in L.A. in 1959, and I told Clyde I thought I could get him into the movies as a cowboy, so he packed up all his gear. Our first stop was in Lubbock, Texas. Everyone knew that Clyde carried guns around—real guns. And Clyde had the kind of personality that made people keep their distance. So we were in Lubbock, and Clyde decided to pay [referee] Willie Smith a visit. In the middle of the night, he knocked on Smith's door. Willie answered and Clyde pulled two pistols out of his holsters and shot Smith—Bang! Bang! I mean real shots. Or at least they sounded real to Willie, who grabbed his gut checking for blood. It turned out they were just blanks, but they nearly scared the life out of Willie Smith.

BOB FERRY: On that L.A. trip, I was a rookie and I roomed with Clyde. He was wearing his six-guns everywhere and talking about his new career as a Western star. I was taking a nap, and I heard a clicking noise. There was Clyde, standing in front of a mirror, wearing nothing but a cowboy hat, his guns and holster strapped to his bare legs. Naked, he was practicing his quick draw in a mirror. Then there was a knock at the door. Clyde had ordered room service and he answered the door still pretty much naked. The room service kid saw Clyde, saw the guns and saw he wasn't wearing anything else. The kid threw his hands over his head and started to shake. He probably figured Clyde was going to shoot him. Clyde just laughed, and the kid took off down the hall, leaving without bothering to collect the money for the food.

4

CROSSING THE LINE

The first black player drafted by an NBA team was Chuck Cooper, a second-round pick by Boston in 1950. When Celtics owner Walter Brown announced the selection of Cooper, one of the other owners said, "Don't you know that he's a Negro?" Brown reportedly said, "I don't care if he's plaid, all I know is that this kid can play." The day after the draft, Brown received this telegram from Cooper: "Thank you for having the courage to offer me a chance in pro basketball. I hope I'll never give you cause to regret it." After Cooper was picked in the second round, Washington selected Earl Lloyd in the eighth round. The first black to sign a contract was Nat "Sweetwater" Clifton, a former Globetrotter who was signed by New York, the deal occurring after Cooper and Lloyd were drafted but before they could sign their contracts. The first black to play in an NBA game was Lloyd, who took the court on Halloween of 1950 with the old Washington Capitols. Lloyd played only seven games before being drafted into the military and the Washington franchise folded at midseason. Cooper made his debut one night after Lloyd's first game and he played the full season, as did Clifton. Also in 1950, Hank DeZonie played five games for Tri-Cities. So the first four black players were Lloyd, Cooper, Clifton and DeZonie. Clifton and Cooper are deceased. In 1951–52, Dave Minor, Bob Wilson and Don Barksdale came into the league. Barksdale was the first black to play on the U.S. Olympic basketball team (1948) and the first to appear in an NBA All-Star Game (1953).

RED AUERBACH: I had been hired to coach the Celtics in 1950, the team wasn't any good and I needed players. Everyone knew that Chuck Cooper was a damn good prospect at Duquesne. When Walter Brown and I talked about the draft, we didn't talk about race, we talked about players. We were aware that Cooper was black, but we were more interested in the fact that he could help us. I scouted him. He was a 6-foot-6 forward with a strong body, long arms and tough on defense. He had good character and came from a good college program—two things I always look for. I can honestly say he was the best player available in the second round, so Mr. Brown and I drafted him.

HASKELL COHEN: Until Red and Walter Brown drafted Cooper, all the good black players went to the Globetrotters. I understand that Red wanted Cooper, but Walter Brown made the final decision. A number of the owners were worried about opening the league to blacks for two reasons.

First, it would upset Abe Saperstein and the Globetrotters. In the early 1950s, the Globies were a huge draw. They played before—sometimes even after—NBA games to help with the crowds. They thought that if the NBA allowed blacks to play, then Saperstein would not play in their buildings.

The second concern was that if a few blacks were signed, the door would be open and within a few years black players would dominate the league. Then this would turn off the white fans. Of course, the opposite was true—black players just helped attendance. Besides, white fans paid to see the Globetrotters, who were all black.

Red Auerbach knew that if he had good players, he'd draw. He didn't care what color the players were. Besides, Red is of the Jewish faith, he didn't worry about anyone's color because he knew about discrimination firsthand.

EARL LLOYD: I had no idea I'd be drafted and was surprised when I was—no blacks had played in the NBA before and I had no clue that the policy was about to change. I had my degree in education [from West Virginia State] and I was planning to become a high school teacher. What I didn't know was that my college coach got a call from someone with Washington and he was told that they might draft me. He didn't say anything to me about it; he didn't want to get my hopes up. I got a chance to tour with the Globetrotters for a week. My coach said that was fine, but not to sign anything with the Trotters until he said so. He didn't tell me why, and I listened to him because he was my coach.

Then Boston took Cooper in the second round and I went to Washington in the eighth round, which meant that teams weren't exactly lined up at my door. I was from outside Washington—Alexandria, Virginia. I had played in a college tournament at [Washington's] Uline Arena, so maybe that was why they took me.

Even after I was picked, I wondered if they were serious. Would they really offer me a contract? They did—for $4,500. I signed immediately.

Nothing was ever said about me being the first black, or how I was expected to act or what I might expect to find in the NBA. They acted as if I was a player, period. Nor was much said in the newspaper about Cooper or me being the first blacks drafted.

LEONARD KOPPETT: Cooper and Lloyd being drafted wasn't much of a story for three reasons:

1. Jackie Robinson had broken the pro sports color line three years earlier.

2. In 1950, pro basketball was so unimportant, literally a minor league in the minds of most sports fans. There were only 11 teams, so who was drafted was news only in those 11 cities. And what went on in the National Football League was 100 times more important than pro basketball. Then there was baseball, which was the undisputed king of the sports scene. No matter what pro basketball did, it didn't receive much attention.

3. In basketball, the color line had not been as rigid. There were prominent black college players. Don Barksdale was on the 1948 Olympic team. Pro basketball also wasn't old enough to have a real history, so there was no sense of any history being made because Chuck Cooper was drafted.

HASKELL COHEN: The Globetrotters were after Cooper and Walter Brown was having some trouble getting Cooper signed. Cooper and I were both from Pittsburgh. I knew a lot of people from Duquesne and I had set up Cooper with a summer job at Kutsher's in the Catskills. Maurice Podoloff asked me to use my relationship with Cooper to get Cooper signed for the Celtics. I talked to Chuck and his coach and we worked out a deal for $7,500, which was the first time a league public relations director ever signed a draft pick. It really wasn't that hard because Chuck wanted to play in the NBA.

RED AUERBACH: Our players didn't give a damn what color Cooper was. Cousy offered to room with him. So did Bones McKinney. I had a policy of changing roommates every so often to avoid cliques, so about everyone roomed with Chuck at some point.

ED MACAULEY: No one ever said, "Hey, we've got this black guy coming to the team, now what do we do?" In fact, no one said much of anything at all. He was just another rookie trying to make the team.

EARL LLOYD: I never had problems with other NBA players, and neither did Chuck or any of the other blacks. I played several exhibition games. There were five rookies on our team and we all got along—we all were trying to find our way.

My first regular-season game was in Rochester. I stepped on the court and the world kept spinning. No one said a word—fans, players, anybody. I don't recall any mention in the newspapers about me being the first black to play in an NBA game. Nor was anything said about Cooper or Clifton.

The guy who was the hero to all of the black basketball players was Jackie Robinson. He blazed the trail. He had guys on his team who said they weren't going to play with him. I mean, Dixie Walker saying, "I ain't gonna play with that guy"? What is that? I can't imagine what that would be like. Baseball had a lot of guys from the South and often the first pair of shoes they got were their baseball spikes, and the opposing players were yelling all that racial garbage at Jackie . . .We didn't have any trouble like that. Basketball players were college people. If they did harbor any racial prejudice, they were smart enough to keep it to themselves.

BOB COUSY: Baseball is a team game played by individuals. Guys can be selfish and still be great players. In basketball, there's a foxhole psychology. Everyone has to work together. If you're in a foxhole, you don't care about the color of the guy next to you. All you care about is if he can help get you out of that mess. Red treated Chuck Cooper like he would any new player and we treated him the same way. Then he showed us that he could help on the court and he was a great guy to be around. He wasn't singled out—he got a fair chance and then he proved himself. That's all anyone wants.

Even Before Chuck Cooper

The first blacks to play any sort of pro basketball were Pop Gates and Dolly King in 1946. They were signed by Lester Harrison, who owned the Rochester Royals of the National Basketball League—one of the two leagues that merged in 1950 to form the NBA.

LESTER HARRISON: Dolly King and Pop Gates played pro basketball before Jackie Robinson played pro baseball. They were really the first black pioneers in pro sports. I signed them with Rochester in 1946. I had a good team, a championship team. I talked to the two players about the hazards of being the first blacks—Gates and King wanted to do it. Then I got a call from Ben Kerner, who owned the Buffalo franchise. Ben said, "Les, you're going to suffer because you signed those two kids. Why don't you let me take one of them, then we can be in this together and we'll be stronger if we run into trouble." I had plenty of guards, so I gave Pop Gates to Kerner. Dolly King was a big man and we needed size. Both of the players ran into trouble at the Craypool Hotel in Anderson, Indiana. They suffered all the discrimination and slights before Jackie Robinson, Chuck Cooper and the rest.

The other owners didn't like us integrating the league, but they never threatened Ben Kerner or me. King and Gates were in the twilight of their careers. We only paid about $500 a month, and they had better jobs outside of basketball. King was an athletic director of a small college. After one season, he quit to go back to that job because he had a family to support. The same was true of Pop Gates. Back then, we didn't have the money to compete with the Globetrotters, or even what guys made as teachers or in business, so it was hard to keep players.

A Globetrotter in the NBA

The late Nathaniel "Sweetwater" Clifton was signed by the New York Knicks in 1950, not long after Chuck Cooper and Earl Lloyd became the first blacks selected in the NBA draft. A 6-foot-7, 235-pound forward, Clifton said he was 28 when he joined the Knicks, but many of his former teammates insisted that he was over 30. He spent his best basketball years with the Globetrotters, but still played eight NBA seasons, averaging 10 points and being named to one All-Star team. But Clifton did tell reporters that people never saw him at the top of his game. He said he could have scored more and been a more colorful player—he had skills from his Globetrotter days such as palming the ball and passing behind his back—but he felt that the NBA wanted him to stick to fundamental basketball.

LEONARD KOPPETT: When the Knicks signed Clifton, race was not an issue. No one was concerned about Clifton being the first black on the Knicks. The issue was the Globetrotters. There was a shaky relationship between the Trotters and the NBA. The league was very aware that the Trotters could help them at the gate, that they guaranteed a near sellout every time they took the court in those doubleheaders. Signing Clifton was not going to make Abe Saperstein and the Globetrotters happy.

DOLPH SCHAYES: In the first five years of the NBA, the Globetrotters helped carry the league. They drew fans who weren't into basketball, they came for the entertainment and then maybe they stayed around to watch the NBA game after the Globetrotters. I played in games where the arena was packed for the Trotters in the opener, then we took the court for the NBA game and half the fans left.

Abe Saperstein felt that he owned the black players because he had been giving them a chance to play when no one else would. And it is very true that Abe did a lot for black players when no one else would give them the time of day. But when the NBA started to sign blacks, Abe was so upset that he stopped playing doubleheaders with some of the franchises.

HARVEY POLLACK: I was at doubleheaders in places such as Fargo, North Dakota, where the NBA game was the preliminary game, then the Globetrotters played the nightcap. Saperstein cut the NBA teams in on the gate almost from the goodness of his heart, and we'd make more from that game than we would from one of our own home games. [Philadelphia owner] Eddie Gottlieb used to travel with the Trotters on their summer European tour, that was how close Saperstein was with Gottlieb, the Philadelphia Warriors and the NBA.

LESTER HARRISON: The Globetrotters drew better than most pro teams and they were able to pay higher salaries to their players. Because of their money and their reputation, a lot of blacks would rather have played for the Trotters than with the NBA in the early days.

HARVEY POLLACK: As the 1950s went on and as the NBA started signing more and more black players, the relationship between Saperstein and the league was strained. The final straw came when the Minneapolis Lakers moved to L.A. in 1960. Saperstein thought that he had been promised the first West Coast franchise by the league. He blamed his close friend Eddie Gottlieb, claiming Gotty should have stood up for him when the Lakers wanted to move. But the world was changing on Abe and the Trotters.

NORM DRUCKER: What most people forget is that in the 1940s and early 1950s, the Globetrotters were a talented basketball team, primarily because they were getting all of the top black players. In the late 1940s, they played a seven-game series against George Mikan and the Minneapolis Lakers and only lost 4–3. They had some super players. Clifton was one, but he was not their best player.

LEONARD KOPPETT: They listed Clifton at 6-foot-8, but that was a Globetrotter height. Also, the Knicks played him at center, so they wanted him to at least sound taller, but he was much closer to 6-foot-5.

When he came to the Knicks, the discussion dealt with the Globetrotters. Were their players just showmen, or did they clown to make a living? Would they have been good enough to play in the NBA? Clifton was not one of their star comics, but some people labeled him a Globetrotter, period. Well, he was good enough to play in the NBA, very capable of playing solid pro basketball. The Knicks told him, rebound, play defense, and anytime you score, it's a bonus. So we began to say that Clifton was a good athlete, but not much of a shooter. Then he showed us that he had an outside set shot and he could score.

CARL BRAUN: Sweetwater never had any ugly incidents like Jackie Robinson did. As for the guys on the Knicks, we liked him. We knew that he lied about his age, he had to be at least 30 when he joined us. But he was a real gentleman and a helluva fighter. I suppose there may have been times when Sweets took an extra bump because he was black and somebody wanted to make a point with him, but if you bumped Sweetwater Clifton, you better be ready because he was coming after you.

EARL STROM: There was a game where [New York coach] Joe Lapchick put Sweets on Bob Harris, who was just a big, strong guy with sharp elbows whose job it was to knock people around. He was working over Sweets, and Sweets was just taking it. Lapchick called a time-out and said, "Sweets, we have you in there to rebound and be physical. You can't let this guy push you around."

Sweets said, "I don't want to start any trouble."

Lapchick said, "You better start some trouble, or there is no reason to have you around. Got it?"

Sweets went back on the floor and told Harris, "You cut this crap out, because the next time it happens, I'm gonna nail you."

Then Sweets cut across the lane, caught a pass, went up for a shot, and Harris drilled him with an elbow. Sweets turned and whacked Harris . . . a 1-2, left-right combination. Sweets's fist was double the size of the ordinary man's. It was lucky for Harris that Sweets didn't hit him square. As it was, he knocked him to the floor.

BOB COUSY: Sweets pounded Harris into the ground. His fists were like sledgehammers. It was not the traditional basketball fight. Harris went down on his knees and Sweets was pounding Harris on the top of the head as if he were going to hammer Harris right into the floor.

EARL STROM: The Boston players came off the bench after Sweets. He turned, took a John L. Sullivan stance and was ready to take them all on. You could hear the rubber screeching from the guys putting on the brakes with their tennis shoes. They just came over calmly, picked up Harris and took him back to their bench.

ED MACAULEY: Harris's face was puffed up for a week. Sweets seldom fought, and after that day no one wanted to fight him.

NORM DRUCKER: Later, Sweets and I were talking about the fight and he told me that he had sparred with several pro boxers—and beaten some of them.

I said, "So why didn't you fight for a living?"

He said, "My mother wouldn't let me."

BOB COUSY: Sweets was never the instigator in a fight. The only time I ever saw him fight was with Harris. He physically dominated games based upon what he could do if he got mad.

MARV ALBERT: The New York fans loved Clifton because he was a friendly guy, because he had played with the Globetrotters, because of the Harris fight and because he had a great nickname.

GEORGE YARDLEY: He was called Sweetwater because he loved to drink Coke, or any kind of soda pop. My wife and I had him over to our house for dinner and we didn't have any soda pop. So he went out and bought six cases—that's right, six cases.

"You know why they call me Sweetwater, don't you?" he asked my wife.

Then he left them with us because he said no house should be without sweetwater. He later told us that this was the first time he had been at a white family's home for dinner.

He was a stickler for hygiene and cleanliness. He brushed his teeth at halftime. He took 2–3 showers a day and used cologne. He wore expensive clothes and had a heart of gold, always a soft touch. If he had $10, he'd give it to you without bothering to ask why. All you had to do was say you needed it.

RICHIE GUERIN: Sweets personally washed his own uniform, because he wanted it to look just right. He was very concerned with having a classy image on and off the court.

CARL BRAUN: Sweetwater wasn't a big scorer, but he was a tremendous clutch player. At the end of the game, he wanted the ball and we looked for him. He was a 60 percent free throw shooter most of the time, but I never remember him missing an important foul shot. Every game he faced guys who were a half-foot taller and he refused to back down an inch. The whole league respected Sweets as much for his character as for how he played.

But Off the Court . . .

EARL LLOYD: The problems the first black players faced were the same that blacks faced everywhere in the 1950s. Kids today, they don't know what it was like before the civil rights legislation, before Martin Luther King and before race became an issue.

My first NBA game was in Rochester. No problems. Nice, quiet town in upstate New York. Then we went to Fort Wayne, Indiana. In 1950, black wasn't beautiful in Fort Wayne. I was allowed to sleep in the same hotel as the team, but I couldn't eat there unless I ordered room service. I wanted to play ball, so what was I supposed to do? I ate room service.

My coach, Bones McKinney, heard about that and he came up to my room and we ate together—a gesture I'll never forget.

I didn't like being closed out of the restaurant, but I also was born and raised in Virginia. Discrimination was a part of life. In a sense, I was amazed that they let me sleep in the same hotel as the team.

These were the days of separate but equal—which was really separate and unequal. In my town, the white kids had the swimming pool, we were supposed to swim in a muddy river. It was separate toilets, sit in the back of the bus and go to an all-black school that was in a run-down building in a bad part of town. These things had steeled me for anything I would face as an NBA player. But I know it was worse for Chuck Cooper, who hadn't endured anything like that growing up in Pittsburgh.

Bob Cousy: Chuck and I were both rookies in 1950. I was from New York, so we had the same basic values when it came to race. We had an exhibition game in Charlotte. He couldn't stay at the same hotel, eat at the same places or even take a piss the same place I did. Chuck was upset by this—and he should have been. In fact, he was taking a midnight train out of town so he wouldn't have to worry about a place to stay. I looked at this garbage and I was embarrassed to be white.

I told Arnold [Auerbach], "Mind if I go home with Chuck?"

Arnold said that was fine.

At the train station, they had "colored" rest rooms and "white" rest rooms, a "colored" waiting room and a "white" waiting room. I was so sick and so embarrassed by what I saw that there was absolutely nothing I could say to Chuck about it. Both of us had been through four years of college and we had heard and read about crap like that— but to be faced with it . . . All I wanted to do was get out of there.

Alex Hannum: I was a teammate of Chuck's in Milwaukee in 1954 and we were playing three exhibition games in Louisiana to capitalize on Bob Pettit's name. At LSU—Pettit's alma mater—they would not allow Cooper to play. They made him sit at the scorer's table. That was better than what they did at Shreveport and New Orleans, where they wouldn't even let Chuck in the gym. Chuck knew that this was how it was in the South. But hell, he didn't like it one bit. Neither did some of the other players and we talked about boycotting the game, but ownership convinced us to play, that this was not the place to make a stand. They put a lot of pressure on us and we played. As for Chuck, he didn't say much. He just took it. It was terrible, but that was what happened.

GENE SHUE: I grew up Catholic, and in the early 1950s I recall certain pews in church that had signs saying, "No colored allowed." I'm talking about in a Catholic church. So it wasn't just hotels and restaurants; the first black players were encountering discrimination everywhere.

JOHNNY KERR: The first blacks to play on a championship team were Earl Lloyd and Jim Tucker with the 1955 Syracuse Nationals. Earl was our defensive enforcer, a guy with a two-handed set shot, a brute-style power forward. If you messed with Earl or any of his teammates, there would be hell to pay because Earl was afraid of no man. But I remember playing in St. Louis and the fans were just screaming all this racial stuff at Earl and it shook him up, as it would anyone. I went and put my arm around Earl, and the fans started spitting on me. It was pretty frightening. The guys on the team didn't care about race, but the fans in some cities sure did.

EARL LLOYD: With Chuck, Sweetwater Clifton and myself being the first three black players, we knew that we were not going to change the world. We also knew that while our teammates were good people, there were only three blacks in the league and we all were on different teams. But we all faced the same problems off the court. So when Chuck Cooper or Sweetwater were playing in my hometown, I'd pick them up at the hotel and bring them to my house for dinner and company. When I was in their town, they picked me up. We were a support group for each other. We wanted the other guy to feel comfortable, and you can't be comfortable sitting alone in a hotel room. What the hell, we got only six bucks a day meal money, so a home-cooked meal with friends meant a lot.

Then the game would come and we'd go out and beat the hell out of each other. The games were the easiest part.

When I played for Syracuse in the early 1950s, I called a few apartments and was told there were openings. Then I went there and suddenly they were full. I knew why they were full, and after a while I found it better to stay with a family in Syracuse. It was a mixed marriage and they lived in a black area. They were great to me, so I found it simpler to live with them during the season.

Adjusting to the NBA was much harder for Chuck than for Sweetwater and myself. I was prepared for anything after growing up in

Virginia. Sweets had traveled the world with the Globetrotters, so he had his share of war stories. But other than having some fans yell racial stuff at him in college, Chuck had very little experience with the rigid racial discrimination in the South. In some towns, you'd walk down the street and wonder, "Will this place serve me or not?" Sometimes, the only way to find out was to walk in and see what happened.

Obviously, it was hard for all the first black players, but the guy who may have had it the toughest was Don Barksdale, who came into the league in 1951. Don was playing in Baltimore, and to the black players, anything south of Philadelphia was considered behind the Cotton Curtain.

No Service: Three Stories

CARL BRAUN: I was with the Celtics in 1961 and we played an exhibition game in Marion, Indiana. They had a big luncheon for us, the mayor gave us keys to the city and it was a nice event.

After the game, I walked into a greasy spoon for a hamburger along with Sam Jones, K.C. Jones and Bill Russell.

The place sat about 40, but there were only 10 people inside. The hostess looked at us and said, "All the tables are reserved."

All the bar stools were empty, so we started walking in that direction. Then she said, "Sorry, those are reserved, too."

We got the message and left. Back at the hotel, I was getting madder and madder the more I thought about it. I remembered the mayor's name, looked it up in the phone book and called the guy about 1 A.M., telling him that I didn't want the key to his rotten city.

TOM HEINSOHN: I went to that joint with Bill Sharman, Frank Ramsey and Cousy. We had just finished eating when Braun, Russell and those guys came in. When they were refused service, Carl came to our table and he was hot. "Some damn town this is. I'll tell you where they can shove the key to their city." Carl wanted to do something. He found out where the mayor lived and about 2 A.M., all the players—black and white—poured into two cabs. We went over to the mayor's house and gave him the keys back. Carl spoke for us and while the mayor tried to apologize, that didn't help Russell and the other black players. They had heard it all before.

Furthermore, Walter Brown said that the black players would not be embarrassed again.

But it was worse the next night, when we played the St. Louis Hawks in an exhibition game in Lexington, Kentucky. It was supposed to be a big homecoming game for Frank Ramsey and Cliff Hagan, who were Kentucky graduates. It also was to be the first game where there would be integrated seating. In the past, black fans were only allowed to sit in certain sections.

When we arrived at a restaurant in Lexington, they wouldn't serve the black players. This came only 24 hours after the incident in Marion, so emotions were very high, as they should have been. I saw Satch Sanders's face. This guy was from New York. He had never been through crap like this. He was heartbroken. Who were these people to treat Satch Sanders like dirt? The black players from both teams held a meeting and they decided that they wouldn't play. Red asked the rest of us to play. He said we had a contract to play the game and that we didn't want to embarrass Frank Ramsey by not playing. It was one helluva spot for everybody. I agonized about playing—should I or shouldn't I? I thought, "They're finally going to integrate the stands, and what if we refuse to play?" We loved Walter Brown and we respected Red. We didn't want to leave them in a business bind by not playing the game. The night before, we had given back the keys to the city. The black players didn't say a word about what we should do. We had traveled together, eaten together and played together. Were we supposed to walk out on a game together? I honestly didn't know. It was very complicated.

Finally, we played. Each team had 6–7 players, all white. We also made a statement protesting the treatment that the black players received and saying that we played only because Kentucky agreed to integrate the stands. But no one felt good about playing or what had happened.

○ ○ ○

HOT ROD HUNDLEY: In 1958, the Lakers set up an exhibition game in my hometown of Charleston, West Virginia. It was supposed to be a big deal for me and I wanted all the guys on the team to be treated well and have a good time. I never thought there would be a racial problem, but you don't think about those things when you're white.

ELGIN BAYLOR: We had played the night before in another part of the country. Our plane connections were messed up and we didn't get to our hotel in Charleston until 4 P.M. The game was at eight.

We didn't go by bus from the airport to the hotel, we took cabs. We were standing around the lobby waiting for our rooms. Because we had spent all day in airports, guys were tired and in lousy moods. We just wanted to get a room and catch a quick nap before the game. Our team captain was Vern Mikkelsen, and he was at the hotel desk. I was about 10 feet away and I could hear that they were giving Vern a hard time.

I had a suspicion about what was the problem, so I went to the desk to ask what was going on.

The clerk acted as if I wasn't there.

Mikkelsen said, "They won't give us our rooms. I don't know why."

It was obvious that the clerk wasn't going to talk to anyone while I was at the desk, so I took a couple of steps away.

The clerk then told Mikkelsen, "You guys can stay here, but the colored guys have to stay somewhere else."

I went back to the clerk and said, "Did I hear you right? Did you say we can't stay here?"

The clerk still acted as if I wasn't there.

Then Coach [John Kundla] showed up. I told him what happened and I said, "Even if they let me in now, I won't stay here. I want an airline ticket home."

Kundla asked me to wait. He went to the phone and called [owner] Bob Short. Short got the clerk on the phone and was screaming. He said that he had agreed to the exhibition game because he was promised that the whole team could stay at the best hotel in town—and that meant everybody on the team. He said he made it very clear that there were blacks on the team, and there better not be any problems with the rooms. The clerk said he could not change policy. Short yelled, "Fine, we'll stay somewhere else."

HOT ROD HUNDLEY: We ended up at a place called Edna's Retirement Hotel, which was a black hotel.

ELGIN BAYLOR: I could tell that some of the white guys weren't thrilled about switching hotels, but no one said anything. At this point, I still planned to play the game because the team had backed me. Then Boo Ellis, Ed Fleming and I went out to get a sandwich before the game, but no restaurant would serve us. We went to several places and were embarrassed each time. Finally, the Greyhound bus station was the only place that would sell us food.

I told Kundla what happened and said, "Coach, I just can't play in this town."

He said, "Elgin, I don't blame you."

HOT ROD HUNDLEY: The people who put on the game wanted me to talk to Elgin about playing. After pregame warmups, I went into the dressing room and he was sitting there in his street clothes.

I said, "What they did to you isn't right. I understand that. But we're friends and this is my hometown. Play this one for me."

Elgin said, "Rod, you're right. You are my friend. But Rod, I'm a human being, too. All I want to do is to be treated like a human being."

It was then that I could begin to feel his pain.

ELGIN BAYLOR: After I told Rod that there was no reason that anyone should be treated like we were, he quickly said, "Elgin, I'll understand it if you don't play."

HOT ROD HUNDLEY: I went to the people who were sponsoring the game and I said, "Elgin isn't playing and I don't blame him. He shouldn't after how he was treated."

That night, we found out that Edna's Retirement Hotel was really a front for a black whorehouse. There were two floors and one bathroom on each floor. I thought, even in my own town, I wind up staying in a whorehouse.

ELGIN BAYLOR: A few days later, I got a call from the mayor of Charleston and he apologized. Two years later, I was invited to an all-star game there, and out of courtesy I went. We stayed at the same hotel that had refused us service. We were able to eat anywhere we wanted. They were beginning to integrate the schools. Some black leaders told me that they were able to use what had happened to me and the other black players to bring pressure on the city to make changes, and that made me feel very good.

But the indignity of a hotel clerk acting as if you aren't there, of people who won't sell you a sandwich because you're black . . . those are things you never forget.

HOT ROD HUNDLEY: Elgin had the personality where he liked to hang around with everyone. I thought he made a point of getting along with the white guys. He was color-blind. He wanted everyone to be team-mates and race was not something we talked about much. But when Ray Charles came out with "Born to Lose," Elgin told me that it was the black national anthem. That comment always stayed with me.

○ ○ ○

ALEX HANNUM: The crazy part about this story is that no blacks were involved—someone just thought one of my teammates was black.

I was playing for the Milwaukee Hawks in 1954. We had an exhibition game in Baton Rouge, Louisiana. It was after the game where they wouldn't allow Chuck Cooper to play because he was black. Several of the players went to a real greasy spoon for some burgers and beer. From where we sat, we could see a statue of Huey Long.

Bob Harrison was with us and he had a dark complexion. A few girls came in and Harrison looked at them for a moment.

While Charlie Share is white, he also could see a problem. He said, "Bob, you better be careful."

But Harrison got up, went over to the bar where the girls were sitting and said something.

There were five guys in the back of the room, and they made some comment about how no black guy—although they used much harsher terms—was going to pick up white girls in their town. The five guys surrounded Harrison.

Then Charlie Share and I went over there. We were upset about how Chuck had been treated at the game. Now this . . . we had had enough racial crap for one night. Beside, Harrison was a white guy.

So we swung into action and it was a terrific brawl, one of those where glass was breaking, bodies were thrown over the bar and wait-resses screamed. It was like the Old West and we were pulverizing those guys, who were fat, out of shape and not ready to deal with three very big pro athletes.

There were sirens and a state trooper came into the bar, and pointed a revolver at my head.

I knew I was in trouble, so I said, "Hey, do you know who Bob Pettit is? We're teammates."

Pettit may as well have owned Baton Rouge after playing for LSU.

The cops led us out of the bar and told us to keep our mouths shut.

CHARLIE SHARE: Since we never did eat that night, we walked away from the bar and asked a lady on the street where was a restaurant that was still open. She started to say something, then saw Bob Harrison. She just turned her back without a word and walked away. She obviously thought Harrison was black and she wouldn't even talk to a white guy who was standing with a black.

ALEX HANNUM: That incident gave me a bit of a feel for what it must be like to be black and take that crap, the anger that is within you. It makes you feel like you're going to explode.

The Quota System

According to Harvey Pollack's statistics, after the 1956–57 season— Bill Russell's rookie year—only 22 blacks had played in the NBA, even though the color line had been broken in 1950. On the 1957 championship Celtics, Russell was the only black player. But the Celtics did have three blacks on their 1959 championship team—K.C. Jones, Sam Jones and Russell. The 1958 St. Louis Hawks were the last all-white champions. By 1960, the situation had improved as 25 of the 96 players—or 26 percent—were black.

HOT ROD HUNDLEY: Even by 1960, the NBA was 80 percent white and that was no accident. The phrase whispered was, "It's a white dollar." Most owners were afraid that too many blacks would keep away the fans. The unwritten rule on most teams was that you preferred to have two black players, but don't have more than three. A black player had to be better than the average white player to make a team. It was racism, pure and simple.

CHARLIE SHARE: Obviously, I don't agree with this. In fact, most white players didn't agree with this. But what we heard was, "Give me two black players and I'll win a title. Three and they'll take over and there will be trouble."

DON BARKSDALE: The feeling among the first black players was that you played defense, you got a rebound, you threw the ball to the guard and that was the last you saw of it. You were there to set picks and hit the boards. If you did score, it was almost by accident—you got an offensive rebound or you ended up with the ball after no one else could get off a shot. You had the feeling that they wanted you on the team, but they didn't want you to score or be a star. In 1953, I averaged almost 14 points, more than any other black player, for the Baltimore Bullets, but I recall a game where I went a full quarter without receiving one pass. I about wanted to cry. It wasn't just selfishness, it was, "Hey, I can help us win some games if I see the ball. We aren't exactly a great team." But I also found that no one was real receptive to that kind of talk. The other black players had the same roadblocks.

They also wanted the black players to guard each other—since we all were forwards. It isolated us. We ran up and down the court and never saw the ball. It was a 4-on-4 game with us as the odd men out. Finally, all four of us got together—Lloyd, Cooper, Clifton and myself—and we went to our coaches and raised hell about the matchups, and they changed it. Was it intentional? They said it wasn't. No matter what was their intent, the result was degrading.

EARL LLOYD: In the early years, I always felt that the quota was one black player—certainly no more than two—on most teams. Two was a good number because the two blacks could room together. If you had three, then one of them had to room with a white boy. Not every team worried about this, but too many of them did.

LENNY WILKENS: When Harry Gallatin took over as coach of the St. Louis Hawks, I roomed with Mike Farmer—a white guy. He changed the rooming list, putting me with a black player and Farmer with a white. Gallatin will deny it today, but that was what happened and I believe it wasn't an accident. A number of the owners, general managers and coaches were prejudiced, and it showed up in small ways such as rooming lists.

EARL LLOYD: You'd walk into a restaurant in St. Louis to order food, and they'd bring it to you on a Styrofoam plate. If you were black, your order always was to go. The fans were vicious—not physically abusive, but they spit a lot of racial venom at you, questioning your ancestry.

JERRY GROSS: The racial climate in St. Louis came to a head in 1961 when the Hawks drafted Cleo Hill. Clyde Lovellette and some of the other veterans, they just buried that kid. Some of the white veterans treated him more like a shoeshine boy than a teammate. Paul Seymour was coaching, and during a time-out he said, "The next guy who doesn't throw Cleo the ball will be fined $500."

The Hawks went back on the court and they still froze Hill out.

Seymour called another time-out and said, "The next SOB who doesn't throw Hill the ball is gonna be punched in the mouth."

About a week after that, Seymour was fired. A number of the veterans went to [owner] Ben Kerner and complained about Seymour—not about Hill, but about Seymour in general. Kerner liked to fire coaches, so he fired Seymour. Hill was a talent, a scoring guard from Winston-Salem State. Some of the Hawks were intimidated by his talent and they didn't want to share the glory. Lenny Wilkens was different. He was a rookie before Hill came into the league, but Lenny was a ballhandler. He made the other guys look better. When Hill was a rookie, Lenny was in the military so Hill was on his own out there.

CLIFF HAGAN: Paul Seymour was determined to make a star out of Hill. He had put his butt on the line when they drafted him, but Hill failed miserably. He played only one year in the NBA, he was traded and didn't make it with any other team, either. So I guess that was the bottom line.

MARTY BLAKE: People said we had a black-white situation in St. Louis, but that's not right. Before Hill, we had Sihugo Green and Lenny Wilkens. They had no problems. Listen, Hill could have been a great player. In his first game, he had 30 points against Oscar Robertson. But he was scatterbrained and he was a runner off the court, too. He settled down and later became an excellent junior college coach, but when he was with us, he was immature and it hurt him.

ZELMO BEATY: I came to the Hawks in 1962 and I had heard about the trouble Hill had and how it was hard for the black players in St. Louis, but I never felt restricted because of my color in St. Louis. No one ever said anything—at least to my face. I enjoyed playing there, but the 1960s was much different from the 1950s in terms of racial attitudes.

AL ATTLES: I came into the league in 1960 and the word was that there could be up to four blacks on a team. When I was a rookie, the Warriors already had four blacks—Guy Rodgers, Andy Johnson, Woody Sauldsberry and Wilt. Then it became apparent that I was going to make the team, meaning there would be five blacks. We—the black players—started hearing that one of us would be traded. The veterans guessed that it would be Sauldsberry who'd go, and sure enough, he was traded. The theory was that black players cut each other. As a black player, you weren't competing for one of the 12 roster spots, you were after one of the four that belonged to black players. There were too many examples of these kinds of player moves for it to have been a coincidence.

NORM DRUCKER: The racial politics that was played by the front office was not reflected by the guys on the court. In all my years of officiating, I never heard one player make a racial remark to another. The fans—you better believe they could get ugly. But not the players.

ALEX HANNUM: The pressure the black players faced off the court can't be minimized. But the white players accepted them. Most of us had played against blacks in college or the military. I also don't believe that there was a color line in the league. I'm emphatic about that—I don't believe there was a quota system. Certainly there never was on any of the teams I coached.

WILT CHAMBERLAIN: The white players were never hostile to blacks. A number of them were ahead of their time in terms of racial attitudes. But there were too many players who didn't know how to handle the situation. Not that they were bigots, it was just that they were content to accept the social rules. A number of them wouldn't say, "Hey, if you don't serve him, then you don't serve me." They ate their meals and let you fend for yourself. They stuck their heads in the sand and pretended nothing wrong was going on.

AL ATTLES: I was introduced to the rules of the road for black players during my rookie year when we had an exhibiton game in a small town in Missouri. The team bus stopped for lunch and most of the guys headed toward a café. Then Wilt and Andy Johnson grabbed me and said, "We're going to Dutch it."

They took me across the street to a little grocery store. We bought a loaf of bread, some bologna and cheese and made sandwiches that we ate on the bus. It took me a while to figure out that Wilt and Andy looked at the place and decided that blacks would not be served there. Rather than go inside and be embarrassed, we all went across the street instead.

WILT CHAMBERLAIN: Remember that the NBA was lily white at the top—owners, general managers, coaches, front office people. They didn't want to make waves, and they didn't want their players to make waves, either.

EARL LLOYD: But things did change. I was the first black assistant coach when Fred Zollner hired me with the Pistons in 1960. Fred was a good guy. He was under no pressure to hire me—I didn't ask for the job, he approached me.

ELGIN BAYLOR: Both black and white players said there was a quota, and I noticed it on some teams who really tried to stay white. But I must say that with the Lakers, race was never an issue. All [owner] Bob Short cared about was winning, and part of the reason we were so successful is that we took the best players, regardless of race. Boston did the same thing.

PETE D'AMBROSIO: The first time five blacks were on the court at the same time was in 1961 with the old Chicago Packers. I officiated the game and the five players were Woody Sauldsberry, Horace Walker, Walt Bellamy, Andy Johnson and Sihugo Green. Nothing much was made of that, but some of the basketball people just mentioned it in passing. The game was changing and finally opening up to black players.

EARL LLOYD: People ask me how I could stand some of the racial slights. I try to explain that was how the world was back then. I would love to take a club, go back through history and settle some scores. But I don't dwell on that. It serves no purpose. I do feel good when I look at the NBA rosters today and see 9–10 black kids. I think about how someone had to be first—how guys like Chuck Cooper, Sweetwater Clifton, Don Barksdale and myself paid the dues so those kids can have the chance they do today. They don't realize what we accomplished, but I do.

AS IT SHOULD BE

A black hand supports
the white body of a fallen teammate.

The ball that scored the winning goal
was placed in motion by a gray hand.

The sweat pouring from our bodies
is neither black nor white.

—TOM MESCHERY

Two Real Teammates

The numbers show that Maurice Stokes played only three years, his career ending after the 1957–58 season. He averaged 16.4 points, 17.1 rebounds and 5.3 assists as a 6-foot-7 center. Yes, a 6-foot-7 center. How can you play center at 6-foot-7? It could only happen in the 1950s, you insist? If that's the case, then you never saw Wes Unseld (1968–81), a Hall of Fame center at 6-foot-7 with the Washington Bullets. Of course, Unseld was wide enough to set a pick on the sun. So was Stokes, who was listed at 240 pounds, but those who played with and against him maintain he was closer to 275. Stokes was the 1956 Rookie of the Year when he was second in the league in rebounding at 16.3. It might also be noted that Stokes was the NBA's first black star, as he came into the league a year before Bill Russell. There were other superb black players in the early 1950s, but they were relegated to what was then called "the defensive forward." But Stokes and teammate Jack Twyman were the heart of the Rochester Royals. The ball went through them, Twyman working outside, Stokes under the basket. Twyman became a Hall of Fame forward, a career 19-point shooter. Stokes would have been a Hall of Famer, too. In his second season, Stokes led the NBA at 17.4 rebounds per game and was third in the league in assists, absolutely remarkable for a center. But at the age of 25 and at the end of his third season, Stokes contracted encephalitis. He went into a coma, regained consciousness, but never played again because of severe paralysis. His legal guardian was Jack Twyman, and their story became the NBA's Brian's Song.

EARL STROM: Maurice Stokes was from little St. Francis College in Loretto, Pennsylvania. I saw him play in college and he just dominated. It was the same when he went to the NBA. Maurice was an innovative player, a very physical center who could handle the ball like a guard. At the high post, he could kill you three ways—by passing to a cutter, by hitting the jump shot, by driving to the basket. He was quicker than he looked. What he really played was point center because of his tremendous passing skills.

CARL BRAUN: People love to talk about the ability and the great size Maurice had, but what impressed me was that this guy was an All-Star from the neck up, too. He did more than play the game; he could think it.

LESTER HARRISON: When I owned the Rochester Royals, I drafted Stokes in the first round in 1955 and then I had to outbid Abe Saperstein for him. Abe didn't talk to me for years after that. He did a lot for the league by playing doubleheaders, with the NBA teams playing the second game, to help the gate. In fact, I had some NBA owners tell me, "Lay off Stokes. Abe has been good to us. We need him."

I said, "Listen, I talked to the Stokes kid. He doesn't want to play for the Globetrotters. He wants the NBA. I want him and I'm going to sign him." So I did. I got Jack Twyman out of that draft, too.

SLICK LEONARD: Maurice came into the league and was an immediate star. He was built like a bull and played with the grace of an antelope. Had he stayed healthy, he was a certain Hall of Famer.

WAYNE EMBRY: The thing that made Maurice so great was that he could get a rebound off the defensive board and then dribble it up the court, leading the fast break like Magic Johnson. That's a Hall of Fame skill. What stood out was his unselfishness; he would rather hit the boards and pass than score.

JACK TWYMAN: I'm coming at this from a biased perspective, but I honestly believe that Maurice had a chance to be perhaps the greatest player of all time. I played with both Maurice and Oscar Robertson, and he could do many of the same things Oscar could, only Maurice was 6-foot-7, Oscar 6-foot-5; he was 275 pounds, Oscar about 220. Maurice's game was evolving to the point where he would have become a bigger version of Oscar Robertson. He could legitimately play forward, guard or center.

JOHNNY KERR: The interesting part of the relationship between Jack and Maurice was that they were not close when they were teammates.

Word around the league was that they both wanted the ball and wanted their shots. They were two great players who came to the same team in the same year and sometimes that leads to friction. Early in their career, you never would have guessed that when Stokes got sick it would be Jack Twyman who'd step up and go to bat for him.

EARL STROM: Jack was a fine shooter who definitely had a scoring mentality. As we used to say, "Jack only shoots the ball when he has it." Oscar and some of the other guys he played with over the years complained about that.

RUDY LaRUSSO: The first time I played Twyman, boy, he just ate me up and spit me out. After that, he would still get his 25 against me, but I would at least make him take 20–30 shots to get it. We called him Pitchin' Jack because he was sort of a gunner and it did seem that he shot it every time he touched the ball. But let me tell you, that man was a great shooter, too.

RON GRINKER: The bottom line on Jack Twyman was that his range was inside the gym. Imagine what the Royals would have been if they could have had Oscar, Twyman, Stokes, Wayne Embry and Jerry Lucas?

JACK TWYMAN: Maurice Stokes was as healthy and strong as any player in the league in his first three seasons. There were no signs that anything was wrong with him. In our final game of the 1957–58 regular season, we played at Minneapolis. Maurice just tripped, fell down and he seemed to lose consciousness for a minute. We gathered around him, and he regained consciousness and seemed all right. No one thought much of it. He was fine until three days later when we played at Detroit in the playoffs. He had a poor game, but none of us who left the floor that night thought anything was physically wrong with Maurice.

LESTER HARRISON: Maurice became ill when we were playing in Detroit. He looked very weak to me during the game. He shot a few airballs, had no energy on the boards. This was a guy who could jump over Bill Russell, and he wasn't leaving his feet. I just figured that he had the flu or something. When we got on the airplane after the game to return to Cincinnati, Maurice went down the aisle to the bathroom and he was moaning, almost a death rattle.

JACK TWYMAN: Maurice wore a tweed sport coat and he started sweating. It was like he had been dunked in a swimming pool. This happened about 10 minutes out of Detroit and it was obvious he was very sick and he passed out. They called an ambulance to wait for us at the airport in Cincinnati.

LESTER HARRISON: That night, Dick Ricketts and myself went with Maurice to the hospital. Jack Twyman was not there. He and Maurice were not very close. Anyway, at seven the next morning, Maurice was having trouble breathing and the doctors wanted to operate. They asked my permission and I gave it. Someone had to speak for Maurice. But the surgery didn't work and the poor guy became a vegetable.

JACK TWYMAN: Maurice's disease was encephalitis and it was caused by a trauma. In his case, when he had his feet knocked out from under him during that game in Minneapolis. When you're unconscious, the brain swells. When you fly, the change of air pressure can affect the brain and that stimulated his attack. It is really unfair to call him a vegetable. Maurice's brain was perfect. He understood everything that was going on and he learned to communicate. But it was obvious that his motor nerves were severely damaged and he would always be under a doctor's care.

RON GRINKER: Jack began to help Maurice by default. Before the illness, those guys didn't have much of a relationship. But when Maurice got sick, someone had to be Maurice's legal guardian and that someone had to live in Cincinnati, where Maurice was hospitalized. Stokes was from Pittsburgh. The Royals had just moved from Rochester to Cincinnati the season Maurice was stricken. Jack was the only player who was a permanent resident of the city.

JACK TWYMAN: It is true Maurice and I weren't especially close friends, but we still were teammates. Also, a few weeks after Maurice got sick Lester Harrison sold the Royals to a Cincinnati group. When he sold the team, the price was $225,000 if Maurice played again, $200,000 if he did not. Maurice became ill on the last day of the season and no one had multiyear contracts then. He was a player without a contract, a man without a team. He had no insurance. He needed to stay in Ohio to get something from workmen's compensation.

When Maurice became ill, he had $9,000 in the bank and a new DeSoto. It was obvious that his medical bills were going to be enormous.

Someone had to become his guardian to gain access to the bank account and to sell his car to pay the hospital. Maurice's parents and family lived in Pittsburgh; they visited him often, but they couldn't move to Cincinnati because they had jobs and we couldn't move Maurice to Pittsburgh. Circumstances meant that it fell to me. I was the logical choice.

RON GRINKER: Jack's entire family threw themselves into taking care of Maurice. What Jack did was to become the front man, the guy raising money, speaking to groups and spending time trying to find a way to pay Maurice's medical bills. His wife, Caroline, along with a local businessman named Phil Margolis, were the unsung heroes. They were with Maurice every day, giving him a lot of personal attention. Jack and a lot of other people made real sacrifices.

JACK TWYMAN: After a while, it became obvious that Maurice was not making the kind of progress we had hoped. My whole family adopted him. At times, it was heartbreaking. Here was an athlete at the height of his physical powers and for him to lose virtually all of his motor skills . . . I mean, he couldn't walk, he couldn't feed himself. At first, he communicated to us by blinking his eyes. Finally, he was able to speak, but the average person could not understand the sounds, although those of us close to him could. Simple communication was so hard, so frustrating for him. You could feel his pain as he tried to tell you something. Yet he retained his intelligence. He read a lot, watched TV and loved to talk about sports, politics, you name it. He never failed to vote. His mind was a sponge and he kept up more on current events than I did.

WAYNE EMBRY: A lot of the players would visit Maurice. He couldn't talk much, mostly he nodded his head. He could utter sounds. Jack and his family usually knew what he said. It was amazing how they did that. There was a real bond between Maurice and the Twymans. It had to be killing both of them because Maurice just didn't make the kind of progress everyone hoped. Unless we've gone through something like that, we can't imagine what it must have been like for Maurice to have his career—and nearly his life—stolen from him. To be confined to a hospital . . . to be a man who was stronger than anyone in the league, and he needed help to feed and dress himself with no real hope of getting better . . . I don't know how Maurice handled it and I don't know where Jack and his family found the patience to be with him every day.

JACK TWYMAN: Of course there were days when it was hard to go see him, because you knew he was hurting and discouraged by the lack of progress. There were days when you asked yourself, "What can I tell him? How can I help him?" But I found that I drew strength from Maurice and his will to go on. I didn't quit because he never quit. I like to think we were there for each other.

WAYNE EMBRY: I had taken over at center for Maurice, and the one thing he would tell me was, "No one gets rebounds." He wanted me to get all the boards. I think he secretly thought one day the disease would end and he'd play again, although he never said it. One of his favorite moments was when they would take him to his own summer game at Milton Kutsher's resort and everyone would make a fuss over him. Myself or some of the other big guys would help carry him on and off the airplane—they had steps back then, not jetways like now. Maurice was a huge guy, and we usually banged his head on something, but he just laughed. He relished any attention and I never saw him in the kind of depression most of us would have been in in his situation.

JACK TWYMAN: The biggest burden for us was financial. As the years passed, the medical bills kept rising. Once I thought we were going to be totally out of money, but a local businessman who never wants his name revealed stepped in and paid a lot of money to cover some of the expenses and buy us time to raise more money. We later moved Maurice to Good Samaritan Hospital in Cincinnati, and they were very good to work with and patient when it came to the bills. In the 12 years that Maurice was alive, the bills ran well over a million dollars. Milton Kutsher was wonderful. He hosted the Maurice Stokes Game each year and that probably raised over $750,000 for Maurice.

HASKELL COHEN: In addition to being the PR director for the NBA, I also did some work for Milton Kutsher. I grew up in Pittsburgh and I knew Maurice from when he was a star at Westinghouse High. He was clean as a whistle, a wonderful kid. He was the kind of person you like to help. His medical bills became astronomical, so Jack Twyman, Milton Kutsher and I put our heads together and came up with the Stokes Game, to be played every summer at Kutsher's to raise money for Maurice, and later for other former players who had problems. For example, we gave the late Gus Johnson $26,000 to help with his medical bills. But when Maurice was alive, the game was a real event. All the top stars played. Now it's more difficult to attract players, even though we have given away over $700,000 to needy players other than Stokes.

JACK TWYMAN: The NBA players stepped in and helped Maurice. Remember, this was when the league wasn't making money, when the average player was earning less than $10,000 and the Players Association really hadn't gotten off the ground. But guys played at the Stokes Game at their own expense. The most dramatic story was when Wilt Chamberlain heard about the first game. He was just out of Kansas and playing with the Globetrotters, before his NBA career had started. He didn't know Maurice. The game was scheduled when the Trotters were touring in Paris, France. Wilt said not to worry, he would be there. He took a plane from Paris to New York City, then chartered a helicopter to go to Kutsher's in the Catskills. He played in the game, took the helicopter back to New York and the plane back to Paris—all at his own expense and he was only 21 years old at the time. So many guys helped—Oscar Robertson, Wayne Embry, Tom Gola . . . the list is very long. The players were very good about stopping by the hospital to see Maurice when they were in town to play the Royals, and that meant a lot to him, especially since Maurice watched all the NBA games on TV.

Howard Cosell had a hot radio show at the time and he'd have me on around Christmastime. We'd talk about Maurice and raise $50,000 that way. In 1958, we were having trouble paying the bills and I mentioned that to Jerry Tax of *Sports Illustrated*. Then *SI* did a piece on Maurice and we received over $200,000 that way. I'd go into different cities with the Royals, and sportswriters and radio broadcasters would interview me about Maurice—we'd get money that way. The great thing was that all these people helped out year after year.

RON GRINKER: You have to understand that Jack Twyman has always been a sharp businessman and he put those skills to work for Maurice. Today, his Super Foods Company in Cincinnati is so successful that Jack could write a check to buy an NBA team all in cash and have plenty of money left over.

JACK TWYMAN: The irony is that his illness didn't directly kill Maurice. He died of a heart attack. His body just gave out. The strange thing was that Maurice had a twin sister—Clarice. She had never been sick a day in her life, but she had a heart attack and died a week after he did.

WAYNE EMBRY: To this day, I get choked up when I think about what Jack and his family did for Maurice. It was every day, for 12 years. Think about that. For 12 years, there never was a day when the Twymans didn't have Maurice Stokes on their mind. It transcended friendship as we know it. It was the ultimate expression of love because love for another person is spending time and helping out when it's not an easy thing to do. I know some people got tired of hearing Jack talk about Maurice, but he had to be persistent to raise the money and pay those medical bills. What Jack Twyman did was one of the best things you'll ever see in pro sports.

5
FORGOTTEN STARS

The Larry Bird of Syracuse

Dolph Schayes was with the Syracuse Nationals for all 14 of their years in the NBA and he's a major reason they won 57 percent of their games and made the playoffs every year in that span. Schayes was a 6-foot-8, 220-pound forward who was among the league's Top 10 in both scoring and rebounding during his first 12 seasons. A member of the basketball Hall of Fame, Schayes averaged 18 points and 12 rebounds in 16 pro seasons. He later coached the Philadelphia Warriors and served as supervisor of NBA officials. His son, Danny, plays for the Milwaukee Bucks.

ALEX HANNUM: In the 1940s and 1950s, there was something called "the New York City player." It isn't like the player from New York you think of today, the guy off the playgrounds with all the dunks and fancy moves. The New York player of the earlier era played a lot of what we called give-and-go basketball, a little like the passing game of today. If you catch a pass, you either shoot, drive or pass the ball and cut. Whatever you do, you don't stand there holding the ball. There were few set plays, nothing but constant movement. In the Midwest and on the West Coast, we played a more structured style with set plays. But Syracuse was a New York–style team. Their coach was Al Cervi, who grew up on the sidewalks and playgrounds. Cervi never went to college. He came up the hard way and it showed. Their star was Dolph Schayes, who epitomized that New York style.

BOB FERRY: In my rookie year, I got off to a great start in the exhibition season with St. Louis. Part of the reason was that Wilt Chamberlain was guarding me. I was an outside shooter and Wilt didn't like to come out from under the basket, so I stood out there making jumper after jumper. Also, since it was the exhibition season, Wilt's heart wasn't exactly in it. I started to think I was a great player. Then we ran into Syracuse. Ed Macauley was coaching St. Louis and he said to me, "Tonight, you're going to guard Dolph Schayes. He's an older guy, all he likes to do is take a two-handed set shot. He's slowed down over the years, so don't worry about it."

The game began and Dolph took off. He ran me up and down the court, in and out exits. He never stood still for a second without the ball. By the end of the first quarter, my tongue was hanging out. I'd never covered a guy like this. Macauley did it to set me up.

TOM GOLA: Dolph was one of the slowest guys in the league, if you were to line the players up and have them run a 100-yard dash. But he never stopped moving on the court. I mean *never*. If he didn't know what else to do, he'd run figure eights out there to drive the defense crazy.

ALEX HANNUM: The shooting. The guy had legitimate 25–30–foot range. You could add five points to his career scoring if they had the three-point shot back then, because he never hesitated to take a 25-, even a 30-footer.

AL BIANCHI: Dolph was a legit 6-foot-8, one of the best rebounders in the league and he couldn't dunk the ball. I don't mean that he refused to do it, like a lot of guys from that era. He couldn't and we'd tease him about it. But the truth was that the guy couldn't jump an inch off the floor, I swear it.

LARRY COSTELLO: Dolph was the first guy I saw who'd get his hand on a rebound, tip it to an open area and then run it down. He was a studied player, as if he thought of every move before he made it.

DOLPH SCHAYES: I was a center at NYU and played the low post. If I was going to play pro ball, it was obvious that I wouldn't be a low-post center. Even in 1948 when I came out of school, 6-foot-8 was small for a center. When I came out of NYU with my engineering degree, there were two pro leagues. The Knicks drafted me and so did Syracuse. I also had an offer to go to work for Boeing. I think the Knicks saw me as a 6-foot-8 center who might have trouble, so they offered me $5,000, take it or leave it. Syracuse brought my father and me in. Danny Biasone and his lawyer, Leo Ferris, really showed an interest. They offered me

$7,000 plus a $500 bonus. People said, how could I pass up the Knicks? Well, it was easy. Syracuse wanted me, but I also knew that if I wanted to be a good pro, I had to learn how to play outside.

DANNY BIASONE: None of my players worked like Dolph. What he enjoyed the most was practicing by himself—running, shooting, dribbling. Our workouts would be over and he wouldn't leave the gym. I had to chase him out.

DOLPH SCHAYES: As I started to work on my outside shot, I saw that I had a good touch. Then I wanted to increase my range so I kept shooting from farther and farther out.

GEORGE YARDLEY: Dolph was compulsive. He was seeking perfection. He's one of my best friends, but even Dolph knows that he was a plodder on the court. What made him great was that he was relentless. We were teammates when he had been in the league 10 years, and he still lived in the gym like some rookie wanting to make the team. He would overwhelm you with effort.

AL BIANCHI: I dressed next to Dolph for six years, and around game time he would sink deep into thought—and all he thought about was the game, even after it was over. After some games, I'd look in my locker and half of my stuff would be gone. Then I'd look in Dolph's bag and there it was. He was so absentminded, he'd leave his things behind and take mine. But the classic Dolph story was before one game when a guy who worked for the team said, "Dolph, did you forget something?"
Dolph said, "What?"
He said, "Your wife is on the phone. She said, 'Tell Dolph that he walked out of the house and forgot to take me to the game.' "

DOLPH SCHAYES: I was consumed by the game, especially what I call true basketball where you don't stand there with your hand up, you move for the ball. You try to get better, learn new shots and moves. That was why I loved practice.

AL BIANCHI: Dolph would do things in practice that drove some of his coaches a little crazy. If he had a bad passing game, then the next day at practice he'd do nothing but pass. Or if he missed a left-handed layup, then the only shots he took were left-handed layups.
Later, when he coached in Philadelphia, he had some strange tech-

niques. One year, we had training camp in Hershey, Pennsylvania, and he'd get us up early in the morning and he'd lead us—yes, I said lead us—on a cross-country run as we smelled the chocolate in the air. He'd lead us in running stairs. Guys half his age would be bitching and moaning as he ran them into the ground.

One year, we trained in Atlantic City and Dolph decided that we should ride bikes on the boardwalk. Again, he led us.

JOHNNY KERR: Chet Walker and I couldn't see a lot to be gained from these long bike rides, so we'd drop back in the pack, let them ride out ahead. Then Chet and I would stop in a greasy spoon for a cup of coffee, wait around the corner and ride our bikes back into the pack as they came around the last turn.

AL BIANCHI: We had a rookie named Jerry Greenspan. He was looking at a girl or something and rode his bike into two old people. That was the end of Dolph's bike-riding drills.

JOHNNY KERR: Dolph also would lead us on a drill where we'd run through the surf at Atlantic City, the idea being to build up our wind. Wilt was on the team then. I remember him driving onto the boardwalk in his Bentley and seeing us ready to run on the beach. Wilt got out of the car and shook his head. You could tell that he found this to be a little off base. He took off his shirt and tie, then his shoes and socks. Wilt rolled up his pants and then ran with us through the surf.

AL BIANCHI: When I played with Dolph, I was inspired by the guy. We'd practice free throws, and I wasn't a very good foul shooter. So Dolph would say, "Any free throw you make counts. Only perfect swishes count for me." We'd play for beer and he'd beat me anyway.

JOHNNY KERR: In training camp one year, they had a little rim—the kind a ball could barely fit through—it was to be used for rebounding drills. Dolph practiced his free throws on that rim.

AL BIANCHI: People remember Dolph's long set shots. His trademark was that after he made a basket, he'd throw his fist in the air and run down to the other end of the court. But what made him great was that he could shoot running one-handers—and make them with either hand. His left was as good as his right.

CHARLEY ECKMAN: That was because he broke his wrist in the middle of the 1954 playoffs. It was his right hand, his shooting hand. He put a cast on it, and played left-handed.

JOHNNY KERR: I asked Dolph how to learn to shoot with my left hand. He said, "It's easy, tie your right one behind your back. That's how I learned."

CARL BRAUN: The only big man who has the shooting range of Dolph is Larry Bird. Dolph's shot was higher, softer. But if you see Larry, then you get an idea of how Dolph was.

TOM GOLA: The Bird comparison is perfect. Both guys were self-made players. Both were great rebounders who couldn't jump. Both had tremendous range on their shots, yet also could shoot off the run with either hand. Dolph wasn't the passer like Larry, but that part of Dolph's game was better than most people thought. It's just a shame because everyone will always remember Larry Bird and more people should appreciate Dolph Schayes.

The Ironman

Johnny Kerr played 11 seasons (1954–66) in the NBA as a 6-foot-9 center. He was the league's ironman, appearing in 844 consecutive games. It's still the league's second-longest streak, as Randy Smith had a streak of 906 from 1972–83. Kerr averaged 14 points and 11 rebounds in his career, and was known as a center whose passing skills rival Bill Walton's.

WAYNE EMBRY: If you were a center in the 1960s and your name wasn't Russell or Chamberlain, no one knew who you were. *Sport Magazine* used to rank the centers every year. Sometimes they had Russell first, other years it was Chamberlain. Then came numbers 3 and 4. One year Johnny would be rated third and I was fourth, then the next year I'd be ahead of Johnny.

JOHNNY KERR: In case you didn't notice, there was a big drop-off between numbers 1-2 and 3-4.

Danny Biasone: Johnny and Dolph became the first two ironmen, Dolph had the record first [706 consecutive games], then Johnny broke it.

Johnny Kerr: When I passed Dolph's record, they gave me 707 Kennedy half dollars in Philadelphia. I wish I had kept those things because they would be worth a lot today, but I gave them to my kids for lunch money each day. I also got a telegram from a friend who said, "707 games . . . Congratulations, John, you're only 1,200 behind Lou Gehrig."

Al Bianchi: The amazing thing about Johnny's streak was how he liked his beer. I could afford to go out after games and have a few because I knew that I wasn't going to play that much the next game. Johnny played over 40 minutes a night and there were some days, I knew how he felt. I knew how much he drank and I wondered how he did it.

Bob Ferry: Johnny and I roomed together in Baltimore. If one of us wasn't around for last call, the other was. Johnny would go to a bar and be content just to entertain the bartender all night with stories. He loved all-night card games. He had parties for the players at his house.

Johnny Kerr: Those parties were great, a case of beer and pizza. Then we'd sit around and talk the game.

Larry Costello: Johnny didn't come to camp in shape, he thought training camp was to play himself in shape, to sweat off all the weight he put on during the summer. He would chase a rookie around and sweat. The man sweated buckets of beer.

Gene Shue: Larry Costello and Johnny had great chemistry. Costello was a player whose first step was his quickest. He started moving at full speed. Syracuse had a back door play where someone would pass the ball to Kerr at the high post, then Costello would cut to the basket and Kerr would throw a no-look pass between his legs to Costello for a layup.

Tom Meschery: Johnny set what we called a "big-ass screen." Instead of picking the defender by facing the man and taking the hit in the chest, Johnny turned sideways, bent over at the waist and stuck out his butt. He had a big enough butt to knock you off balance, then he could go to the basket and catch a pass for an easy layup.

AL BIANCHI: Johnny played through everything. Now, if a guy has a hangover, they call it a "virus" and he takes a couple of days off. Back then, you threw up and you played. There were a lot of nights when Johnny could barely stand up in the bar and you know it killed him to get out of bed the next morning, but he played.

He had a swayback, or curved vertebrae. That affected his feet. One of his toes overlapped the other. I told him, "You're the only guy to play a million games in a row and one of your toes never touched the floor."

JOHNNY KERR: I didn't think about the streak until I got close to Dolph's record and people began writing about it. I played every game because that was what you did. You played until they carried you out, so I played with broken fingers. I played with a broken nose and wore a hockey mask for protection. I learned to fall without using my hands so I wouldn't break a wrist or a finger. One game, I stepped on Dick McGuire's ankle and I thought I broke my ankle. It was just a serious sprain, but my foot swelled up like the Goodyear Blimp. We were in Syracuse and my wife, Betsy, would go outside, fill a pail with snow and ice and then stick my foot in it. Betsy had a lot to do with the streak. She rubbed me down, she bandaged me up, she was my personal trainer. She took as much pride in the streak as I did.

There were mornings when I couldn't move from the bed. I'd lie there and my feet would be shaking and jerking—they were telling me something. Even driving to the arena, I didn't think I could make it. During warmups, I'd feel a little better. But what made it special was the national anthem and then hearing my name announced as the starting center. It went on for 12 years, but my heart pounded away at my chest and my palms would sweat. I wanted to play so badly right then and it happened before every game for 12 years.

BOB FERRY: I was the one who started the night Johnny's streak ended. We were with Baltimore and Paul Seymour was the coach, the same guy who played guard on Johnny's championship team in Syracuse. There was no reason for Johnny to sit out that night. He didn't feel any worse or better than normal. But Seymour got a thing in his head that Johnny's streak was somehow disruptive to the team. He thought it was a problem and he could eliminate it by not playing Johnny.

JOHNNY KERR: We lost 128–119 to Boston. Seymour just told me that the streak had to end sometime and it was "best" it was over. I didn't know who it was best for, but not me. The irony is that I started the next game, so I easily could have gotten into the loss to Boston without disrupting anything. It hurt me to lose the streak that way, but Betsy was really mad. She wanted to punch Seymour in the nose.

BOB FERRY: The players did not like how Johnny was treated that night, and I think Johnny was especially hurt because Seymour was his old teammate.

JOHNNY KERR: Rather than dwelling on the end of the streak, I'm proud that I did it. I held the record for 17 years until Randy Smith broke it. It's still the second longest. But I guess when it did end, it also made me think that maybe it was time for me to listen to my feet, which had been telling me to quit for years. My last game was in St. Louis when Baltimore was knocked out of the playoffs. I spent a long time in the dressing room, just taking off my uniform. Finally, I was down to only my stocking feet. I could look out the door and see that Kiel Auditorium was nearly dark. Guys were folding up the chairs, sweeping up the garbage and I heard the popping of paper cups. I put on some clothes, went into the arena and watched them dismantle the floor. I began to think that there would be no more nights after the games, drinking beer with the guys. No more parties at the house with Betsy and the players and no more times when my name was announced and people cheered. I was 34, I had never made more than $30,000 as a player, and I cried that day in St. Louis. Not because I wouldn't play again; my body was hurting too much to play anymore. But because I wouldn't be a basketball player.

The First Sixth Man

Frank Ramsey never scored 20 points in a season and averaged only 13.4 points for his nine-year career, all with Boston. Furthermore, his game was offense. So why is the 6-foot-3 guard/forward in the Hall of Fame? Because those 13 points came in 23 minutes per game.

FRANK RAMSEY: Red Auerbach drafted Cliff Hagan, Lou Tsioropoulos and myself all in 1953, even though we each had a year of eligibility left at the University of Kentucky. The NCAA had put Kentucky on probation for a year—our senior year. Actually, it was the death penalty. In 1952–53, Kentucky did not field a basketball team, we just practiced. But Red drafted all three of us anyway. We were allowed to play the following season at Kentucky, and we all played knowing we had been drafted by Boston. So Red got the jump on the rest of the league by finding the loophole that allowed him to draft us early. We all had played under Red one summer at Kutsher's in the Catskills, so he knew us well.

In the summer of 1954, I had already graduated from Kentucky and I was on a summer tour with a group of college all-stars who were playing the Globetrotters. The Trotters carried a portable floor with them and we played outside. This game was at Fenway Park, and I saw Red Auerbach sitting in the Red Sox dugout.

Red said, "Let's talk about playing next year."

I said, "I'm due to go into the service sometime in the next year, so I don't know when I can play."

Red said, "Suppose you can play."

I said, "I'd like to."

Red said, "I'll give you $6,500."

I said, "No, I need $8,500."

Two minutes later, we had settled on $8,000. I signed the contract right there in the Red Sox dugout.

I went to camp and there were no plans to make me into a sixth man. The fact was that Sharman and Cousy were the starting guards and they were better than me. Red made a big deal about my coming off the bench and scoring, but it wasn't by design. I just wasn't good enough to start.

TOM MESCHERY: Ramsey was the first designed shooter off the bench in NBA history. Red gave him the green light to take any shot. In fact, Red wanted Frank to score as quickly as possible, and Frank was never shy. He'd be on the floor for three seconds, catch a pass and launch one. He drove me crazy because I would have perfect defensive position and just stand there with my hands up. He'd leap into me, take the shot and make it and I'd get called for the foul. He was one of those guys with all the tricks, and he pioneered the sixth-man role, passing it on to [John] Havlicek.

JOHN HAVLICEK: Frank was a "cute" player. By that, I mean he knew how to hold on defense, how to cheat on a fast break to get an open layup and how to make a defender foul you. People kept track of how long it took Frank to score after he came into the game. I believe his record was three seconds. Frank played a lot of forward in college, so when we faced small guards Red would put Frank into the game and he'd post-up the little guard under the basket. Red used Ramsey a lot to create mismatches. The ultimate sixth man is a guy who can make an immediate impact in the game, both offensively and defensively, and do it at guard or forward. That was Frank's role, and then he taught it to me.

FRANK RAMSEY: I never needed many shots in warmups to get loose, 10–15 would do it. Guys like Tommy Heinsohn needed to shoot for a half hour. I sat on the bench with my warmup jacket open, so I could rip it off as I ran to the scorer's table the second Red called my name. I went into the game looking for a shot. People said I had no conscience. Red told me, "When you're open, shoot it. That's why you're here."

TOM HEINSOHN: Ramsey was nothing but business from the moment he joined the Celtics. He was involved in several successful businesses in [Madisonville,] Kentucky. He wore a suit and tie all the time, even to practice. One of his great thrills in life was to find a new tax loophole. Money and winning were always on his mind. The story everyone tells is that after Ramsey lost his first game as a Celtic, he cried. The other guys looked at him and asked what was wrong. He said at Kentucky, they never lost. The players told him, well, you'll lose some games here. He said, "That doesn't mean I'll ever learn to like it."

BOB RYAN: When the playoffs would start, Ramsey would write $5,000 on the blackboard. That was what a championship was worth to each player.

GENE CONLEY: Frank knew if you talked money to guys who didn't make much, they played a little harder. That $5,000 is a lot to guys making $8,000–$12,000.

CARL BRAUN: I spent the 1961–62 season with the Celtics and we had clinched first place with a few weeks to go in the season. When we should have been getting sharp for the playoffs, we were playing sloppy. After this one loss, Auerbach had left and the dressing room was silent. Then I saw one tennis shoe sail through the air and slap against the wall. Then came a second tennis shoe and *bang*—against the wall.

It was Ramsey.

He said, "Gentlemen, I'd rather live year-round in Kentucky, but I come to Boston to make money. My business is here and we're screwing around with my business and my money. If we're not ready for the playoffs, it will cost me money, and if that happens, we'll really have it out."

He was standing up, staring all of us in the eye.

No one said a word.

I thought, "So this is it. This is what it means to be a Celtic."

FRANK RAMSEY: Yes, I wanted to win and I wanted the playoff money. But the only contract I ever negotiated was my first one with Red in the Fenway Park dugout. After that, I signed a blank one and let Mr. [Walter] Brown fill in the amount. I never made more than $20,000 a year, but that was more than fair for that time. I had nursing homes, construction companies, a lot of businesses back in Kentucky. I played until I was 34, my knees were shot and I had worked with Havlicek. That was the thing about Red, he wanted you to train the guy who'd take your spot. I was proud to do it, proud of every moment I wore that Boston uniform. And if people want to credit me with creating the sixth man, I'm proud of that, too.

Bob Pettit: He Lived on the Foul Line

In 11 years, Bob Pettit scored over 20,000 points—and over 6,000 came from the foul line. That meant on nights when he scored his usual 26, eight of those points were free throws. That is what most opponents remember about the 6-foot-9, 220-pound forward who played for the St. Louis Hawks from 1954–65. That's 11 years an All-Star; the league's MVP in 1956 and 1959. Pettit also was one of the game's remarkable rebounders, averaging 16.2.

CHICK HEARN: Bob Pettit is one of those great players who is forgotten. He was a guy who couldn't make his high school team, a guy whose features were soft, almost feminine. He just developed into a helluva scorer and rebounder, and from just looking at him, you never would have believed it.

BOB PETTIT: Basketball never came easy to me. I grew up in Baton Rouge and I was very tall and thin, but not coordinated at all and had very few skills. Even though I was taller than most kids, I still was cut from my high school team as a sophomore. I stayed with basketball because I wanted to earn a letter in something. Being tall, I figured basketball was my best chance. We had no summer AAU leagues, no basketball camps and very little coaching. My high school coach is a dear friend of mine, but he also was the assistant football coach and football was his sport. So I taught myself to play, through trial and error. I learned to shoot one-handed because that was the way the ball went in most often. I had no idea how you were supposed to shoot. I made the team as a junior, and didn't become much of a player until my senior year. By then, I was 6-foot-8 and I had about six college offers—LSU, Tulane, Mississippi State and some smaller schools. I grew up only a few miles from the LSU campus, and it wasn't until I was 19 years old at LSU that I got any real coaching.

CLIFF HAGAN: Bob and I were tremendous rivals in college, him at LSU and me at Kentucky. In December of 1953, I scored 51 points against Temple, which broke an NCAA record that Bob had set. But a few months later, Bob scored 60 against Louisiana College, which we're still trying to find on the map. Both of our teams were 14-0 and we met on a neutral court in Nashville and we beat LSU in a close game. That's why I found it ironic that we both ended up on the same team and became roommates and such close friends.

BOB PETTIT: I was the second pick in the 1954 draft, behind Frank Selvy, who went to Baltimore. No one from any NBA team ever spoke to me before the draft. I don't think anyone scouted me until the postseason all-star games in Madison Square Garden. Ben Kerner owned the Milwaukee franchise and we met in a hotel room in Milwaukee. I asked for $15,000. He offered $9,000. I was afraid to move from my offer. I figured if I dropped down first, then I'd lose even more money before we settled. Mr. Kerner would not move, either. So we sat there for two hours, barely speaking to each other. It may have been the longest two hours of my life. Finally, he waited me out and I said, "Mr. Kerner, I want to play pro ball. How much is fair?" We settled on $11,000.

BEN KERNER: I knew that Pettit was a top college player and everyone had heard of him, but never in my wildest dreams did I think he'd have such a great career.

BOB PETTIT: In my first training camp, Red Holzman made a move for which I'm eternally grateful, switching me from a college center to a pro forward. I just wasn't strong enough to play center in the NBA, especially at that point in my career.

SLATER MARTIN: Bob was very weak when he came into the NBA and had real problems hanging on to the ball in traffic under the basket. At 6-foot-9, Bob was a big, big forward for his time. But the pushing and grabbing bothered him, and then he learned to push and grab with the best of them.

BOB PETTIT: I was one of the first basketball players to go on a weight program. Coaches always told us not to touch weights, that weights would ruin our shooting touch. I was 24 years old and had won the rebounding title, but I also was 215 pounds. I wanted to be the pounder, not take a pounding every night. I worked with a guy named Alvin Roy, who was a strength coach at LSU. My coach and owner didn't like it, especially when I showed up at 240 pounds. But I felt my hands, my arms, everything was stronger. With today's conditioning programs, I'd play at 265.

CHARLIE SHARE: The biggest break of my career was to be the Hawks' center when Bobby Pettit came to our team. I was a limited player, but for six years I set picks for Bob. Through his dogged determination, we became a very good team. Bob Pettit was the reason I had a 10-year NBA career.

LARRY STAVERMAN: If you guarded Pettit, then you had to deal with the likes of Charlie Share and Clyde Lovellette. You'd rather run into a brick wall than a pick from Share. And Lovellette, if you ran past him he'd always nail you with a hip or an elbow. There were times when

Lovellette would hip you into Pettit right after Pettit shot the ball and he'd end up at the foul line, going for the three-point play.

RUDY LARUSSO: If he got the ball inside the foul line, he owned you. He was so tall, he could shoot the ball over you. He also had one-dribble moves to either side. And he was protected by the refs. It was horrible. Bailey Howell told me that he was at a game where Pettit made a free throw and the announcer said, "That's Pettit's 15,000th career point." Bailey said, "Yeah, and 12,000 of them came at the foul line."

JOHNNY KERR: We always said that Pettit had two shots—a jumper and a free throw.

TOM MESCHERY: When Pettit wasn't shooting free throws, he was scoring on offensive rebounds. He probably averaged eight points a game on the offensive boards. He wasn't that physical. He didn't hurt you. But you'd think you had him blocked out, and you'd feel his elbows in your back and shoulders, pushing you out of the way. He was a very sneaky rebounder.

ZELMO BEATY: Bob was the greatest offensive rebounder I'd ever seen. He showed me some of his tricks, how he always stayed on the side of his defender, not his back. But I never could do it.

BOB PETTIT: My offensive rebounding was not an accident. When my teammate shot the ball, I never watched the ball hit the rim. The first thing I did was look at the defender trying to block me out. By not watching the ball, it gave me a chance to make the first move and my first move was to block out my defender, then look up to see the ball hit the rim. I made it into a science and it reached the point where I didn't believe anyone could block me out. I also held my arms up and my elbows out when I jumped. Usually, my elbows were over my defender's shoulders, so when he jumped for a rebound, he carried me up with him. The offensive boards were worth 8–12 points a night to me, then I'd get another 8–10 at the free throw line. All I had to do was make a few jump shots and I was on my way to a good night.

JERRY GROSS: I'd watch Pettit night after night and think, "This guy never has two bad games in a row." He was so consistent. Every move he made was under control. One of his tricks was to keep the ball over his head. He'd catch a pass about head level, and he'd go right up with his jumper from there, not bringing the ball down where the defender could knock it out of his hands.

LENNY WILKENS: Bob's hands were like vises. He'd get the ball and you couldn't knock it loose. He wasn't a graceful player, but he was a smart player who would still be damn good today.

ED MACAULEY: There was a game when I was coach where I found myself yelling at Pettit during halftime. Right in the middle I stopped and thought to myself, "Why am I yelling at Bob Pettit? He plays over his head every night." No one ever had a bad word to say about him.

Twenty Rebounds a Game, and He Can Count 'Em

The greatest rebounders the game has ever seen? The record book says that they are Bill Russell and Wilt Chamberlain, and those who played against them won't disagree. There were 12 seasons where Chamberlain averaged 20 rebounds, nine when Russell did it. Another player to do it was Nate Thurmond, who topped 20 in two different seasons. There probably were 15–20 more missed shots per game in the late 1950s and 1960s than today, but 20 rebounds a game is a lot for any man, especially if the man in question isn't a center. Bob Pettit managed it in 1960–61, when he averaged 20 rebounds and 27.8 points. But consider that in four seasons from 1964–68, Jerry Lucas averaged 19.8 rebounds. The Cincinnati Royals' 6-foot-8, 230-pound forward broke the 20-mark twice. In 1966, he averaged 21.5 points and 20 rebounds—the only man besides Chamberlain and Pettit to average 20 points and 20 rebounds in the same season. An Ohio State product who was the National Collegiate Player of the Year in 1961 and 1962, Lucas was also a terrific shooter, hitting 50 percent for his 11-year pro career, most coming from at least 20 feet. Lucas also was known for his incredible memory and ability to figure complex math problems in his head, which came in handy as he kept track of his rebounds.

JERRY LUCAS: You can talk about eras all you want and how guys shoot for a higher percentage today and there are fewer missed shots, but the players of my time simply wanted to rebound more and we rebounded better. I went into games expecting to get 20 rebounds. So did Wilt, Russell and Nate Thurmond. Now, when a guy gets 20 rebounds, it's an event. Back then, it was just doing your job. There were many games where I got 30–35 rebounds, and that felt normal. Only four men ever got 40 rebounds in an NBA game: Wilt, Russell, Nate Thurmond and myself. In my opinion, those are the four greatest rebounders ever to play the game. We grunted, sweated all over the arena. We would rather get a rebound than eat.

WAYNE EMBRY: I never saw anyone as obsessed with rebounding as Jerry Lucas. I played center next to him, and I'd get a rebound and he'd get mad at me and fight me for it. I'd say, "Hey, Jerry, I'm on your side." He wanted to outrebound everybody on both teams.

JERRY LUCAS: One reason I'm the only forward to get 40 rebounds in a game is that I played with Wayne Embry.

I'd tell Wayne, "You just block out the big guys, I'll get the rebounds."

Wayne would put his wide body on Russell, Wilt or whoever, take them out of the play, then I'd have a clear path to the boards. Wayne was a very unselfish player.

But I was also absolutely manic about rebounds. I had great timing and a sixth sense. I knew where the ball would come off the board when a guy shot it, because I had studied tendencies—where certain rebounds went when they were shot from certain areas of the floor. About everyone could outjump me, and they would just rely on their legs to get the rebounds. But that wasn't good enough. I always could outrebound guys who just lived off their legs.

LARRY STAVERMAN: There is no question that Jerry was a great rebounder, especially for his size. But those of us who played with him would notice that when a guy would take a 50-foot heave with two seconds left in the quarter and it would bang against the board as the buzzer sounded, Jerry would run the ball down in the corner. As he came off the court at the end of the quarter, he would remind the stat crew at the press table, "That's a rebound." It seemed like he was counting the rebounds in his head, and given his incredible intellect, maybe he was. What I remember most about Jerry was his high, high arcing jumpers from 25 feet. He may have been the best long-distance shooter of any big man who ever lived, and he certainly had the highest arc.

JERRY LUCAS: I shot the ball that high for a couple of reasons. First, I'm convinced that 95 percent of the shots that are missed are missed short. The more arc on a shot, the less likely it will be short. But there is a common sense aspect to it. Imagine that you're trying to throw something into a garbage can. If you drop it straight in, the hole is pretty big. But if you are trying to throw it in from the side, the hole is smaller. The reason I performed as I did was that there never was a shot or a rebound I saw where I didn't ask, "Why . . . why didn't that shot go in? Why did the rebound go where it did?" That shows rebounding is more than a physical act.

6

BOSTON BEFORE RUSSELL

The Magician Came Out of a Hat

He was pro basketball's first legitimate gate attraction, a normal man thriving in the land of giants. That was Bob Cousy, who sensed that basketball was as much entertainment as a sport. George Mikan was the league's first superstar, but he was 6-foot-10. Cousy was the fun guy to watch and to write about. He was a magician, a now-you-see-it, now-you-don't dribbler and ballhandler. He didn't just put the ball through the rim, but through his legs and around his back. Most of Cousy's moves are commonplace today—a good high school point guard can dribble behind his back and through his legs—but in the 1950s no one did as many different and mesmerizing things with the basketball as Cousy.

Yet, Boston coach Red Auerbach initially didn't want him, didn't like his game and tried to get rid of him. When Auerbach became the Celtics coach in 1950, the first decision he had to make was about the skinny, 6-foot-1 guard from Holy Cross. The Boston press and fans demanded that Auerbach make Bob Cousy his No. 1 draft pick. Auerbach had other ideas, which is why Celtics critics point to the acquisition of Cousy and say, "That's the thing about Red Auerbach— even when he's wrong, it turns out right. Talk about a lucky stiff. Where would the Celtics have been if Auerbach had his way about Bob Cousy?" Auerbach probably would have been looking for a new job by 1953. Instead, Cousy became the first piece of the Celtics Dynasty, and with Cousy running his offense Auerbach was on his way to becoming a genius.

RED AUERBACH: I saw Cousy in college. I knew what he could do, that he was a great talent. But I looked at my roster and I didn't need a guard, I needed someone to get the ball off the boards. I tried to explain this to the reporters, but all they wanted to talk about was Cousy. Walter Brown also was interested in Cousy because Mr. Brown believed Cousy would help the gate. I understood that, but I told Mr. Brown that winning is what helps the gate the most and we needed a big man to win. Without a good big man, we couldn't win with Cousy, and I told the press that when I drafted Charlie Share over Cousy.

[Actually, what Auerbach told the press was, "I don't give a damn for sentiment or names. That goes for Cousy and everybody else. The only thing that counts with me is ability. I'm not interested in drafting somebody because he happens to be a local yokel."]

LEONARD KOPPETT: Pro basketball was ruled by George Mikan. At 6-foot-10 and with only a six-foot lane, he determined how the game was played. If you were going to win anything, you had to overcome Mikan. I don't think Red liked or disliked Cousy. All he cared about was finding someone who could play against Mikan.

BOB COUSY: If I were Arnold [Auerbach], I would have done the same damn thing—draft for size. Arnold had never seen me play. In effect, Arnold had taken over an expansion team and if you talk to any coach today, he'll tell you that you like to start an expansion team with a big man, not a guard. In the 1950s, 6-foot-1 guards were considered a dime a dozen. So that was how Arnold felt.

My feeling was that unless I played for Boston, I wasn't going to play pro basketball. I'd had four good years academically at Holy Cross. I had a partner and we had opened up a gas station and a string of driving schools in Worcester. The driving schools were going great and unless I got $10,000 to play pro basketball, I couldn't quit. I had never seen a pro game when I was in college; the league had little prestige and received little publicity. I figured my basketball days were over and I was going into business.

I got a call from Ben Kerner, who owned the Tri-Cities franchise. He said he drafted me. I was honest and told him that I didn't even know where Tri-Cities was. He said he'd pay me $7,000 to play for him.

I said, "Mr. Kerner, I'm going to pump gas and teach ladies to drive."

He thought I was using this as a negotiating ploy, but I wasn't interested in leaving the area. Either I would play in Boston, or I wouldn't play.

CHARLIE SHARE: I was attending Bowling Green in Ohio when the Celtics drafted me. I found out when I read it in the *Toledo Blade*. I was contacted by Boston and I signed, I forget for how much. Then I was contacted by a team from Waterloo, Iowa, that played in the National Professional Basketball League. They put $2,500 on the table and said, "If you sign with us, you can take this money with you now." I was engaged and $2,500 was a lot of money, so I signed with them, too. I even played with Waterloo for a month, then the league folded.

My rights went back to the Celtics, and Auerbach sold me to Fort Wayne. I was told he got $50,000, which was a huge sum in those days. But Fred Zollner owned Fort Wayne and he was the richest owner in the league, so $50,000 probably was true. As it turned out, I had to sit out the rest of the 1950–51 season anyway.

RED AUERBACH: There was some cash involved, but I also got the rights to Bill Sharman and Bob Harris in the deal.

BOB COUSY: I spent the summer of 1950 teaching ladies to drive. One day I got a call from a newspaperman who said Tri-Cities had traded me to Chicago. I said that was fine with me. I had no plans to play in Chicago or anywhere else but Boston. A month later, I got a call and they said the Chicago franchise had folded. The season still hadn't started, and I'd already been with two teams and was headed for a third.

RED AUERBACH: Chicago was one of the [six] teams that folded, and I ended up with Ed Macauley, who had been with St. Louis the year before. If I'd had Macauley before the draft, then I probably would have taken Cousy over Share. When Chicago folded, they had three guards who became available—Max Zaslofsky, Andy Phillip and Cousy. The three teams that were going to get these players were Philadelphia, New York and us. I had a real interest in Zaslofsky and Phillip because they had been in the pros and were All-Stars. Cousy didn't have their track record.

DANNY BIASONE: There was a lot of debate about who should get those players. All three teams really wanted Zaslofsky. Then they would take Phillip. Cousy was third on the list. The owners couldn't decide how to divide up the players and the argument went on most of the night. Finally, we said, "Let's pull the names out of a hat." I took off my hat.

Maurice Podoloff wrote down the names on slips of paper and dropped them into my hat. New York picked first and Ned Irish got Zaslofsky. Eddie Gottlieb drew Phillip for Philadelphia and that left Boston with Cousy, which is who Red should have drafted in the first place.

BOB COUSY: I got a call from Walter Brown saying I belonged to the Celtics. I got in my car and drove to his office.

I told Mr. Brown I wanted $10,000 and why I needed $10,000 to play. He thought about it and said, "We can give you $9,000."

I said, "Okay, you've got a deal. I'll take $9,000 to play close to home."

[Auerbach was not overjoyed to have Cousy in training camp. He told writers, "Cousy has to make the team like anyone else." At the first practice, he jumped all over Cousy for wearing a Holy Cross T-shirt.]

RED AUERBACH: Cousy always was an excellent passer. But sometimes, his passes were too good. By that, I mean that the guys didn't see them coming. Well, a pass that doesn't work isn't a good pass.

I sat him down and said, "Look, I don't care how you pass the ball, behind your back, through your legs or whatever, but someone had better catch it. We can't have turnovers. The ball is in your hands, now make sure we don't turn it over."

BOB COUSY: I was blessed with long arms and big hands, which helped me when it came to passing and dribbling behind my back. Really, they're moves you see 12-year-old kids doing on the playground today, and some of those kids are smoother than I was as a pro. But my vision was my greatest gift. People would say, "You have eyes behind your back." What I'm blessed with is great peripheral vision. That was what gave me a tremendous sense of where everyone was on the court.

JIM LOSCUTOFF: Cooz was almost like a freak. He was just over 6-foot and he was so skinny, but he had huge hands, long arms and big feet. He also had that French accent and he couldn't say his Rs.

He would say, "I have great po-whiffel vision."

Once, he did a commercial for Roman Meal Bread, but he called it "Wo-man Meal Bed."

We teased him about that stuff all the time.

ED MACAULEY: Cousy was not the first player I ever saw dribble behind his back. That was Bob Davies of Rochester. But Cooz did things with the ball we'd never seen before. We never considered him a showboat because he got us the ball. I was on the other end of a lot of those behind-the-back passes and he set me up for a lot of layups.

BOB COUSY: There was a reason for those spectacular plays. Ninety percent of my game was conservative. I've been associated with the unorthodox because I was the only one doing it, so those few times a game when I did go behind my back, it really stood out. In my mind, that kind of pass also was the best pass in that situation. I get annoyed when I watch a game and see a guy dribbling the ball through his legs for no reason other than to do it.

SAM JONES: What made Cooz great was that he'd go behind the back with the ball and everyone expected him to pass it, but he'd hang on to the ball with those big hands of his and make a layup. No one in basketball had that move before Cousy did.

FRANK RAMSEY: Because Bob's hands were so large, he'd dribble the ball and then just throw a pass all in one motion with one hand, and throw it nearly the length of the court directly off the dribble. And he'd whip the ball, about waist high. It would go through about four different guys right into your hands. I never figured out how he was able to do that.

SLATER MARTIN: Cousy was never a good shooter, but he had guts. He'd miss five shots in a row, but if he was open, he'd take and make that sixth shot, and that was the shot that usually broke your back.

[Cousy shot 37 percent for his career and never shot 40 percent in any season. He had a running one-hander that he often shot off balance. One of his favorite shots was a running hook off the backboard. He did average 18.4 points and led the league in assists eight times.]

BILL SHARMAN: Cousy was a lot like Magic Johnson, in that he was an innovator and his first instincts were to get you a good shot. On the fast break, he was an artist, inventing something new—he was way ahead of his time.

LEONARD KOPPETT: Fans were attracted to Cousy because he was an ordinary-sized person competing against all these giants, and a lot of the time he made them look silly.

HOT ROD HUNDLEY: The first time I played Cousy, it was a thrill for me. He was my idol and when he said hello, it was as if my heart stopped beating. In that first game, he scored 20 points on me in the first half. George Mikan was my coach and Mikan said, "Hundley, I told you to watch Cousy, didn't I?"
  I said, "I did and he's great, isn't he?"

DON BARKSDALE: Cousy is one of my favorite people. His hands were so quick. He'd just flick the ball away from the other team. He revolutionized the game. The black players had a lot of respect for him because of how he treated us. He's a very sensitive guy.

ED MACAULEY: The biggest adjustment Cousy had to make was in dealing with Red, whose personality could be pretty difficult. Early in his career, I think Red and Bob had some problems, but you could see that they grew to respect each other as the years went on.

BOB RYAN: When I did a book with Cousy, I sensed that he was biting his tongue when it came to certain things about Red. He considers Red a great coach and an interesting figure. He calls him Arnold, which is a term of endearment. But some of Red's crudities offended Cousy; Red's brashness offended Cousy's Gallic sensibility, if you will. But Bob has never strayed from the Celtics family. While he does not buy the whole package that is the myth of Red Auerbach, Cousy does have great respect for Red as a coach and basketball mind, which is why they were able to overcome their differences.

ED MACAULEY: Red is never one to second-guess himself or admit that he made a mistake, but I guess even he'd have to say that Cousy wasn't exactly some local yokel.

Cousy's Roomie

For 10 years, Bill Sharman and Bob Cousy not only were a Hall of Fame backcourt for Boston, they were roommates. Sharman was a 6-foot-2 shooting guard, a career 18-point scorer and 88 percent free throw shooter. He also was the first NBA player to make 50 free throws in a row. He later became a coach, winning titles in three pro leagues—with the 1971 Utah Stars of the ABA, the 1972 L.A. Lakers of the NBA and the 1962 Cleveland Pipers of the ABL. As a pro coach, he had a career winning percentage of 57 percent.

BILL SHARMAN: What most people don't know is that I started my pro career as a baseball player in the Brooklyn Dodgers' farm system in 1950. I was an outfielder in their system for three years. I also was playing pro basketball in the winter, and I planned to stay with both sports until I saw what was best for me. In the early 1950s, pro basketball was considered a minor sport, one that could fold any day. In 1950, I played for the Washington Capitols and coach Bones McKinney. Bones refused to fly, so we'd spend 12–18 hours on a train, going from Washington to Minneapolis. It was awful. There were times when we drove—four guys to a car—and actually changed from our street clothes into our uniforms while in the car because the dressing rooms in some arenas were so poor. I didn't think basketball had much of a future, especially when Washington folded in the middle of the 1950–51 season.

[Sharman was promoted by Brooklyn to the majors at the end of the 1951 season. He never appeared in a big-league game for Brooklyn, but he was in the dugout when the Dodgers blew the 1951 pennant to the New York Giants on Bobby Thomson's legendary home run, although his name does not appear anywhere in The Baseball Encyclopedia. *Sharman played pro baseball until 1953—five seasons.]*

RED AUERBACH: I caught all that hell for taking Charlie Share over Cousy, but if I didn't draft Share, we never would have gotten Sharman. Fort Wayne wanted Share and I knew that, so I was able to get the rights to Sharman, who everyone thought was going to stick with baseball. But I talked to the kid, saw him shoot, and could he ever shoot. We surprised the entire league by signing him.

[Sharman received a $14,000 bonus from the Celtics. The first night in which Cousy and Sharman played together, they combined for 44 points.]

SHARMAN: Red and Cousy changed my feelings about the NBA. Red was a great coach, an innovator who emphasized conditioning. We had the same philosophy. Cousy made the game easy for me. All I had to do was get open and he got me the ball.

BOB COUSY: Bill was a unique pro player for the time. He was the first to believe in a structured exercise program. Before the game, we'd sit around the dressing room, talk, maybe drink some water, and there would be Sharman on the floor doing situps, pushups, stretches and everything that is common to most teams today.

CARL BRAUN: One summer Sharman and I worked at a basketball camp. I went out for an early-morning walk and saw Bill. He was running behind a car, which was driven by his wife. He did that every morning, and it was long before everyone started jogging.

TOM HEINSOHN: Red made us do pushups and other exercises, but the minute Red turned his back, most of us would stop. Not Sharman. He'd do every pushup in perfect form.

GENE CONLEY: My rookie year was 1952, and on one trip Red told me to room with Sharman. I had no idea about his routines. Every morning of a game day, we had to find a gym so Bill could shoot around. He was the first coach to use a shootaround, but he also did it as a player. He held his own shootaround. If the main arena was closed, we'd go to the YMCA. Mostly, he shot and I rebounded for him.

At exactly 2 P.M., we took a nap. He'd pull down the shades and that was it—lights out. About five, we'd have tea and toast. Tea with honey, because he believed that gave you energy.

Finally, he had these index cards with little notes on them. One dealt with his jump shot, reminding himself to square off, follow through and all that stuff. He had notes on opponents, and he'd take those cards to the arena and then look them over before the game.

BOB COUSY: Bill was the most structured person I've ever seen. He put the same clothes in the same places in the room. I always literally lived out of my suitcase, but Bill had to hang up everything even if we were going to be in a town for only 12 hours. I'd watch him take everything out of that damn suitcase, and then a few hours later watch him put everything back into the suitcase—in the exact spots where he took them out. I never asked him why he did the things he did. Your roommate is like your wife. She wants to do that, fine, as long as it doesn't bother you.

FRANK RAMSEY: At home, I know that Bill liked to eat a steak every day, and every day at exactly 3 P.M., his wife would make him a steak.

BILL SHARMAN: I believe that details make a difference. There were a lot of players with more talent than I had. I believed that if I could do the little things, I could beat them.

BOB COUSY: We hated to play HORSE with Sharman. When most of us played, we took crazy shots from behind the backboard, with our eyes closed. Not Sharman. He played that game like he practiced. He'd want to shoot free throws—and it was nothing for him to make 50 in a row. Or he'd take his favorite 12-foot bank shot, and make 50 of those. So he'd always win, but he was no fun at HORSE. We just let him practice by himself.

TOM HEINSOHN: We always thought Cousy and Sharman were some pair. Bill had all his eccentricities, and poor Cousy had nightmares. Once we were at a hotel where they didn't have enough rooms, so they put three of us in a room—Cousy, Conley and myself. Conley met some buddies and went out for a few pops. Cousy and I went to bed. The next morning, I woke up and there was no Conley.

At 6 A.M., we were meeting in the lobby to leave and there was Conley sleeping on the damn sofa. I said, "Geno, you had a room with us."

Conley said, "I know. I went into the room, Cousy stood straight up in the bed and screamed at me, 'Get out!' He scared the hell out of me, so I went downstairs."

Cousy didn't remember a thing. But he told me that he had these nightmares where he was being chased.

ED MACAULEY: Cousy and I were in a car. I was driving and talking to him for quite a while, but he never responded. I looked at him, his eyes were wide open. I said something to him. He didn't move—he just stared straight, wide-eyed and fast asleep.

JIM LOSCUTOFF: I roomed with Cousy once. He walked in his sleep. He came to the side of my bed, looked down and screamed. I don't know how Sharman roomed with him all those years, but when we asked Sharman, he'd act like he had no idea what we were talking about. Maybe Bill just slept through everything.

BOB COUSY: Bill and I gave each other a lot of room and that is why we got along so great. Also, we had great respect for each other. Bill was the most disciplined son of a gun I've ever seen. On the court, he never took a bad shot. Never. He was in constant motion, running the court in a circle and running his defensive man into picks. Eventually, he either ran his man into the ground or wiped him out on a pick and was open. Then his shot was automatic.

GENE SHUE: I hated guarding Sharman, absolutely hated it. He never got tired. He ran you into Loscutoff or one of the big guys, and they'd nail you with an elbow or a hip, and back then there was very little switching on defense. If you were guarding Sharman and you got picked, tough luck.

DON BARKSDALE: Sharman was the opposite of Cousy. He wasn't a flashy player at all. He did the same things, took the same shots over and over. He wasn't very fast of foot, but he had a quick release on his shot and his knowledge of the game was a bitch. You'd look at the box score and see he had 20 points and ask, "Just how did he do that?" Whereas you could remember every one of Cousy's baskets.

BOB COUSY: Bill was known for his offense, but his defense . . . his defense was extreme. He would blanket players. He had this thing about Andy Phillip. I don't know what, but it was obvious Phillip once pissed Bill off, and Sharman would guard Andy full court. He'd dog him every step, every minute on the court. If Bill sat out for a minute and Phillip scored a basket on me, Bill would be all over my ass. There were other examples of how focused he'd get on something, and he was so intense it could be scary. He got into a lot of fights, and never with guys his own size. Usually, he'd start flailing away at some seven-footer. The fans would come storming out of the seats and most of us with common sense just wanted to head for the hills, but Bill would take on everybody.

He had two personalities. Off the court, he was the most compassionate, gentle and polite man I've met. Something would happen when he pulled on that uniform and he'd switch into a killer mode.

RUDY LARUSSO: Bill coached Golden State when I was there and everyone bitched when he made us get on the court for a morning shootaround after we got in at 3 A.M. from somewhere. He drove us nuts with all the exercises he wanted us to do. But by the end of the year, I could see that he had made us a better team.

RICK BARRY: I'm sorry, but I don't buy all that shootaround crap. In my second season, I played under Bill and averaged 35 points. People said it was because of Bill's programs, but that just wasn't true. The players hated the morning shootaround. Bill said it was so we could get used to the baskets we'd play on that night. But one time we had a game in L.A. and couldn't get into the Forum, so Bill scheduled a shootaround for Loyola Marymount.

I said, "Bill, did they change the game for tonight? Are we playing here? Is that why we're getting used to these baskets?"

He ignored me. Bill wanted to impose his will on you, to make you do the same things he did as a player. I just don't believe that drinking tea with honey in it before a game makes you a better player.

TOM MESCHERY: I think there was a genius to Sharman's system. I played under Bill when he coached the Golden State Warriors. He replaced Alex Hannum, who was very popular with the players. With Alex, guys smoked at halftime. Our pregame meal was a steak or a hamburger and a beer. Bill said we should lay off the red meat. Like everyone else, I'd say, "What do you mean, no beer and a steak?" He was constantly keeping up with the dietary changes, and he was saying we needed to eat pasta. He said smoking was terrible for us. He had morning shootarounds, aerobic exercises and film sessions. At first, we thought he was nuts, but as we began to win we listened to him even if we didn't like what he was saying. He was a pioneer. As much as anyone, Bill is responsible for how coaches approach pro basketball today.

The Patron Saint

Boston had come into the basketball business in 1946 when Walter Brown—a hockey fan who owned part of the Ice Capades—purchased *the team. Brown and public relations man Howie McHugh began considering nicknames. The final four were the Olympics, the Whirlwinds, the Unicorns and the Celtics, which Brown liked because he was Irish and Boston had a large Irish population. In their first two years, the Celtics were coached by John "Honey" Russell, then Alvin "Doggie" Julian. In their first four seasons, the Celtics had no winning records and were losing more than games; by 1950, Brown was $500,000 in the red, a staggering sum. He had sold much of his Ice Capades stock and remortgaged his house to stay in business. In 1950, Brown hired Arnold "Red" Auerbach as coach. Auerbach was the son of a Brooklyn dry-cleaner. He played basketball at George Washington University, under Bill Reinhardt. In 1949, Auerbach coached at Tri-Cities under Ben Kerner, but quit. Auerbach immediately coached the Celtics to their first winning season—39-30 in 1950–51. But it would be seven years before Bill Russell and the first NBA title came to Boston.*

BOB RYAN: The Celtics came into existence because Walter Brown was one of the original hockey arena owners and he wanted something to put in his arena when the Bruins were out of town. Brown knew nothing about basketball, but he quickly fell in love with it. When he needed a coach, he accepted the recommendations of people he knew, including newspaperman Sam Cohen. In 1950 on the advice of Cohen and others, Brown hired 28-year-old Red Auerbach, who had coached in Washington and Tri-Cities.

RED AUERBACH: When I came to the Celtics, Walter Brown was honest with me. He told me about all the money he'd lost and it was obvious that he didn't have much left. I didn't know if Walter had the money to make it in the basketball business, but he had great integrity. His word was his bond and he said I had complete control over the basketball, which was something I wanted. I had coached in Tri-Cities the year before under Ben Kerner. Ben wanted to trade John Mahnken to Boston for Gene Englund. I said, "Ben, you can't do that. Mahnken is my center. Englund is 6-foot-5. We don't need another 6-5 guy." But Kerner's whole life was wrapped up in basketball, and when your life is basketball, it's hard to keep your hands off it. So he made the trade while we were on the road. I was devastated. I liked Kerner, he built a damn good team with the Hawks in St. Louis, but he goofed on Mahnken and I told him so.

Then I heard from Walter Brown about the Boston job. Walter was a basketball fan, but he knew enough to know that he didn't know the game, so he hired me. Naturally, I had to tell Walter the moves I planned to make, but the final decision was mine.

BEN KERNER: We were struggling to make money in Tri-Cities. Walter Brown offered Red more money and I released him. The reason Red left me wasn't a trade, it was a chance to coach in Boston and make more money.

MARTY BLAKE: Walter Brown's team was in such sad shape that he told Ben Kerner that he had to have Red to straighten things out or Walter might be forced to fold the franchise.

CHARLEY ECKMAN: I don't know all the details of why Red went to Boston, but no one went to the Celtics in those days for money. Hell, Red was lucky to make 10 grand in the early years, and they couldn't sell a ticket in that town.

RED AUERBACH: When I came to Boston, it was all baseball and hockey, the Bruins and the Red Sox. When it came to basketball, they thought it began and ended with Holy Cross. I had sportswriters tell me that Holy Cross was better than the Celtics.

I said, "Guys, you don't know what the hell you're talking about."

What saved us early was getting Bob Cousy. Then I set up some scrimmages with Holy Cross and invited the press to watch. We beat the hell out of Holy Cross, and that shut up that talk about a college team being better than the Celtics. But it still was hard to sell basketball to the fans.

ED MACAULEY: Ted Williams couldn't step on the street without being mobbed. In the early 1950s, our whole team could walk through downtown and no one would notice us.

RED AUERBACH: I wanted a team that would run and would play an exciting brand of ball. Cousy, Sharman, Macauley and those guys gave me that, but you could tell we still had something missing.

ED MACAULEY: For a number of those years, our front line was Bob Brannum, Bob Harris and myself. I was a 180-pound center. I had some of my greatest scoring games against George Mikan, but George used his size and strength to have some of his best games against me. Cousy and I were usually in the Top 5 in scoring. We were a smart team, but not very physical.

TOM GOLA: You'd get into a lot of 140–135 games with those old Boston teams. They tried to outscore you. When they were hot, they could score at will but they never could stop anyone.

BOB COUSY: Macauley, Bill Sharman and myself were the so-called catalysts of the team and we won as many games as we should have, but we were never a threat in the playoffs. We couldn't control the backboards and Auerbach knew that until he found someone who could do that, we were never going to be a legitimate championship contender.

CHARLEY ECKMAN: When you played the Celtics, Cousy would get 20 and Sharman and Macauley would get their 20, but you still could beat them by 20.

BOB RYAN: Walter Brown was just trying to keep the team alive with a cult following of about 4,000. They played hockey and basketball doubleheaders, or doubleheaders with high school teams—anything to draw a few people.

FRANK RAMSEY: We all were aware that the team had financial problems. In my first season [1954–55], Walter Brown said that he just couldn't afford to give us our playoff shares—about $400 each. He asked us to wait until the start of next season, which we all did, and then he paid us. That's because Walter Brown was the most honest man in the game.

TOM HEINSOHN: One time I ran into Walter Brown in the men's room, and he asked me how much I wanted. I told him and by the time we had both flushed the toilets, we had a deal. All of the players wanted to negotiate with Walter and not Red, because Walter would make a deal in five minutes. He loved his players. With Red, it was a war for every penny and it would go on all day.

RED AUERBACH: I had a contract with Walter when I first came to the Celtics, but never after that. He just gave me his word on what I'd be paid, we'd shake hands and that was it. Not a word in writing between us for 16 years.

JERRY GROSS: When I was just a sophomore in college and trying to land a job as an NBA broadcaster, I sent a tape to Walter Brown. Mr. Brown told me, "Even if you were better than my announcer, I wouldn't hire you because Johnny Most is my announcer and that isn't going to change. But if you write me a letter every other month, I'll help you find a job." I had never met this man before and there was no reason for him to care about some college kid. But I wrote him a letter every two months. One day, I got a call from one of Marty Blake's flunkies with the St. Louis Hawks. The Hawks had heard about me from Walter Brown and wanted to listen to a tape. I sent them a tape I did while sitting in the stands at Cincinnati Gardens, talking into a tape recorder. They hired me, more on the strength of Walter Brown's word than that amateurish tape I sent them.

[Brown did have a temper. He once threatened to trade the entire team, including the revered Cousy. He called Commissioner Maurice Podoloff "the NBA's biggest mistake." He lashed out at Heinsohn at a banquet and also said his team "was a bunch of chokers." But the next day, Brown invariably apologized and was embarrassed by his outburst.]

BOB COUSY: I knew that there were several times in the 1950s when Walter Brown's friends advised him to get out of basketball. People were afraid that the team would bankrupt him, but Walter stayed with it. He believed in us and he believed in his coach. And one day in December of 1956, Arnold came to me and said, "Don't worry, everything is going to change next season. I've got a guy I'm going after who is exactly what we need." At the time I didn't know who he meant, but Arnold was talking about Bill Russell.

Russell Is Drafted

During his last two years at the University of San Francisco, Bill Russell's teams won 55 games in a row and two NCAA titles. That would seem to ensure that the 6-foot-9 center would have been the

No. 1 pick in the 1956 draft. But he wasn't. Rochester took Sihugo Green, a 6-foot-2 guard from Duquesne. St. Louis had the second pick and a shot at Russell. Instead, they traded it to Boston for Ed Macauley and Cliff Hagan.

PETE NEWELL: Most people don't know that Russell was a late bloomer. He played only one year of high school, actually a half season. Phil Woolpert and I were teammates in college and he became my assistant coach at San Francisco. When I left USF to become the head coach at Michigan State, I recommended Phil to take my place. Phil's assistant was a guy named Hal DeJulio, and he was the only major college coach who liked Russell. It was Hal who told Woolpert to offer Bill a scholarship.

I saw Bill as a freshman, and even then he had the great gift of being able to block a shot without fouling and without knocking the ball out-of-bounds. Woolpert played a pressing defense with the accent on the fast break and rebounding, which was perfect for Russell.

LESTER HARRISON: Basketball in 1956 was different than today. We couldn't afford scouts or assistant coaches. Nor was there any real television coverage of the college game. We had a coach and a general manager and we relied on the word of college coaches we knew. The real scouting was done after the college season at the East-West All-Star Game at Madison Square Garden. There was a week of practices and then games for the best college players, and I went to them all. Naturally, I knew about Russell and what his team had accomplished, but this was my first time to see him. Russell looked like a bum. He didn't do anything, he just moped around. One New York sportswriter did an article saying the guy would be lucky to make the league, and I was supposed to make him the No. 1 pick?

LEONARD KOPPETT: Russell played in two tournaments in New York during his senior year and there were a lot of guys saying, "Nah, he can't score. He's not that strong. All he does is block shots." But there also were those of us who said, "What the hell are you talking about? This guy's defense is changing the game. We've never had a player like this." To me, seeing a young Bill Russell was like seeing a young Willie Mays or Cassius Clay for the first time—you knew this was a unique athlete.

RED AUERBACH: Bill did not play well in New York. In my files, I have articles that said he would be another Walter Dukes—at best. They said Walter was bigger and had a better shooting touch, and the only thing Russell had on Dukes was rebounding. But I had talked to coaches I knew. The first was Bill Reinhardt, my old coach from George Washington. He told me, "This Russell kid is going to be super." Pete Newell was coaching at California during Bill's senior year, and Pete was watching him closely for me.

PETE NEWELL: Red had his heart set on Russell early. Red knew that I was close to Phil Woolpert, and he asked me to see what kind of money Russell wanted and if he had any interest in playing for the Globetrotters. There were rumors that the Trotters would offer Bill $50,000, which was an astronomical sum at that time. So I talked to Woolpert and learned that Bill wanted the NBA and he was looking for something like $25,000. I called Red with this information.

DON BARKSDALE: At the end of my career, I played for Red and then I retired to San Francisco. The Celtics asked me to send in a scouting report on Bill. I said that he couldn't score, but he blocked shots like no one we'd seen before. He'd also get 12–15 rebounds a game. I said he'd be a good pro, but I had no idea that he'd make the impact he did. Then Red asked me to find out more about Russell, the Celtics were worried about the Globetrotters. I got to know Bill's father well. I told them how the Trotters played 230 games a year, Bill would play only 70-some in the NBA. I said with all the clowning and stars the Globies had such as Goose Tatum, Bill would get lost because the things Bill did best did not translate into the entertainment business. I also talked to Bill and immediately could tell that he was not the kind of person you could overwhelm with a bunch of bull. He was smart, and his personality would not be right for the Globetrotters, and I told the Celtics that.

LESTER HARRISON: The real truth about this draft was that Auerbach and Russell set me up. You ever hear about a horse race where a 3-to-5 favorite finishes dead last? That was what happened to me. I was cheated out of Russell, who played poorly at the All-Star Game because he didn't want to play in a small city like Rochester. We weren't drawing well in Rochester, and it looked to me as if Russell couldn't play. Green was a solid prospect. We had Maurice Stokes at center, and he would have been as good as Russell if he hadn't gotten ill. Listen, what was I supposed to do?

LEONARD KOPPETT: Russell was going to play for the 1956 Olympic team. The Games were in the late fall and Russell would miss the first third of the NBA season. I don't think Harrison wanted to wait for Russell. It also was common knowledge that Russell was looking for a lot of money, and Harrison couldn't afford him. Harrison drafted Sihugo Green because Green was a player he could sign.

PETE NEWELL: Some people considered Russell difficult because he was a young man who knew what he wanted and said what was on his mind. The man who had a huge impact on Russell was Phil Woolpert, who was about four decades ahead of his time in terms of human rights and racial consciousness. He had three blacks starting—Hal Perry, K.C. Jones and Russell—when most teams would not play more than one, if any. I know that Phil took a lot of heat for this, but he didn't care. His parents were so liberal that in the early 1950s they probably would have been considered Communists.

I wasn't there, but I was told that when Abe Saperstein came to talk to Woolpert and Russell about Bill playing for the Globetrotters, all Abe did was talk to Woolpert. This didn't sit well with Phil or Russell.

[Russell told Sports Illustrated: *"All Saperstein said was hello and goodbye to me. He just talked to Woolpert, telling him what the Globetrotters could do for me and how much money I could make. He never said a word to me, treating me like an idiot who couldn't understand what the conversation was about. I made up my mind that I'd never play for that man."]*

RED AUERBACH: Once I knew that Rochester couldn't pay Russell and I was sure he wasn't going to play for the Globetrotters, I had to get the second pick that belonged to St. Louis.

NORM DRUCKER: In 1956, St. Louis was an antiblack city. The black players who played there from other teams—the fans called them such names . . . if those words were said today in public, you'd have a riot. All you heard was "Nigger . . . Monkey . . . Coon." That garbage. I don't know if Ben Kerner was willing to bring a black player into that environment, although I do know that Ben himself got along very well with his black players in the 1960s.

BEN KERNER: Don't ask me why Lester Harrison passed on Russell. Green was an Eastern guard and Lester liked those kinds of players.

But I knew I couldn't afford Russell. I heard that he had turned down $50,000 from the Globetrotters. I heard he wanted $25,000 or $50,000— it didn't matter because to me, it may as well have been a million. We didn't have the money. I had been in St. Louis for only one year [with a 33-39 record] and I needed immediate help. Then [GM] Marty Blake and I heard from Red, who mentioned Ed Macauley.

MARTY BLAKE: When Red called, I was convinced—and I still am— that he thought he was making a deal for Green because Russell would be off the board. Macauley had been a star at St. Louis University and was a good player with Boston. He would help our gate, even though he was coming to the end of his career. Listen, before the draft, we could have bought Macauley for $2,500, but we didn't have it. I was making $85 a week as general manager.

RED AUERBACH: Macauley had been my center and he was taking a beating because he was 6-foot-8, but only 185 pounds. He would have been a great forward playing next to Russell. Ed was one of the best trailers on the fast break that I've ever seen. We knew that St. Louis wanted him, and we knew that Ed lived in St. Louis. But Walter Brown and I never would have traded Ed unless he agreed.

ED MACAULEY: Our son Patrick had problems with his kidneys from the day he was born and it developed into spinal meningitis. He had such a high fever that it destroyed part of his brain. He was a cerebral palsy boy until he died at 14. I was living in St. Louis, making $17,500, which was a lot of money for the time, but I also was having to deal with a lot of medical bills.

Walter Brown called me and said, "Red has a deal that would send you to St. Louis. But we won't do it unless you agree. I can't imagine the Celtics without you."

If it had been anywhere but St. Louis, I would have said, "No way."

But I told Walter, "With Patrick so sick, I don't even know if I want to play basketball next year. I do know that I want to keep Patrick near his hospital and doctors in St. Louis."

Walter said that Lester Harrison didn't want Russell. He said Kerner didn't want him, either. Neither of those guys could pay him. Walter said, "We think Russell can be a great player for us, but if you want to stay with us, you stay."

I said, "Walter, you'd be doing me a favor if you sent me to St. Louis."

I know that Red had his heart set on the trade and he would have screamed and stormed, but Walter Brown would not have let the deal go through without my permission.

BEN KERNER: Auerbach told me that he'd give up Macauley for the pick. I said I wanted Cliff Hagan, too. Marty Blake had seen Hagan and liked him. I said, "Red, I need bodies. Macauley is not enough. It's Hagan and Macauley or no deal."

RED AUERBACH: Kerner played it cute and asked for Hagan at the last second—I thought I'd get Russell for Macauley. I loved players from Kentucky and knew Hagan would be good, but Kerner stuck to his demand for Hagan.

BEN KERNER: Yes, that trade made Boston great, but it also made us a contender and led to our championship in 1958, when we beat Russell and Boston. Macauley and Hagan were important players for us.

MARTY BLAKE: Macauley brought us credibility and class. He may be the only player I ever went to dinner with who picked up the check. Hagan was a Hall of Fame forward. The team that ended up with nothing was Rochester. Instead of Russell, they ended up with Green, who needed knee surgery. *[He played only 59 games in his first two seasons.]* In 1959, we worked a deal for Green while he was in the operating room. Kerner was saying, "Dead or alive, Green is ours." Green then went on to play decently for us for four years.

Over the years, people like to forget. Harrison would like to forget that he passed up Russell. Red likes to forget that when he was dealing with the Hawks, it was for Green, not Russell.

PETE NEWELL: You listen to Marty Blake and you start to think that the only time Marty ever made a mistake was the one time he thought he did, but it turned out he was right after all.

RED AUERBACH: Hagan and Macauley for Green? Are you kidding me? No way. Listen, most people don't know it, but we had assurances from Rochester that they would not take Russell. Lester Harrison was having trouble booking the Ice Capades. At one time, Walter Brown owned part of it. So Walter told Harrison, "If you pass on Russell, I'll help you get the Ice Capades." That clinched the deal.

MARTY BLAKE: I never heard the Ice Capades story.

LESTER HARRISON: There are a million stories about that draft. It is true that I had the Ice Capades for two years, then I was in jeopardy of losing them. I was having trouble with the people who ran our building in Rochester, and Walter Brown did come down to talk to them, saying I should have the Ice Capades. But this had absolutely nothing to do with the draft. Walter and I were friends and we did favors for each other all the time.

Russell the Rookie

Because he played on the Olympic team, Bill Russell didn't join the Celtics until December 22, 1956, after signing for $17,000. Boston had a 16-8 record. In his debut, Russell played 21 minutes, grabbed 16 rebounds and scored six points as Boston beat St. Louis 95–93. Boston was down by 16 points heading into the fourth quarter and won on a Bill Sharman jumper at the buzzer. Russell played a key role down the stretch, blocking three Bob Pettit shots in the fourth quarter. In his fourth pro game, Russell had 34 rebounds against Philadelphia's Neil Johnston. A week later, he held Johnston scoreless in 42 minutes; Johnston averaged 23 points that season. That caused Warriors owner Eddie Gottlieb to complain to the league that Russell was "committing legal goaltending," and he was "playing a one-man zone." Those charges were filed under sour grapes. Ironically, Gottlieb found himself on the other end of those complaints when he signed Wilt Chamberlain in 1959.

BOB COUSY: Trading for Russell was a ballsy move by Red because Ed Macauley was a bona fide All-Star center. Cliff Hagan became what everyone said he would—an All-Star small forward. Red told us Russell could rebound and that much was obvious. But as a kid, Bill couldn't hit a bull in the ass. He had no real offensive game.

TOM HEINSOHN: Unlike most of my teammates, I had played against Russell before he joined the Celtics. That was in the Holiday Festival when I was with Holy Cross and Bill was with San Francisco. There were about five straight plays in which I made my usual fake, blew by him like I did against most guys and went up for what should have been an open layup. But Russ somehow blocked all five of those shots. Believe me, that shook me up. I couldn't figure out where he was coming from. And he owned the boards. But offensively, Russ had a hard time hitting the backboard. He either scored on an offensive rebound or when Cousy threw him a lob and he'd jump over everyone and stuff it. But I knew he'd be great because I had never seen a player his size with that much athletic ability. And winning—you could tell from day one, all he cared about was winning. I was a rookie the same year as Russell and at the press conference where I signed my contract, I told everyone how great Bill would be. When he showed up, people tended to dwell on how skinny he was and how he was limited on offense. There were stories written that Red had made a mistake.

[Boston sportswriter Tom Carey wrote, "Is Russell worth $17,000? No, because I can name four rebounders that Russell fears. . . . In plain basketball sense, he is a vastly overrated competitor. He has ailments, too. Too tired to play more than 24–25 minutes a ballgame. In the assist department, William pays little attention to where the ball is. . . . Russell owes a great deal of his rebounding to Heinsohn, who is forever blocking out, which automatically forces Russell into rebounding position."]

LEONARD KOPPETT: In Russell's first game at Madison Square Garden, Harry Gallatin ate Bill up. I mean, Harry destroyed him. Bill had come in late because of the Olympics and he was new to the league, so that was the reason he had a few rough games early. But it also was an opportunity for his critics to jump on him and it became pretty unbelievable after a while, all the comparisons to Walter Dukes.

ED MACAULEY: No one was in awe of Russell in his first year or two. I don't think people understood how defense could change the game. It wasn't until he started winning championships that fans and writers began to appreciate Russell.

[As a rookie, Russell averaged 14.7 points and shot 43 percent and only 49 percent from the foul line. But he also averaged 19.6 rebounds. Blocked shots were not kept.]

CHARLIE SHARE: I was the opposing center in Russell's pro debut, and I held my own against him. Bill was so excited that all I had to do was fake a shot and he was up in the air and I was open for a layup. But he still blocked a lot of shots. I thought to myself, "I am seeing the pro game change right before my eyes." After that game, I had more reporters waiting for me than I did at any time in my career. I told them, "I played well against him, but I'd be perfectly happy if I never faced him again." When I did play Bill again, the move that worked the first time didn't. He remembered and adjusted—that was what made him great.

JIM LOSCUTOFF: There was a lot of pressure on Bill when he joined us because we were in first place by 7–8 games. If we won the title, people would say, "Well, they were going to win anyway before they got Russell." If we lost, they'd say, "Russell came in and messed things up."

RED AUERBACH: I told Bill that I didn't care how many points he scored. What I wanted him to do was get me the ball—rebounds, block shots. Then get the ball to our shooters: Sharman, Cousy, Heinsohn, Ramsey. These guys can put the ball in the basket. Just do what you do best.

PETE NEWELL: We coaches in the West knew that Russell was a unique player. But I'd run into guys in the East—even after Bill turned pro— and they'd tell me that he was another Walter Dukes.

I'd say, "Listen, basketball is played with a basket at each end of the court. You have to guard one of those baskets in order to win. Russell will guard that basket better than anyone ever has. Red knows this and that is why he drafted him."

BEN KERNER: When Boston beat us for the title [St. Louis in 1956–57], we began to realize the greatness of Russell was in the playoffs. In big games, no one was better. In the fourth quarter, he'd get every defensive rebound. How are you supposed to win when you get only one shot and there's Russell sweeping the backboards?

JIM LOSCUTOFF: Most people assume that Russell was the Rookie of the Year in 1957. But Heinsohn won the award, primarily because he played the full season. It turned out that the rookie award was the only major award that Russell never won. Bill has a lot of resentment about that. Tommy deserved it [16.2 points, 9.7 rebounds], but I think that Bill felt slighted that he didn't get it.

SLATER MARTIN: Russell was the first player to dunk regularly; he did it off lob passes from Cousy and he did it with little flamboyance. He just caught the ball and dunked it, no big deal, and we accepted that because it was Bill's shot. There was no finger pointing or talking like you see today. We didn't consider the dunk a skilled shot. If you could jump high, then you could throw the ball through the rim. So what?

LEONARD KOPPETT: Before Russell, the NBA was a vertical game— nearly all the plays went directly to the basket. Russell made basketball a horizontal game because his shot blocking took away the layup. He forced teams to pass the ball from side to side to set up the medium-range jump shot, and that meant outside shooting became more important.

JACK TWYMAN: Russell coming to the NBA was a monumental event. The reason I point to Russell is that Boston invented the modern fast break after he joined the team. They didn't just run, they went out to annihilate the competition and that aggressive style carried over to other teams. There was a study in the late 1950s that showed the average time of possession was 11 seconds. The league went from one dominated by large, somewhat slow centers who set a lot of back picks, used the pick-and-roll play and threw a lot of passes, to one that was made up of the pure athletes and the jump shooters.

Red's First Title

Ten months after Boston and St. Louis made the trade that changed the course of the NBA, the two teams met in the NBA Finals and played what has to be considered one of the greatest seventh games in the history of the league. The two franchises also were winning as they never had before.

When St. Louis agreed to trade the draft rights of Bill Russell to Boston for Cliff Hagan and Ed Macauley, the Hawks had no idea what Russell would mean to the Celtics. Nor did they even guess that Hagan would one day go into the Hall of Fame. The Hawks were owned by Ben Kerner, known behind his back as Bennie the Boob. He was a guy whose love of basketball was bigger than his wallet. In 1951, Kerner moved his Tri-Cities team to Milwaukee, figuring at least Milwaukee had a new 11,000-seat arena. But the Hawks were losing, and losing big. Not even a sniff of a .500 record or the playoffs. In 1953, the Boston Braves moved to Milwaukee; with a new major league baseball team in town, no one cared about a lousy NBA team.

So Kerner packed the truck again and moved his franchise, this time to St. Louis in 1955. St. Louis was supposed to be a barren ground for pro sports. The baseball Browns had moved east to Baltimore. St. Louis had an NBA team named the Bombers, but they went belly-up in 1951. People in St. Louis cared about the baseball Cardinals and only the baseball Cardinals. That's why Kerner was dubbed the Boob.

In his first season in St. Louis, the Hawks were 33–39—their best record in six years under Kerner. It also was the Hawks' first playoff appearance since Auerbach coached them in 1949–50 back in Tri-Cities.

Things were better for Kerner, but the cash register wasn't singing loud enough. He wanted a gate attraction, a local hero. The perfect guy was Ed Macauley, a native son who had played with the ill-fated Bombers before moving on to Boston after basketball folded in St. Louis in 1951. Bill Russell? He wasn't even a name to Kerner. He certainly didn't sound like box office. If Boston and Auerbach wanted this tall kid from San Francisco, they could have him.

When the 1956–57 season opened no one expected St. Louis and Boston to wind up playing for the title six months later. St. Louis stumbled under coach Red Holzman. Kerner did not handle stumbling well. He had gotten Bob Pettit in 1954, and now he had added Macauley. By God, the team should be doing better. When Kerner thought the team should be doing better, he meant the coach should be doing better. And when he thought that, the coach should pack his bags, which Holzman did after the Hawks hit 14-19. Point guard Slater Martin coached the team—under protest—for two weeks. He refused to do double duty any longer, and told Kerner to put bench-warming forward Alex Hannum in charge. Hannum was Martin's roommate. Hannum's nondescript career was nearly over and he wanted to coach. Kerner was not a big Hannum fan, but someone had to coach the Hawks and at least Hannum was willing to finish out the season.

Under Hannum, the Hawks were 15-16. They ended up with a 34-38 record. So did two other teams—Minneapolis and Fort Wayne. There were only four teams in the West, and the top three all had 34-38 records, so they could all say that they shared first place. At 31-41, you could say Rochester finished last; you also can say they had second place all to themselves.

Anyway, St. Louis prevailed out of this mediocre mishmash to win the Western Division playoffs and face Boston in the Finals.

Boston was clearly the premier regular season team at 44-28. The Celtics were 16-8 when Russell joined them after playing for the 1956 Olympic team, then went 28-20 with Russell. Averaging 19.6 rebounds, Russell would have led the league but did not play in enough games to qualify. Maurice Stokes (17.4) was recognized as the NBA's top rebounder in 1956. No one kept track of blocked shots, but no one came close to Russell in this area. As Auerbach said, "Players just didn't block shots until Russell came into the league."

But lost in the hype of Russell joining the Celtics was the fact that Auerbach would have had a great 1956 draft even without Russell. He picked Tom Heinsohn as a territorial choice from Holy Cross. Another selection was Russell's San Francisco teammate, K.C. Jones, although Jones was in the military and would not join the Celtics until 1958.

As the 1957 Finals opened, Boston was the overwhelming favorite. Their roster included future Hall of Famers Sharman, Ramsey, Cousy, Heinsohn and Russell. Then the Hawks went into Boston Garden for Game 1 and beat the Celtics 125-123 in overtime—so much for the homecourt advantage. Pettit scored 37, Macauley and Slater Martin each had 13. That game also served notice: this series was going seven games.

The games in St. Louis were especially heated as some of the Southern crowd had no use for black players, especially almost-Hawk Russell. But another guy who caught their wrath was dark-skinned official Mendy Rudolph. According to Leonard Koppett, the fans thought that

Rudolph, a Jew, was Puerto Rican and they showered him with racial taunts. Of course, St. Louis wasn't thrilled with Jews, either. Add in the fact that Rudolph was an official, and he simply didn't stand a chance.

In Game 3 in St. Louis, Auerbach complained that a basket was too low, holding up the start of the game. Kerner thought his old coach was showing him up, so he went on the court and challenged Auerbach, who decked Kerner with a right hook. Bloodied, Kerner staggered off. The floor was mopped up and the game began, the Hawks winning 100–98 on Pettit's shot in the final seconds.

The series was inevitably moving toward a final, climactic last game. Game 7 was in Boston.

With six seconds left, Boston had a 103–101 lead. Pettit was fouled. With the Boston crowd screaming at him, Pettit coolly dropped in both free throws.

That set up overtime No. 1.

Hawks guard Jack Coleman swished a jumper in the final seconds to send the game into a second overtime. The score was 113–113.

At this point, fouls were taking a toll. Heinsohn went to the bench with 37 points and 23 rebounds, while Macauley, Coleman and Jack McMahon fouled out for the Hawks.

Boston had the edge in the backcourt for most of the series, but not this game. Cousy shot 2-of-20, Sharman 3-of-20. Think about that— two Hall of Fame guards banging away at the rim at 5-of-40 in a seventh game of a championship series.

In the second overtime Boston had a 125–123 lead with two seconds left.

"We had the ball out under our own basket, which meant we had to go the length of the court to win," said Bob Pettit. "Alex Hannum called time-out. He was very confident. He had just put himself into the game [when Ed Macauley fouled out] a minute earlier."

"Alex hadn't played for a month," said Cliff Hagan. "He wore a uniform, but by playoff time he had become strictly a coach."

The Hawks gathered around Hannum and wondered what he had in mind.

Ed Macauley remembered, "Alex said, 'All right, I'm going to take the ball out-of-bounds. Pettit, I want you to stand at the opposite foul line. I'm going to throw the ball the length of the court, it's going to hit the backboard. Then, Pettit, you'll get the rebound and tip it in.' There were nine guys around Hannum and we all were nodding like we knew what he was talking about. But I was like everyone else. I was thinking that Alex had a hard time hitting the backboard from 15 feet, so how was he going to do it from 94 feet?"

As Pettit came onto the floor, he was dazed by Hannum's plan. "I kept thinking that I'd never heard anything like it before. And Alex was so sure of himself. He looked right at me and said, 'Pettit, you'll get the rebound and tip it in.' "

Hannum said, "It was a gamble, but Pettit was the greatest offensive rebounder I'd ever seen. I figured if I could get the ball on the board, we had a chance."

The remarkable aspect is that Hannum's heave did bang against the backboard and the rim—an incredible feat in itself. Then Pettit crashed the boards and got the rebound.

"I caught the ball in midair and shot it before I came down," said Pettit. "The ball rolled around the rim and came out. Really, as crazy as it sounds, I should have made the shot. Alex's pass was perfect."

Pettit played 56 of a possible 58 minutes, scoring 39, snaring 19 rebounds. But he shot 14-of-34, not a great percentage for a big man in a big game. Hagan scored 24, Martin 23 for the Hawks. Russell had 19 points and 32 rebounds for Boston, who won despite shooting 37 percent.

A relieved Red Auerbach ran off the court. There was no cigar lighting until after the final buzzer this time.

"Winning your first championship always is the hardest," said Auerbach. The Celtics celebrated by having a few beers and shaving off Russell's beard in the joyful dressing room.

They had no idea that they were to do this again and again and again—nine times in 10 years under Auerbach.

7

THE LOYAL OPPOSITION, PART I

Meet Coach Hannum

Alex Hannum had been a part of pro basketball from 1948, when he played for Oshkosh, Wisconsin. Hannum was a six-point scorer, a 35 percent shooter from the field as a 6-foot-7, 230-pound power forward who seldom started. By the time he came to the St. Louis Hawks in 1957, Hannum had been with seven teams, including an earlier stop in St. Louis. Few knew that this classic journeyman player was about to become one of the greatest coaches in pro basketball history. Starting in 1957, Boston won 11 NBA titles in 13 years. The other two belonged to Hannum-coached teams—the 1958 St. Louis Hawks and the 1967 Philadelphia 76ers.

MARTY BLAKE: We opened the 1956–57 season with Red Holzman as our coach in St. Louis. We didn't get off to a decent start, and Ben Kerner wanted to make a change. Benny was never afraid to change coaches. He hired and fired some of the best.

CHARLIE SHARE: Toward the end, Holzman gave us a pep talk where he pulled out pictures of his wife and kids and asked us—pleaded with us—to win so that he could keep his job and feed his family. We knew that he was in real trouble.

MARTY BLAKE: After we fired Holzman, Kerner went to Bob Pettit and offered him the job. Pettit said he'd take it for a game or two, but we better find someone else because he didn't want to coach. Next, we went to Charlie Share, and he wasn't interested. So that was two players who wouldn't coach. Next was Slater Martin, who said he'd take it for a while, but he didn't want to be the full-time coach.

SLATER MARTIN: We had lost in Rochester, and the next night we got beat at home to someone who wasn't very good. Mr. Kerner told me to be in his office the next morning at eight.

I knew what he wanted—he had been looking for one of the players to agree to coach the team.

I told Mr. Kerner that I couldn't coach and play at the same time, and that he needed me more as his point guard than he did coaching the team on the bench.

I said, "Why don't you make Alex Hannum the coach?"

I roomed with Alex and I knew that he had tremendous insight into the game. I knew he was the one player on the team who wanted to coach.

But Mr. Kerner didn't like Alex personally.

He said, "Slater, you're the coach, period."

That night, I sat down with Alex and said, "Sit just tight for a few weeks. You can help me from the bench, and after a while I'll talk to the old man and get him to put you in charge."

ALEX HANNUM: Slater said, "How am I supposed to keep track of time-outs, substitutions and everything else and play, too? You've gotta help me. We'll coach the team together."

We had a good couple of weeks and Slater was leaving most of the coaching to me.

SLATER MARTIN: After eight games [the Hawks were 5-3], I went to Mr. Kerner and said, "Make Alex the coach. I'll still help him and we'll coach the team like we've been doing, but give him the title. I don't want it."

I didn't want any part of coaching, but I wanted to make it so that Mr. Kerner would put Alex in charge, which he finally did.

ALEX HANNUM: Until I became the coach, I was just another piece of meat to Kerner, a body for his bench, and I don't think he ever looked at me as anything else. Buddy Blattner was our radio announcer and a confidant of Kerner's. Slater went to Buddy and said, "Tell Mr. Kerner that Alex can handle the team. Tell him that if Alex doesn't get the job, I quit."

MARTY BLAKE: Benny and I were talking about what to do with Alex— we either were going to make him coach or put him on waivers. Finally, Benny made Alex coach because he was the one guy who wanted the job.

BOB PETTIT: When Alex took over, we knew he was a tough son of a gun. He had very strong convictions and the guts to try anything. He even tried starting himself over me, the idea being he'd play 8–10 minutes, pick up four fouls and beat up the opposing forward. Then I'd play the rest of the game after he had softened the other guy up. That didn't last long, but it was an example of his innovative thinking. He wasn't afraid to try something different, nor was he afraid to say he made a mistake and junk his plan.

ED MACAULEY: Alex was a man's man. You had a feeling that if you challenged him, he'd say, "Let's lock the door and see who comes out of here." You knew that Alex would fight you if that was what you wanted, and if he did fight, he'd win.

JOHNNY KERR: When Alex coached in Syracuse, we had a guy named Lee Shaffer who was complaining about his playing time. At halftime and in front of the team, Alex went up to Shaffer and said, "I want you to know that the sun doesn't rise and set in your asshole."

Then he stood there, daring Shaffer to do something about it. Of course, Shaffer backed down. But later that night, I saw Shaffer and Alex in the bar, talking it out and throwing down the beers.

AL BIANCHI: I remember a game against the Celtics where there was a fight on the floor, and here came Alex leading the charge from the bench. He threw a cross body block into a couple of Celtics.

JOHNNY KERR: I've seen Alex walk into the room where the wives waited after the game and he'd say, "Okay, who's mad at me because I'm not playing your husband?"

CHARLIE SHARE: There were a couple of sides to Alex. He could get into your face and be as stubborn as a mule. We called him Old Iron Head.

I thought I had a pretty good set shot, especially for a center. Alex had another opinion.

"Charlie," he told me, "when we need a seven-foot set shooter, I'll let you know."

Alex put in his own set of plays and designed an offense to get the ball to Cliff Hagan and Pettit. He studied their favorite spots on the court and made sure they got shots from those areas.

The other side of Alex was that he told us, "Listen, I can't see everything on the court and I can't hear everything. So tell me what you think. I won't always use it, but I will listen."

After games, Alex would take guys out for beer and he'd talk over the game and the team. He wanted to know what we thought, and there were times when he did change things.

ED MACAULEY: It was Alex who had the guts to make the move that both made Cliff Hagan a great player and made us a great team. It also meant that Alex had to put me on the bench, which wasn't easy because I was very popular in St. Louis. When Holzman was the coach, Hagan was a rookie and he had been playing Hagan at guard. All of us could see that Hagan was not a guard.

CLIFF HAGAN: I had been a center in college at Kentucky, even though I was only 6-foot-4. The Hawks had Charlie Share in the middle, Pettit and Macauley at the forwards, so they asked me to play guard. I didn't understand the position. When a shot went up, I went to the boards. I wasn't playing until garbage time. I was very insecure. I had signed a one-year, nonguaranteed contract for $6,500. I also had a knee problem. I wondered if I would make it through my rookie year. My break came when Holzman got fired and Alex took over. At the same time, Pettit got hurt and Alex started me at forward for a few games. I felt at home, played well, and he never took me out of the lineup after that.

BOB PETTIT: I broke my arm and missed a few weeks, when Alex gave Hagan his chance. At guard, Hagan was a fish out of water and there was some talk that he might even get cut. Everyone but Alex Hannum said Hagan was too small to be a forward, and then Hagan became a great forward. If not for Alex, who knows what would have happened to him.

[Hagan played 10 years with the Hawks, averaging 18 points, 7.1 rebounds and making four All-Star teams.]

BOB FERRY: Hagan made it at forward because he had a great hook shot. I'm talking about a running hook that he could make with either hand from 18 feet away on the dead run. He knew every trick and was all business on the court. I always thought he was the kind of guy who could flip the switch on the electric chair. You just didn't mess with him.

CLIFF HAGAN: I learned that hook shot in junior high and it was my way of dealing with taller players. I was a solid 215 pounds. Even though the men I covered were usually bigger than I was, I often was just as strong and usually a lot faster.

LENNY WILKENS: Cliff had the hands of a much larger man. When he held the ball, it was like a grapefruit in one of his hands. He and Elgin Baylor never liked each other. They beat the hell out of each other when they played—incredible physical battles. Not dirty, but these were two great players who locked horns out there.

JERRY GROSS: There was a game where Cliff took his hook shot and Chuck Noble just decked him. Cliff hated to show he was in pain on the court, it was a badge of honor with him. But you could see Cliff was really hurting and he thought it was a cheap shot. For the rest of the game, nothing happened. But a year later, we played Noble's team for the first time since the incident. Noble drove to the basket and Cliff just bashed him in the skull. There was blood all over.

Norm Drucker was working the game and Norm told me that after Cliff hit Noble he said, "That's for last year."

BOB PETTIT: People say how can a guy 6-foot-4 play forward, especially when he wasn't a great long-range shooter. I say, look at Charles Barkley. He's only 6-foot-4, but he's like a rock. Hagan had a lot of that fierce spirit in him, believing he could outscore or outrebound anyone on the court. I roomed with Cliff for nine years and I can't say enough good things about him. He was the toughest competitor I've seen, but he also was a man who collected antiques and would take me to antique shows on the road.

MARV ALBERT: We all knew Cliff as one of the toughest SOBs on the court, but one day I was backstage at Kiel Auditorium in St. Louis and there was Cliff sitting behind a baby grand piano. He was wearing his Hawks uniform and playing this wonderful classical piece. I thought, "Well, there is some real depth to this man."

Red's Playoff Punch

In the third game of the 1957 Finals en route to his first NBA title, Boston coach Red Auerbach punched St. Louis owner Ben Kerner. It happened before the opening tap. Auerbach was not ejected, although he later was fined $300. St. Louis won that game, 100–98. But the Celtics eventually won the series.

MARTY BLAKE: There was some bad blood between the Hawks and Celtics, part of it having to do with Red once working under Ben Kerner, and the other being that these were the two best teams in basketball. The teams had split the first two games. When the Celtics were in our building, a couple of their players had been hit by eggs thrown from the fans. So Red was not in a good mood before Game 3.

BOB COUSY: Auerbach blames me for what happened, but I believe the whole setting was a factor. At Kiel Auditorium, the players had to walk down from a stage area to get from the dressing room to the court. The fans were right on top of you, and the St. Louis fans could be very vulgar, and especially vicious for the black players.

As we were warming up, I sensed that there was something wrong with the basket.

I said, "Arnold, that basket's not 10 feet."

Red was out on the court, pointing to the basket and yelling about it being the wrong height. Marty Blake grabbed a 10-foot pole and was checking it.

FRANK RAMSEY: It was Bill Sharman who first complained about the basket. Bill, being the meticulous fellow that he is, was shooting free throws and they kept coming up short. Sharman went up to Red to complain about the basket, and Red was out in the middle of the court, standing with Heinsohn, when I saw Ben Kerner leave his courtside seats and walk toward Red.

BEN KERNER: I just thought it was another of Red's stunts, things he did to annoy people. This was right before game time and I didn't want to start late.

I went out there and said, "What the hell is going on, Red?"

He said the basket was off.

I said, "That's bush. It's just a cheap trick."
Then he punched me.

BOB COUSY: Kerner took Arnold's questioning the basket as a personal affront. He was screaming obscenities at Arnold, questioning his integrity. Arnold had his back turned to Kerner. As Kerner came closer, Arnold just turned around and leveled him. He really cold-cocked Kerner, put him right down at midcourt with a sold-out crowd waiting for the game to begin.

FRANK RAMSEY: Kerner's nose was bleeding, so one of his friends came out on the court and wiped it with a handkerchief. Meanwhile, Red just walked away from the whole thing. Then Kerner got up and went back to the stands and we played the game.

BILL SHARMAN: I believe Red wanted us to see that he wasn't about to back down from anything. He knew that St. Louis was a tough place to play and that the crowd was hostile. And there he was, socking the owner right in front of the fans.

BOB PETTIT: The players on both teams didn't think much of it. We had seen Kerner and Red go at it before. There was one night when those guys ended up wrestling. They were rolling around on the floor, yelling at each other about something.

RED AUERBACH: Ah, that was no big deal. Not worth talking about.

BEN KERNER: We all had our fights back then, and not just the players. I love Red. He lit up the building every time he stepped into the arena. He was a great coach, he was in charge. He was great for the game. He may have punched me, but I had a night for him in St. Louis the year he quit coaching.

The Hawks Hang On

It seemed that the 1957–58 season was spent waiting for the Celtics and Hawks to play for the NBA title again. Boston won the Eastern Division by eight games, St. Louis won the West by eight games, and they seemed to play the 72-game regular-season schedule with one eye on each other.

Red Auerbach thought the hardest title to win was his first, until he tried to repeat. St. Louis was convinced that no team ever came closer to a championship than it did, losing in two overtimes in the seventh game at Boston Garden in 1957.

Both teams returned with nearly identical rosters. Auerbach had Bill Russell for a full season, and he set an NBA rebounding record, averaging 22.4. Maurice Stokes was second at 18.1, followed by the Hawks' Bob Pettit at 17.4. When it came time to pick the MVP, the NBA players voted for Russell (until 1979–80, it was the players who voted for the league's MVP). But the NBA writers, who never fully comprehended the importance of rebounding and defense, placed Russell on their second All-NBA team. Pettit was picked as the center, even though he actually was a forward as the Hawks played the wide-bodied Charlie Share in the middle. It was these early slights—not being Rookie of the Year in 1957 and then being second-team center in 1958—that set the tone for much of Russell's bitterness and anger about his career and the men—the white men, to be exact—who wrote about the NBA.

The one negative note as the Celtics approached the playoffs was that they were without Jim Loscutoff, who played five games and then went down for the year with a knee injury. Loscutoff was a guy who supplied the Celtics' muscle from the power forward spot. He started some fights and finished the rest that were begun by someone else. As the playoffs dawned, it would have been nice to have a healthy Loscutoff, but not necessary. Not as long as Boston had Russell.

As for the Hawks, Alex Hannum was now the full-time coach, wearing a suit and tie instead of a sweatsuit and tennis shoes on the bench. The core of the team remained the same—Slater Martin and Jack McMahon in the backcourt, the front line of Cliff Hagan, Charlie Share and Bob Pettit. Hagan had emerged as a star, averaging nearly 20 points, leading the league in shooting percentage at .443. Auerbach later said that "Hagan was the Adrian Dantley of his era." As usual, Pettit (24.6 points, 17.4 rebounds) was simply great.

As was the case the year before, the 1958 Finals opened in Boston. Once again, St. Louis won the opener on the Celtics' parquet floor, Boston winning Game 2 to even the series.

But in Game 3—the first in St. Louis—Russell sprained his ankle while blocking a Pettit shot early in the first quarter. He was called for goaltending on the play. His ankle forced him to the dressing room for the rest of the game and, naturally, the Celtics lost. In Game 4, Russell didn't dress. The Hawks were home and in position to take a commanding lead in the series. Instead, the Celtics went with dinosaur Arnie Risen in the middle, and they beat the Hawks 109–98.

No one was sure what to make of the series at this point. St. Louis had won the opener, a game everyone figured it would lose. Yet the Hawks lost Game 4 at home to a Celtics team without Russell. Game 5 was in Boston with Russell still out. This time, the Hawks made sure to pound the ball inside and beat Boston.

With the series at 3–2, Game 6 was in St. Louis. Russell taped up his ankle, but limped through 20 minutes, scoring only eight points. Even with Russell virtually ineffective and playing on the road, the Celtics stayed right with St. Louis as Bob Cousy, Tom Heinsohn and Frank Ramsey did the damage from the outside. In the middle, Risen was feeling all of his 33 years—he would retire after the playoffs. Auerbach found himself wishing he had one more big body—or wishing that Loscutoff had not ripped up his knee five games into the regular season.

Early in the fourth quarter, the score was 93–93. But the Hawks kept putting the ball in Pettit's hands and he kept putting it in the basket. Pettit scored 19 of the Hawks' last 21 points. His medium-range jumper with 15 seconds to play put St. Louis in command at 110–107.

Pettit finished with 50 points, a playoff record. Cousy also had 50 in a playoff game, but that was in 1953, in a game that went four overtimes as Cousy scored 30 of his 50 from the foul line. Pettit had done his damage in 48 minutes. Sports Illustrated said that Pettit "blocked at least a dozen shots."

The Hawks would be the NBA's last all-white championship team.

After this game, there would be much debate about what would have happened if Russell had been healthy. The answer—to an extent—came in the Finals of 1960 and 1961, as St. Louis and Boston met again. Boston won both times.

BEN KERNER: I knew I had a good team in the middle 1950s with Pettit, and then I traded for Macauley and Hagan. But the guy who got us into the Finals was Slater Martin.

MARTY BLAKE: Martin was a great little guard at 5-foot-10. He got the ball to George Mikan, Vern Mikkelsen and Jim Pollard when Minneapolis had that great front line. But the Lakers never appreciated Martin. They'd tell him, "We could get two bellhops to play the backcourt and we'd still win." But we knew that Martin could be our missing piece, and we made a move to get him.

SLATER MARTIN: Everyone knew that Ben Kerner wanted to win so badly in St. Louis, but the rest of the league also knew that the Hawks would never do it with their backcourt. When I was with the Lakers, we would press them and their guards couldn't handle it. We'd disrupt their offense, and they couldn't get the ball to Pettit and Hagan. I remember seeing Hagan in the backcourt, and it was a joke. I told Red Holzman, "Red, put that kid at forward and forget about him. But he'll kill you at guard." I don't want to sound arrogant, but looking at it from the outside I knew that what the Hawks needed was a player like me.

I had been the point guard on the four Lakers teams that won titles in the early 1950s, but they never wanted to pay me. By September of 1956, I was holding out for $14,000—I wanted a $1,500 raise. Things had reached the point where I told the Lakers that I quit and I had opened a sporting goods store in Houston.

Ben Kerner called a sportswriter who was a mutual friend. He told the writer that the Lakers would not trade me to the Hawks because St. Louis was in their division. But Kerner had a way to get me if I would agree to go to a team in the East for a while. He also said I'd get the $14,000. So I was traded to New York, all the while knowing I'd eventually end up with the Hawks. Mr. Kerner and [Knicks owner] Ned Irish and I were the only ones who knew that I wouldn't stay in New York. I was with the Knicks for three weeks and played in several games. We had back-to-back games against the Hawks. The first night, I played for New York and we beat the Hawks. But the next night, Mr. Kerner used his influence with Ned Irish and the Knicks held me out of the game, saying I was injured. Three days later, I was traded to St. Louis for Willie Naulls.

When I came to the Hawks, I told the players, "When they press us, don't worry. Dribbling the ball is the easiest part of the game for me. Putting it in the basket is easy for you. We're a perfect match."

BOB PETTIT: After Slater came to the team, we jelled. We had a lot of very unselfish players. He had played with all those big men with the Lakers and he understood how to get them the ball. It was no accident that winning followed Martin around. He also was a real fighter. He might have been 5-foot-10, but he took no foolishness from anyone, and he often got into fights with guys a foot taller. I loved his feistiness. Charlie Share was our center and he set the picks to get Hagan or myself open. I mean, he'd do whatever it took—an elbow to the throat—and it might be brutal or a bit mean, but he got us open. He was a totally unselfish center. In the backcourt with Martin was Jack McMahon, who also liked to pass. Those three guys—Share, Martin and McMahon—usually never took more than five shots each because their main concern was getting shots for Hagan and me.

CHARLIE SHARE: I was the captain of the Hawks and I knew my role. I also understood that the game was changing on me. Before Russell came into the league, I averaged 12–14 points. After Russell, I was under 10 a game. I just didn't have the athletic ability that Russell and the other young centers had. Compared to them, I was almost inert. That is why facing Russell in the finals and us winning that title meant so much to me.

[Share played in the Finals with a broken jaw that was wired shut.]

RED AUERBACH: I take nothing away from St. Louis, but Russell was hurt. You could see it wasn't the same Russell, and we almost won anyway.

CHARLIE SHARE: Russell and I went up for a rebound, and naturally I came down first. Then he landed on my foot and turned his ankle. He wasn't 100 percent, but we won that title because Bobby Pettit would not let us lose. He had 50 points, and nothing the Celtics can say can take that away from Pettit.

ED MACAULEY: Pettit's 50 points in a game of such magnitude was the most amazing performance I had ever seen. In the fourth quarter, he scored 19 of our last 21 and he did it under constant defensive pressure, against 2–3 guys. Slater Martin and Jack McMahon kept feeding Pettit the ball, and he made every conceivable kind of shot. You can't dismiss the fact that the one year Russell was hurting, Boston didn't win. But that should not put a taint on our championship or Pettit's greatness.

BOB PETTIT: That game was a once-in-a-lifetime thing. In the last quarter, I wasn't sure what was happening. I was getting the ball, shooting it, and it was going in. The whole thing happened in a blur and I don't remember any of the individual shots or plays. I just knew that I wanted the ball because I didn't think they could do anything to stop me. I also remember feeling totally exhausted when the game was over.

Look, injuries are part of the game. Earlier in the season, I broke my arm and played with it in a cast. Charlie Share was hurt for us, but he played. Russell wasn't 100 percent, but he was on the court in that last game. I just don't think it's fair to say that we won only because Bill was hurt. The year before, we took Boston into double overtime in Game 7 and lost to a healthy Russell. We had a great team.

BOB COUSY: Everyone knows how great Russell was and what he meant to us. He was severely hampered by that ankle. All I know is that without question, the Hawks were the second-best team that year.

CLIFF HAGAN: The Celtics were fortunate to win the title in 1957. Listen, we beat them in six games—not seven—in 1958. It is senseless to ask, "What if?" I mean, what if Boston had never made that trade and Russell was with the Hawks while Ed Macauley and I were with Boston? Then what? You only know for sure what actually happened, and in 1958 Russell was on the court and we beat his team in six games.

CHARLIE SHARE: When the last game ended, Macauley threw the ball about 60 feet straight up in the air. I caught it and was running off the court protecting it from the fans who had come out of the stands. I nearly ran over my wife. I later gave the ball to a very good friend.

MARTY BLAKE: After we won the title, the players threw me into the pool at Kiel Auditorium. I had over $400 from program sales in my pockets and the dollar bills came floating up. The players were jumping in after the money, sort of like diving for dollars.

SLATER MARTIN: Back then, the NBA had no official championship ring. We won all those titles in Minneapolis, and they wouldn't even buy us a lousy belt buckle. They gave us a team picture, but that was it. Mr. Kerner let us design our own rings and he paid for them—all very first-class.

BOB PETTIT: A few days after we won the title, we started a 21-game exhibition tour around the country. I look back at that season and count up all the exhibition games and the playoff games and I bet we played in over 140 games.

ED MACAULEY: The bad thing was that after we won the title, Alex Hannum got into a contract dispute with Ben Kerner. Alex liked to play cards, but was always a poor poker player. He thought he could write his own ticket after the championship year and he asked for a big raise, and supposedly said he would not coach the team unless he got what he wanted.

Kerner said, "You mean if you don't get that much, you quit?"

Alex said, "Yes, I quit."

Kerner said, "Marty [Blake], write up a press release and say that Alex has resigned."

This was a case of two very strong-willed guys butting heads, and neither was about to give an inch. Money was one question, but control of the team also was something Kerner believed that Alex wanted. Ben Kerner was not about to give up control of his team to anyone.

He Owned Murderers' Row

Ben Kerner went back to the roots of the NBA, owning the Hawks franchise that began in Buffalo in the pre-NBA days. He made his money in the game program and concession business. In the tradition of Danny Biasone and Eddie Gottlieb, Kerner was a one-man show.

He picked the players, hired and fired the coaches. In Milwaukee, he hired Marty Blake as his staff—anything Kerner couldn't do, Blake handled, ranging from publicity to the public address system to scheduling to scouting. Bob Pettit recalled Blake arriving in Milwaukee wearing a pink shirt, an orange tie, blue pants, a brown coat and white socks. "He had a voice that would shatter an anvil and a mile-long cigar," said Pettit.

MARTY BLAKE: My first season with Ben Kerner [1954–55] in Milwaukee, the team was $94,000 in debt. He was ready to pull out of pro basketball and wanted $75,000 for the franchise, but the best offer he got was $50,000 from a group that wanted to move the team to Indiana. When we moved to St. Louis, they promised us that we'd have a base of 1,000 season ticket holders. We had 55. So we scrambled for money. We played a million exhibition games. We promoted before promotion was fashionable. I mean, we had acts such as Count Basie, Guy Lombardo, the Four Freshmen, Tommy Dorsey—all big names and they all played after our games. We gave away prizes.

ED MACAULEY: The Hawks were Ben Kerner's life. He didn't have a dime when he brought the team to St. Louis and built the franchise from the sweat of his brow. He had his fingerprints on every aspect of the operation, so it was very hard for him to let anyone control anything.

Ben was very close to his mother, and Ben's mother didn't want him to marry a gentile. He was in love with his secretary, who was not Jewish. So they never married until his mother died, and now they have two children. But I believe that all those years when he was living and dying with the team and when he had no family life, it helped him develop a very tough, dog-eat-dog personality.

JERRY GROSS: The Hawks scrambled for every penny and that meant a lot of exhibition games. We played in small towns in North Carolina and Georgia. Marty Blake always got a cashier's check or cash before the game—none of this splitting the gate stuff. Marty would wear a big cowboy hat, clench a cigar between his teeth, and as we'd walk out of the gym he'd wave goodbye to some poor Rotarian who sponsored the game. Then out of the side of his mouth, Marty would say, "Well, we just blew another town."

CLIFF HAGAN: One of Marty's tricks was to sign a rookie and then play a game in the rookie's hometown or his college town. He'd collect the money for the game, and the next day he'd cut the rookie.

JOHN VANAK: Marty would read a lucky number over the public address system, "Tonight's winner of the pony is 2334." Of course, Marty had that number in his hand. I don't know if they ever actually gave away a pony in St. Louis.

SLATER MARTIN: Money was an overriding concern to Mr. Kerner. One day, the Cardinals owner August Busch asked Mr. Kerner, "Ben, how do you make your money?"

Mr. Kerner said, "I own this team."

Busch said, "I know that, but how do you make your real money? I've got a little baseball team, but my brewery pays the bills."

But the team was all Mr. Kerner had, and as far as I'm concerned he was always fair with me.

ZELMO BEATY: As a man, I'd give Mr. Kerner an A. When I was a rookie, Clyde Lovellette was on the team. We had a scrimmage and Clyde hit me in the back. It was a blow that could have cost me my career, because I went face-first into the backboard. I was all right, but Mr. Kerner came running out of the stands screaming at Clyde about trying to hurt his No. 1 draft choice. Within a week, Mr. Kerner traded Clyde to create a spot for me.

Mr. Kerner was very good about taking his players out to eat when the team was on the road, and he took us to first-class places. He also would buy one of his veterans a new car every year. After he sold the team to Atlanta, he called me and said that it was still my turn, to go pick out a Caddy and send him a bill.

But negotiating a contract, now that was something else.

He would say, "You don't sign this, you don't play. I won't trade you. You'll just sit and get nothing." He always paid Pettit well, but in my last three years with the Hawks I was the highest-paid player at $37,500.

RUDY LaRUSSO: It was common knowledge that St. Louis was the lowest-paying franchise in the league. We heard that Kerner would tell you, "Either you take this or you work at the car wash. Now make up your mind."

CLIFF HAGAN: Because of the reserve clause, you were bound to a team forever, so you had no leverage. Mr. Kerner would tell you that he was just trying to survive, so he couldn't pay much. Well, we players were trying to survive, too. But he had the upper hand.

CHARLIE SHARE: One year, I decided that the best way to deal with my contract was to send it in blank and let Mr. Kerner fill in my salary. I thought I got a decent salary raise that way. It's what you do when you have faith in a man. It also is what you do when you don't have an agent to advise you.

BOB PETTIT: Mr. Kerner put the team first. If we needed a guard, he went out and traded for Slater Martin when Minneapolis wouldn't sign him. He made one good trade after another. People can complain about him, but he was more generous than most owners. He bought me three cars and a lot of other guys got cars and other gifts. He gets a bad rap from some people.

ED MACAULEY: Ben Kerner was a brilliant assembler of talent. You look at our 1958 championship team and everyone except Pettit was acquired through trades and acquired on a very tight budget.

CHARLIE SHARE: Mr. Kerner liked to play poker, but he wasn't very good. Pettit used to say, "Let Ben in the game and we'll subsidize our salaries."

BEN KERNER: I couldn't afford to pay my players a lot of money. Back then, the NBA was a hand-to-mouth operation. Basketball was my only business. I had to watch every penny. I could afford to give them cars and nice dinners, but I couldn't pay high salaries.

EARL STROM: At every game in St. Louis, Ben sat at halfcourt, in the first row across from the benches. He was there with his mother, his dentist, his lawyer, his doctor and other friends and they reacted to every call against the Hawks. They earned their name as Murderers' Row for officials.

There was a game I worked with Willie Smith. Kerner really got on Smith and before the game I said, "Willie, just take it easy. Don't let Kerner get to you."

He nodded, but late in the first quarter, he made a couple of calls and Kerner went crazy, screaming at him. There was a time-out and

Kerner really worked Smith over. Willie pointed at Kerner and yelled, "You . . . screw you!" Then he turned and walked away from Ben.

Willie was in the middle of the court, and here came Kerner. He had picked up a folding chair, raised it over his head and was heading onto the court after Willie.

I cut off Kerner and said, "Ben, do you realize what you're doing?"

Ben said, "I'll kill the son of bitch. I want to kill him, that's what I'm doing."

I said, "Benny, just get off the floor."

Smith yelled, "Let him go, Earl. If he hits me, I'll own his franchise."

With that, Ben lowered the chair and got off the court. He wasn't suspended or fined. Hey, that was just another night in St. Louis.

PETE D'AMBROSIO: Kerner just made a jackass of himself during games, jumping up and down and all the while he was sitting next to his elderly mother.

NORM DRUCKER: Kerner's mother got into the act, too. She wouldn't like one of your calls and she'd yell in her Yiddish accent, "You . . . this will be the last game you ever work in the NBA!"

RUDY LaRUSSO: [Official] Richie Powers told me this story. Bill Bridges was with the Hawks and he drove to the basket on Gus Johnson of Baltimore. Bridges went up for the dunk, slammed it through and Johnson came down on Bridges's back. The force of those two guys hitting the backboard caused the whole thing to shatter. Now, there's glass everywhere, absolute chaos. Then Kerner came running out of the stands screaming, "It's a three-point play. Richie, he got fouled, it's a three-point play."

EARL STROM: One of Kerner's best ideas was to have the first and last night any team has ever had for an official. It was Jim Duffy Night. The year before, Kerner had hammered Duffy in the papers, just killed him.

The next year at an exhibition game, Kerner wanted to get back on Duffy's good side, so he decided to have a night for Duffy.

NORM DRUCKER: Duffy and I were walking off the court at halftime and Jim said, "Wait a minute, they're going to give me something."

I said, "What?"

He said, "I'm going to get something."

Then Marty Blake was on the court and giving Duffy a TV and some other stuff.

EARL STROM: Duffy held up his whistle and told the crowd, "May this whistle never blow another sour note in St. Louis."

NORM DRUCKER: Duffy always liked Bob Pettit. He called him "Mr. Bob."

RUDY LaRUSSO: We called Duffy "Pettit's guardian angel." You would just look at Pettit hard and Duffy would blow the whistle.

LEONARD KOPPETT: Ben knew he shouldn't yell at officials. He told me, "I'm the owner and I'm screaming at the refs. It's stupid. It's as if I opened a restaurant, and then ran outside to tell everyone, 'Don't come in, the food stinks.' That's what I'm doing every night, but I can't control myself."

MARTY BLAKE: Ben loved to hire and fire coaches. His biggest mistake was Andy Phillip—hiring him in the first place. Andy held practices at 8 A.M. because he wanted to get home to make breakfast for his wife. We started the season 5-2, but lost a home game by 28 points to Syracuse. The players were telling us something.

ED MACAULEY: After Alex Hannum quit, I was offered the job. I turned it down because I wanted to keep playing. So Andy Phillip was hired. He was once late for an exhibition game because the baby-sitter was late. That did not sit well with Ben Kerner. It was just a matter of time before Andy was fired.

He called me in and said I had three choices:

1. I was playing poorly and I could retire.

2. He could trade me to Philadelphia, and he knew that I was very attached to St. Louis and would quit rather than leave.

3. I could coach the team.

I wanted to stay in St. Louis, so I reluctantly agreed to coach. Ben would sit on the sidelines and yell instructions to me. I had a meeting with him and told him that I would not tolerate that. He cut it out.

You see, Ben's style wasn't to second-guess coaches. He just fired them. Poor Andy Phillip, he found out he was fired when he was driving to practice and heard it on the radio.

BOB PETTIT: Mr. Kerner always wanted me to coach, but I wasn't interested. I was the designated interim coach until he found a new one. I played for 11 coaches in my 11-year career.

CLIFF HAGAN: Today, the TV cameras would love Ben Kerner at courtside—yelling at everyone, firing a coach about every year.

MARTY BLAKE: Say what they want about Benny Kerner, he built a franchise from nothing, won a championship and then sold the team for $7 million. Here was a man who understood the basketball business.

8

A CAST OF CHARACTERS

A Hot Dog Named Hot Rod

He was the first pick in the 1957 draft and was considered by many scouts and sportswriters to be the best college player ever. If nothing else, basketball had never seen a player quite like Hot Rod Hundley from the University of West Virginia. His father was a pool shark and gambler; his mother reportedly was a madam at a brothel. He grew up with different relatives and family friends in Charleston, West Virginia, and he grew into a 6-foot-4 guard who went to the foul line at Madison Square Garden in the NIT tournament and made two free throws— one a left-handed hook, the other a right-handed hook. Playing on the West Virginia freshman team, he averaged 35 points and there were six games where he didn't bother to take a shot, preferring to pass and dribble. His heroes were Bob Cousy and the Globetrotters' Goose Tatum, and he never believed in throwing a bounce pass unless he could bounce it between his legs—or at least throw it behind his back. Hundley played all six of his NBA seasons with the Lakers, averaging 8.4 points. He did make two All-Star teams, but was known more as an entertainer than a player. He was also the first of three great college guards from West Virginia—the others being Jerry West and Rod Thorn—who played for the Mountaineers three years apart. Today, Hundley is a broadcaster with the Utah Jazz.

JERRY WEST: Hot Rod was the first real basketball hero in West Virginia. He commanded attention not just because of his basketball ability, but his personality. He was like a Pied Piper; people were just drawn to him. They thought he was crazy, but they liked him anyway. His game was the same way. He did things on the court—I mean, I couldn't imagine myself doing that stuff—but those things turned the fans on. He set the stage for all of us to come.

Rod Thorn: Jerry West was a basketball player first and last. Hot Rod was a basketball player and a showman, and it was hard to know what came first with him. But Rod became a legitimate folk hero in West Virginia. He came up the hard way and he played and lived hard. The bottom line on Hot Rod was that he always had a good time.

Hot Rod Hundley: Because my parents were divorced and left West Virginia when I was very young, I grew up in a lot of different places with different people. I found a home on the playground and I stayed there day and night. I was blessed with good size and a feel for the game—I always was better than kids my age. I looked at basketball as a way out of the ghetto, and I was getting recruited early. Right after my sophomore season, Everett Case, the coach at N.C. State, brought me down to Raleigh. They bought me some clothes, gave me a job as a lifeguard at the pool on the N.C. State campus. For three summers, I worked at N.C. State, at basketball camps and stuff like that. But the NCAA caught up with them and questioned me about what I was getting from Case. This was in 1953 after I had 45 points in a high school all-star game between the best players from West Virginia and Kentucky. The NCAA suggested that it might not be wise for me to go to N.C. State. I told Coach Case that and he said, "I understand . . . You can keep all the clothes we bought you, but I want the suitcase back."

Rudy LaRusso: Hot Rod told me that he didn't do that fancy stuff in high school. He saved it for the playground. But in one freshman game, his team was way ahead and the fans were starting to fill the seats to watch West Virginia's varsity play. Hot Rod said he came down the court on the fast break, instinctively went behind his back and threw a no-look pass that led to a layup. Then, boom! The crowd went crazy and Hot Rod loved it.

Hot Rod Hundley: That's true. I never saw Cousy or the Globetrotters play, but I heard about the things they did and I worked on it. I thought that stuff belonged only on the playground. But in my freshman year, we had such a good team and we were killing the small colleges and junior colleges on our schedule. I got bored. So one night I'd score 60, the next I wouldn't score at all. Then I tried a couple of ballhandling things and the fans ate it up. So once in a while, I'd be at the foul line, and I'd spin the ball on my finger and then shoot by punching the ball. Or I'd shoot a free throw with my back to the basket, straight over my head. I made a 20-foot shot from my knees, and I threw the ball in from 20 feet away—behind my back, and it was a bank shot. I didn't do it to show the other team up, but just to have a good time and make the fans happy.

RUDY LaRUSSO: Lou Mohs told me that when he scouted Hot Rod for the Lakers, Rod would hang on the rim and play monkey. Lou said that once during the NIT, Rod had a great game, and with a couple of minutes left to go, the coach took him out of the game and he received a nice hand from the fans at Madison Square Garden. But Rod stopped dead at midcourt, put out his hands palms up and raised them, asking the crowd for a standing ovation. Lou Mohs told me, "So the crowd stood up and cheered Hot Rod."

FRED SCHAUS: I was hired to coach at West Virginia after Rod's freshman year. In fact, Rod wanted to quit school and play in the NBA, but the rules didn't allow players to come out early. So he talked to [Philadelphia Warriors owner] Eddie Gottlieb, who was close friends with Abe Saperstein. Abe was going to hire Rod to play for the team that played against the Globetrotters—Rod's act would have been perfect for them. But Rod had a cartilage problem in his knee. Gottlieb called me and said, "I think Rod should come back to school and I told him as much."

So I had Hot Rod, and he was great for college basketball. He never embarrassed an opponent, nor did his antics ever cost us a game. In the middle 1950s college basketball was coming off the scandals and it needed a shot in the arm, someone to bring the fans back. That's what Hot Rod did.

RUDY LaRUSSO: One of the famous Hot Rod stories was at the Dixie Classic or some tournament in the South. Rod needed two points to set a tournament scoring record. He went to the foul line, did his spin-the-ball-on-the-finger routine and punched it at the basket. He missed both shots.

Somebody said, "Jeez, Rod, if you made those free throws, you would have set the record."

Rod said, "Yeah, and if I broke it, then a year from now someone else would come around, break my record and I'd be forgotten. Now, they'll remember me."

These were his words to live by. He didn't care what you said, just print his name.

HOT ROD HUNDLEY: The Lakers made me the first pick in the 1957 draft. I told the Lakers I wanted $11,000, they said they couldn't do better than $9,000. We settled on $10,000. I figured I'd be the greatest pro who ever was. When I went to training camp, I hooked up with Slick Leonard and we were two of a kind—we smoked, drank beer, stayed out all night. George Mikan was coaching the team and he wanted to go with us, but we didn't want the coach along. George would say, "Listen, guys, let me come. I'll pay for it." George missed the life of a player. He was the one who named Bobby Leonard "Slick," because George lost so much money in cards to Slick.

SLICK LEONARD: Hot Rod and I were just two kids, getting in and out of trouble. In fact, he got us called in to see [owner] Bob Short and I thought we really blew it.

HOT ROD HUNDLEY: Slick and I had missed some curfews, and one day we missed a flight from New York to Syracuse. Actually, we had been at some friend's house in Philadelphia at an all-night party. We spent two hours drinking coffee and smoking cigarettes trying to cook up a story that would get us off the hook with Bob Short. We settled on the old "We got lost and had a flat tire" line.

Short called me in first and he didn't buy a word of it. He said, "You guys have been warned and warned again. I have no recourse but to fine you $1,000. Have you anything to say?"

I said, "It's your team," all the while I was also thinking that $1,000 was 10 percent of my salary. It was even more to Slick, who was making $8,500.

SLICK LEONARD: Hot Rod came out of the office, his face as white as a sheet.

I asked, "What did they hit you for?"

Rod said, "The big one."

I said, "A hundred."

Rod said, "No, baby, a grand. One thousand dollars."

My heart sank.

HOT ROD HUNDLEY: Slick got that kind of scared look you get when you think, "How can I ever explain this to my wife?"

SLICK LEONARD: Short liked us and he never took the money. He just wanted to scare the hell out of us, which he did . . . for a while anyway.

RUDY LaRUSSO: To Rod, going out at night was the same as breathing. He had to do it to live. We were roommates in Minneapolis during my rookie year and got to be great friends. I'd be going to bed at midnight, then I'd hear his car starting up. About seven in the morning, I'd get out of bed and Rod would come in from wherever and he'd catch a couple of hours of sleep before practice. On the road, we'd come into a hotel lobby, he'd dump his Lakers bag and head out somewhere. You'd walk into the lobby the next morning and the bag would still be there—exactly where he'd left it. The interesting thing and it's a comment on society is that no one would even consider stealing his bag.

When Rod did open his bag—two days later—everything would be wet and smell. I'd say, "Rod, you've got to wash things out once in a while."

HOT ROD HUNDLEY: Rudy likes to come across as the straight guy from Dartmouth, but when we went through the Detroit airport there was a shop that had this huge stuffed tiger, as big as Rudy. And Rudy would grab the tiger and start rolling around on the airline concourse with it in a wrestling match. He also had his own sound effects. Listen, he was my friend, so he couldn't be all sane, right?

EARL STROM: Hot Rod loved to draw attention to himself. There was a game where Elgin Baylor drove to the basket, got knocked down and had his bell rung. Hot Rod came off the bench, picked up Elgin and dusted off his pants.

I said, "Rod, what the hell are you doing on the court?"

He said, "Just taking care of my meal ticket, baby."

FRED SCHAUS: Once we had a game at the L.A. Shrine Auditorium, it was literally played on a stage and Hot Rod was super. We all said, "He should be good here, a stage is the perfect place for him."

SLICK LEONARD: A lot of people got on Rod because he didn't match his college greatness in the pros. They blamed his lifestyle and said he wasn't serious about the game. But the basketball clown image wasn't him, not on the court. He did very little messing around as a pro, and none when it mattered in a game. He played his ass off. He cared. His greatest attribute was his heart. But he was a step slow and not a good leaper, and that showed up as a pro.

CHICK HEARN: Rod played hard and was a great ballhandler, but he couldn't guard *me* and I can't go to my left.

Fred Schaus: I know Rod's background and I admire him as much as any player I've ever coached. I had Rod in both college and with the Lakers. I know he never got a college degree, but the things he learned in terms of social graces and dealing with people . . . listen, there is a reason he has been so successful and so well liked as a broadcaster. I am so proud of how he turned out because most guys who grow up like he did don't amount to anything.

Hot Rod Hundley: I look at my NBA career and I realize that I lost my outside shot and my confidence in it. I don't know why. I do know there were things I should have done differently. But I don't dwell on that. What the hell, I went into the NBA making $10,000 and came out making $11,000, and in between I made two All-Star teams. I was like a guy who goes into the army as a buck private and six years later he comes out as still a buck private, but he's got some great stories to tell.

He Played the Games

Gene Conley was the first man to play both major league baseball and basketball, and he did it the longest. For 11 years, Conley was a right-handed pitcher with four different teams, compiling a 91-96 record with a 3.82 ERA. He was a 14-game winner with Milwaukee in 1954, an All-Star with Philadelphia in 1959 and a 15-game winner with Boston in 1962. Conley was a decent-hitting pitcher, batting .192 and occasionally being used as a pinch hitter. In six NBA seasons—four with Boston, two with New York—the 6-foot-8 Conley was primarily a backup center, averaging 5.9 points and 6.8 rebounds. In 1961, he was the only man to pitch to Roger Maris the year he hit 61 homers and guard Wilt Chamberlain the year Wilt averaged 50 points.

Gene Conley: Bill Sharman was the reason I ended up with the Celtics. In the early 1950s, Bill played basketball at Southern Cal, and for one year I played basketball at the University of Washington. Then I ran into Bill again, this time in minor league baseball. I was pitching for Milwaukee, Bill was an outfielder with St. Paul of the Class AAA American Association. Bill told me that he mentioned my name to Red Auerbach, who was looking for guys with size. In 1952, Red made me his last draft pick even though he never saw me play—it was done purely on Sharman's word.

I was the 1952 Minor League Player of the Year. Red called me that fall and I had never even heard of him.

Red said, "I just drafted you to play for the Boston Celtics."

I hadn't played basketball for two years and I had no idea why any NBA team would draft me. But I also could use some extra money.

I said, "What do you pay?"

Red said, "Come to Boston and find out."

I had nothing to do after baseball season, so I went to camp with the Celtics and made the team. But I hardly played. I didn't see myself as a basketball player, it was just something to do until spring training. At the end of basketball season, I went to spring training and I figured that was the end of my basketball career.

RED AUERBACH: After his first season with us, I didn't hear from Conley for six years. Then I got a call and he said he wanted to play basketball again.

GENE CONLEY: In 1958, I'd had some arm problems [he was 0-6] and the Milwaukee Braves wanted to cut my salary 20 percent. I told them that I was going back to basketball because I was losing money. The Braves didn't like the idea, but I called Red.

Red said, "Gene, I don't know. A lot has happened since you played. We've got a 24-second clock. We've got Russell, Heinsohn, Ramsey . . . we're loaded with players."

I said, "Would you give me a tryout? I just bought a new house in Milwaukee for $20,000 and I don't have enough money to finish the work on it."

Red said, "You can come down to Boston, but if you don't make the team you'll have to pay your own way back to Milwaukee."

I showed up at Boston Garden with my big footlocker. I went to see Walter Brown, and Walter and Red were in the office.

Walter Brown said, "Red, I don't know if he can make the team, but that footlocker makes me think that Gene plans to stay."

Later, Walter called me into his office after Red had left. He was a big baseball fan and he liked to talk baseball.

Then he said, "Gene, what do you want for a salary?"

I said, "I made $20,000 in baseball."

Walter said, "Twenty thousand is fine."

But $20,000 was a lot of money in the NBA for 1958, especially for a guy who hadn't played anything but some pickup basketball for six years.

I made the team and four games into the season, Red told me, "You're the 11th man on a 10-man team. We can't pay you $20,000. What did you tell Mr. Brown?"

I said, "Red, all I did was sign a contract."

Red said, "We're sending you home."

He could do that because contracts weren't guaranteed. I went home for a week, then Red called and asked me to come back. I said I was glad to do it.

Red said, "But we have to cut your pay in half."

That was Red's way of getting out of Walter Brown's contract.

FRANK RAMSEY: After Gene came back to the team, he played about 10 minutes a game behind Russell. But there was a game where Russell was hurt and Gene started. In the middle of the second quarter, Gene was winded and he said, "Red, we've got to renegotiate my contract. You never said anything about playing me this much."

GENE CONLEY: From 1958–64, I played 13 straight seasons of basketball and baseball. I never went to a training camp in either sport. I was 6-foot-8, 225 pounds and I was a strong guy. I had a wife and three kids to support. Still, I don't know how I did it. Red would not allow me to touch a baseball when I was with the Celtics. Once during the playoffs, I asked Frank Ramsey to play catch with me because I knew that in a few weeks I was going to baseball. Red found out about it and went crazy—I never did it again.

In baseball season, I never shot baskets. In basketball season, I didn't touch a baseball. I went one day from wearing my low-cut Chuck Taylors to my baseball spikes. When we beat St. Louis for the 1959 title, the next day I was on a plane for Florida. The regular baseball season had started, but I'd work out with a high school team in Florida for a week and then join the team. Ten days after the Celtics won that 1959 title, I was with the Red Sox and pitched a shutout against Washington at Fenway Park and hit a double off the left field wall while Russell and K.C. Jones were in the stands.

RED AUERBACH: The newspapers gave me some crap about letting Conley play basketball. I said, "We ain't paying the guy peanuts. The question is, should we let him play for the Red Sox, because we're paying him better." Gene was a backup center, strong as a bull with a lot of enthusiasm. He liked to swing his elbows and his offense was crude. Because Conley was so physical, Russell hated playing against him in practice.

FRANK RAMSEY: Gene never knew his own strength. In warmups, he swung his elbows and accidentally hit Bill Sharman in the eye. Gene was so upset and kept saying, "Oh, no, Bill, look what I've done."

WAYNE EMBRY: Conley loved to fight. Not long after he signed with the Celtics, I ran into him in the hotel lobby. I was with the Royals and we were playing Boston that night. I had never met Conley before, but he talked to me like we were old friends. He seemed like the nicest guy in the world, then that night, he started a fight with me. I couldn't believe it was the same guy. But what I remember most was that long after Gene had retired, he was at a Celtics game. Wally Jones and Larry Siegfried got into a fight, and here comes Conley running out of the stands and onto the court, screaming at Jones, "You can't do that to my teammate."

FRANK RAMSEY: Gene got into a fight in Syracuse. He punched someone with his right hand and hurt his little finger. I was rooming with Gene, and at the hotel the trainer gave Gene a glass of Epsom salts to set on the commode so he could soak his finger that night, and then do it again in the morning.

Gene got up in the middle of the night, went to the bathroom. He didn't turn on the light and I heard him drink a glass of water.

I figured out that Gene had drunk the Epsom salts. I told everyone else, but I didn't tell Gene.

He said, "I've got the bad boiler, my stomach really hurts."

We were playing in Philadelphia's Convention Hall that night. During warmups, he had to leave the floor to go to the bathroom, which was up behind a stage on the second floor.

Red put him into the game in the second quarter and we waited to see what would happen.

JIM LOSCUTOFF: Gene got a rebound, threw a pass to Cousy and filled the lane on the fast break. Gene caught the return pass from Cousy, made a layup and then the Epsom salts kicked in.

Early NBA play was physical and largely earthbound, as demonstrated by this photo of Bob Cousy's drive against the Knicks in the 1952 playoffs. The Knicks are Ernie Vandeweghe (leaping), Harry Gallatin (11) and Nat "Sweetwater" Clifton (behind Cousy).

Walter Brown, owner of the Boston Celtics, whose "number" 1 hangs from the Boston Garden rafters.

3

Chuck Cooper of Duquesne (*above*) was the first black player drafted by the NBA. But the first black to sign a contract was "Sweetwater" Clifton (*below*), who joined the Knicks after a stint with the Harlem Globetrotters.

4

Philadelphia owner Eddie Gottlieb
may just be gesturing, or he may be
offering assistance to an impoverished
referee unable to afford proper vision
correction.

5

Johnny "Red" Kerr was a prototype
1950s center: large, skilled, tough.

6

Cliff Hagan's hook shot was a key
weapon for the champion St. Louis
Hawks in 1958.

7

This free throw gave Dolph Schayes his 19,000th point in his fifteenth year with Syracuse.

Bob Pettit receives a portrait from Hawks owner Ben Kerner after going Schayes one better, becoming the first player in NBA history to score 20,000 points.

8

9

10

Bob Cousy dishes off to an open Tom Heinsohn, as Slater Martin (22) and Ed Macauley of the Hawks defend in action from game two of the 1957 NBA finals.

11

12

Bill Russell scores a negotiating point with Red Auerbach in the stands of Madison Square Garden in December 1956 as his wife, Rose, looks on. Russell signed his first Celtics contract the next day.

Frank Ramsey created the role of sixth man, coming off the bench to give the Celtics an immediate lift.

13

Eddie Gottlieb finally gets his big man as Wilt Chamberlain, the Warriors' 1955 territorial draft pick out of Overbrook High in Philadelphia, signs a contract to play for the club in 1959.

Alex Hannum signs on to coach Syracuse, clearly pleasing owner Danny Biasone.

Sid Borgia, the godfather of referees.

Red Auerbach, nose-to-nose with Norm Drucker, was a constant irritant to the referees.

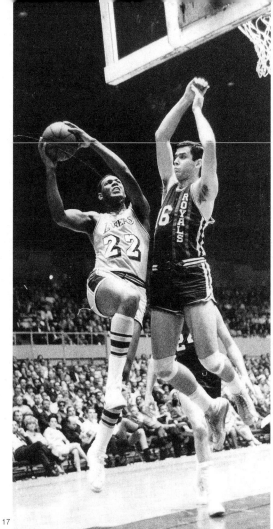

Elgin Baylor drives to the basket as Jerry Lucas tries to intercept him.

17

Norm Drucker and Earl Strom, in 1962.

18

Wilt Chamberlain and Jack Twyman welcome Maurice Stokes to his first game after falling victim to encephalitis. The game, on January 24, 1960, was Stokes's first time out of the hospital since he was paralyzed nearly two years earlier.

Jerry West and Oscar Robertson accept congratulations from their Soviet and Brazilian opponents at the 1960 Olympic games in Rome.

The third rookie guard of the class of '60, Lenny Wilkens, dribbles around Bill Sharman of the Celtics.

21

Wilt scored the points, Harvey Pollack wrote down the number, and there are *still* 46 seconds to go in the most famous game ever played in Hershey, Pennsylvania.

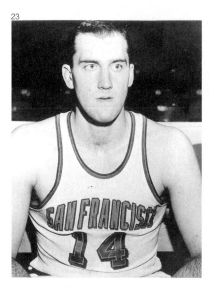

Tom Meschery: the hardest-fighting poet in NBA history.

Al Attles, another great NBA battler, passes off to a teammate and blocks out Jerry West at the same time in a game from 1967.

Oscar Robertson loses Sam Jones to a solid Wayne Embry pick, but Bill Russell is waiting, April 1963.

Jerry West shows the classic form of his jumper, shooting over Richie Guerin in the 1964 playoffs.

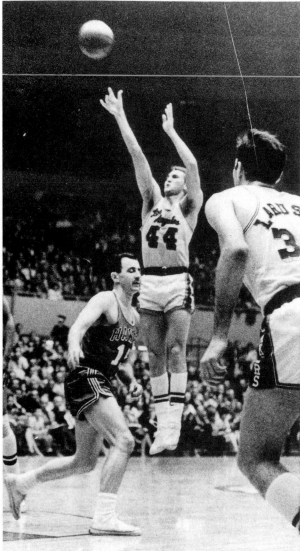

Hot Rod Hundley's number hangs proudly today in the Great Western Forum (albeit under the name Abdul-Jabbar).

A happy Red Auerbach hugs Bill
Russell after Red's last game gave
Boston its eighth straight champion-
ship.

28

29

The two faces of Gene Conley:
Braves pitcher, Celtics center.

30

32

John Havlicek gives K.C. Jones a chauffeur's cap to go with a new car given to him at the ceremonies to retire his number, March 1967.

On a team filled with players who could take the last shot, Sam Jones was the most deadly.

Wilt Chamberlain and Don Nelson wrestle for the ball under the close scrutiny of Bill Russell, Luke Jackson, Bailey Howell and Chet Walker in the 1968 Eastern finals.

The 1969 playoffs were the last battleground for Russell and Chamberlain—the two men who defined pro basketball for a generation. Who was better? The debate rages on.

FRANK RAMSEY: Gene ran right off the floor and onto the stage, leaving a trail of yellow droplets behind him, all the way up to the second-floor bathroom.

GENE CONLEY: There are a lot of stories about me. People said I once ripped the door off a cab—I wish I was that strong. Another time, I was supposed to have punched out a Doberman pinscher. I'd like to say it was true, but when I see a cocker spaniel, the hair on my legs goes up because I'm afraid of dogs. I can't live up to my own legend. Besides, I really did enough crazy things, especially toward the end of my career. Playing the two sports was driving me nuts. My arm hurt and I was taking cortisone. I once took 10 cortisone shots in a day and was dizzy from it. But I was afraid if I didn't take the shots, then they'd give me two weeks' pay and send me home.

EARL STROM: No matter what he says, Gene did try to leave baseball and go to Israel. I was working a game in Madison Square Garden and Gene was with the Boston Red Sox, who had a game in Yankee Stadium. I walked past a hotel bar and Gene yelled to me, "Earl, come on in here. We'll have a drink and then we'll head to Israel."
I said, "Why there?"
He said, "Because I want to get closer to the Lord."

GENE CONLEY: That story is true. It was in 1962 and I was mentally worn out from going from baseball to basketball and then back to baseball. I started a game at Yankee Stadium and they took me out in the fifth inning. I was with the Red Sox and I started throwing down the beers in the visitors' dressing room. After the game, we were going to take a bus from New York to Washington. We got stuck in traffic on the George Washington Bridge.
I was sitting next to Pumpsie Green and I said, "Pumpsie, let's get off the bus and take a leak. We're not going anywhere in this traffic."
We got off the bus and I heard Frank Malzone tell Billy Herman, "We won't see those guys for a couple of days."
When Pumpsie and I got back, the bus was gone. So we decided to forget baseball and just tie one on for a few days.
We were in a bar and I said, "Pumpsie, I don't know about you, but I'm going to Jerusalem."
He looked at me as if I'd lost my mind.

I said, "Israel. Listen, I'm exhausted. I'm going to the Holy Land to seek a high power."

Pumpsie said, "Then you're going on your own."

I was determined to go. The hotel manager knew me and he lent me $1,000 so I could buy a ticket, which I did. I was half loaded and I went to Toots Shor's, where I told everyone in the bar that I was going to Israel.

Soon reporters showed up, and they took my picture and wrote I was leaving the country.

I even went to the airport with my ticket, but thank God I got stopped at the gate because I didn't have a passport. People talked me out of leaving, so I went back to New York, hid out at the Waldorf-Astoria for a few days.

Then I sobered up, called my wife and told her how ashamed I was. I had been missing for four days and I had become national news. When I went home to Foxboro, there were all these reporters waiting at my house. I couldn't believe what a jerk I had been.

I was no lily on the pond. I drank too much. I got into scrapes too many times in bars. I played hard and lived hard, but after a while I got disgusted with myself. I quit drinking over 20 years ago, and I just wish I had done that earlier because I could have played longer.

Poet with a Punch

No NBA player has ever published more poems than Tom Meschery, who moved from pro basketball to the prestigious University of Iowa writer's program. Meschery has since published a book of poetry, Over the Rim, *with the Saturday Review Press in 1971. It's a safe bet that no other NBA player grew up in a Japanese concentration camp during World War Two. But what his friends remember most is not Meschery's verse, but his verve. They say he lost more fights than any player in NBA history. Meschery disagrees, insisting that "Bob Ferry was really the league's punching bag." Well, no statistics are kept in that area. The numbers do show that Meschery played 10 seasons and never averaged more than 16 points. But he had his number retired by the Golden State Warriors. And for the record, he did foul out of 20 of his first 100 pro games. He is now a high school teacher in Reno.*

TOM MESCHERY: What I remember most about being a kid is the bombing raids. I spent six years in a Japanese concentration camp—five during World War Two. By the last year of the war, the U.S. was hitting Tokyo very hard and we were continually hiding in a basement that served as a bomb shelter. Our concentration camp was for children and displaced people—so we weren't tortured by the Japanese. In fact, several of the guards were good to us. There were missionaries in the camp who taught us. When the bombs would hit nearby, the ground would shake. I'd climb up to this window in the basement—it was really nothing more than a crack that would let me see outside. I'd pull the curtain back, see the searchlights crossing the night sky and then passing over the planes as they made their bombing runs.

I was about seven when this happened.

My real last name is Mescheriakoff. It was changed to Meschery when we came to the U.S. after World War Two. The Joseph McCarthy era was starting. My parents were Russian immigrants and my father felt that a last name that ended with a "koff" was a tip that we were Russian, and that would make things very tough for us.

My father was a real Russian—he fought with the White Army after the 1917 Russian Revolution. He had to flee the country with most of the men who fought at his side when Lenin took over. They went across Siberia and into Manchuria, a town called Harbin, which is now in northern China. That's where he met my mother and where I was born in 1938. Our plan was to immigrate to the U.S. My mother spoke some English and she was able to secure a visa for my father and found someone willing to sponsor him in the U.S. Our plan was for him to go to the U.S., settle in his job and then send for us. By the time that happened, it was early December of 1941. We were actually preparing to board a ship that would take us to the U.S. when the Japanese bombed Pearl Harbor and then they stopped all ships leaving China. The Japanese took my mother, sister and me to Tokyo, where we spent the duration of the war in the concentration camp.

I didn't speak English until I went to the concentration camp. The missionaries taught the language to my sister and me—they were from France and England and there were also some Canadian nuns. We stayed in one huge dormitory room and slept on cots. Our diet was pretty simple—one day, it was rice and fish and then the next it was fish and rice. The closest we came to getting hit was when the church next door to our building was bombed and then the wind blew the fire into our building. We had to evacuate and then spent the rest of the war in a hospital.

When the war ended, we were able to join my father in San Francisco. Actually, when I saw him, I would not have known my father from Joe the Barber. He had left us when I was less than a year old. He had been a dentist in China, but he was never able to master English well enough to pass the U.S. dental exams, so he worked in the shipyards and later as a dental technician. In my home, my father spoke a mixture of English and Russian. My mother spoke English to us, Russian to him. So I naturally learned both languages.

They talk about people who are DPs—Displaced Persons. Well, that really was us. I even wore short, knicker-type pants when I first went to school and was teased unmercifully about that. Being old-fashioned and from "the old country" was how people looked at us. That also is why I clung so passionately to sports. Being a good athlete is a way to become immediately accepted as an American. I was a big guy and coordinated and I gravitated toward basketball, where my size worked in my favor. Then the game became a part of me. I was a high school All-American and was recruited by most of the big schools. My mother wanted me to go to St. Mary's [of California] because there were a lot of Catholic brothers in the concentration camp who were good to us. Those guys used to carry my sister and me around. They played with us. They made an impression that my mother and I never forgot. St. Mary's was a Catholic school run by the Christian Brotherhood. It was small and seemed like the right place for me.

FRANK MCGUIRE: Tom was our first-round pick with the Philadelphia Warriors in 1961. He was the classic power forward for the time— maybe 6-foot-7, 220 pounds, and he loved to defend, rebound and fight, not necessarily in that order.

RICK BARRY: Tom was the Mad Russian. His eyes would get wide. He'd scream, "No one drives down the damn middle. Anybody drives, I'll kill them." And that was how he acted in practice.

WAYNE EMBRY: Tom would take on anybody. As a rookie, he went after me and I had to outweigh him by . . . well . . . a lot. Still, he wanted to fight. I told him to settle down, but he was swinging, so finally I just grabbed him in a headlock and squeezed a bit. That cooled him off.

TOM MESCHERY: I got into a helluva brawl with Tommy Heinsohn in my rookie year. He was elbowing me and I was throwing elbows back. Tommy was a veteran and I could tell that if I didn't do something, he was just going to kick my ass. I threw a punch at him and hit him in the side of the head. Then Jim Loscutoff grabbed me from behind and said, "Slow down, Ruskie." Like me, Loscutoff is a Russian from San Francisco. But while he was holding me, Heinsohn hauled off and belted me. I needed eight stitches over my eye.

FRANK McGUIRE: Tommy got the eight stitches during halftime and then he came back to the bench. He wanted to play. The doctor told me to keep Tommy out. I stood in front of him and said, "If you're going to play, you have to go through me." Tommy had that wild look in his eye, and then just pushed me aside and went back into the game.

AL ATTLES: Tom was completely consumed by basketball. It was a total emotional and physical experience for him. He could be a wild man. His eyes would roll around in his head and you'd think, "Oh, no, he's losing it. He's starting to go off."

Once, in practice, we all were getting tired and Tom caught an elbow over his eye. Blood was streaming down, but he would not wipe it off. He just stood there, the blood dripping to the floor and screaming, "That's it. No one drives on me again. No one, you guys hear that?"

We sort of backed away and practice petered out.

ROD THORN: Off the court, Tom was a gentle, intelligent guy. I played with him at the end of his career. Tom was writing poetry when athletes just didn't do that. In fact, he liked doing things that went against what we considered to be conventional for basketball players. He wore tweed jackets with elbow patches and smoked a pipe. But between the lines, he would fight, scratch, anything. He would get so wrapped up in the game that he is the only player I know who couldn't remember the plays where he was supposed to shoot the ball. Al Bianchi would say, "Gee, Tom, we only have one play for you, how could you forget it?"

AL ATTLES: Meschery loved to rebound. He wanted every rebound and was especially tough on the offensive boards. But one game, he knocked over two guys, got the ball and put it back in. The only problem was that he shot it into the wrong basket. He couldn't figure out why the announcer said, "Basket by Heinsohn."

ALEX HANNUM: Meschery wasn't the most talented player I coached, but he may have been my favorite. He always played with such fire, it was infectious. He loved to fight but he couldn't. He threw a lot of punches, but I don't think any of them landed. His heart was willing but his hands were too slow. Off the court, he was a thoughtful guy, a real poet, a flower child. I'm a big conservative and we'd have some great heated debates long into the night. But what I loved about Tom was his passion for the game. I guess you could say he was the only flower child who loved to fight.

ROD THORN: Tom went up for a shot and Wilt Chamberlain blocked it back in his face. Tom went up again, and Wilt blocked the second shot. He pump-faked about five times trying to get Wilt to jump, then Tom tried a third shot—Wilt blocked it. Tom went nuts. He dropped the ball and started throwing punches at Wilt, swinging from the floor. Wilt and Tom were friends and Wilt was talking to him, trying to cool Tom down. At the same time, Wilt had his hand on Tom's head and was holding Tom off.

WILT CHAMBERLAIN: I looked at Tom and said, "Who are you kidding?" Tom would get mad as hell, but he didn't know what he was doing. He was blinded by his Russian temper.

TOM MESCHERY: I was pissed off, but Wilt was smiling and he used his long reach to put his hand on my head. It was like a cartoon, his hand was on my head and I was swinging away and hitting nothing but air because my arms weren't long enough. I wanted to kill him and Wilt was laughing at me.

RICK BARRY: The Meschery fight I remember best was when he went after Zelmo Beaty with a chair.

TOM MESCHERY: I don't remember anything about a chair, but it was a great brawl with Zelmo and me trading punches and we both ended up in the chairs. Zelmo was going to destroy me, but Al Attles stepped in.

ALEX HANNUM: That fight started when Lenny Wilkens drove and Tom knocked him down.

LENNY WILKENS: Tom stood over me and just glared like he wanted to eat me alive.

ALEX HANNUM: Then Zelmo Beaty stepped in and that was no match. Zelmo was clearly getting the best of Tom, when Al Attles came to the rescue. Al was about six inches smaller and 50 pounds lighter than Zelmo, but he picked up Zelmo, I mean right off the floor, and Al flung him down and jumped on him. He pinned Zelmo, who was trying to get Attles off him by pushing Al in the face. What happened was that Zelmo got his fingers in Al's nose, I mean a finger in each nostril, and he was starting to rip off Al's nose when Al finally got off and they broke it up.

TOM MESCHERY: I never set out to fight. I didn't say to myself, "Hey, this is great. I get to play basketball and fight with guys, too." But I was so intense, maybe even so weird about basketball, that when something happened on the court, I couldn't hold back. I had a temper but I guess the bottom line was that I wasn't a very good fighter.

I was motivated by the competition and the camaraderie. Pro basketball didn't just begin and end with the game. It started with that wonderful high I'd get before the game, just thinking about playing. Then it came to fruition during the game, which was a thrill, and I was able to have that thrill 100 times a year as a pro basketball player. The romance with basketball didn't end at the buzzer. What meant so much to me was to go out with the guys, teammates and opponents, have some beer and relive the game. It would be myself, Bob Ferry, Johnny Kerr, Al Bianchi . . . a lot of different people. We'd wind up in the same bar. We didn't go there together, but we all knew where you'd find guys after a game. There would be a lot of beer and a lot of basketball talk.

Playing basketball is like writing poetry. I didn't do it for the money, I did it because there is something inside me that made me do it. In my home, poetry was written and read. Russians love poetry, so I occasionally wrote poems during my career, it was a way of expressing the romance that I felt for the game. The emotional bind to basketball also made me a lousy negotiator. They would hand me a contract and say, "Here, sign this." Even though guys were starting to get big money by the end of my career, I'd look at the first offer and say, "This seems reasonable to me," and I'd sign. I was always amazed that I could play basketball for a living.

9
HEADING WEST

In the early 1950s, the Lakers dominated the NBA. By 1955, they were in decline for two reasons: the retirement of George Mikan and the advent of the 24-second clock. After sitting out a season, the 6-foot-10 Mikan tried to stop the Lakers' slide by making a comeback in 1955–56. He played only half the season, averaged 10 points and was "a ghost of a great player," according to one newspaper account. By the late 1950s, the Lakers and owner Bob Short were looking for a new home.

RUDY LARUSSO: I came to the Lakers in 1959–60, their last year in Minneapolis, and hard times had set in. *[The Lakers had had one winning season since Mikan's retirement in 1954.]* John Kundla had coached all those great Minneapolis teams and he no longer wanted to stay in the NBA. Bob Short was running the franchise by telling people, "The check's in the mail." We needed a coach, so Short hired John Castellani. It was Elgin Baylor's second year with the Lakers, and Castellani had been Elgin's college coach at Seattle. When Short wanted a coach, he liked to hire guys who had coached his stars in college. And John, was he ever a peach. When training camp opened, Elgin was doing a six-month hitch in the army, so we had Castellani but no Elgin. Poor Castellani. We knew we had problems from how he ran practices—he rolled out the ball and watched us scrimmage for two hours. He might have put in a play or two, but I can't recall any. We had one of those incredible exhibition schedules. We went through New England playing the Celtics 13 straight nights in 13 different towns. We were in Maine for a potato festival. We'd get up at the crack of dawn, four of us would pile into a rental car and drive to the next town. Today, the union would go bonkers if they tried something like that. *[NBA records show the Lakers-Celtics tour was 10 games in 13 nights.]*

Anyway, we were getting our asses kicked every night and one day Castellani sat down next to me and said, "You played for a great college coach."

He meant Doggie Julian, who had coached me at Dartmouth and is in the Hall of Fame.

Then Castellani said, "You got any good plays from college?"

Here was a pro coach asking a rookie forward for a couple of plays. Even I knew we were in deep trouble. What the hell, he wanted some plays, so I gave him some plays.

Believe me, it didn't help.

ELGIN BAYLOR: I never went to Bob Short and said, "Hire John Castellani." He did ask me about Castellani and I told him that I had a tremendous amount of respect for John as a person, but I didn't know he would be the next coach.

RUDY LARUSSO: Castellani had this idea of how to celebrate a win— he'd come into the dressing room, slowly loosening his tie. Then he would take his tie off as he walked around the room, looking at everyone. I guess he thought he was building up the tension, because he'd look at us for a while, then put the tie over someone's neck. I guess he meant that the guy was the Player of the Game. Players would be sitting there, trying not to bite through their lower lips as they held back the laughter.

SLICK LEONARD: I was just a young player back then, but I could tell that Castellani would never last the season. He was a good person, but he did some dumb stuff for a pro coach.

RUDY LARUSSO: At midseason, Bob Short burst into the dressing room after we had lost yet another home game. He had these small slips of paper in his hand.

"We're going to find out who's going to coach this team," said Short as he was handing out a piece of paper and a pen to each player.

"We're gonna vote right now," said Short. "I want you to rank the guys 1-to-5, based on who you want to coach. I don't care what name you write down. You can vote for John . . ."

Then Short looked at Castellani, who was standing in the corner looking like a guy who was getting beat over the head with a sledgehammer.

"Like I said, it could be John, Al Cervi, Larry Foust . . . I don't care," said Short.

A couple of the players who hated John yelled, "Give me that piece of paper."

Castellani got one vote—from Frank Selvy.

A couple of us went to Frank and asked, "How the hell could you vote for that guy?"

Frank said, "He played me. He's the only coach in five years who played me."

I don't think he won the vote, but Short did hire Jim Pollard, who had been a great player with the old Lakers and was retired and living in Minneapolis. He was a dignified, classy guy who had the respect of the players. He put in all of his own old plays from the George Mikan era, but instead of Jim Pollard coming off a screen for a shot, it was Pollard setting up the play so Elgin could shoot.

[The Lakers were 11-25 under Castellani, 14-25 under Pollard.]

HOT ROD HUNDLEY: Short was running the franchise month-to-month. He had several investors and they were dropping out. Finally, he told us that to save the franchise from folding, he had to pool his resources and buy it. When Bob said that, I thought, "If the players put all their money together, we could outbid Short for it, and we're broke."

FRED SCHAUS: Bob Short's favorite line was, "Call me for anything, but don't call me for money."

ELGIN BAYLOR: In Minnesota, we didn't draw. The days of the great Mikan teams were over. We even went from building to building, playing in three different places.

LEONARD KOPPETT: Short and Frank Ryan put together some investors and bought out what was left of the old owners for about $10,000 each. It was a real bargain. The main thing was that he had to assume the debt, which was substantial. Anyway, Short had other ideas for the team. He saw baseball teams move to California and make a lot of money and he planned to be the first basketball team on the West Coast.

HOT ROD HUNDLEY: Before we moved to L.A., Short told me that he would have taken $200,000 for the team. Instead, he bought the whole thing for about $85,000 and then took it to L.A.

ELGIN BAYLOR: I guess I should have been tipped off that we might move to L.A. because in the middle of our last season in Minneapolis, we played a game out there. It was snowing and below zero when we left Minnesota, and it was sunny and 76 when we got off the plane in L.A. But back then, you played regular-season games everywhere to make money, so I didn't think anything of it. But I remember telling everyone how beautiful and how pretty everything was out there—nice and green in the dead of winter. The L.A. Sports Arena was also a state-of-the-art facility at that time.

Elgin Baylor: The Test Pilot

One reporter described Elgin Baylor's style by writing, "He never broke the law of gravity, but he's awfully slow about obeying it." Or as John Castellani, his former coach at Seattle University and the Lakers, said, "Elgin has more moves than a clock." Baylor led Seattle to a No. 2 ranking in the NCAA in the spring of 1958 and was the first draft pick of the Lakers, who viewed him as a true franchise player, given owner Bob Short's statement, "If Elgin had turned me down, I'd have gone out of business." A 6-foot-5, 225-pound forward who made 10 All-Star teams, Baylor retired in 1972 because of bad knees. The fact that Baylor was a career 27-point scorer comes as no surprise. But he also was a fine passer and led his team in assists in three of his first five pro seasons.

CHICK HEARN: I saw Elgin Baylor play while he was in his first season at Seattle. I was doing a UCLA game at the University of Washington. [UCLA coach] John Wooden and I were invited by John Castellani to watch Elgin practice. Their gym was nothing more than an old barn. Baylor was talking to his coach, telling Castellani that his foot was bothering him and he didn't want to practice. Castellani said, "I want you to meet Chick Hearn from CBS." Elgin said, "I'll get my shoes on and give it a shot."

I had never seen a player like this—all his high-flying moves and how he used reverse English on the ball to make a layup from unbelievable angles. He would hang in the air for so long that you'd worry that he'd get hurt when he came down. He was the pioneer for the kind of athletic players we see today. A lot of the moves people say were invented by Michael Jordan or Julius Erving, I saw Elgin do first. People ask me how good was Elgin . . . well, he may have been the greatest player ever.

PAT WILLIAMS: I saw Elgin while he was in college playing in the Holiday Festival in New York. He was mesmerizing. He had both the physical gifts and the creative mindset that no one had before him. He was the one who came first, the one who set the standard for Connie Hawkins, Julius Erving and then Michael Jordan—all of those players did things no one had seen before.

ELGIN BAYLOR: I don't know why I played like I did. I had never seen anyone else do my moves. It starts with talent, you have to be able to jump. But more than that, things I did were spontaneous. I had the ball, I reacted to the defense. The important thing to me was making the shot. I saw a lot of guys make great moves to get to the basket, but then they missed the layup. So what good was it? Making the move, then making the shot. That's what made me feel good—seeing those two points go up on the board.

HOT ROD HUNDLEY: Elgin Baylor was a 6-foot-5 Karl Malone, I'm talking about that kind of knock-bodies-out-of-the-way strong. Just like Karl, he'd pound the boards for a rebound, throw an outlet pass to a guard, fill the lane on the fast break, catch the return pass and go to the basket like a steam engine, daring anyone to get in his way. One look at him in training camp and our whole team was saying, "Elgin is going to be great."

ELGIN BAYLOR: I never saw an NBA game until I played in one, so how would I know how good I'd be? The pro game was hardly on television. Very few college games were broadcast. Everyone said I'd be a high pick in the NBA draft, but the only GM I talked to was Fuzzy Levane from New York. The day before the draft, Bob Short called me and said, "We may draft you." But as far as I know, the Lakers never scouted me.

Seattle was a small school and I knew the NBA would be a big step. I figured I'd make the league, but I had doubts. Was I good enough to start? How would my moves work? After a couple of weeks of practice, I knew I could play.

JOHNNY KERR: Elgin was stronger than a bull, it really was one of those men-against-boys situations when he was a young player. But the strange thing was that he had a nervous facial twitch, kind of a tick. You didn't know if it was a head fake or what was going on.

ZELMO BEATY: He mostly definitely had a head twitch. It was different than a head fake, more pronounced, and you'd end up just staring at him, wondering, "What was that?" Then the next thing you knew, he was gone. Elgin took what could have been a handicap and made it into an asset.

SLICK LEONARD: That twitch helped him on the court, but it killed Elgin in poker. When he had a good hand, he'd twitch and all of us would know that it was time to fold.

ELGIN BAYLOR: Mostly, it just happened to me on the court. I don't know why. I saw some doctors, they said it was a nervous reaction, nothing was wrong and not to worry about it, so I didn't worry about it.

RUDY LARUSSO: During our last training camp in Minneapolis [1959] Elgin was in the army. These were the days when there were no rules about when training camp could start. You could have camp anytime, anywhere. Elgin was going into his second season, so they decided to move our entire training camp to Elgin's army base in San Antonio. This was in late August and they gave us a barracks to live in. Late August in San Antonio is hot, and we didn't have any air conditioning, just screen windows. At six in the morning, soldiers were marching and counting right outside our window, and we're screaming, "Shut the hell up out there." Our barracks was like Animal House. Beer cans everywhere. Dirt everywhere. No one made a bed. It smelled. One of the generals came in and said, "Listen, you guys gotta clean this place up and keep quiet when the soldiers are marching." Elgin got us a TV set from somewhere. He wore a uniform and everyone called him Private Baylor. We were down there for a week or so for practices, then we went back to Minnesota for regular training camp.

ELGIN BAYLOR: I was doing my basic training when the team came down. We'd go to play at night and I was tired from all the stuff I had to do during the day for the army.

RUDY LARUSSO: Elgin missed all of training camp, all the exhibition games, and we opened the season at home against Detroit. He walked into the dressing room the day of the game, put on a uniform and went for 52 points. I sat there in complete awe. I kept thinking, "He doesn't even practice and he gets 52."

ELGIN BAYLOR: All I could do was shoot around by myself. There wasn't anyone to practice with at the base. Besides, I was in the army and they kept me busy right until I was let out just as the regular season started.

FRED SCHAUS: Elgin had to go back into the army for six months during the 1961–62 season and he played only half the season [48 games]. He got out on weekend passes and still averaged 38 points and 18 rebounds even though he never practiced with the team.

ELGIN BAYLOR: That time, I was at Fort Lewis in Seattle. I would get a weekend pass that began on midnight Friday and I had to be back on midnight Sunday. I'd take the red-eye on Friday night to wherever the team was, play the weekend games and then kill myself to get back by midnight Sunday.

RUDY LARUSSO: We had this incredible record when Elgin played and we were pretty ordinary when he was in the army. Elgin could score so easily. People don't have a full appreciation of it because he was playing at the same time Wilt was putting up such huge numbers.

[Baylor had 64 points vs. Boston on November 8, 1959, breaking Joe Fulks's record of 63 set in 1949. A year later—November 15, 1960— Baylor set another NBA record with 71 at New York on 28 field goals and 15 free throws.]

LEONARD KOPPETT: I covered Elgin's 71-point game and I never was conscious that he was piling up that many points. There were no Doctor J, high-flying dunks. It was steady, basket-after-basket, one good solid play after another. Every point he scored came within the framework of the game.

RICHIE GUERIN: I was with the Knicks when everyone was setting scoring records against us. Elgin scored his 71, and a few months later Wilt had his 100-point game against us. By far, Elgin's was the better performance, and that 71-point game remains the greatest individual effort I have ever seen. In Wilt's game, they set out to get him the record. There was nothing artificial about Elgin's 71. He got all the points in a natural flow.

ELGIN BAYLOR: When I broke Joe Fulks's record in Boston, Red Auerbach had four guys on me at the end of the game to stop me from getting 64 points. He kept telling them not to let me shoot, but the irony was that I caught a pass, they fouled me and I got the record at the free throw line.

SLICK LEONARD: Elgin is right. Red tried to smother him and make anyone else shoot the ball, but Elgin broke it anyway. That's because a young Elgin Baylor was capable of going for over 50 on any night.

ELGIN BAYLOR: The New York game was a little different because I was not aware that I was getting near a record. I was just scoring. But I noticed that the guys were passing up open shots and feeding me the ball. I thought, "Okay, they don't want to shoot it, I will."

HOT ROD HUNDLEY: The night Elgin had the 71 points, he also had 25 rebounds. Bob Short gave every member of the team cufflinks with a "71." We all wore them proudly.

FRED SCHAUS: When Elgin got 71, [GM] Lou Mohs told me, "Too bad he didn't score five fewer points. Then we could have gotten Phillips 66 as a sponsor."

ELGIN BAYLOR: I was excited about the 71 points, but I knew it wouldn't last long, not with Wilt averaging 50 a game that season. I told reporters, "Listen, Wilt will get 100 points one day. I tell you, it's inevitable."

CARL BRAUN: A great game Elgin had was when he scored 61 against Boston [April 14, 1961] in the playoffs. Red had the whole team guarding him that game too, including Bill Russell. He was such a physical specimen, he played so hard and so smart. He was one of the best passing forwards in the league. And his rebounding . . . he killed you on the offensive boards.

JERRY WEST: Elgin is the best I have ever seen when it comes to getting his own missed shot and putting the ball in.

LARRY STAVERMAN: You'd guard Elgin and you'd think you forced him into a bad shot because he would sometimes just throw the ball at the backboard, not even hitting the rim. Then he'd blow by you, get his own rebound and score. No one else did that.

ELGIN BAYLOR: That was by design. One of the coaches I had early in my career drilled "follow your own shot" into my head. Then I learned you could create your own shot by missing one and getting the rebound. Suppose the shot clock was running down and I had the ball on the right side of the court and the defense was all over me. I'd bang it against the backboard so that it would bounce off to the left. Then I'd run over, get the rebound and score. Since I shot the ball, I had a better idea of where the rebound was going than the defense did. I don't know why guys don't use that play today.

ROD THORN: The man was so strong. You would try to lean on him and he'd fend you off with his left arm, using it like a hammer.

BARRY CLEMENS: He'd put that left forearm out, jump into your chest, and he'd really hurt you physically as he scored.

ZELMO BEATY: I would be guarding him, he'd go up and he looked as if he had to be out of control when he jumped, but he would get his balance in midair. I had never seen anything like it. The thing to remember about Elgin is that he was the first NBA player with hang time.

There Almost Were No L.A. Lakers

The closest a professional sports team has come to being lost in an airline crash was on January 18, 1960, when the Minneapolis Lakers landed in a Carroll, Iowa, cornfield at 2 A.M.

HOT ROD HUNDLEY: We had played an afternoon game in St. Louis and lost (135–119) and we were heading back to Minneapolis. We had our own DC-3. It had two seats on one side of the aisle, one seat on the other. It didn't make time like jets today; it was going to take us

3–4 hours to go from St. Louis to Minneapolis. So we settled in and had our usual poker game going, a blanket down on the floor to catch the cards as we played. We noticed that it started to snow, but weren't worried.

ELGIN BAYLOR: Then the lights went out. We didn't think much of it because strange things had happened before on that plane.

HOT ROD HUNDLEY: When we lost the power, most of the guys bitched because it meant we had to break up our poker game. We were yelling at the guy, "Hey, turn the lights back on." When the pilot said the power was down for a while, we figured we'd go to sleep.

ELGIN BAYLOR: I got worried when the heat stopped. It got very cold in that plane.

SLICK LEONARD: We had run into a dad-gum snowstorm and the pilot told us, "Boys, we've lost our power." Our pilot had flown missions in the South Pacific during World War Two. He said that he had lost the radar, too, and that we were lost because he couldn't see a damn thing through all the snow. The co-pilot had opened a side window and was scraping the snow off the windshield so he could see. In fact, the poor guy got frostbite on his ear from that. All the players were wrapped in GI blankets. I was sitting next to Tommy Hawkins and he said, "Slick, do you think we're gonna die? I'm so scared that my hair is standing on end."

Up in the cockpit we heard the pilots talking. One said, "If we don't put this thing down soon, we're gonna run out of gas."

HOT ROD HUNDLEY: The plane was bouncing around in the snow. We had been gone a few hours and should have been back in Minneapolis. The co-pilot opened the door and came back to talk to us. As he did, a rush of cold wind filled the plane. The co-pilot had a flashlight in his hand and he said that they had been flying with one of the windows down trying to see. He said, "We've lost all power and communication. We're in a snowstorm. We have about 30 minutes of gas left." He said we were over Carroll, Iowa. "There's a cornfield down there," he said. "We have two choices. We can try to look for another airport, although we have no idea where one is. Or we can land in the field."

The guys yelled, "Put this SOB down now."

SLICK LEONARD: I got worried when I heard one of the pilots say, "If we're gonna land in this field, we gotta make sure we clear those high-tension wires." At this point, we were so low that the noise from the plane was causing people to wake up and turn on the lights in their houses. We saw red lights from a firetruck and ambulance. We actually were following a car down a road, about 300 feet above him. Then the car started going uphill, and the pilot yanked the plane straight up, which scared the hell out of everybody.

HOT ROD HUNDLEY: We heard the pilot say, "Eighty . . . Seventy . . . Sixty . . . Take it back up, take it back up." They thought they were going to hit the car driving up the hill.

ELGIN BAYLOR: We made several passes, up and down, up and down. Each time it happened and we didn't land, each time was worse than the last.

HOT ROD HUNDLEY: They did it again, "Eighty . . . Seventy . . . Sixty." Then they cut the engines and we floated down into the cornfield. We bounced a few times, but it was no worse than any other landing.

ELGIN BAYLOR: To me, it was the smoothest landing I had ever had. There was 3–4 feet of snow over the corn and it was like landing on a blanket.

HOT ROD HUNDLEY: It was a perfect landing. The guy didn't put the wheels down. He flew through a blinding snowstorm, between a water tower and power lines and got us down without a scratch. When we were on the ground, it was absolute silence for a moment. All you could hear were a few knees knocking because we were so cold, yet our foreheads and palms were soaked with sweat from fear. Before we landed, Elgin had left his seat and lay down on the floor at the back of the plane. Maybe he figured he could slide right out if we crashed.

ELGIN BAYLOR: After the initial silence, there was a knock on the door of the plane. It was then that we realized we'd made it and everyone just started cheering and screaming.

HOT ROD HUNDLEY: We opened the door and saw a guy with a hatchet. He was going to whack away to get into the plane.

ELGIN BAYLOR: The first thing I saw out that door was a hearse, with the town mortician standing next to it. We had buzzed his house and he figured he better get out there to get a jump on some possible business.

SLICK LEONARD: We rushed out the back of the plane. The snow was up to our ass, but we were jumping in it, throwing snowballs at each other. We were like little kids, just glad to be alive.

HOT ROD HUNDLEY: We walked about a half mile through that snow to a place called the Carroll Hotel, which was nothing but a fleabag joint.

SLICK LEONARD: Really, it was a hotel for the elderly. As we walked in, the first thing a couple of us spotted was a liquor cabinet. There was a padlock on it. Our big center, Larry Foust, just ripped off the lock like they do in the movies. Then he opened the door, took out a bottle of V.O., poured himself a big glass and drank it straight down.

HOT ROD HUNDLEY: We stayed up all night, drinking coffee, eating doughnuts, calling people on the phone and reliving the whole damn thing.

SLICK LEONARD: The next morning we went back to Minneapolis . . . by bus.

RUDY LARUSSO: I was the only Laker not on the plane. I had gotten sick and had been diagnosed as having an ulcer, so they slapped me in the hospital for tests. The nurse came in and said, "Did you hear what happened to your team?"

I said, "Yeah, we lost."

She said, "But on the way back, they crashed in a cornfield." Then she gave me a newspaper story.

But the real newspaper to see was one that someone gave Rod later. It was a paper from West Virginia and the headline was: "Lakers Land in Cornfield: Hundley Safe."

JOHNNY KERR: The Lakers getting out of that crash then became fodder for jokes around the league. The best one was that as they were going down, Hot Rod wanted to do something religious, so he stood up and started a bingo game.

SLICK LEONARD: A few days after the crash, Bob Short hired a bull-dozer to clear a runway in the field. He sent a couple of mechanics to Carroll to fix the plane, then they flew the plane out of there.

RUDY LARUSSO: About a week after the crash, we had one of those tryout games in L.A. We got to the Minneapolis airport and there was the DC-3.

Guys were going crazy, telling Short, "Bob, we gotta go over the Rocky Mountains. Let's take a commercial flight."

Bob said things like, "Boys, I don't mind losing a game or two, but the way we're going, I'm losing $20,000 a night . . . Listen, I know some of you think that I went out and fixed this thing in my garage, but I really had some of the best . . . blah, blah . . ."

SLICK LEONARD: We said, "Bob, we're just not taking that plane."

He said, "You get on that plane or you're out of a job." So we got on.

HOT ROD HUNDLEY: A couple of weeks later, the players pitched in $20 and bought the pilot a trophy with the inscription: "May you have eternal safe landings." We presented it to him at halftime.

RUDY LARUSSO: The upshot of the crash was that the farmer in Carroll held up the Lakers for $10,000 because he said the plane ruined his crop. Ruined his crop? It was the middle of January and there was three feet of snow on the ground.

Making the Move

The first game in L.A. was between Wilt Chamberlain's Philadelphia Warriors and the still–Minneapolis Lakers, the Warriors winning 103–96, during the 1959–60 season. There were 10,202 fans at the Sports Arena and a preliminary game between a navy team from Los Alamitos vs. "The Vagabonds, an All-Negro All-Star Team." There were two other NBA games in L.A. with crowds in the 5,000 range. At the 1960 NBA meetings, Short's motion to move the team to L.A. was originally voted down by the other owners, who worried about the cost of travel *to the West Coast. Then Short agreed to pay any extra cost a team would incur in a formula that worked like this: suppose it cost $300 to fly from New York to Minneapolis, but $500 from N.Y. to L.A.; Short would pay the extra $200. He won on a second vote, with the only opposition coming from Ned Irish of the Knicks. Irish was hoping that Short would continue to have financial problems, and that would force Short to sell Elgin Baylor to the Knicks.*

LEONARD KOPPETT: Never underestimate Bob Short's persuasive ability. This was a man who once convinced Ted Williams to manage the Washington Senators, so he had no trouble with the other NBA owners.

SLICK LEONARD: When Short got the green light for the move, he told the players, "You guys can sell all your furniture. They have different furniture in L.A. I'll give you what you paid for your old stuff; just sell everything—your house, your furniture, your clothes. Hold an auction at your house and watch them carrying everything out the door. Then get in your car and drive out there, we're all starting over."

I sold everything like Short said and bought a new Buick station wagon with air conditioning. Short said to be sure to get a car with air conditioning. My wife and I piled our three kids into the station wagon, and about halfway through the desert, the air conditioner broke and my kids started crying.

RUDY LaRUSSO: Hot Rod Hundley and I decided we were going to be the first two Lakers in L.A. We both had new cars and we drove from Minnesota to the West Coast, stopping in Salt Lake and then Las Vegas, where we gambled and played blackjack for something like 24 straight hours. I said I needed a bath. Hot Rod said, "Let's just jump in the pool, our clothes are wash and wear, right?"

HOT ROD HUNDLEY: We drove across the country, bumper-to-bumper. He had an Olds, I had a new Bonneville. We raced right through downtown Salt Lake and got to Vegas in the middle of the night. I had never been to Vegas before, and we were like guys let out of jail. It ended with us both jumping into the pool outside a casino with our clothes—our wash and wear clothes—still on. But we did have sense enough to take off our shoes.

RUDY LaRUSSO: Short had a trucking company and a hotel in Minneapolis, so he needed someone to run the team in L.A. for him. He hired Lou Mohs as GM, a good guy but very tight. Short's partner and attorney was Frank Ryan, who spent time in L.A. They were both great Catholics, Short had seven kids, Ryan had about 10.

Then Short and Mohs needed a coach. In the 1960 draft, they took Jerry West. Then they hired Fred Schaus, who was West's coach at West Virginia. On the surface, it was like Baylor and Castellani all over again, but Schaus was a former pro player and he had an idea what the game was all about.

FRED SCHAUS: People just assumed that Jerry and I came to the Lakers as a package deal. But I had no idea that the Lakers were interested in me coaching their team when Jerry was drafted. It wasn't until late in the summer, Jerry was with the 1960 Olympic team, when Bob Short called me about the job. Their GM was Lou Mohs, who was a basketball nut. He was former circulation manager with the Hearst newspapers based in St. Louis. He knew that we had good teams at West Virginia and he made the suggestion to Short. Then Short offered me a two-year contract at $18,500 a year. I was making less than $15,000 at West Virginia. I thought about coaching the first team on the West Coast, about building a team around Elgin Baylor and Jerry West. I also had coached Hot Rod Hundley in school and I liked him very much. So I took it.

HOT ROD HUNDLEY: Our biggest problem was travel. When teams came to L.A., we played them twice—say, Friday and Saturday—to cut the travel. Then we'd head east on these long trips for two to three weeks at a time. Remember, St. Louis was the farthest team west at that time. In that first year, Short and those guys had no money. Mohs watched every paper clip.

SLICK LEONARD: At first, the crowds weren't big *[4,008 for the opener, a 111–101 loss to New York]*. The Sports Arena had all these neat things—escalators, a fan that blew wind through the flag during the National Anthem, and an attendance counter. In the corner of the arena was a scoreboard that showed the attendance. Every time someone came through the turnstile, it kept count on the board. Early in the season, the crowds were 2,500–3,000. The fans sat and watched, like it was a game on a neutral court. By playoff time, we were close to selling out.

CHICK HEARN: I was hired to do the Lakers games during the end of their first season in L.A. I was working for NBC, doing some national college games. Bob Short called me in the middle of the night and asked, "Can you go to St. Louis tomorrow for a televised game?" We had an overtime game that was carried back to L.A. Even though they had Baylor and West, the fan interest wasn't there. There were nights when the Sports Arena was booked and we had games at different colleges in the area. I felt I had to sell the game of pro basketball on the West Coast. In our early years, sportswriters seldom traveled with us, so the radio was the only way to follow the team. But what we had going for us was Baylor and West, two great superstars in a town that loves stars.

SLICK LEONARD: In the early 1960s, some Hollywood stars did adopt us. There was a team of stars who played preliminary games—Pat Boone, Gary Crosby, Gardner McKay. Doris Day sat courtside. Then there was the team—West and Baylor—and that's who people came to see.

10
THE CLASS OF 1960

Only once in the history of the NBA have three future Hall of Famers at the same position entered the league at the same time. But that description is deceptive; Jerry West, Oscar Robertson and Lenny Wilkens may all have played guard, but their differing styles showed the diversity that could exist at a position before roles were firmly ingrained.

West was the consummate Mr. Outside, with a deadly jump shot, fine ballhandling and passing skills, and a fierce defender; West was also relentlessly self-critical, demanding nothing less than perfection from his own play. Robertson, a strong, punishing all-around player whose position could almost be described as "power guard," could shoot, drive, pass and often outrebound his own center. And Wilkens, the pure point guard, played a low-key, no-frills game that was easy to overlook, unless you were on the court with him. According to the folklore of the game, West had trouble going to his left, Wilkens never went to his right, and Robertson could go left or right but would just as soon go straight through you. The three traveled routes into the league and on to All-Star prominence as varied as their styles of play.

Before Jerry West Was a Laker

Jerry West was a 6-foot-2 guard from Cabin Creek, West Virginia. Myth has it that West was a coal miner's son. Actually, he was a coal miner's grandson. His father, Howard West, worked for an oil company until it went out of business. Then he worked for a coal company as an electrician. In West's three years at the University of West Virginia, the Mountaineers were 81-12 and never lost a home game. As a senior, he was the NCAA Player of the Year as he averaged 29 points.

JERRY WEST: I was a very shy kid and basketball was something I could do by myself. It was just me, the ball, the hoop and my imagination. I played on a neighbor's hoop on a dirt surface and I practiced for hours upon hours. Most people don't realize it, but basketball can be a very solitary game, and that was the early appeal of the sport to me. I've developed a great love for golf and if there had been a golf course in my hometown, maybe I never would have touched a basketball because golf is the ultimate solitary game. But there was no golf, so it was basketball. To me, playing basketball by myself was very soothing.

The other factor in my attraction to the game was that West Virginia has a strong basketball heritage. When West Virginia University played, the games were broadcast around the state. I grew up outside of Charleston, and our reception wasn't very good. At night, I'd fiddle with the dial, getting the game when the score was 50–40. Then I'd lose it for a few minutes, get the signal back and the score would be 60–56. It was frustrating, but it also heightened the anticipation for the morning newspaper so I could read about what happened.

The culmination of my interest in basketball came when I was about 12 and my brother-in-law took me to a West Virginia game in Morgantown. It took us four and a half hours to get there because it was all back roads. We spent the night after the game in a hotel, and I couldn't sleep. I was caught up by the excitement of the crowd and the game. That really started me fantasizing. I began to believe I could play for the university and that it would be me in the middle of that excitement.

ROD THORN: Jerry's hometown of Cabin Creek had about 20 people when he was a kid. But he went to East Bank High, which may have been the second-largest school in the state, with over 2,000 kids. When I was a high school freshman, my father took me to the state playoffs. Jerry was a senior at East Bank. I had never heard of Jerry West, and his team was playing Mullens, which was considered the best in the state.

This was a state semifinal game and Jerry was incredible. He carried his team and he was already drilling that line-drive jumper of his. Back then, you were allowed to block shots after the ball hit the backboard. Jerry would wait until a guy shot a layup off the board, then he'd jump up and swat it away. Now that's goaltending. Then it showed you what a great leaper he was, even though he was a little over 6-foot and rail-thin.

[West had 43 points and 23 rebounds as his team beat Mullens, 77–73. Then West had 39 points as his team beat Morgantown, 71–56, to win the state title.]

JERRY WEST: The reason I was able to block those shots off the board was because most guys took one look at me and thought, "This kid is too skinny. He can't jump that high."

FRED SCHAUS: I first heard about Jerry when he was playing for Pratt Junior High. Someone told me that this kid was skinny as hell, but a player. He had a major injury in his sophomore season and wasn't fully recovered until he was a senior. I scouted Jerry in the state tournament, and believe me, Jerry's team was Jerry and four very nice students. He just carried them to that title.

HOD ROD HUNDLEY: It was such a big deal when Jerry's school won the state title that East Bank High changed its name to West Bank High for a while.

JERRY WEST: Our school had never won a state title before and what made it more dramatic was that our victory was a major upset. We had a parade and received a lot of attention, which was terribly embarrassing to me. I was so shy to the point that it was painful. Inwardly, I was very proud. But I didn't enjoy all the notoriety.

FRED SCHAUS: To this day, Jerry is embarrassed about the accolades he's received. He has a shyness and humility that I admire.

JERRY WEST: As a junior in high school, I scored a lot of points but got only one letter from a college. I used to say to myself, "Obviously, I'm not that good." I didn't have many expectations about college. But as the state tournament went on, I was deluged with letters. I'd come home from school and 3–4 coaches would be sitting on my doorstep talking to my mother. I honestly didn't understand all the commotion. I just didn't think I merited all the attention. I even had some incredible financial offers that would have helped my family. But all along, I was going to West Virginia. My mother and I told them as much, but they didn't believe us. I went to West Virginia because it was where I always wanted to go. I never got a dime extra, but people don't believe that, either.

FRED SCHAUS: There were about 70 schools after Jerry. The final four were Duke, Maryland, Kentucky and us at West Virginia. Jerry lived in a nice, white-painted home in a coal mining area. No one had much money and most of the other homes weren't as neat as Jerry's. The thing you immediately noticed when you walked into the home was how clean and neat everything was. I liked Jerry and his family a lot. Later he told me, "Coach, I was never going anywhere but West Virginia." I just wish he had said that right away because he would have saved me a lot of grief. Maybe Jerry didn't think he'd be a great college player, but I knew otherwise.

When Jerry was a freshman, his freshman team played against our varsity with Hot Rod Hundley. I was pulling for the freshmen to play well, but suddenly it appeared that they were going to win the game. Our varsity was ranked in the Top 10. If the freshmen beat them, then the varsity's confidence might be shaken and there would be too much pressure on the freshmen the following season.

HOT ROD HUNDLEY: I was everybody's All-American and I had to work like hell to stay with Jerry. We beat the freshmen by four points. Afterward I thought, "If they would only have let Jerry play varsity. With the two of us in the backcourt, we would have been national champs." What most people don't know is that Jerry's leaping ability meant he played forward in college. He didn't move to the backcourt until he was drafted by the Lakers.

[As a 6-foot-2 forward, West averaged 17 rebounds a game in his senior year.]

JERRY WEST: I had a good college career, but I wasn't "storied," like Hot Rod Hundley. To me, he was a great player. Then I saw him go to the pros and he didn't dominate the league. That made me wonder what kind of NBA player I'd be.

HOT ROD HUNDLEY: While I was at West Virginia, I'd tell Jerry, "You see this field house and all the fans? I'm making the payments." When Jerry became my teammate with the Lakers, he told me, "Remember the payments you made on the field house? Well, it's paid in full."

I had more talent than Jerry, but he had more dedication. I was a much better ballhandler than he was in college, but I also knew that his attitude would make him great. We became great friends even though

I'm an extrovert and he's an introvert. I liked to drink. I'd have 10 beers, he'd have one. I wanted to go through the front door to let everyone know I was there, Jerry wanted to sit in the back booth. To me, basketball was a game. I loved it. I wanted to win, but I also saw it as entertainment. To Jerry, it was a war, a mission, and he was totally wrapped up in it. That is the secret to his greatness.

[The Lakers made Jerry West the second pick in the 1960 draft, Oscar Robertson going No. 1 to Cincinnati. West signed for $16,500 and did not start until the 20th game of his rookie season. He averaged 17.6 points, the only season he would average under 20. He also averaged a career-high 7.7 rebounds in 1960–61, as he was converted from forward to the backcourt.]

FRED SCHAUS: When Jerry was a rookie, he was madder than hell at me for not putting him in the lineup right off the bat. I went with Hot Rod Hundley and Frank Selvy in the backcourt because they had experience and I wanted to break Jerry in gradually. I had seen too many rookies come into the league with high expectations, be immediately thrown to the wolves and get eaten alive. They never developed and lost their confidence. I always believed that was the case with Darrall Imhoff [the third pick in 1960] in New York. I also took into account Jerry's personality. Since I had coached him at West Virginia, I knew he was a perfectionist. I knew he would eat himself up inside when he didn't live up to his own expectations. I still played him a lot of minutes, but he just didn't start right away.

I don't know if Jerry ever came around to my way of thinking. I've been told that he still sort of holds a grudge about that, and also because he thought there was a point in his career where I wanted to trade him. But Jerry's name never came up in trade talks. I would have traded my wife before Jerry.

HOT ROD HUNDLEY: I know that Jerry had to make some adjustments from being a college forward to a guard in the NBA, but Jerry didn't have problems learning to handle the ball. He was great immediately. He should have started opening night. All the guys knew it, and Jerry knew it, too. I was starting and averaging 11 points, and he was scoring 17 off the bench. Jerry hated sitting, but he never bitched about it.

RUDY LaRUSSO: Fred Schaus got it into his head to break Jerry in slowly and all of us—even Hot Rod—were saying, "Enough of this crap, when the hell is Fred going to start West? We got a star here, let's put him on the court."

JERRY WEST: I've always respected Fred as a coach and I've never had any problems with any coach. But early in my rookie year, we were playing this silly shooting game in practice, taking shots we wouldn't in a game.

Fred said to me, "Look, you can't afford to do this. You're not as talented as other people."

That made me think that Fred believed I wasn't that good, and it probably did change my relationship with him from then on. Not starting was frustrating, especially because the team was floundering early in the season. Also, Fred was my college coach. We had a relationship, yet he wanted me to learn from sitting. That's all right for a while, but the only way to improve is to play.

CHICK HEARN: Jerry obviously was pissed off about not playing, and when he did get his chance, look out. He rose to unimaginable heights and it became apparent that we had a star on our hands. Since I had to sell pro basketball to fans who had never been exposed to the pro game, the fastest way was with stars. Elgin was a legitimate superstar before the team moved to L.A. Jerry gave us another one. At first, I called him Zeke from Cabin Creek, which was Elgin's nickname for him. Jerry had a crew cut and a thick West Virginia accent, and it seemed to fit. But Jerry's first wife asked me not to use it on the air, so I stopped.

[Baylor also called West Tweety Bird, because of West's high voice and skinny legs. West wore a green sport coat from his college days and Baylor would say to him, "That's a nice coat, Tweety Bird. Does it come in men's sizes, too?"]

CHICK HEARN: By the end of Jerry's rookie season, I began to notice that he was making a lot of shots at the end of the game. This wasn't an accident. He wanted the ball under pressure, then he produced. So I started to call him Mr. Clutch, and it stuck.

RUDY LaRUSSO: We'd get into a tie game with 15 seconds to go and we'd give the ball to Jerry, clear out the side of the floor. He'd take one dribble, then another, then go up with the jumper and we'd go home with a win.

ROD THORN: What Jerry did right before he went up for his jumper was take a hard dribble—*bam*—then take the jump shot, and the guy guarding him was dead meat.

LARRY STAVERMAN: You could see it in Jerry's eyes. He'd look at the clock and his facial expression told his teammates, "Give me the god-damn ball. I'll win the game for you."

JERRY WEST: I always thought that if we needed a basket, I could score. I didn't care who was guarding me or what the defense was, I could get the ball in the basket. As my career went on, it became easier and easier to score in clutch situations because my confidence grew. In fact, I would be irritated if someone else took a shot in those situations, because I knew that if I took it, we'd score.

EARL STROM: Jerry worked hard to make himself a great player. Early in his career, he never drove left. But I'd tell people, "It's too bad Jerry can only go right because he can only average 30 points that way." But he taught himself to go left. He couldn't dribble the ball more than twice as a rookie without getting into trouble.

JERRY WEST: The summer before my second season, I practiced the weakest parts of my game. I ended my rookie year on a high note and went to camp in the best physical shape of my life. A lot of people would have been delighted with my rookie year, but I felt it was a mixed season. It was true that I never went left early in my career. Later on that worked to my advantage; the defenses would shade me to the right, but I had been working on dribbling with my left hand and I could drive around them.

ELGIN BAYLOR: Jerry was going to be a great pro, no matter what. But in his second season, he was able to really take command because I was in the military and only played on weekends. That meant the team looked to Jerry to score and that speeded his development.

[West had only one 30-point game as a rookie, but he scored at least 30 in each of the first four games of his second season, averaging 31 for the season. On January 17, 1962, he scored a career-high 63 on 22-for-36 shooting vs. New York before only 2,766 at the L.A. Sports Arena.]

JERRY WEST: I had a virus and a temperature before the 63-point game. I think I played only 39 minutes and I wasn't conscious of scoring 60-some points. I've had other nights where I know I played better, I just didn't shoot that much. I became a better shooter later in my career. Early, my jumper was very flat. As I got older, I had more height to it. In my first three seasons, I never shot 80 percent from the free throw line; after that, I never shot under 80 percent.

RED AUERBACH: What people don't realize is that Jerry was one of the greatest defensive guards ever.

JOHN HAVLICEK: Red used to say that you don't judge a player by only his height, you need to consider the length of his arms. Jerry had something like a 39-inch sleeve. He was 6-foot-2, but had the arms of a man 6-foot-7. That made him so tough when he guarded you. He could use those long arms to poke away your dribble, I mean really pick your pocket.

LENNY WILKENS: I wish they had kept track of steals when Jerry and I played because we would have been the league leaders. He had hands that were as quick as a snake's tongue.

JOHN VANAK: Jerry was so methodical. He wore you out with his jump shot, his relentless defense, and unlike a lot of guards, he had enough guts to go under the basket for rebounds. He seldom complained about an official's call, and when he did you had to ask yourself, "Did I kick that one?" He commanded that much respect in the league.

Oscar

In the modern NBA, the measure of a complete player is the triple-double: at least 10 points, rebounds, and assists in a game. To most of

*us, that's the Magic Line because most of us believe that Magic Johnson
was the first player to do it consistently. But Johnson never came close
to averaging a triple-double for a season. Oscar Robertson did just that
in 1961–62, and came very close in three other seasons in which he just
missed because he averaged slightly under 10 rebounds. As a rookie in
1960–61, he averaged 30.5 points, 10.1 rebounds and 9.7 assists. Yes,
he was a 6-foot-5 guard who was 10th in the NBA in rebounding as a
rookie—and that turned out to be a typical season for Robertson.*

WAYNE EMBRY: When Oscar Robertson walked into the ninth grade,
he was a great player—not just for junior high, but for anywhere. The
thing to remember about Oscar is that he was always great. When I
played for the Cincinnati Royals and Oscar was a freshman at the University of Cincinnati, we had already heard about him and that was
before freshmen were allowed to play varsity ball. After his freshman
year, Oscar was shooting around in a gym. Jack Twyman and I were
there. Twyman was an NBA All-Star, a future Hall of Famer. He said
to me, "I'm going to teach that kid a lesson." So Jack challenged Oscar
to a 1-on-1 game and Oscar won 21–0, that's how great Oscar was.

RON GRINKER: Oscar and I went to the University of Cincinnati together. He was on the basketball team. Because I had a knee injury
and couldn't play any sports, some friends convinced me to try out for
cheerleading. I couldn't see myself as a cheerleader, but I ended up
being the Cincinnati Bearcat mascot, and that meant I traveled with
the team and got to see all of Oscar's games. He made you fall in love
with basketball. Oscar was from Indianapolis and I think he went to
Cincinnati because it had a good basketball program and was only a
few hours from home. He took business, and the business department
had a program where students could work at local businesses, get paid
and receive college credit at the same time during the school year.
That's what Oscar did during the season. Now it would be illegal under
NCAA rules, but back then it was what most athletes did in order to
have a more flexible schedule during the season and to get some prac-
tical experience and some spending money, too.
    There was a lot of pressure on Oscar from the moment he stepped
on campus because he was considered by many to be the best high
school player in the country. When he was a freshman, the fans would
fill the 7,800-seat arena for his games. Then the varsity would play and
about half the fans would go home. And at 18, Oscar played like a
seasoned pro.

CARL BRAUN: No one at 6-foot-5 could control a game like Oscar, and he did it even though he never took the ball behind his back, he never dunked, he never took a stupid shot. He killed you with fundamentals.

OSCAR ROBERTSON: I could dunk, dribble around my back and all that flashy stuff. I dunked once in high school and my coach got all over me, so I never did it again. Dunking is overrated, a showboat play. All the stars in my era could dunk, but we saw no reason to do it. We had too much respect for each other to try and dunk in each other's face. The dunk, the behind-the-back garbage—those aren't great plays and they aren't skilled plays. I never played that way and I never changed my game from high school to college to the NBA. In high school, I learned to take a good shot, to get as close to the basket as possible before you shoot, and that each possession was important. You didn't waste a possession by forcing a shot from too far out or with two guys on you.

RON GRINKER: In his pregame warmups, Oscar never practiced a shot that he wouldn't take in a game. He was like a robot. He'd practice his right-handed hook, his left-handed hook, and then he'd go from spot to spot in a circle working on his jumper. He once told me that he would never practice a shot unless it was something he would take at the buzzer when his team was behind by one point.

BOB FERRY: People forget what a great athlete Oscar was. I was a center at St. Louis University and having a helluva game against Cincinnati. They were trying all their different big guys on me and no one could stop me. Then they put Oscar on me. I had about six inches on him, but in the last 10 minutes of the game he was all over me. He wouldn't let me catch a pass. That was why I've always insisted that there is nothing on a basketball court that Oscar could not do.

RON GRINKER: As a sophomore at Cincinnati, he walked into Madison Square Garden for the first time and scored 56 points against Seton Hall. It was almost as if he was telling the New York media, "Well, guys, here I am." I felt he could put up those numbers anytime he wanted, but Oscar was more interested in the team game.

OSCAR ROBERTSON: I was taught to think basketball, to know where my teammates were on the court, where they should have the ball and where they shouldn't. Do you want to run, and when should your offense run the fast break? In virtually every game I played, the opposition pressured me full court. I don't care who you are—Oscar Robertson, Jerry West, Magic Johnson, anybody—you don't like to face a pressure defense. But that became a challenge to me. They thought that pressure would wear me down, but I believed I had the greatest stamina of anyone who ever played. So I felt, "You come at me, I'm coming right back at you and we'll see who's still going 100 percent at the end of the game."

BOB FERRY: The first time I got to know Oscar was when we were on the Pan-American team, and boy, could he be an intimidating presence. He was so good and always made the right play—and he expected you to do the same. When you didn't, he let you know and he could make you feel about two inches tall.

WAYNE EMBRY: Some guys were afraid to play with Oscar. He had such quick reactions. You'd get open and zip, the ball came at you. You'd never figure that anyone could throw a pass through there. If you missed, he let you know. Poor Hub Reed, he hated to play with Oscar. Oscar would throw him a perfect pass, Hub wouldn't be ready, and Oscar would say, "Sheet, Hub, you gotta catch them balls."

RON GRINKER: A lot of people saw Oscar as moody and difficult, and he could be that way. One day, he would act like your best friend, the next he may walk past you like he didn't know you. I think some of it was a defense mechanism. He was the first black basketball player at the University of Cincinnati. On the court, everyone cheered for him. But there was a movie theater a half block from the campus that would not sell a ticket to a black, even if the black was the great Oscar Robertson. This was the late 1950s and there were restaurants in town that would not serve the great Oscar Robertson. That embittered him.

I know Oscar played a game in the deep South in his sophomore season where they threw some black cats on the court when Oscar came out of the dressing room.

But the most pronounced incident came when Oscar made Gary Phillips a first-round draft choice. Phillips played for the University of Houston and he "held" Oscar to 13 points, Oscar's worst college game.

What people don't know is that when Oscar checked into his Houston hotel room the night before the game, he found a sign on the door that read, "No Niggers Allowed."

Oscar was really upset, and for good reason. The coaching staff knew about it and they should have gone to the front desk and said, "Gentlemen, our team is not staying here."

Instead, they told Oscar to ignore it and I think he felt that he wasn't supported. He thought the team should have moved to another hotel and he was right. When Oscar walked onto the court the night Gary Phillips "held" him to 13 points, I don't think his heart was in it. I could have held him to 13 points that night, because it was a disheartened Oscar Robertson who stopped himself, not Gary Phillips or anyone else.

WAYNE EMBRY: Because they had the territorial draft back then, we knew that Oscar was coming to play for the Royals. We also knew his game because we used to play with him during summer pickup games while he was still in college. In a sense, he was part of our team even before he graduated.

RON GRINKER: Most territorial choices considered it an honor that the NBA team in their area wanted them, and down deep I believe that Oscar felt the same way. His first-year salary was $22,000, which was pretty good considering most of his teammates were making between $8,000–$12,000.

JERRY WEST: Oscar was great from Day One in the NBA. He is the most advanced player I've ever seen at such an early stage of his career. He had good coaching when he was young. He was a hard worker and dedicated. His greatness was his simplicity. He made every play in the simplest way because his skill level was enormous. It took me a long time to catch up with him.

HOT ROD HUNDLEY: Oscar and Jerry West played on the 1960 Olympic team together and they started their NBA careers at the same time. Jerry would tell me, "Jeez, Oscar is great." If you know Jerry, then you know that he is not one to throw around accolades. I believe that he always thought Oscar was better than him—and he was a little in awe of Oscar because Oscar had so much talent. To Jerry West, the greatest player ever was Oscar Robertson.

OSCAR ROBERTSON: People forget that I did have to make adjustments to the NBA. I was a forward in college. I should have been a guard and I handled the ball, but the team also needed me on the boards. So I came into the NBA with the idea that I was there to rebound, too.

That was part of my job. I averaged 15 a game in college, so I wasn't surprised when I got 10–12 a night in the NBA.

WAYNE EMBRY: Much to my disgrace, it is true that in his second season, it was Oscar Robertson, a guard, not me, Wayne Embry the center, who led the Cincinnati Royals in rebounding.

OSCAR ROBERTSON: I played the total game because we weren't into specialization like they are today. We didn't have all this point guard and off guard nonsense. A guard was a guard. If you were a guard, you were expected to be able to handle the ball, to score and to play defense. Now the shooting guard is really a 6-6 forward from college who can't dribble and all they do is run him off picks to get him open. Pass him the ball and he shoots it. No one ever made my life that easy.

JACK TWYMAN: Before Oscar, the offense revolved around me. I went from averaging 31 points to 24 in Oscar's rookie year. In effect, I became a supporting player to him. But you could see right away that Oscar was a franchise player. We went from 19 wins without him to 33 when he was a rookie to 43 in his second season.

TOM GOLA: I always guarded the other team's best scorer and the first time I faced Oscar, he got only 14.

WAYNE EMBRY: That's right, and Gola told some reporters, "He's not that great. From all I had read and heard, I thought he'd be better." The next time they played, Oscar went for 45 points and talked to Gola the whole night.

TOM GOLA: After that first night, Oscar just wore me out. He had the ball 90 percent of the time for the Royals. He would run you into Wayne Embry, and big Wayne would put a hit on you. He was Wayne the Wall, no one could move him, and because he was so wide it took forever to get around him.

WAYNE EMBRY: Oscar didn't just talk to Gola, he talked to everybody. He loved to score over Wilt and say, "Too late, big fella." Or he'd drive around Wilt and make a layup and say, "You can't get that one, can you, big fella?"

FRANK MCGUIRE: When I coached Philly, I'd let the players make the defensive matchups. Gola would say, "Okay, I'll take Oscar, but he's going to get 36." I remember distinctly that the first time Gola said that Oscar scored 36. It was eerie.

JERRY LUCAS: The people who appreciate Oscar the most were the ones like Wayne Embry and myself who played with him every day. But it is true that Oscar was a perfectionist and he'd yell at you if you messed up. Then you saw that he yelled at everybody, so you learned not to take it personally.

BARRY CLEMENS: There was a game where John Tresvant missed a layup and Oscar gave him the kind of tongue lashing I never heard before on the court. It was totally X-rated and it went on and on. After a while, Tresvant yelled at Oscar, "Man, cut it out. I ain't a damn dog." When you played with Oscar, you had the feeling that if he fed you on the fast break and you blew the layup, forget it. You can run the lane all night, you aren't going to see the ball. You'd just have to get it off the boards and get back into his good graces.

EARL STROM: I officiated a game where Oscar threw a perfect pass to somebody, who dropped it out-of-bounds. My wife was at the game and Oscar cut loose with a bunch of F-words. I was 50 feet away and I could hear it, so I hit him with a technical.

He said, "I wasn't yelling at you."

I said, "Oscar, see that lady sitting under the basket?"

He nodded.

I said, "Oscar, that's my wife. If I don't talk like that in front of her, neither do you."

He just nodded and shut up.

JOE GUSHUE: There were three guys I called the Debating Team. Every time you blew the whistle, they debated it. Rick Barry, he was a crybaby. Tommy Heinsohn, another crybaby. Then there was Oscar Robertson, a real big crybaby.

ZELMO BEATY: I would have loved to have played with Oscar because he would have made me so much better. But he was such a perfectionist that I never could have lived up to his expectations. The way he'd scream at Wayne Embry: "You dummy, catch the ball . . . I put the ball right in your hands, how can you drop that one?" I felt sorry for Wayne.

WAYNE EMBRY: Oscar was so far ahead of the rest of us humans that you could never come up to his level. But because of his greatness and what he meant to the franchise, you hated to fail him.

LARRY STAVERMAN: The thing about Oscar was that in his mind he never made a bad play. If a pass was missed, it was your fault. He was so good 1-on-1 that sometimes it became like playing with Michael Jordan. You were afraid to cut to the basket because you didn't want to mess him up. The temptation was to get him the ball, get out of the way and let him have room to operate, and that would lead to people standing around—which was not what Oscar wanted.

RON GRINKER: Oscar had a big behind and he used it to get in position for the shot he wanted—he just used his butt to back the defender out of the way. He loved the baseline right. You'd go to block his shot, but he'd put the ball behind his head, wait until you came down and then shoot it. He could score with his left hand or his right. I once said to him, "Oscar, you're averaging 30, but I know you can get 50 anytime you want to."

Oscar winked and said, "Yeah, Ron, but I know I'll still be able to get my 30 when I'm 50 years old."

WAYNE EMBRY: On that fallaway, Oscar would put the ball right in your face, then pull it back and score as if he was toying with you.

PETE NEWELL: I coached Oscar on the 1960 Olympic team and he was the first player I saw who consistently used the pump fake. He continually had his defender off his feet and that move became his trademark.

AL BIANCHI: Here's a testimony to Oscar. Everyone knows what a competive, hard-nosed coach Alex Hannum was. Well, we were ahead by a point with a few seconds left and Oscar's team had the ball. In the huddle, Alex said, "We know Oscar can make it with two guys on him. So Al, you just wave at him and say, 'Go ahead and take it.' I don't know what else to try on him." Well, I did—and he made it anyway.

WAYNE EMBRY: Oscar's greatness sometimes overwhelmed Adrian Smith. We called him Odie, and Odie would tell Oscar, "Please, O, you know I'm trying, I really am. You gotta believe me, O."

BARRY CLEMENS: I mentioned that Oscar could be hard on his teammates. Well, he also knew how to take care of them. There was the All-Star Game [in 1966] when the Big O set out to make Adrian Smith the MVP. Everyone knew that Adrian Smith couldn't shoot off the dribble, he had to be set up. Since Adrian was the "other guard" in the Royals backcourt, the Big O set up Smith all night and he got 24 points and was the MVP. But it happened only because Oscar decided to make it happen.

OSCAR ROBERTSON: That game was in Cincinnati. Adrian Smith is one of the finest pure shooters ever and he never got much publicity, so I went to him. It made me feel good to see him get the award.

RON GRINKER: That was the other side of Oscar. He would rather let Smith have a moment in the sun and talk to the reporters. Oscar hated doing interviews and I know he liked the idea of making stars out of guys. Obviously, it was a day Adrian Smith will never forget because he still has the '66 Mustang Convertible he won in his garage.

BARRY CLEMENS: I was on the other end when Oscar made a star out of Jack Twyman. It was at the end of Jack's career and they were having a night to honor him. He wasn't starting then, but he did that game. I also got a rare start and I was on Twyman. Oscar worked me, forcing me to cover him and then feeding Jack, over and over. I'd switch off to cover Oscar as he penetrated, then he'd dish to Twyman and boom—15-foot swish. He made sure that Jack had a real night and Twyman ended up with about 35 that game.

WAYNE EMBRY: Oscar and I were roommates for six years. I know what he did for my career. *[Embry was an All-Star in five of the six years he roomed with Robertson, the only times he made the All-Star team.]*

When a new big man would come to training camp, O would say, "You're not going to let him take your job, are you, big fella? You're gonna knock him down, right?"

So I'd go out and knock him down.

Once Oscar decided that we needed to draft George Wilson out of U. of Cincinnati. He used to say, "We needed somebody to get some ballboards." Ballboards was what he called rebounds. Oscar wasn't close to Jerry Lucas and he thought that Wilson could help out at forward. So we drafted him, Wilson came to camp and had a tough time. In the middle of a scrimmage, Oscar stopped and said to Wilson, "Sheet, get outta here. You can't get no ballboards."

Poor George was scared to death, but it broke up the rest of us. That was Oscar. You just had to know him.

When we were on the road, our routine was to get a bag of cheeseburgers, a couple of beers or Cokes and take them back to the room. We'd eat and Oscar would watch television. He'd stare at the TV until the test pattern came on. By then, I was usually asleep.

OSCAR ROBERTSON: When I came to the Royals, they had no plays for Wayne. They just left him out there. I convinced Wayne to do what he did best—take his wide body to the basket and I'd get him the ball. Wayne was the smallest center in the league [6-foot-8], so we'd pull the opposing centers away from the basket with our pick-and-roll play.

WAYNE EMBRY: On that play, Oscar would say, "When I throw it, you got to go get the ball, big fella." I knew I had to or else I'd hear about it.

JOHN VANAK: Wayne just worshiped Oscar, you could see it in his face. He also was like a blocking back for Oscar—he'd set a pick and clear out Oscar's man.

ZELMO BEATY: Wayne was so low and compact, you couldn't move him. When he drove and you tried to get in his way, he'd just throw you into the basket support.

FRANK McGUIRE: Because he was so strong and worked so hard, Embry gave Wilt as much trouble as any center.

RON GRINKER: When they played, Wilt and Wayne went at it like two sumo wrestlers.

JOHNNY KERR: Oscar would yell at Wayne to lean on me. Then Wayne would, and my coach would be screaming, "Hold your ground." I'd say, "Hold my ground?" I'd look down on the court and there were skid marks from where I held my ground and Wayne pushed it out from under me.

BOB FERRY: One time, poor Wayne fell down in the key, Oscar was yelling at him to get out of there and I was screaming, "Three seconds" to the officials. All the while, all 300 pounds of Wayne was crawling on his hands and knees to get out of the lane.

WAYNE EMBRY: People still don't appreciate Oscar. They talk about triple-doubles. He *averaged* them. He outrebounded *centers*.

SLATER MARTIN: The thing about Oscar's triple-doubles was that they didn't throw around assists like they do today or he would have gotten 15–20 most nights. And if they let him palm the ball like they do today, Oscar probably never would have missed a shot.

OSCAR ROBERTSON: I wish I had played in a wide-open style like guys do now and where guards don't even bother to try for rebounds. If I could have shot every time I felt like it, I would have liked to have seen the numbers I would have put up. In my first seven years in the league, I don't think I ever got a basket off the fast break because I was always the guy in the middle, running the break and passing off to someone else. Come playoff time, I was on the court for all 48 minutes. That was a given, and today no one can imagine doing it.

AL BIANCHI: Oscar often comes off like a bitter guy, but he really was that good. I mean, he about averaged a triple-double his whole life and now it's a big deal when a guy does it once a month. So in his view—which is correct—few guys could play like him.

OSCAR ROBERTSON: The triple-double is blown out of proportion. No one noticed it when I played. Today, they are so cheap. An assist used to be a pass that led to a basket without a dribble. Now, you pass to a guy, he takes a dribble, makes a 25-footer and that's an assist. Guys worry about getting one more rebound or assist for the triple-double—it's ridiculous. What matters is a guy who plays the total game. He's not after stats, but because that's how you should play the game, period.

The Quiet Man

Lenny Wilkens had a 15-year career as a point guard with St. Louis, Atlanta, Cleveland and Portland. He later coached in Seattle, Portland

and now at Cleveland. But when the 6-foot-2, left-handed-shooting Wilkens came to the St. Louis Hawks in 1960, he had no idea what to expect. His experience then was more typical of rookies at that time than those of the expected stars West and Robertson.

LENNY WILKENS: I've worked nearly all of my life—I'm talking about getting my first job at the age of seven when I hung around a vegetable market in Brooklyn and carried home people's groceries in exchange for tips. Later, I pulled a wagon and made home deliveries from the store.

To me, this was not a hardship. My father was black and a chauffeur, but he died when I was five. My mother was an Irish Catholic, and when my father died she was left with having to raise five kids. She worked at a candy factory, packing boxes. We also went through a period when we were on public assistance. But even when we were getting aid, I worked—on Saturdays, I'd clean this lady's house from top to bottom, and she had a three-story brownstone. After high school, I was stocking shelves and I was in charge of the vegetable department at a grocery store, weighing the produce, figuring out what to charge people and all that.

My mother was a strong presence. If she said be home at a certain time, you had better be there. If not, she'd track you down and it would be terrible. Once, I went to a party and stayed late. She found me and embarrassed me in front of my friends. I was truly mortified and never was late again. Because of how I grew up, the fact that I didn't have a father and that my family did spend some time on welfare, I guess I don't have a lot of patience with some people who use their background as an excuse not to try and achieve. I saw a man shot in my neighborhood. There were gangs—not as violent as today because we didn't have the drug problem, but there was violence. A good thing was that even though we were a mixed family, it was not a problem in our area of Brooklyn. It was a racially mixed neighborhood, and everyone was pretty much accepted. That was why going to St. Louis was such a culture shock to me after I was drafted by the Hawks.

Because my mother was a strong Catholic, I went to a Catholic elementary school, Holy Rosary. I was an altar boy and it was a priest named Father Manion who first got me involved in basketball in the CYO program. I never played high school basketball until my senior year at Boys High. I had made the team as a sophomore, but they had 15 players and I was the 15th guy. I also was working after school at the grocery store, and I wasn't going to sacrifice my job just to sit on the bench, so I quit the team.

I learned my basketball on the playgrounds of Brooklyn. Today, being a playground player is an insult—it means all you want to do is go 1-on-1, it means your fundamentals stink and you don't understand the game. But the playgrounds I knew were tremendous training grounds. The older guys were in charge of the games, most had played in high school or college. They knew the game. If you took a bad shot, made a selfish play or played lousy defense, they got all over you and they wouldn't pick you to play again. Saturdays were big at the playground. People came to watch the games, and a guy who was selfish, they'd hoot him right off the court. The fans were astute. They wanted to see team ball.

As a pro, one of my favorite plays was the pick-and-roll, and I learned how to run it on the playgrounds. Also, I used a running hook. That came from the playgrounds because I couldn't get all the way to the basket against the big guys, so I had to develop an in-between shot. I watched guys who were the point guards, how they read the floor and hit the open man, and I emulated them. Father Manion took an interest in my basketball and he gave me some drills to do such as dribbling around chairs, switching hands. Ballhandling is not natural like jumping. It's a learned skill and it was the reason I had success.

The only reason I got a college scholarship was that Father Manion wrote the athletic director at Providence College, and he passed the letter on to Joe Mullaney, who was the coach. But I had graduated in January from Boys High, which meant that I didn't play the second half of the basketball season. Coach Mullaney came to Brooklyn to scout me, but I was already out of school. We met, he gave me a catalogue and an application. I filled it out and never heard another word. That summer, I played on a summer team that won a major tournament, and I had 36 points in the final game. Joe Mullaney's father happened to be at that game. He sent Joe a note about it, asking Joe if I was the same kid he had talked to in Brooklyn. It was only then that I got my acceptance to Providence. So I had to take the SAT—I believe I got a 1230—and I was accepted.

In school, I studied economics and was planning to teach on the college level. In the summers, I had construction jobs and a job carrying 50-pound bags of sugar. Even though I played well, the NBA was not on my mind. Pro ball just wasn't a big deal in the 1950s, and I never even saw a game. I averaged about 14 points as a senior and ran the offense. I didn't look to score until we got into the NIT and we needed offense from me. I averaged about 25 and won the MVP. That was when I first received some attention. I was invited to play in the East-West All-Star Game in New York. Oscar Robertson was on the West team. Jerry West and I were the guards for the East, and Jerry and I were picked as co-MVPs for the game.

I suppose I was aware that I would be drafted by the NBA, but I had no idea where and I didn't worry about it. I was offered a fellowship to go to Boston College and teach economics while I pursued my master's. I also had an offer from the Technical Tape Company in New York, which fielded an AAU basketball team. They offered me a job and I was supposed to play ball for them, too.

The NBA draft was in May, and I got a call to stop by the athletic department after one of my classes. They told me that I was the first-round pick of the Hawks. A couple of writers and TV people stopped by to interview me and that was it. Players of my generation saw the draft as nothing more than an invitation to play pro ball, that's why we're astounded by all the attention the kids out of college get now. And the money? To us, it's inconceivable that these kids are paid like they are before they even play a game.

I never saw an NBA game in person until after I was drafted and went to one of the playoff games between St. Louis and the Celtics at Boston Garden. I watched the Hawks, especially their guards, and I decided that I was as good as they were. The Celtics were double-teaming Hagan and Pettit, leaving the Hawks guards open for medium-range jumpers, and those guys couldn't make a shot. I also liked the excitement of the crowd and it was only then that I decided to try the NBA.

Technical Tape offered me $10,000, which was more than the Hawks. I've often thought that if I hadn't gone to that NBA game, I probably never would have taken less money to sign with the Hawks. Ed Macauley was the Hawks GM and I probably was the easiest sign he ever had. His first offer was something like $7,500. I wanted more, but we settled on $8,500. The big issue was that I wanted it guaranteed. They refused at first, then finally agreed. My mother wasn't thrilled about me playing pro basketball; she wanted me to go to graduate school. Then I explained to her that most CPAs made about $6,500, and I was getting $8,500, so she realized it was a good deal.

When I joined the Hawks in 1960, Slater Martin had retired. He had been the point guard on their 1958 championship team, which also was the last all-white championship team. The first impression I got was a cold reception from most of the veterans. They saw rookies as guys trying to take their jobs, or the jobs of their friends. The rookies were separated from the rest of the team, even dressing in a different room. Before regular training camp, the Hawks held a minicamp at Kutsher's in upstate New York. The rookies along with a few of the veterans were there. I sprained my ankle the first day, and then I tried to play on it. I didn't tape my ankle because I had never taped an ankle in my life. I didn't move well and they probably saw me as a big disappointment. When I arrived in veterans camp, there were stories that I'd be cut or traded—before our first practice! I know that Fred Schaus heard the Hawks were unhappy with me, and he tried to get the Hawks to trade me to the Lakers. That probably saved me with the Hawks—the fact that the Lakers wanted me. In training camp, I learned that the Hawks were exclusively a front-court team. The ball was supposed to go to Pettit, Hagan or Lovellette. They didn't have a single play for the guards to shoot the ball, so when I scored, it was almost by accident.

The only other black player on the team was Sihugo Green. One day after practice during training camp, I went across the street with a few other black rookies to have lunch. The place was just a greasy spoon, but they wouldn't wait on us. Rolland Todd was a white player with us, and they went up to him and said they would not serve the black players. I was demoralized by this. I had spent my life in the Northeast, and I never had it happen to me before. I couldn't help but take it personally. I was college-educated, I had worked hard my whole life, I had accomplished far more than those people who were telling me that I wasn't good enough to eat in their lousy restaurant. I was both angry and embarrassed, and I just left.

Sihugo Green set me up in an apartment. It was the upstairs of a house owned by an Italian couple who lived downstairs. The place had hardwood floors and scatter rugs. If you picked up a rug, there was a sign on the floor that said, "Rug Goes Here." It was a mostly black neighborhood. I got to know a guy named Hank Reed, who owned a local grocery store. He brought me to his house for dinner, and he told me where blacks would be welcome.

I was not in the starting lineup at the beginning of the season. Paul Seymour was the coach and it seemed whenever I made a mistake, I got a quick hook out of the game. He called me Rook, and only Rook. He wasn't a teacher and didn't have much patience. About 25 games into the season, I had a good practice and right in the middle Seymour said, "Why don't you play like that when you get into the game, Rook?"

I yelled, "I'm never in the game, so how would you know how I play?"

As soon as I said that, I thought, "Great, now I'll never play."

But after practice Seymour asked me, "Rook, what's on your mind?"

I said, "When I make one mistake, you take me out. I'll see some of the older guys make the same mistake 3–4 times and you leave them in."

He shook his head and left. I figured I was in even deeper trouble. But the next night, Seymour went to me early in the game. The first time I got the ball, I saw Hagan run down the court and I fired a pass right into the stands. I looked over my shoulder, figuring he'd pull me. But he left me in. I scored 14, had a lot of assists, and started every game after that. The veteran players saw that I could get them the ball, so they were nicer to me. Cliff Hagan was the first to invite me over to dinner, and that meant a lot. Bob Pettit began taking me to the airport with him when we started road trips.

I adjusted to St. Louis and I played well there. Kiel Auditorium was a pit. You were lucky to have hot water in the shower. But what I liked was that it also was connected to an opera house, only separated by a curtain. Before some games, I'd pull back the curtain and just listen to the music. It was very relaxing and hearing that music was one of my favorite memories of my rookie year.

11
WILT AND THE WARRIORS

To Edward Gottlieb

When we first met
I was reminded
Of a Jewish Falstaff
Stubby legs, clothes askew
You shuffled into my hotel room
And stabbed me
With your fiscal swords.

I still live
With the scars
Of our first encounter
And the memory of you
Little gruff man
Who carried pro basketball
In his pocket.

—Tom Meschery

Eddie Gottlieb was born in Kiev, Russia, in 1898, an unlikely beginning for the man who in 1946 helped organize the Basketball Association of America. Gottlieb also was the driving force in merging his BAA with the National Basketball League to form what became the 11-team NBA in 1950. His involvement with basketball began in 1918 when he founded the SPHAs—an all-Jewish team that was called the South Philadelphia Hebrew Association. Later, the team became open to players of all faiths and began beating the best professional teams in the country during the 1920s and 1930s. He served as a coach, president and owner of the Philadelphia Warriors. Gottlieb had tremendous power within NBA circles. He sold the Warriors to San Francisco in 1962, then went to work for the NBA as a consultant and schedule maker until his death in 1979.

LEONARD KOPPETT: Gottlieb was the brains of the league. Maurice Podoloff was the first commissioner, but to his dying day, Podoloff never understood basketball. Gotty knew the game—how to sell tickets, how to get the arena cleaned, how to promote, how to sign up talent like Wilt Chamberlain, and the man also was a coach of the Warriors [until 1955]. He made the league's schedule. When anyone inside the league or outside had a question, they went to Gotty.

HARVEY POLLACK: Gotty saved the Warriors from bankruptcy in 1952. He was coaching and running the team's front office when the original owners were about to fold it. Eddie bought the franchise for $25,000—$15,000 was his own money. He borrowed $5,000 each from two other guys. Ten years later, Eddie sold the team for $875,000, so you have to say he made a good investment.

TOM GOLA: Gotty believed in the star system. It began with Joe Fulks, who was one of the first jump shooters and set an NBA scoring record [with 63 points in 1949], and it continued with Paul Arizin and then Wilt. He liked guys who scored big numbers because he thought that was how you attracted fans.

The man was a maven. It seemed as if he knew everything and he always had an angle. I played at La Salle in Philadelphia, which meant I was a territorial pick of the Warriors. This was in 1955, when the best Ford was $2,200 and the top-of-the-line Caddy was $4,500. For $20,000, you could buy a great house. I took all of that into consideration and decided that $17,500 was what I deserved.

Eddie about dropped dead when I said that. He kept repeating, "No way. No way."

We went back and forth, and finally he said, "All right, I'll give you a salary of $11,500. You're a local kid so we'll have a night for you, and you'll get enough in gifts to get your $17,500."

Eddie went to a lot of local merchants and got them to donate everything from some nice suits to a custom Dodge Royal Lancer.

But the next year when I went to negotiate a contract, I said my salary was $17,500 so that was the starting point. He said, "Oh, no. You made $11,500 last year. That's your salary."

AL ATTLES: When I was a rookie, meal money was $7 a day. Eddie would meet us at the airport gate and hand out the money. On one trip, we were supposed to get $14. When it was my turn, all he had left was three $5 bills. He handed them to me and said, "Give me a dollar."

I said, "I don't have one. Catch up with me later."

Later, I forgot about it but Eddie didn't. He waited a month for me to give him that dollar. When I didn't, one day he said to me, "You still owe me a dollar."

HARVEY POLLACK: With the exception of Ned Irish in New York and Fred Zollner with Fort Wayne, Gotty was like all the other owners in the league—he had no other income besides basketball and he'd fight you for every dollar.

TOM MESCHERY: I was drafted by Philadelphia in 1961 and didn't find out about it until I read about it the next day in the newspaper when I was playing at a college all-star game in Kansas City. Later that day, Eddie knocked on my door. I was rooming with a player from Missouri named Charles Henke. I had never seen Gotty before in my life. He came into my room, pointed at Henke and said, "You, get the hell out. We gotta talk."

The kid was so surprised that he left the room.

We started talking contract right then and I settled for $15,000 with a $1,000 bonus that I used to buy a Plymouth convertible. He just stormed into my room and signed me.

AL ATTLES: I was a fifth-round choice with the Warriors in 1960 and I went to training camp without a contract. I played 20 exhibition games without a contract. After it was over, Gotty said, "We're gonna keep you."

Notice, he didn't say, "You made the team." That might have given me some negotiating power. By saying, "We're gonna keep you," he made it sound like, "You're lousy, but we're going to keep you around anyway . . . for now."

Then he told me to go home, talk to my mother and then come back the next day to talk contract. I had been offered $4,500 to teach high school, so I figured that $7,500 was not too much to play pro basketball.

I figured wrong.

I was in Eddie's office and while he talked to me, he never looked up. He was shuffling through some papers when I said, "Seventy-five hundred."

He said, "Too high . . . too high."

He still wouldn't look at me and he still was moving around the papers on his desk.

I had no idea what I was supposed to say next, so I said, "What do you think?"

He still wouldn't look at me. He grabbed a small piece of paper, wrote down something, folded it in half and slid it over to me. I felt like I was in a poker game getting a face-down card.

As I opened the paper, he finally looked at me. He had written down $5,000 and he could tell from my face that I was disappointed.

Then he said, "I'll give you $500 more."

I leaned over and grabbed the pen right out of his hand and signed the contract for $5,500. At that point, I was afraid he would change his mind.

While Gotty watched every penny, I also found him to be very honest and even generous. That same year, he gave me another $900 as a signing bonus and then $900 after the playoffs. Add it up and I got $7,300 that year, which was almost what I had asked for.

TOM MESCHERY: In the poem I wrote about him, I called Eddie "a Jewish Falstaff." Today, I'm not so sure. He was an incredible penny-pincher and a tightwad in every aspect of business. I couldn't negotiate with him—I just signed for what he offered me. He would go crazy if you left the hotel on the road and forgot to pay for a phone call. He'd get the money from you if it took all season. But the year my father died, Eddie came up to me and wrote me a check before I left the team to go to the funeral. I didn't even ask for it, he just did it.

AL ATTLES: Wilt and I liked Eddie and we wanted to set him up with a deal. We used to appear at a clothing store in Philadelphia and the owner would give us $500 in clothes. Actually, the owner really wanted Wilt, but Wilt would bring me along so I could get the clothes, too. Back then, 500 bucks went a long way and we were like kids in a candy store, picking out mohair coats, hats, everything. Eddie asked us about all our new clothes, so Wilt called the store and told them to take care of Eddie. The next day, we saw Eddie with a new brown suit.

He said, "That was great, and I got five more suits, too."

We asked, "What color?"

He said, "Brown." All six of his suits were identical.

HARVEY POLLACK: Everyone who ever worked for Gotty has a story about how he was first hired or signed. I was a sportswriter for the *Philadelphia Bulletin* making $26 a week after World War Two when he approached me about being the Warriors' assistant PR director. But what he said was, "Keep your newspaper job, too."

He knew it would be easier to get stories into the *Bulletin* if I still worked there than if I was with the Warriors full-time. The PR director was Herb Goode, who also was a sportswriter at the *Philadelphia Record*. So Gotty had two sportswriters also working for him. Later, Goode quit and I became the PR director. In the 1950s and 1960s, our front office was Eddie, myself, a ticket manager and Dave Zinkoff, who did the PA and also typed up Eddie's letters. We never had a full-time secretary until Alex Hannum was hired to coach in 1966, and we hired his wife.

AL ATTLES: Even though Neil Johnston was the coach when I was a rookie, Eddie sat at the end of the press table, right next to the bench. He never looked at Neil and said, "Do this."

But Eddie would stare straight ahead and say loud enough for Neil to hear, "Hey, get that guy out of there."

Once, I missed a jumper and Eddie said, "Who told him he could shoot? Him—Attles? Who said he could shoot?"

CHARLEY ECKMAN: When Eddie was coaching, he didn't just sit on the bench, he owned it. He'd take off his coat and throw it on the floor if he didn't like an official's call. In some games, he was throwing so many clothes around you had a feeling he would be down to his drawers by the time it was over.

JOHN VANAK: Eddie was an owner by the time I was an official, but you'd hear him yell at you from the press table. You knew the power that he had in the league, and with one phone call you could be history. Eddie knew it, too, and he used that to try to intimidate you.

DOLPH SCHAYES: If the fans yelled at Gotty, he'd cuss right back at them. You could not win an argument with the man. He was brilliant, opinionated, and when you disagreed with him, you got the feeling he was thinking, "How can you be so stupid not to see that I'm right?"

NORM DRUCKER: There was a game in Philly where a sportswriter named Jack Kiser yelled, "Drucker, you must have a bet on Boston tonight."

I let it go, but the next time down the floor, Kiser yelled at me again, "Drucker, how much do you have on Boston?"

I stopped the game, went to the press table and told Kiser to get out.

Kiser said, "You can't throw a sportswriter out."

He had a point, but I told him to get out of there. He wouldn't move. Then Gotty came over and I told him that I wasn't going to take that garbage from anyone.

I said, "Eddie, the guy leaves or I forfeit the game to Boston."

That was the second thing I wasn't allowed to do.

Gotty looked at his arena, which was packed. I could see him thinking, "If the game is stopped, I've gotta refund all these tickets."

Then Gotty looked at me. Finally, he turned to Kiser and said, "Jack, you're outta here."

Kiser left. That was how it was with Gotty: he acted as if he ran the team, the building, even the league. Everyone just accepted that as fact.

AL ATTLES: Eddie came from the era when he needed boxing matches, the Globetrotters, dances—anything to help bring in a few extra people. He never had a dime, and he sold the Warriors to San Francisco because he was scared when salaries started to go up. He didn't believe he could compete financially and thought that guaranteed contracts would be the death of the NBA.

DOLPH SCHAYES: Gotty went to work for the league office after he sold the Warriors. He missed running a team a lot. When Ike Richman put together a group to buy the Syracuse Nats and move them to Philly, Eddie wanted to be the general manager. But since he was the guy who sold pro basketball out of Philadelphia, that wasn't a good idea. So he put together the schedule for the league, stuffing his pockets with little notes that he got from all the teams about when they did and did not want to play at home. One year, the league had a computer company work on the schedule and they also had Eddie do it. When both were finished, the company admitted that it could not put together the schedule as well as Gotty did.

AL ATTLES: Eddie would spread all those little notes out on his desk—these crumpled pieces of paper. No one else could even begin to guess what he was doing.

PETE NEWELL: Eddie Gottlieb symbolized those owners of the 1950s. Those guys were street fighters. One minute, they were ready to kill each other. Then they'd calm down, shut the door, put their heads together and come up with the rules and ideas that made this a great game.

Gottlieb's Greatest Move

Many high school seniors believe they will eventually be picked in the NBA draft. Wilt Chamberlain knew it, because he was a territorial selection of the Philadelphia Warriors—while still a senior at Philadelphia's Overbrook High in 1955.

LEONARD KOPPETT: In the early days of the NBA, the emphasis in the league by the owners was more on survival and staying in business than competition. That's what led to the territorial draft, a rule that went back to 1946. The idea is simple and logical: suppose there is a college player in your area who is very popular—and in the 1940s, people were far more interested in college basketball than the pros. If Tom Gola is a star with La Salle in Philadelphia or Oscar Robertson is a dominant player with the University of Cincinnati, forget putting them in the regular NBA draft. Let them play for the NBA teams in their cities. So a pro team can ride piggyback on the success of a college player— that will bring in more fans, and in some cases even get better dates from the arena owner. Of course, the draft also eliminates bidding for college players between teams, but this carried that concept further. The only way any other NBA team could have drafted Oscar Robertson would have been if the Cincinnati Royals first passed on him, and that was not going to happen.

[Territorial draft picks preceded the first round, and a team using a territorial pick gave up its first round pick for that year. The definition of a team's territory was crucial; the Knicks only allowed Syracuse to move to Philadelphia in 1963 after it was agreed that Princeton was in the New York territory, guaranteeing them the rights to Bill Bradley.]

Then there was Wilt Chamberlain, who was a huge star in high school right in Eddie Gottlieb's backyard. There were about 130 colleges after Wilt, which was absolutely unheard of in those days. Word was that

Red Auerbach was angling to get Wilt to attend a college in the Boston area, so the Celtics would have him in their territory. But Eddie Gottlieb was not about to permit that to happen.

HARVEY POLLACK: Eddie went to the league and said, "Our territorial pick is Wilt Chamberlain."

The NBA said, "Hey, you can't take him. He's still in high school."

Eddie said, "Why not? Listen, I guarantee that Wilt will be our first-round pick after his senior year in college and I'm taking him now. If he breaks a leg, if he can't play—I still get him. I'm taking a gamble on the guy."

LEONARD KOPPETT: Eddie's argument was that no matter where Wilt went to college, he was still from Philadelphia. He would always be from Philadelphia, and Philadelphia was where he should play.

Gottlieb was a power in the league, one of the founding fathers. So they gave him the rights to Wilt.

RED AUERBACH: The league felt sorry for Eddie, so they made a special provision for him. We didn't like it in Boston, but back then deals were made all the time.

[Gottlieb feared and respected Auerbach. He often said, "If Red had coached my Warriors with Wilt and someone else had the Celtics and Bill Russell, we would have won all those titles. Red would have gotten more out of Wilt than any other coach.]

WILT CHAMBERLAIN: It was a coup when Eddie Gottlieb drafted me while I was still in high school. He may have done it because he got word that I had played under Red Auerbach at Kutsher's Country Club in the summer. Red wanted me to attend Harvard so he could have my rights. It was late in my junior year at Overbrook when I first learned that Eddie planned to draft me. It didn't faze me to know that I was drafted by an NBA team while still in high school. In the summer, I had played against Tom Gola, Paul Arizin, Guy Rodgers and John Chaney. These guys were great college and pro players, and I was a high school kid. They taught me the game, how to play it correctly. But I also played against Neil Johnston, who was the Warriors' starting center, and I was kicking his ass while I was in high school, so I knew I could play in the NBA.

[One other player was taken as a territorial pick out of high school: Jerry Lucas, out of Middletown (Ohio) High School, selected by Cincinnati. Lucas then attended Ohio State, which was in Cincinnati's territory anyway. The territorial draft was abandoned in 1965.]

VINCE MILLER: I've known Wilt since the third grade and we've been close friends ever since. Wilt was a great athlete and would have been a star in track, football, about anything he wanted. But he loved basketball and the thing people don't understand is that he worked at the game. He wasn't just a big guy. He was lifting weights before anyone else did. In the summer, they would close several Philly recreation centers because it was so hot inside, but we'd get a key and Wilt and I would go in there and work on his outside shot. It would be 90-some degrees, he'd be drenched with sweat and he'd be jumping up and down, touching the rim a hundred times.

Eddie Gottlieb was a wise man. He not only recognized Wilt's obvious physical gifts, he saw Wilt's desire. If he could have found a way, Eddie would have signed Wilt directly out of high school.

ALEX HANNUM: It was common knowledge that Eddie also encouraged Wilt to go to college at Kansas in order to keep him away from any of the NBA cities. He did this for two reasons: First, he didn't want Wilt at a Philly school such as La Salle, where he would be drawing fans away from Eddie's Warriors. Second, if Wilt went somewhere such as Kansas, no other NBA team could contest Eddie's territorial pick of Wilt while he was still in high school.

WILT CHAMBERLAIN: I went to Kansas because they had a great basketball tradition and they were very good to me. I'll leave it at that. But it wasn't that much of a challenge. Freshmen weren't eligible for the varsity and our freshman team didn't have a separate schedule. All we did was play the varsity and kick their ass. Because of all the great players I had faced in the summer, there wasn't much of a transition to college ball. After my junior year, I was ready for something else. In fact, Eddie Gottlieb came to me in 1958 and said he thought he could get the NBA to waive the rule that required a player to wait four years after high school before turning pro. I made it clear that I was leaving school a year early to play for someone. Eddie Gottlieb and I met in a Detroit hotel room—it was all supposed to be very secret—and Eddie wanted me to forget the Globies and go to the NBA. He was worried about losing me to the Globetrotters forever. What Eddie was doing was very illegal because NBA people were not supposed to talk to underclassmen.

He offered me $25,000 to sign with Philly after my junior year. He said, "Listen, that's $3,000 more than anyone in the NBA makes."

At the same time, I had another option—Marques Haynes and Goose Tatum had left the Globetrotters and formed their own team, the Harlem Magicians. They first approached me after my sophomore year at Kansas. They had a black businessman from Michigan tell me, "I'll give you a cashier's check for $100,000 to play for the Magicians."

I was so naive that I didn't even know the difference between a cashier's check and any other check. Also, $100,000 was absolutely unheard of at this time—Bob Pettit was making about $18,000. The whole thing didn't sound right, so I passed.

Finally, my third option was the Globetrotters, and I signed with them because they had a great tradition. In the 1940s and early 1950s, it was the Globies who had the best black players. Playing for them was something that a young man of color often dreamed about. I was studying French and I wanted to travel in Europe. Also, the Globies just seemed like a lot of fun, so I signed with them for a base of $50,000 plus bonuses for attendance. Very early in my career, I learned to count the house and figure out what the crowd was worth to me.

HARVEY POLLACK: After Wilt signed with the Globetrotters, Eddie knew that he had a great chance of bringing him to the Warriors. He didn't think Wilt would be happy with that kind of basketball for more than a year.

WILT CHAMBERLAIN: Eddie Gottlieb and Abe Saperstein were close friends until they started bidding against each other for me. Finally, I signed for about $65,000, which was far more than the figure [$35,000] that was announced. The last thing Eddie wanted was for everyone else in the NBA to know what I was making out of college. This was a pattern that continued through my career. Eddie and I were very close, and I was always making more—two or three times more—than what people thought. We kept it quiet to eliminate jealousy or any other problems.

VINCE MILLER: After Eddie signed Wilt, he tried to get the league to approve a rule whereby the visiting team would get a cut of the gate receipts. Wilt was packing arenas all over the NBA and Eddie wasn't getting a dime from it because the home team kept it all. Eddie told the other owners, "Listen, I'm paying this guy and you're getting rich off him." But this time he didn't get his way. It was one thing to let Eddie have the draft rights to Wilt—that didn't cost them anything. But they weren't about to give up any cash, too.

WILT CHAMBERLAIN: Eddie tried to get around that by playing a heavy exhibition schedule where he got to keep the gate. People don't believe me, but in my rookie year we played 31 exhibition games before the season began. Hey, the Globies prepared me for the NBA—playing every day in a different city.

AL ATTLES: During the season, rather than letting us practice on a day off, Eddie would put us on a bus to Amish Country and we'd scrimmage—I'm talking about a full 48-minute game—so he could sell tickets. The players would pick the sides and no one wanted to draft Wilt. He was playing 48 minutes a night during the regular season, so you weren't going to see the true Wilt in these scrimmages. The first pick was Joe Ruklick, who hardly played during the season but would get 40 points in these games. Meanwhile, Wilt would play guard and bring the ball up the court, dribbling behind his back in one of his old Globetrotter routines.

Game of the Century

Wilt Chamberlain said scoring 100 points in a game was "inevitable." Of course, Wilt has also said it was "a fluky thing." Actually, it was a metaphor for the changing game of pro basketball, the emergence of not just the black athletes such as Elgin Baylor, Oscar Robertson and Chamberlain, but great athletes, period—certainly Jerry West and John Havlicek could run with anyone.

The NBA had become a teenager, feeling its legs, testing its limits and often taking things to extremes, as was the case the night Wilt scored 100. Players fell in love with the fast pace, with getting up a lot of shots in very little time. They were cut free of the ball and chain that was college basketball without the shot clock, and were making up for lost time (and shots) in the pros.

Baylor came into the league with the Minneapolis Lakers in 1958–

59. He averaged 25 points as a rookie, but had a night where he scored 55, the third highest total in NBA history.

Baylor was just a rookie, but he was scoring in ways no one had seen before—off the run, gliding through the air and changing hands on his shot, even changing the direction of his whole body in midair to beat the defense. At the end of Baylor's rookie season, his Lakers got into a 94-foot track meet with Boston, the final score being Boston 173, Lakers 139; Boston's total was the highest for a 48-minute game in NBA history.

It was just beginning.

In 1959–60, Chamberlain came into the league and the NBA became infatuated with scoring. The young Wilt broke league records for scoring (37.6) and rebounding (27.0), and he did it in his rookie season. Baylor averaged 29.6 points, but that only placed him third in scoring—Jack Twyman (31.2) was second to Chamberlain. Twyman and Chamberlain became the first players in NBA history to average 30 points a season. The Hawks' entire front line averaged 20 points—Bob Pettit (26.1), Cliff Hagan (24.8) and Clyde Lovellette (20.8). The average NBA team was scoring 115 a night, Boston leading the way at 124.5.

Danny Biasone had dreamed of a quicker game when he invented the 24-second clock, but he'd never imagined this. Most teams got off a shot within 10 seconds. Rather than worry about shooting percentages, most teams approached the game like Billy the Kid. Billy was a blaster, not a marksman. His idea was to swiftly empty both of his six-shooters, figuring that at least one of the 12 bullets would hit the target.

In 1960–61, West and Robertson entered the NBA—and Robertson averaged 30.5 points as a rookie. Chamberlain led with 38.4, followed by Baylor at 34.8. The lowest-scoring team in the league was New York, and the Knicks averaged 113.7 points.

By 1961–62, a star scoring 40–50 points was not big news. Chamberlain didn't even draw much attention unless he scored over 70. That was the setting on the night Chamberlain did the unthinkable.

During the pregame warmups, Chamberlain was laughing and singing as he shot around. That's because the 7-foot-2 Chamberlain had recently cut his first and last record, "By the River," and it was blaring over the public address system. Wilt could dig it, even if everyone else was underwhelmed. There were five games left in the 1961–62 regular season, and Chamberlain's Philadelphia Warriors were securely in second place. The New York Knicks were dead last as they took the court in Hershey, Pennsylvania, on March 2, 1962. They had no way

*of guessing that Chamberlain would shoot 36-of-63 from the field
and a remarkable 28-of-32 from the foul line. Wilt also had 25 rebounds that night—a great game for most guys, but one under his
season's average.*

*He started fast with 23 points in the first quarter and was 9-for-9 on
free throws. He also made his first six jump shots as his team jumped
to a 19–3 lead. To reach the century mark, Chamberlain scored 31
points in the fourth quarter, 12-for-21 from the field and 7-for-12 from
the foul line. He played all 48 minutes in the Warriors' 169–147 win.
While Chamberlain took 63 shots, the rest of his teammates combined
for 52. Chamberlain's 63 shots and 21 in a quarter are both NBA
records. In NBA history, there have been eight games in which an NBA
player has scored at least 70, and six of those eight belong to
Chamberlain.*

WILT CHAMBERLAIN: What I like best about the 100-point game is that
there is no videotape or film of it. There is just a scratchy radio tape.
The game is shrouded in myth and mystery, and over the years people
have been able to embellish it without facts getting in the way. As I've
traveled the world, I've probably had 10,000 people tell me that they
saw my 100-point game at Madison Square Garden. Well, the game
was in Hershey and there were about 4,000 [actually 4,124] there. But
that's fine. I have memories of the game and so do they, and over
the years the memories get better. It's like your first girlfriend—the
picture you have in your head is always better than how she looked in
real life.

HARVEY POLLACK: It is a mythic game because Wilt scored exactly
100, no more, no less. And the game ended after Wilt scored his 100th
point even though there were 46 seconds left on the clock. Those things
will never happen again.

PETE D'AMBROSIO: I officiated that game with Willie Smith and there
was nothing special about it. The season was almost over. The playoff
spots had been decided. The only reason it was played was because it
was on the schedule. The last thing anyone expected was basketball
history.

HARVEY POLLACK: This was supposed to be the classic NBA nonevent.
Hardly any New York reporters were there. The biggest paper in Philadelphia—the *Inquirer*—didn't even send a reporter. I was the public

relations man for the Philadelphia Warriors and I also was covering the game for the *Inquirer*, Associated Press and United Press International. I also was keeping the stats and my son sat next to me at courtside, keeping the running play-by-play.

I remember hearing Wilt say before the game that he had been out all night with a beautiful woman. In the Hershey arena lobby, they had a pinball machine and one of those target practice machines, and Wilt said he set records on both of those.

WILT CHAMBERLAIN: I lived in New York and I was out with a friend. I mean, I got no sleep at all before that game. I was up for at least 24 hours. I drove from New York to Philly, where we caught a bus to Hershey. I tried to sleep on the bus, but I couldn't. You should have seen me on the rifle machine—I was hitting everything. I'm talking about a world record.

FRANK MCGUIRE: Eddie Donovan was the coach of the Knicks and he is a special friend of mine. I had said earlier in the season, "Just you wait, Wilt is going to get 100 one of these nights." But that was because Wilt was the greatest offensive force this game has ever seen. Sixty, 70 points was common for him. We did not set out to get Wilt the 100.

TOM MESCHERY: Hershey had one of those dreary, old, dungeonlike arenas with overlapping rafters. Because the Hershey Company was there, the whole town smelled like fresh chocolate. We had trained in Hershey, so we were acquainted with the gym. Right away, I knew Wilt was in for a big night because he was making all of his free throws.

WILT CHAMBERLAIN: To me, the 100-point game was inevitable that season. I was averaging 50 points. I had 78 in a game [three months earlier]. In high school, I once scored 90 [in 32 minutes] and shot 36-for-41. I always scored a lot, so I figured that 100 would come. But I certainly did not decide to go for it that night in Hershey. Even by halftime, I had 41 and it wasn't that big a deal. I had scored 40 in a half before.

AL ATTLES: Wilt just kept scoring. He had 69 after three quarters. Dave Zinkoff was doing the PA and after every basket Wilt scored in the fourth quarter, he'd announce, "That's 82 for Wilt." So everyone in the game knew the situation and it just evolved to the point where we wanted Wilt to score 100.

WILT CHAMBERLAIN: When I got into the 80s, I heard the fans yelling for 100. I thought, "Man, these people are tough. Eighty isn't good enough. I'm tired. I've got 80 points and no one has ever scored 80." At one point, I said to Al Attles, "I got 80, what's the difference between 80 and 100?" But the guys kept feeding me the ball.

TOM MESCHERY: By the fourth quarter, the Knicks were waiting until the 24-second clock was about to expire before they shot. When we had the ball, they were fouling everyone except Wilt so he wouldn't get 100. So we would take the ball out-of-bounds and throw high lobs directly to Wilt near the basket. When Wilt wanted the ball, he was big enough and strong enough to go get it. Guys were hanging on his back, and he was still catching the pass and scoring. I knew it was going to happen when with about five minutes left Wilt dunked one and nearly threw two New York players into the basket with the ball, and Dave Zinkoff yelled over the PA, "Dipper Dunk for 86!"

RICHIE GUERIN: They can complain about us fouling people, but Frank McGuire sent some subs into the game and they were fouling us immediately to get the ball back and give Wilt more chances.

PETE D'AMBROSIO: The game was a real pain in the neck to call. The last three minutes of game time took about 20 minutes. The Knicks were jumping on guys just to keep the ball away from Wilt. Then New York would get the ball, and Philly would foul.

AL ATTLES: Frank McGuire told Wilt, "You bring the ball up the court." Wilt liked to think he could play guard, so he loved it. But Frank did that down the stretch so that if New York wanted to foul someone, it had to be Wilt.

HARVEY POLLACK: Darrall Imhoff started at center against Wilt, but he fouled out and played only about half the game. By the end of the game, all of their big men had fouled out.

[Chamberlain was guarded by Cleveland Buckner, who was listed as 6-foot-9 but was closer to 6-foot-7. Chamberlain scored his 98th point with 1:19 left.]

MARV ALBERT: The irony is that Darrall Imhoff's strength as a player was his defense, but he is forever the butt of the joke that "Here's the guy who held Wilt to 100 points," even though he wasn't on the court when it happened.

HARVEY POLLACK: There are several fascinating things about the end of this game. First, the few reporters who were there disagree on how the final basket was scored. Some say it was a dunk, others say it was a tip-in.

PETE D'AMBROSIO: I was looking right at the play, and I don't remember what happened.

WILT CHAMBERLAIN: I keep trying to remember, but I can't. I do know that they built a fort around me when I caught the ball. It seemed like about 30 of my 36 field goals were on fadeaway jumpers, because that was all I could take. What does stick in my mind was that I made 25 of my first 26 free throws, then I missed two.

HARVEY POLLACK: Here is exactly what happened for the 100th point. Wilt took a shot and missed. It rebounded out to Joe Ruklick. Even this has been disputed, because the NBA said it was Paul Arizin, but I called them and they changed it.

Ruklick got the ball, passed it to Wilt and Wilt made a layup, not a dunk as some people reported.

The ball went through the rim with 46 seconds left, the fans rushed on the court and the game ended right there.

FRANK MCGUIRE: After he scored 100, Wilt was trying to get off the court and there were four little kids hanging on to his shoulders and waist. It was as if he were giving them a piggyback ride.

AL ATTLES: After the game, Wilt was in the dressing room and he wasn't celebrating like the rest of us.

I said, "Wilt, what's the matter."

He said, "I never thought I'd take 60 shots in a game."

I said, "But you made 36—that's better than 50 percent."

He said, "But Al—63 shots, Al."

Then he just shook his head.

FRANK McGUIRE: I do think we were more excited about the game than Wilt was. I do recall him sitting in that little locker room—it was nothing more than a high school dressing room with one long wooden bench in the middle where everyone sat. Wilt was holding the stat sheet, sweat pouring off his face, just staring at it.

HARVEY POLLACK: The one famous picture from that game is Wilt in the dressing room holding up a little sign that said "100." The photographers wanted something special and I just grabbed a piece of paper, wrote 100 on it, Wilt held it up and it went all over the country.

WILT CHAMBERLAIN: The 100-point game will never be as important to me as it is to some other people. That's because I'm embarrassed by it. After I got into the 80s, I pushed for 100 and it destroyed the game because I took shots that I normally never would. I was not real fluid. I mean, 63 shots? You take that many shots on the playground and no one ever wants you on their team again. I never considered myself a gunner. I led leagues in scoring because I also led them in field goal percentage. I've had many better games than this one, games where I scored 50–60 and shot 75 percent.

AL ATTLES: Wilt gave me the ball that he scored the 100th point with, even though some kid claimed to have run off with it.

WILT CHAMBERLAIN: I wanted Al to have that ball because he's a great friend and he spent his whole career sacrificing to make other guys better players.

RICHIE GUERIN: I'm not saying this to take anything away from Wilt. I think Wilt Chamberlain is the best big man to play the game—ever. I am convinced that he can go out there today at 50-some years old and be better than most of the guys starting now.

But that game was not played as it should have been played. The second half was a travesty. I don't care what the Philly people say, I'm convinced that during the half they decided to get Wilt 100. He took nearly every shot. In the normal flow, Wilt would have scored 80–85 points, which is mind-boggling when you think about it. I'm sorry, this may be basketball history but I always felt very bad about that game. I got so sick of it that I intentionally fouled out.

ALEX HANNUM: I think the only guy who feels a stigma from that game is Richie Guerin. He is a combative ex-marine who never took any crap from anybody, and having Wilt score 100 against his team had to hurt. But there was no stigma against him or the Knicks. The rest of us in the league knew that Wilt was going to score 100; it just happened that night.

PETE D'AMBROSIO: Wilt was such a phenom that we took it for granted. When he scored 100, it was mentioned on the news and in the papers, but it wasn't the kind of huge event that it would be today. That's because we weren't able to put Wilt into context like we can now.

WILT CHAMBERLAIN: I have to admit that as the years have passed, I like the 100-point game more than I did at the time. To me, averaging 50 points in a season or being the only center in NBA history to lead the league in assists are more indicative of the kind of player I was. But the 100-point night . . . The good thing is that everyone has their stories and I can't disagree with many of them because I don't even know how I scored the last basket. It has reached fabled proportion, almost like a Paul Bunyan story, and it's nice to be a part of a fable.

The Year Wilt Averaged 50

In 1961–62, Wilt Chamberlain did more than score 100 points in a game. He averaged 50.4 for the season. He set an NBA record for field goals attempted and made, averaging 38 shots per game, making 20. He became—along with Walt Bellamy—the first NBA player to shoot 50 percent from the field in a season. He even shot a career-high 61 percent from the foul line. He also had games of 78, 73, 67 (twice) and 65 points. In an eight-day stretch in January, he scored exactly 62 points three times. He averaged 48.5 minutes per game and led the league with 25.7 rebounds per game. His Philadelphia Warriors were 49–31 and lost in seven games to Boston in the Eastern Conference Finals. That season, Chamberlain played every second of every game except when he was ejected with 8:33 left in one contest by official Norm Drucker. And yet, after the season Chamberlain was criticized. As Leonard Koppett wrote, "He was castigated for shooting too much, for being selfish and paradoxically, for not making more use of his size by going to the basket. . . . He was blamed for playing all 48 minutes, and then blamed for loafing while he did it. . . . How could he be scoring too much and still loafing? . . . What Wilt did was exactly what his employer wanted." It was Chamberlain's third season. He averaged 37.6 and 38.4 in his first two years under coach Neil Johnston. Then Warriors owner Eddie Gottlieb hired Frank McGuire.

WILT CHAMBERLAIN: Early in my career it was made very clear to me, "Wilt, you've got to score a lot of points." Eddie Gottlieb believed it was good for his franchise and for the league for me to set records. That was nothing new to me—I had always carried my teams. I averaged close to 50 a game in school, and those were 32-minute games and I usually played only 28. I played against pros and semipros in the summer and it was not unusual for me to come home and say, "I scored 75."

But in my first two years, I was coached by Neil Johnston, who had been the Warriors center before me. I don't mean to say anything disparaging about Neil Johnston, but he was a guy Eddie Gottlieb felt sorry for and he knew that his days as a center were over, so he gave him a job coaching the team. This man knew nothing about basketball or how to deal with a superstar coming into the league. He had no sympathy for me because I used to kick his butt on the playgrounds in Philly and because I now was playing his old position. Eddie Gottlieb later admitted to me that Neil Johnston as a coach was a mistake.

That changed in my third year when Frank McGuire came in. He was a unique man, not just because he allowed me to score 50 points a game. Rather, he was very sensitive to this young black man and all things that surrounded me. He never told me to score points, he let it happen in the natural flow of the game. He did tell the team, "Gentlemen, if Wilt has to score 50 a game for us to win and if he can do it, then gentlemen, that is how it will be."

FRANK McGUIRE: I first coached against Wilt in the 1957 NCAA championship game when my North Carolina team beat Kansas. During my pregame talk, I never even mentioned the Kansas team, I just talked about how we'd defense Wilt. I challenged my players, "Are you afraid of Chamberlain?" I had Tommy Kearns—who was a foot shorter—jump center against Wilt. We put five guys on him and he still scored 26 points, but we won. But that wasn't Wilt's fault.

From that day, I had been intrigued with Chamberlain. I had read that he was uncoachable and a bad guy, but I refused to believe that. He didn't strike me that way. I was at North Carolina for 10 years when Eddie Gottlieb talked to me about the Warriors job. I looked at films of Wilt and the more I saw, the more I wanted to coach him. Even though I had been very comfortable at North Carolina, I couldn't resist the temptation of working with Wilt.

WILT CHAMBERLAIN: The first thing Frank did after he got the job was sit down and talk to me, man-to-man. No coach had ever treated me that way before.

FRANK McGUIRE: During our first day of training camp in Hershey, I said, "Wilt, how long do you want to play?"
   He said, "Forever."
   I said, "I mean in the game."
   He said, "Coach, when you take me out, I sit on the bench and I look at you. I don't get any rebounds. I don't get any points. You keep me out for three minutes, then put me back in and it takes me about five minutes to get loose again—so you lose eight minutes."
   I asked, "Can you play all the time?"
   He said, "That's what I want to do."
   I never took him out of the game. The only time he didn't play was one game where he had a fight and was ejected. He got hit in the mouth more than any player I'd ever seen, but he wouldn't come out for a second.
   People told me that he wasn't tough enough. My God, steamrollers like Wayne Embry . . . he put a kneecap into Wilt's crotch to push him out of there. In fact, I ran on the court and screamed at the officials, "You can't let Embry do that!"
   They told me, "If we let Wilt stand under the basket, he'll ruin the game."
   I said, "But he's getting killed out there."
   Through it all, he never complained.

WILT CHAMBERLAIN: Frank stood up for me. If he was my coach in my first two years, the league would not have been allowed to push around Wilt Chamberlain like it did. But I had a weak coach in the beginning, and that set the tone, so I decided not to complain about the pounding I took.

TOM GOLA: Frank didn't try to control Wilt. Some of Wilt's early coaches, they kept telling him what to do. But Wilt thought he knew more about basketball than they did. By not telling Wilt things all the time, when Frank did talk to Wilt, Wilt listened.

FRANK MCGUIRE: I had meetings with each of the players. We talked about their careers and about the team. I said that Wilt was the most dominant force in basketball history and I wanted him to get the ball two-thirds of the time. Guy Rodgers said to me, "Coach, whatever you say is fine, but will you sit in with us when we go to talk contract with Eddie Gottlieb?" One of the problems back then was that guys were paid according to their scoring averages. But that also is why I respected the players—they ran the offense I wanted.

TOM MESCHERY: Frank never wavered from his plan to center the offense around Wilt. He never said, "We've got to get away from Wilt for a while and try this." Our second option was Paul Arizin—he'd take a jump shot off the break. So that was our offense, Arizin on the break or set it up and work the ball to Wilt.

HOT ROD HUNDLEY: When Wilt was a kid, he shot the ball every time he got it. The Philly offense was throw the ball to Wilt and watch him. Once, I stopped in the Warriors' dressing room before the game and I saw Tom Gola throwing the ball against the wall.

I asked, "What are you doing?"

Gola said, "Practicing our offense—throw the ball to Wilt and then stand there."

Actually, Tom Gola and Wilt have always been great friends and Tommy was just messing around when he told me that. Back then, Wilt was almost too good. He scored about every time he shot it. He really pounded the boards and when he got an offensive rebound, people just cleared out and gave him the dunk. Why try to block it and have him break your arm?

TOM GOLA: I first played with Wilt when I was in college and he was a 6-foot-8 junior high kid. He held his own with all these hotshot players from Philly, even at 13 years old. If Wilt had come into the NBA and not scored 50 a night, he would have been booed. Those were the kinds of expectations he faced—not just from the fans, but the other players. No other player ever had to deal with the kind of pressures that Wilt did. He was expected to be perfect.

EARL STROM: There were games when Wilt would block a shot, Tommy Gola would pick up the loose ball and instead of taking it down the court on the fast break, he'd hold it.

Wilt said, "Tommy, somebody has to help me score."

Tommy said, "Hey, big fella, you got the hot hand, we're working it to you."

AL ATTLES: I probably played 500 games with Wilt and never once did I hear him say, "Get me the ball." When you have a talent on your team like that, no one has to say a word, you know where to throw it. That season, Arizin still scored his 22. Gola got his 14. Tom Meschery and I were in double figures. We averaged 125 points a game, so other guys got their shots. But the temptation always was to get Wilt the ball and get out of the way.

WILT CHAMBERLAIN: Along with Frank McGuire, the other reason I averaged 50 that year was Guy Rodgers. He was as good a ballhandler and passer as anyone, and that includes Bob Cousy.

PAT WILLIAMS: As a kid, I went to a lot of Warriors games. With Rodgers and Wilt, you had the ultimate passer and the ultimate scorer. Guy was about 6-foot-1 and built like Kevin Johnson. He was an imaginative passer in the middle of the fast break with a flair for theatrics— some of his passes took your breath away. Was he the best point guard in the league? No, but I'm sure Wilt would say he was because Guy set him up for about 8,000 stuffs.

TOM MESCHERY: Guy had a million ways of getting the ball to Wilt. There was a part of Guy that was very insecure. He considered himself an elite player, but he had some weaknesses that he didn't like to admit. Guy was not much of an outside shooter and not a good defender. He had Al Attles next to him all those years, saving his butt in the backcourt on defense. But on the fast break and getting the ball to Wilt, no one was any better.

CHICK HEARN: In the early 1960s, guys were scoring huge numbers. The most entertaining game I've ever broadcast was December 8, 1961, when Wilt scored 78 and Elgin Baylor had 63. The Warriors jumped to a 15–0 lead in Philadelphia before about 4,000 fans. But the Lakers came back and it turned into one of the greatest games ever—triple overtime, and the Lakers won 151–147. I remember all the numbers—

Wilt scored 78 on 31-for-62 from the field and he had 43 rebounds. I said 43 rebounds, in case you missed it. Elgin had 63 points and he had 31 rebounds, and Elgin was only 6-foot-5 for God's sake. It was a tremendous shootout between two superstars. This also was one of those games that haunted Wilt. People would say, "Yes, he scored 78, but Wilt's team lost." Going into the game, Elgin had the NBA scoring record with 71, so Wilt broke it. But afterward, I was talking to Elgin about the record. He took a puff on his cigarette and said, "Hey, don't worry about it. The big fella is going to get 100 one night real soon."

WILT CHAMBERLAIN: I just wish that I could have played for more than one year for Frank McGuire. He and Alex Hannum were my favorite coaches.

TOM GOLA: Frank was just not prepared for the life of the NBA. His basketball background was college, and in our first meeting he gave a pep talk about no smoking and no drinking.

After, Paul Arizin asked me, "What does he mean, no drinking?"

Wilt didn't drink. But Arizin, Meschery, myself and most of the other guys did. I told Arizin that he was the team captain, so he should go talk to Frank. I guess they had a meeting of the minds, because Frank came back and said he didn't want guys buying beer in the lobby of the arena where kids would see it. As for smoking, the guys toed the line—they were closet smokers, lighting up in the back of the airplane when Frank wasn't around. But Frank also was smart enough not to make an issue of it.

Frank was a first-class guy. He wore starched, white shirts, silk ties and nice jackets. He lived at the Cherry Hill Inn, which was very exclusive. His favorite drink was a J&B Mist.

FRANK MCGUIRE: I was amazed at how small-time the NBA was, compared to college. On the road, it was just me and the players.

I asked Eddie Gottlieb, "No trainer travels? Who is going to tape the ankles?"

Eddie said, "Tell the other team's trainer to do it, and give him two dollars."

I said, "Two bucks? We paid the kids who worked in our dressing room at North Carolina more than that. I tipped the trainer $10." Once, we were on the road for two weeks and ran out of tape. Wilt was making a hundred grand and we had no tape for his ankles. I went to the Syracuse trainer for some, but he wouldn't give it to us.

AL ATTLES: Frank couldn't believe that the players had to wash their own uniforms and jocks in the sinks of our hotel rooms after games.

We had an exhibition game in Omaha and they sent an old school bus to pick us up. Everybody got on the bus, but Frank just stood there, staring at the bus. When he got on, he wouldn't sit down because he said the seats would mess up his pants.

The next morning, Guy Rodgers and I saw him in the hotel lobby and Frank said, "Boys, you almost lost your coach. I called Eddie Gottlieb and tried to quit, but he talked me out of it."

FRANK McGUIRE: I had over $10,000 in expense money and gate receipts with me during the exhibition season. I threw that in a bag with all the players' wallets and watches. There was no security in the dressing rooms, so during the games I put everything in that bag—probably $15,000—and put the bag under my chair on the bench, figuring no one would steal it out from under me.

When we traveled, I split up some of the money with the players, so if I got mugged I'd only lose half of it.

MARTY BLAKE: When Frank called Gottlieb to say he quit, he told Eddie, "I'm carrying around $15,000. I've got two suitcases full of dirty clothes. I've got no trainer. We played in Winston-Salem last night and tonight we're in Portland, Oregon. I quit."

Eddie said that he'd send someone to meet the team in Portland.

When the team arrived, Frank saw a guy who said he was from the Warriors. As they took a cab from the airport to the hotel, Frank was telling the guy, "Can you tape the guys' ankles in your room, or do you want to do it at the arena?"

The guy said, "Frank, my name is Vince Miller. I'm a friend of Wilt's. I was in Eddie's office when you called and Eddie sent me out to see you guys. But I can't tape any ankles."

JERRY GROSS: I was broadcasting an exhibition game between St. Louis and Philly in some jerkwater town. The game was over and both teams shared the same dressing room. Suddenly, we heard all this swearing and yelling. Two Hawks players—Johnny Green and Richie Guerin—were about ready to beat the hell out of each other in the shower.

Frank said, "Jeez, I've never seen anything like that—and those guys are on the same team."

AL ATTLES: Frank's son, Frank Jr., had cerebral palsy and he was living in North Carolina. Frank was very close to his son and worried about him a lot. There were times when Frank would tell us, "Look, I've got to go home and see Frank Jr. I want you guys to have practice. Just do the things we normally do." Wilt and everyone would show up, we'd scrimmage and guys didn't mess around. We had a lot of respect for Frank. We won 49 games—a lot for the Warriors.

[Their 49 regular-season wins are the third-best total in the history of the Warriors franchise starting in 1946 in Philadelphia and continuing today in Golden State.]

FRANK McGUIRE: In the playoffs, we took Boston to seven games and lost when Mendy Rudolph called a very questionable goaltending on Wilt. We got beat 109–107 and had a chance to win because we caught Boston on a bad day.

Wilt was so great. He shook my hand after that game and told me how much he appreciated my coaching.

I would have come back for a second season, but Eddie Gottlieb sold the Warriors to San Francisco and I was not about to move to the West Coast and be that far away from Frank Jr., so I quit and went back to coaching in college. But in that one year, I'm very proud to have been the coach when Wilt averaged 50 and scored 100 in a game. I wish I could have coached him for his whole career.

Foul Line Blues

Wilt Chamberlain says he shot 80 percent from the foul line in high school. The stats say he was a 62 percent free throw shooter in college, 58 percent as an NBA rookie and a career-best 61 percent in 1961–62. For his pro career, he was a 51 percent free throw shooter and shot under 50 percent in six different seasons, his worst being 38 percent in 1967–68. In the NBA playoffs, he made only 46 percent. Yet he holds the NBA record for most free throws made in a game (28), which happened the night he scored 100. A Philadelphia Inquirer story of March 18, 1991, listed six reasons given by Chamberlain over the years for his poor free throw shooting: 1. Arthritic knees. 2. Too much English on his shot. 3. Too tall, which ruins his shooting arch. 4. Lifting weights made him too strong. 5. His hands are too big. 6. It's all in his head.

DOLPH SCHAYES: Wilt will say he's the greatest at everything—basketball, bowling, pinball, you name it. But not foul shooting, and he desperately wanted to be a good free throw shooter. The two of us would go to the gym by ourselves and practice, shooting 100 free throws. That's a lot in one set. He'd make 80–85 of them. But in the games, he'd tighten up, shoot 1-for-10, 3-for-11. He'd line the ball off the rim. He worked so hard and got nothing out of it.

WILT CHAMBERLAIN: I always believed I was a good free throw shooter in high school. Now I know I was because a guy gave me a scrapbook with clippings from my days at Overbrook. They'd write, "And then they started to foul Chamberlain, which was a mistake." I looked at the box scores and saw games where I was 7-for-8, 11-for-12. I asked myself, "What the hell ever happened to those days?"

ALEX HANNUM: When we won the title in 1967, Wilt shot 44 percent at the line. He had reached the point where the last place in the world he wanted to be was at the foul line. He'd tell me what a great free throw shooter he was in high school. He'd practice his free throws all the time and probably shoot 75 percent. Then the games would come and it would be so embarrassing for him. There was nothing anyone could do. I coached Dolph Schayes and Rick Barry when they shot 90 percent, and I coached Wilt when he shot 38 percent in 1968. Dolph worked with Wilt. Everyone did.

FRANK McGUIRE: The best year Wilt had at the line was 61 percent in our one season together. I never mentioned free throws to him. I figured talking about it would make it worse. About a month into the season, Wilt sat next to me one day and said, "Coach, how come you never say anything about my foul shooting?"

I said, "I'm not a magician. You missed over 500 last year. I know you work at it."

He said, "But what do you think I should do?"

I said, "Well, I'd try underhanded, because it gives you a softer shot."

He shot underhanded the rest of that season, but then he got away from it.

AL ATTLES: People loved to see Wilt at the foul line, because it was something he couldn't do. Wilt could score 100 in a game, he could get 50 rebounds, he could block shots, but he couldn't make a free throw. Fans would say, "Even I can make a free throw and the big fella can't do it."

People had theories. One guy said Wilt's hands were too big. Well, what was he supposed to do? Make his hands smaller? Get a bigger ball?

He shot with two hands, with one hand, underhanded. It was said he was too close to the basket, so he stood about three feet behind the foul line. He tried shooting from off to the side.

ALEX HANNUM: Wilt had an excellent fadeaway jumper from the side, an 18-footer off the board. I said, "Wilt, take your fadeaway from the foul line. It's your best shot."

Wilt would say, "Hannum, I can't do crazy stuff like that."

He was afraid that people would laugh at him.

LARRY COSTELLO: The fans would start yelling when Wilt went to the line. He'd grab the ball and shoot it quick, almost as if he wanted to miss the shot and get it over with so he could get away from the free throw line.

EARL STROM: Wilt said, "Everybody tells me that free throw shooting is nothing but concentration. Damn it, I concentrate more at the line than anywhere else and I still miss."

But I'd watch him and you could see Wilt holding the ball and thinking to himself, "I'm gonna miss . . . I'm gonna miss."

People would say, why would a big guy like Wilt take a fadeaway jumper? That's easy—if he faded away from the defense, then he wouldn't get fouled.

Once, I handed him the ball and right in the middle of the game he said, "Earl, what am I doing? Why can't I make free throws?"

NATE THURMOND: Wilt wanted to be the greatest basketball player ever. That's why he developed the fadeaway. It was a difficult, highly skilled shot. But the free throws . . . that bothered him. And sportswriters and fans dwelled on it, which just made it worse because it went right to heart of Wilt's pride.

WILT CHAMBERLAIN: After a while, it didn't matter how much I practiced, how I shot, I wasn't going to shoot well. It was all mental. In practice, I'd make 80 percent. Then the games would come . . .

BOB FERRY: Wilt's free throw shooting led to some funny moments. At the end of the game, I'd tell Wilt, "The minute you touch the ball, I'm gonna foul you." That would piss him off.

There were games where I'd try to foul him even when he didn't have the ball. I'd go after him and he'd run away as if we were playing tag. When I finally did foul him, I'd say, "Wilt, you're gonna miss."

That really pissed him off. Then he'd go to the line, miss the shot and get even madder.

Cliff Hagan and a lot of other players used stickum on their hands to get a better grip on the ball. Wilt claimed that was why he missed foul shots—the ball was too sticky. The league had a rule against stickum. So we started to hide the stuff on the side of our shoes, on our shorts. We'd go to the line, rub the side of our shoes, and Wilt would yell to the officials, "Those guys are putting stickum on the ball."

The officials would check us and find nothing. Half the time, we didn't have anything. We just acted like we did to annoy Wilt.

WILT CHAMBERLAIN: Bad News Barnes was with Baltimore and he was a big, rough-and-tumble guy, about 6-foot-9. We were in a close playoff game with them and Barnes's coach told him, "Every time Wilt gets the ball, foul him."

I knew what was going on, so I set up about 35 feet from the basket. I caught a pass and Barnes came running at me. I put the ball down on the floor and said, "You put your hands on me just once and I'm gonna knock you on your ass."

He stopped like he ran into a wall. I picked up the ball and passed off.

ALEX HANNUM: In Johnny Kerr's first year coaching the Bulls, he ordered his team to foul Wilt every time in the fourth quarter, and the game became a travesty with Wilt running around and two Bulls chasing him even though the ball was nowhere around. Finally, I took Wilt out for the last few minutes. He was so damn tired from running from those guys just so he wouldn't get fouled.

ROD THORN: Wilt was the reason they put in a rule to stop players from intentionally fouling away from the ball. Everyone was just grabbing Wilt and making the game last forever.

RICK BARRY: Wilt would have shot 75 percent from the line if he had stuck with shooting underhanded and learned the proper technique. But he experimented so much that he never had a feel for how he wanted to shoot free throws. Can you imagine the records he would have set if he'd shot 75 percent from the foul line?

[If Wilt had made 75 percent, he would have averaged three more points per game—33 instead of 30 for his career. The season when he averaged 50 points, it would have been 54.]

RUDY LARUSSO: A few years ago, Wilt and I were watching a game and James Donaldson went to the line. He was a 7-footer who shot 70 percent.

I said, "It seems like big guys today are better free throw shooters than we were."

Wilt said, "Oh, man, don't you know why? They didn't have to shoot in those dinky gyms like we did. Our gyms were dark, the rims were tight, the floor sagged, the balls were lopsided." He had a 10-minute litany of foul shooting problems from 30 years ago.

WILT CHAMBERLAIN: The only ones who didn't mention free throw shooting to me were my teammates. Not Jerry West, not Billy Cunningham, no one. They saw me make them in practice and they knew it was a damn mental thing with me. I give them credit for not saying a thing, because it was bad enough just with the things going on in my own head.

But let's talk about one thing that no one ever remembers. I may have missed a lot of foul shots, but by me going to the line so much, that meant my team got into the penalty situation faster and my teammates got to shoot more free throws.

Besides, if I did make 75 percent, then what would people have had to talk about?

When Wilt Did Get Mad . . .

JOHN HAVLICEK: In my rookie year, Wilt was involved in a pick-and-roll play and suddenly Bill Russell was off Wilt and guarding someone else, and I had Chamberlain. Wilt took me down near the basket and caught a pass. Being the bright kid out of Ohio State I thought I was, I figured, "No problem. Wilt isn't a good foul shooter. I'll grab him." Well, Wilt didn't like being held. I reached around from behind and held both of his arms. He wasn't going to let some rookie stop him, so Wilt took the ball—and me—up. He dunked the ball and I hung there on his arms, both of my feet off the ground and hanging on to Wilt's arms for dear life until he put me down. Then Wilt went to the line and made the free throw for the 3-point play.

JOE GUSHUE: Havlicek shouldn't feel bad. I saw Russell grab Wilt from behind—riding him piggyback—and Wilt still dunked the ball.

BILLY CUNNINGHAM: The greatest play I've ever seen was one of the last games of the 1966–67 season and we were playing Baltimore. We [Philadelphia] were going for the best record in NBA history. There was a play earlier in the game where Gus Johnson had dunked one over Wilt. Gus was a very strong player. I weighed 220 pounds, and with one hand Gus could push me out of the lane. The man was a physical specimen [6-foot-6, 230 pounds], all muscle. He loved to dunk and was a very colorful player. When he slammed it on Wilt, he really threw it down, and you could tell that Wilt didn't like it one bit.

Later in the game, Gus was out on the fast break, and the only man between him and the basket was Wilt. He was going to dunk on Wilt—again. Gus cupped the ball and took off—he had a perfect angle for a slam. Wilt went up and with one hand he grabbed the ball—cleanly! Then he took the ball and shoved it right back into Gus, drilling Gus into the floor with the basketball.

Gus was flattened and they carried him out. It turned out that Gus Johnson was the only player in NBA history to suffer a dislocated shoulder from a blocked shot.

JOE GUSHUE: I had that game where Wilt dislocated Johnson's shoulder. To put it in today's context, Gus Johnson was like Charles Barkley. He was flat on the court, his eyes had that look of, "Did what I think just happened really happen?"

BILLY CUNNINGHAM: Luke Jackson was 6-foot-10, 275 pounds and considered one of the strongest men in the NBA. We set up an arm wrestling contest between Luke and Wilt. The first time, it was no contest. Wilt just slammed Luke's arm down. So Wilt decided to give Luke an advantage. Wilt started with his own arm halfway down, at a 45-degree angle. Wilt said, "Ready?"

Luke grunted.

Then Wilt slammed Luke's arm to the table.

JOHNNY KERR: Once Wilt got upset with me and dunked the ball so hard that it went through the rim with such force that it broke my toe as it hit the floor.

BILLY CUNNINGHAM: Johnny was embarrassed to let everyone know that he got a broken toe from one of Wilt's dunks, so he went down to the other end of the court, acted as if he tripped, grabbed his foot and went out of the game.

TOM HEINSOHN: In the 1960 playoffs—Wilt's rookie year—Red Auerbach devised a play where I was to get in Wilt's way whenever Wilt's team scored a basket. For example, a Philly player would make a foul shot and when Wilt turned to get back on defense, I was to run in front of him, to delay him so Russell could get down to the other end of the court and get an open layup. That's because we ran fast breaks off free throws, something you never see today. So Russell was scoring at the other end of the court while Wilt was trying to run around me. Then Wilt caught on and said, "You do that again and I'll knock you on your ass."

I said, "We'll talk about this later at lunch."

I didn't want to get him mad, but I also knew that Red would be all over my ass if I didn't keep getting in Wilt's way. After the next free throw, I stepped in front of him and Wilt shoved me—I must have slid 20 feet. I got up to fight and Wilt was coming after me, he had his arm cocked to punch me. Just as he swung, Tom Gola stepped between us as a peacemaker. But it was too late. Wilt couldn't pull the punch and what he did was belt Gola in the head. Gola staggered away, Wilt was holding his right hand and I'm hitting Wilt with a few punches. Wilt acted like he didn't even know I was there, he just held his hand. It turned out that he had broken it. Gola was dazed, but all right.

RUDY LARUSSO: Larry Foust was not about to get near Wilt's dunk. Wilt had this windup dunk, where he'd sort of crouch to get ready for his dunk. On the PA, Dave Zinkoff would yell, "A . . . Dip . . . per . . . er . . . er . . . Dunk!" When Foust heard Zinkoff say, "Dipper," he'd turn and run down to the other end of the court, giving Wilt all the room he wanted.

TOM MESCHERY: Most of Wilt's dunks weren't scary. He would finger-roll the ball in, just a little flick of the wrist and the ball gently dropped through the rim. But there was a time when Gene Wiley thought he was going to block one of Wilt's dunks. He got a hand on the ball, and Wilt dunked the ball and Wiley's wrist into the rim. No one could figure out how Wiley didn't end up with a broken wrist.

JOE GUSHUE: There was a young player named Paul Hogue who put his hand above and in front of the rim as Wilt went for a dunk. All Wilt had to do was slam it, and the kid's hand would be in a cast. Instead, Wilt used his left hand to brush the kid's hand away and then Wilt dunked the ball with his right.

FRANK McGUIRE: Wilt just looked at that kid as if to say, "Who are you kidding? You could lose your arm trying to block one of my dunks."

ALEX HANNUM: Wilt is the most dominant force this game has ever known. When I coached against him, I'd put four guys on him at the end of the game. My guys would beat the hell out of him, and Wilt would get frustrated. While he was an aggressive player, he certainly took a lot more of a pounding than he gave out. Above all, Wilt was always a gentleman. Later, I coached him and I said, "Wilt, these guys are bashing you, holding your arms and trying to hurt you. Just once, all you have to do is smash the ball down their throat and break their wrists. Just once, that's all it would take and they would back off." But he wouldn't do it. He knew his own strength and he knew how dangerous he could be. But in those rare instances when he got mad, it was a truly frightening sight.

NORM DRUCKER: It wasn't just that Wilt worried about hurting someone. I also believe he was sometimes embarrassed by his own strength. That was why he didn't like to dunk the ball hard—he'd rather take his fallaway jumper or his finger roll. He didn't want to be known as a seven-foot giant, but as a basketball player with basketball skills.

LEONARD KOPPETT: People tried to diminish what Wilt accomplished by saying he was so big, so he should score 50 a night. But that was taking away from his ability and his dignity, and I think that also was why he didn't dunk as often as you'd have thought he would.

KENNY HUDSON: Wilt liked the game of basketball, not fights. When things got rough on the court, he was the peacemaker, the guy who stepped in the middle and said, "That's enough." When Wilt said, "That's enough," that was more than enough.

EARL STROM: The one time Wilt really punched someone was in the 1964 Finals. Clyde Lovellette was at the end of his career and playing backup center for Boston. Wilt was with San Francisco and there were only a few minutes left in the game. The game was at Boston and the Celtics were way ahead, ready to win the title. Red pulled Russell and sent in Lovellette, who thought he was going to put on a show for the Boston fans. Clyde was bumping Wilt, throwing some elbows.

Wilt said, "Look, Clyde, the game is over. You guys are the champs. We just want to get out of here. So cut that crap out or I'll knock you out."

Lovellette never saw Wilt hit anybody, so he figured Wilt wouldn't do it. With about 25 seconds left, Wilt caught a pass in the pivot and Clyde stuck him with an elbow. Wilt turned, put the ball on the floor, then reared back and punched Lovellette in the jaw. Clyde went down in sections, he was out cold.

NORM DRUCKER: Clyde was about 6-foot-11 and at that stage was carrying close to 290 pounds, mostly around his middle. He was always a bit of a clown and he clearly provoked Wilt. Even after he was down, he started to get up and George Lee yelled from the Warriors bench, "Clyde, take the 8-count, don't get up."

EARL STROM: The Boston players came onto the court, but none of them were going near Wilt. Red yelled to me, "I want Wilt out of the game."

I said, "Red, get this stiff [Lovellette] out of here so we can finish the game."

Red said, "We're not going to finish the game until you throw Wilt out. You saw him throw the punch."

It went on and on. Finally, Wilt came over, touched Red on the shoulder and said, "Red, if you don't shut up, I'm going to put you down there with Clyde."

Then Red looked up at Wilt and said, "Oh yeah, why don't you pick on somebody your own size?"

NORM DRUCKER: We refused to throw Wilt out. We just called a technical and finished the game.

EARL LLOYD: I think of Wilt's strength and I remember how guys would beat on him, pull his pants, and he just took it. The fact that Wilt was so even-tempered made you believe in the Lord. If he had been mean, the league would have had to take up a collection for protection money.

Wilt's Bodyguard:
As If He Needed One

Al Attles was a 6-foot-1, 180-pound guard who played 11 years, all with the Warriors—the first two when the team was in Philadelphia, and then when they moved to the Bay Area. He never averaged more than 11 points, he never made an All-Star team, yet his number has been retired by Golden State. Obviously, there was more to Al Attles than numbers.

ALEX HANNUM: We called Al the Destroyer. He wasn't big and he is one of the friendliest people in the world. But when something would set him off, it was frightening. The most scary fight I've ever seen in the NBA came when Bob Ferry got into it with Al. Ferry had about 10 inches and 50 pounds on Al, but Al had Ferry down and hit him about 50 times in a minute. It was so bad that Wilt had to come to Ferry's rescue and pull Al off Ferry or he might have killed the guy.

JOHNNY KERR: For some reason I'll never understand, Bob Ferry liked to annoy Wilt. He'd do little things to piss him off. For example, Wilt always wore a rubber band around his wrist as a good luck charm. Ferry would wear one, too, just to infuriate Wilt.

BOB FERRY: I probably led the league in getting into fights with Wilt. Once in Baltimore, Wilt chased me into the stands. The reporters asked me when I thought Wilt was serious about the fight. I said, "When I ran out of the arena and crossed Howard Street."

Thank God, Wilt never punched me. It would just be pushing and shoving, then Al Attles would punch me.

WAYNE EMBRY: I'd get into a shoving match with Wilt, and here would come Al, stepping between us and wanting to take me on. Guy Rodgers also liked to start something, then take off. If you played with Al Attles, you never had to worry if you got into a fight because you knew the Destroyer would be right next to you.

AL ATTLES: I never planned to be a pro basketball player. I went to North Carolina A&T with the goal of becoming a teacher. The reason I was drafted was that a writer from the Greensboro paper, Irwin Smallwood, did a lot of nice stories about me and sent them to the wire services and to the NBA teams. A&T was a small black school— we got no national publicity. The other reason Philadelphia took me in the fifth round was that Vince Miller, Wilt's childhood friend, played on the team. Vince had Eddie Gottlieb's ear and he kept bugging Eddie to the point where Eddie probably said, "I'm just drafting Attles to shut Vince up." I wasn't even going to attend training camp—I figured I wasn't good enough—but Vince convinced me to give it one week.

I was the kind of guy that when the coach said, "Run through that wall," I bulled my neck and ran right into the wall. I wouldn't dare ask, "Why should I run through that wall?" Neil Johnston was the coach my rookie year and one day he was screaming at us. Then he said, "Okay, go run some laps."

I jumped up, took off and suddenly saw that I was the only one running. The other players just sat there. Then Neil said, "All right, practice is over."

I knew that I couldn't be like the other players. I wasn't that gifted. I was smart. I played hard and I understood why I was there.

NATE THURMOND: Al came to every game, every practice, every flight and every team function on time. He was always tenacious. Name a great guard and he'll tell you that the one guy he didn't want to see step on the court was Al Attles. Al wasn't dirty, but he was so strong and so relentless.

RON GRINKER: Oscar Robertson told me that it wasn't even close— the guy who guarded him the best was Attles.

NATE THURMOND: Al and I were teammates for six years and I never saw him start a fight. But I also never saw a fight we had that he didn't try to finish.

ZELMO BEATY: The Warriors used to think I tried to hurt Wilt. That wasn't true, but I had to push and grab and do everything I could to try and negate Wilt's overwhelming size advantage. I would never punch anyone because I was afraid of breaking my hand and not being able to play. But I did everything else I could get away with. One night in Omaha, Wilt and I were in a shoving match and Attles ran headfirst into me and knocked me into some chairs. I got up and he jumped on me again. It was the fiercest fight I'd ever been in, and I was a center and Al was a guard.

AL ATTLES: I would talk to Wilt about all the players pounding on him. Sometimes, he said he didn't notice it—he was so strong. But I also believe that there were two sets of rules. By that, I mean because Wilt was so strong, the officials let the man guarding him get away with more—almost trying to equalize the game. I also believe that Wilt just took it because he didn't want to get thrown out, and because it had always been like that with him. But I'd watch it and I'd get mad. It takes me a while to get my temper going, but when it does—look out. I'd see what the other players were doing to Wilt and what the officials were allowing, and I'd get more upset than if it were happening to me. So I jumped in there. It wasn't that Wilt couldn't defend himself. If he ever got really hot, he'd kill people, so he let things pass. But I didn't have to worry about that. I was strong for my size, but I was not about to do anything like the kind of damage Wilt would.

BOB FERRY: Against Wilt, you'd try anything you could get away with. My favorite tactic was to push him in the stomach when he went up for a shot, hoping to knock him off balance.

WAYNE EMBRY: Forget pushing. I almost gave him a karate chop to the stomach. Half the time, he acted like he never felt it.

SID BORGIA: Wilt was never one to complain to officials. Only once did he get on me. It was during a time-out, and Wilt yelled, "If I wasn't black already, I'd be nothing but black-and-blue."

RICK BARRY: Wilt seldom even threw an elbow, but once he came down with a rebound and casually threw out an elbow—he wasn't trying to hit anyone—but he nailed me and I was sure he broke my rib cage.

FRANK MCGUIRE: I told Wilt, "Get your elbows out a little bit, these guys are all over you."

Wilt said, "Coach, if I threw an elbow, I'd kill somebody."

WILT CHAMBERLAIN: I didn't think about hurting people. I thought about winning the game. When I was in the tenth grade, I played in a church league and an older guy came into the game, started throwing elbows and trying to get me to fight.

My coach called time-out and said something I'll never forget.

"Wilt, you need to remember this forever. Teams will always send players after you to provoke you, because no one can play like you. They want you to foul, to fight, to get you out of the game. If they have to sacrifice a player to get into a fight and get ejected with you, that's fine with them. That guy who gets thrown out with you isn't one-fifth the player you are. So we lose you and they lose nobody. This is just the beginning, you'll have to learn to deal with the cheap shots. Now, here's what you do. You put the ball in the basket that much harder. You score more points, get more rebounds. When he tries to score on you, you ram the ball down his throat. That is how you re-taliate."

So the fear of injuring someone was not as important as being sensible. My payback was humiliation in terms of scoring and rebounding. I couldn't do what the ordinary player would because Wilt Chamberlain was never an ordinary player.

12
THE DYNASTY

By the 1962 playoffs, the NBA had become big-league, or at least more major league than ever before. Knicks owner Ned Irish still had to live with the fact that Syracuse was in the same division as New York, and the folks in Syracuse took delight in the fact that the Nats regularly beat the Knicks. But Syracuse was the league's smallest city.

In the summer of 1957, Rochester moved to Cincinnati and Fort Wayne switched to Detroit.

In the summer of 1960, the Lakers went west from Minneapolis to Los Angeles.

In the summer of 1961, the league expanded, adding Chicago. Not as in the Chicago Bulls, but as in the Chicago Packers. (Chicago Bears fans could have told them that name would be unpopular.) They lost 62 and 55 games in their two seasons in Chicago—changing the name to Zephyrs for the second season—before moving to Baltimore as the Bullets. The Bullets, in defiance of all logic, kept Chicago's place in the Western Division for their first three years on the East Coast.

By the 1962 playoffs, the nine-team league looked like this:

Western Division: Los Angeles, Cincinnati, Detroit, St. Louis and Chicago.

Eastern Division: Boston, Philadelphia, New York and Syracuse.

The league had a network TV contract with NBC that featured a game—usually a Celtics game—every Sunday afternoon. The NBA Finals were broadcast to most of the nation, but very little attention was paid to the earlier rounds. Basketball was still the third sport behind pro baseball and pro football, but it was a solid third. The league was not about to fold and most of the franchises were staying put.

On the court, not much had changed. The Celtics were still winning titles. St. Louis had supplied the loyal opposition in 1957, 1958, 1960 and 1961.

The Lakers took over for St. Louis in 1962, losing to the Celtics in seven games.

The 1962 finals would typify the frustrations felt by the Lakers, and show why the mere mention of the name Red Auerbach could cause Lakers coach Fred Schaus to turn Celtics green with envy. The reason was simple: Auerbach had Bill Russell in the middle, while Schaus had Jim Krebs and Ray Felix.

The 1961–62 Celtics lost Bill Sharman to retirement, but in typical Celtics fashion, they had Sam Jones prepped and ready to take over at shooting guard. Jones spent four years sitting behind Sharman. He also had spent two years in the military, so he was 28 when he finally became a starter, playing next to a 33-year-old Bob Cousy.

Sharman was a great guard, but Sam Jones was greater.

Boston's bench wasn't exactly depleted. Another Hall of Famer, K.C. Jones, was the third guard. Frank Ramsey was still the consummate sixth man, and Jim Loscutoff backed up Russell. Auerbach's one notable pickup was convincing Carl Braun not to retire after having been fired as player-coach of the Knicks.

The Celtics had to fight to make the Finals. In the second round, they tangled with Philadelphia and Wilt Chamberlain, coming off his 50-point season. The Celtics and Philly went to a seventh game in Boston Garden, the Warriors even holding a 70–61 lead late in the third quarter. But the Celtics came back, and with 16 seconds left the score was 107–107. Boston had the ball, milking the clock. K.C. Jones found Sam Jones open for a medium-range jumper, Sam's shot was true with only two seconds left, and Boston won, 109–107.

In the West, the Lakers were liking L.A. just fine. They had a 54-26 record, even though Elgin Baylor could play in only 48 of the 80 games because of his military duty. Baylor still averaged 38.2 points in a season where he was never around to practice with the team. In the games where Baylor was absent because he was keeping America safe for democracy, second-year guard Jerry West stepped up and became a star. He averaged 30 points for the season. West had a career-high 63 against New York, but that went virtually unnoticed in the middle of Chamberlain's scoring barrages.

The Lakers played at the new L.A. Sports Arena on the campus of Southern California. Doris Day was the Dyan Cannon of the early Lakers, a star who was a regular at courtside.

As the playoffs came, Schaus had Baylor on leave and starting at one forward. The blue-collar Rudy LaRusso was the other forward, with West and Frank Selvy in the backcourt.

Selvy was a 6-foot-2 guard who once scored 100 points in a game while at Furman. But when he came to the NBA in 1954, he was much like a forerunner to Rick Mount. Yes, he could shoot, but he needed time to do it, and don't ask him to do much else. Selvy bounced from Baltimore to St. Louis to Minneapolis to New York to Syracuse and finally back to the Lakers—six teams in five years.

Schaus kind of liked Selvy, believing he could be a viable guard next to West. The reasoning was that West would demand so much defensive attention that Selvy would benefit with a lot of open shots. Selvy came through for Schaus with his best season in 1961–62, averaging 14.7 points and shooting 42 percent. The Lakers' third guard was Hot Rod Hundley.

But Schaus's real concern was the pivot. Poor Jim Krebs and Ray Felix. Krebs was 6-foot-8, Felix 6-foot-11, and neither was very good. Schaus hoped to take two very mediocre centers, juggle them, and come out with one guy who was average.

It didn't quite work that way. Chamberlain feasted on the Lakers, scoring 78 against them once, 60 twice, and 57, 56 and 48 points in his six games against the two-headed Krebs/Felix.

Schaus could take solace from the fact that Russell would not run up those kinds of numbers against his centers; Russell wasn't interested in scoring those kinds of numbers. But he still went to bed at night wondering how he was going to cope with Russell in the middle.

The first two games were in Boston, and the Lakers came away with a split. In Game 3 at L.A., the Lakers stole a 117–115 decision when West swiped the ball from Cousy, drove the length of the court and scored right before the final buzzer.

Boston won Game 4, to make the series 2–2. But the Lakers won 126–121 in Boston as Baylor tossed in 61 points. All the Lakers had to do was win Game 6 on their home court to become the champs. Instead, Boston ripped them, 119–105.

Game 7 was in Boston. At this point, no one was sure what—if anything—the homecourt was worth. Boston was 1-2 at home, and so was L.A.

The seventh game started close and stayed that way. The Celtics were ahead 53–47 at the half, but glad to be in front as Sam Jones was 1-of-10 from the field. In the first half, Baylor and West combined for 41 of the Lakers' 47 points.

The third period ended at 75–75. In the fourth quarter, foul trouble *struck Boston. Satch Sanders fouled out, then Loscutoff, both picking up most of their fouls trying to stay with Baylor. With 4:40 left in the game, Tom Heinsohn went to the bench with his sixth foul on Baylor's 37th and 38th points. Heinsohn had a miserable game with eight points, six fouls and 3-of-13 shooting.*

Auerbach needed someone to attempt to shadow Baylor. He went with Braun, a 6-foot-5 guard by trade. Braun had been in the league 13 years, and Auerbach figured that his experience and the fact that the officials knew him would keep Braun away from cheap fouls.

It turned out to be a key move: Baylor would only score three points in the last four minutes.

With 40 seconds left, Boston had a 100–96 lead, but Selvy drove 94 feet and scored, cutting it to 100–98.

Boston brought the ball in-bounds, but West pilfered a Cousy pass. West found Selvy open, and he scored again.

That made it 100–100 with 18 seconds left.

Boston worked the ball to Frank Ramsey, who cut loose with a running hook that banged off the rim and was collared by Rudy LaRusso.

With five seconds left and the score 100–100, the Lakers had the ball and the ballgame in their hands. In the Boston huddle, Auerbach patted Braun on the back and told him to take it easy—Russell would now take care of Baylor.

Schaus wanted to get the ball to West or Baylor—which didn't exactly surprise anyone, especially the Celtics. Boston blanketed the two stars, leaving Selvy wide open on the baseline, about 10 feet from the basket. He got the ball, took the shot, and it skidded off the rim. The rebound was snared by Russell as the buzzer sounded.

Even though there was still a five-minute overtime period to be played, Boston could feel the confidence seep out of the Lakers, and the Celtics put them away, 110–107.

Russell would not let the Celtics lose. He played all 53 minutes, scoring 30 and hauling in 40 rebounds. The battered Krebs and Felix combined for 10 points and 14 boards.

After his 1-for-10 start, Sam Jones was 11-for-21 in the second half and finished with 27 points. Cousy had an awful time, scoring eight and shooting 3-of-13 from the field and 2-of-10 from the foul line. Yes, he made only two out of 10 free throws.

Baylor scored 41 for the Lakers, but shot only 13-of-40. He also had 22 rebounds. Like Russell, West played all 53 minutes, scoring 35 on 14-of-30 shooting.

And Selvy? The two field goals he scored in the final minute of regulation were his only two of the game, as he was 2-of-10 for 10 points in 49 minutes.

The Celtics and Lakers would meet again in the finals—in 1963, 1965, 1966 and 1969—but the Lakers would never come as close to an NBA title as the day of Selvy's shot. As the years and the Finals frustrations mounted, Selvy's shot would assume an even more tragic place in Lakers history than it originally had on April 18, 1962. West would be especially haunted by it. He would not win an NBA title until 1972, when the Lakers defeated New York in five games. That would be his only championship as a player, and he'd retire knowing that he never beat Boston in the Finals, a thought that gnaws away at him to this day.

The Loyal Opposition, Part II

ELGIN BAYLOR: Logically, I understand why we lost the titles to Boston. The Celtics were better. Then I think about the games and I see them as clearly as if they happened yesterday—Frank Selvy missing that jumper at the buzzer; he makes that shot, there's no overtime and we're champs. Frank said that Bob Cousy fouled him, but there was no whistle. I was in perfect position to go up and tap in the rebound, but Sam Jones shoved me out-of-bounds—again, no whistle.

In 1965, I hurt my knee and Jerry West played great [averaging 40.6 points in the playoffs], but he couldn't do it alone and it was lousy timing for me to be injured.

There were all these things . . . we were so close . . . I know the difference was Russell. We had no one who could play with him, but still . . .

ZELMO BEATY: The Lakers were a two-man team in the 1960s—Elgin and Jerry. In St. Louis, we'd play well enough to get to the Western Finals, but Elgin and Jerry would go out and score 30, 40, sometimes even 50 a night against us. They just wouldn't let the Lakers lose, but those two guys weren't enough against Boston.

HOT ROD HUNDLEY: We relied on Jerry and Elgin to a fault. Fred Schaus was in love with them, which is understandable, but Fred made the rest of us afraid to take a shot. We'd miss a jumper and Fred would yell, "Hey, what are you doing?" What he meant was, "Get the ball to Elgin and Jerry."

RUDY LARUSSO: We never had a center to compare with Russell, but we went to seven games with Boston in 1962 and 1966. I remember a couple of talks Schaus gave us in the playoffs that were along the lines of, "We know what Jerry and Elgin are going to do. They'll have big nights. We can count on them. But we need it from the rest of you guys . . ."

Then I'd look at Auerbach and he was using 8–9 players and he built up the confidence in all those guys. We had a star system; they had a great team.

FRED SCHAUS: The success of the Celtics was not due to Auerbach, but to No. 6—Bill Russell. I respect Red's ability to coach and judge talent, but not his attitude. Not too many people in the NBA liked it when he lit up the cigar, and when you play and lose to him in the Finals four times as I did—it can get to you because the cigar wasn't necessary. If Frank Selvy makes that shot, then we win even though they have Russell. Then no one says anything.

CHICK HEARN: We had some good players besides Elgin and Jerry. I always admired Rudy LaRusso. He was a blue-collar forward who played defense and fought bigger guys for rebounds. He knew his job was to get the ball for Elgin and Jerry and he did it without complaining.

RUDY LARUSSO: Because we didn't have a talented center to occupy Russell, he could roam around on defense and help guard West and Baylor. I guess I can't come down on Fred too hard. He was a pretty decent coach, even if he wasn't the warmest guy in the world.

JERRY WEST: The thing about the Lakers was that we always had these frustrating endings with losses to Boston. Then the second-guessing of the coach would start, which is simply not fair. Fred coached us for seven years and familiarity can breed contempt. I'm sure there were days when he didn't like me or the other guys.

JOHN VANAK: You could see Fred getting frustrated in the playoffs. He always was kind of a grump because he never smiled, and he certainly wasn't going to smile when playing Boston. He didn't yell a lot, but he'd take those size 16 shoes of his and stomp on the ground. We officials called him the Stomper.

FRED SCHAUS: I tried to trade for a center a couple of times, but I wouldn't give up Elgin or Jerry. Those guys were great players, the guys who got us to the championship. Once, I thought we had a trade worked out for Walter Bellamy, but that fell through. Walter was no superstar, but put him in the middle and we would have been a different team.

Even without a big-time center, we nearly beat them in 1966.

[The Celtics were ahead by 10 points with 45 seconds left and Auerbach lit the cigar. With 15 seconds left, the lead was six. The final score was 95–93, Boston.]

RED AUERBACH: Fred Schaus was a helluva coach and he had damn good players, but I think we had a psychological edge because he tended to focus on me and the moves I was making.

FRED SCHAUS: I admit it, I didn't admire some of the things Red said and did. It would have been nice to make him choke on that cigar, but I don't think any of that affected my coaching.

ELGIN BAYLOR: I was never offended by Red's cigar but it would have been nice to beat him, take it out of his mouth and puff on it once . . . Yeah, I just wish I could have done that once. You have to understand, we worked so hard in those games.

FRED SCHAUS: I do realize that over the years, there was so much pressure on Elgin and Jerry—and I admire how they handled it. With two stars of that magnitude, you could have trouble on your team, but not those guys. Part of the reason was Jerry played guard and Elgin forward, Mr. Outside and Mr. Inside. It gave us a balanced attack.

RUDY LaRUSSO: Jerry and Elgin were on everyone's list of superstars. There might have been a bit of a rivalry, but I never sensed any jealousy. Both guys knew they were going to get the shots and get the headlines and the rest of us knew they deserved it. The big thing was that they were good to their teammates. Okay, we didn't win any championships in the 1960s, but we had a damn good team and that was because Jerry and Elgin worked together and the other guys got along and played their roles.

HOT ROD HUNDLEY: I think there was some strain between the two guys—they both were so intense and so talented. They didn't socialize much. To me, that's natural because they were such huge stars. But what I also sensed was the tremendous respect they had for each other. You never heard them complain because the other was shooting too much or crap like that. When we lost, they both took it to heart.

ELGIN BAYLOR: We never had problems playing together. History shows we were a very good combination and I've always considered Jerry a great player.

JERRY WEST: Elgin was a super competitor with a great instinct for the game. His whole effort was aimed at winning. I felt that I approached the game the same way.

When I look back at those playoffs, I think, "Maybe we should have gotten the other guys involved more." But that also went against the makeup of the team and the coaching philosophy. The coach has to determine if he has enough talent to attack the opposition on all fronts, or if he has to rely on a couple of guys to carry the load.

When the season was over, I'd ask myself, "Did I contribute as much as I should have?" It took me 5–6 years to become a truly confident player. Sometimes, I was too hard on myself and I blamed myself for the team's failure. For years, I battled with the high expectations I set for myself. That was what pushed me to excel, but maybe I did it to a fault. That's the thing about losing, it causes you to go over and over the same ground, trying to find the answer to what went wrong and then the frustration builds year after year. During my career, I had nine broken noses, three broken hands, a broken thumb, a knee injury and all the other injuries athletes endure. I think every player leaves the game with scars on himself, but all the scars I have came from losing.

Two Guards Named Jones

Sustaining a championship string like the Celtics' takes either great luck or great foresight. The Celtics showed the latter throughout their run; whenever a key player reached the end of his career, there was someone ready and able to take his place—with the exception of the irreplaceable Russell, whose retirement ended the dynasty. The clearest example of this is how they made the transition in the starting backcourt from Cousy and Sharman to Sam and K.C. Jones.

A third-round draft choice by Boston in 1956, K.C. Jones had to spend two years in the army before he could begin his pro career in 1958. He went three more seasons before he became a starter in 1961–62. Sam Jones was the Celtics' No. 1 pick in 1957; he reported to the team and did a four-year apprenticeship before starting in 1961. K.C. is a career 7.4 scorer; Sam scored 17.7 per game. Both are in the Hall of Fame.

JIM LOSCUTOFF: Red knew about K.C. Jones because he played with Russell at the University of San Francisco. He found out about Sam Jones from Bones McKinney, who had played for the Celtics and later coached in North Carolina and saw Sam play for North Carolina Central.

SLICK LEONARD: We should have had Sam Jones with the Lakers. I played against Sam when we were both in the army and I could see that he'd be great. I ran into Sid Hartman, a sportswriter from Minneapolis. He asked me if there was anyone I knew who the Lakers should draft. I mentioned Sam. Sid then told the Lakers about Sam.

SAM JONES: After one game in the army, Slick and I were sitting in a beer hall. He said he had played for the Lakers and wanted to know if I wanted to get into the NBA. This was in 1956 and I told Slick that the NBA was not something I thought about. After I got out of the service, I went back to North Carolina Central to finish my degree. One day, I heard that the Lakers had taken me [in the eighth round]. I told them I wanted to get my degree. They said if I didn't sign, I'd go back into the draft and they'd pick me again in 1957. The Lakers got the first pick in 1957 and they took Hot Rod Hundley. They were going to take me in the second round, but Boston took me with their first-round pick.

I never heard from anyone from Boston before the draft. Even after the draft, I wasn't sure I'd go to camp. They had just won a world championship, and you don't cut people after you win a world championship. Also, there weren't too many black players in the NBA, so I figured there were two strikes against me.

BOB COUSY: Sharman and I were still the guards when we drafted Sam and K.C. I know it had to be frustrating for them, knowing they were good enough to start on most teams but backing us up. But I never heard them say, or did I ever believe they'd even think, "I wish that guy would break a leg so I could get a chance." Maybe I'm naive. Maybe I'm looking at it from a white perspective. I was so used to people telling me that they loved me that I'd never believe that everyone didn't love me as a player.

Sam had great skills, he was 6-foot-4 and a better basketball player than K.C. I could understand if Sam said, "I should be getting more minutes." The point is that on our team, it was never an issue. They never went to Red, they never grumbled to the other players. They busted their ass in practice, but they waited for their chance. It's hard to imagine players today being that patient.

JOHN HAVLICEK: When you join the Celtics, you hear the stories of what happened before. Players said that Sharman and K.C. didn't just practice against each other, they nearly had bloodbaths. Neither guy was dirty, but both were tough as rusty nails. They bodied each other and battled each other on every dribble. The fact that Sam and K.C. played behind Cousy and Sharman for several years had to make them better players.

SAM JONES: Winning was the answer. K.C. and I understood the situation. Cousy and Sharman were established. So was Frank Ramsey— all three of those guys played ahead of us and those guys won championships together. When you're winning you're willing to sacrifice. We knew we could play. K.C. could have been an even greater player, but he wouldn't shoot the ball. I didn't say couldn't shoot—he could—but he'd rather let someone else do it. He handled the ball, played the best defense of any guard in the league, and he let me shoot, so I won't argue with that.

LENNY WILKENS: K.C. stuck to you like glue. He was with you, right on you, every step. He'd bump you, hold you, get in your way. And with Boston, all he had to do was think about defense because they had so many other guys to score.

RUDY LARUSSO: K.C. did the best job of anyone on Jerry West. He'd play right on top of Jerry—overplaying Jerry, daring him to drive to the basket. K.C. could do that because he knew that he had Russell behind him. K.C. symbolized the defense the Celtics played: they pressured you all over the court and they could play tight because they had Russell roaming behind them like a free safety, there to challenge anyone who drove to the basket.

GENE SHUE: Today, very few guys play you the length of the floor like K.C. did. And it didn't matter if you had the ball or not, there was K.C. in your face.

BOB RYAN: K.C. was a 6-foot-1 Dennis Rodman, getting right in your jock and guarding you. When they needed someone to foul Wilt, it was K.C. who'd do it and K.C. would clobber him. K.C. was like Al Attles—he was small but he feared no one. Red once told me that when K.C. first joined the team, "I'd put him on one team during a scrimmage and that team would win. Then I'd put him on the other team, and again K.C.'s team would win. K.C. never scored much, but he made any team better."

WAYNE EMBRY: The Jones boys were a great backcourt, because K.C. and Sam complemented each other. K.C. is recognized as one of the fiercest defensive players ever. No one ever mentions Sam when they talk about super offensive players, but they should. Sam averaged 20-some points, but in big games he could go for 40 or 50. I was with Cincinnati when Sam got into a shootout with Oscar Robertson. Oscar had 43, but Sam had 47 and Boston won the game by four. Later in my career, I was with Boston and Russell was in foul trouble all night during a playoff game. He barely played, I filled in and scored 15. I got all the attention from the reporters, but it was Sam who won it for us—he scored 51.

JOHN HAVLICEK: From my era, the greatest guards were Jerry West and Oscar Robertson. But third on my list would be Sam Jones. He was only 6-foot-4, but he wore the same size pants as Bill Russell—

which tells you how long Sam's legs are. That meant his first step wasn't just quick, it was long. He was always under control. He had no weaknesses and was a great, great clutch player.

LENNY WILKENS: Sam had all the shots, from a two-handed set shot that would be well beyond the three-point line today to driving hooks to medium-range jump shots. And bank shots—he banked in about everything. No good shooter has ever used the board as much as Sam.

SAM JONES: I just started shooting off the backboard and liked it. I never understood why more players didn't use the board because it makes it easier to score—you can be a little off and your shot still goes in. I was a 6-4 guard and my height was a big advantage. A lot of guys who guarded me were much smaller, so I just took them under the basket and shot a hook over them—Magic Johnson is the only other guard I've seen use the hook as much as I did.

JOHN HAVLICEK: It was as if Sam had divided the court up into sections. Most shooters have gray areas where they get the ball and wonder, should I bank it or shoot it straight? There was never a moment of doubt with Sam. He always took his bank shots from the same spots.

LENNY WILKENS: Sam liked to mess with your head during the game. He'd say, "You can't guard me."

Or he'd say, "Where's your shot? How come they never let you shoot the ball? Don't they think you can shoot?"

GENE CONLEY: Sam loved to talk to Wilt. He'd drive the lane, arc a shot over Wilt and as the ball settled into the net, he'd tell Wilt, "Too late, baby."

WAYNE EMBRY: Sam would say, "Wilt, you can't get that. What makes you think you can get my shot?"

SAM JONES: I respected Wilt. I never challenged him by trying to drive right on him—he'd just block your shot. I'd drive in, making sure there was still plenty of room between myself and Wilt. Then I'd stop in front of him and shoot over him. Then I talked to him. I talked to everybody on the court, but it was a lot of fun to say things to Wilt because he'd react to them.

NORM DRUCKER: One day, Wilt just had had enough. *[It was the fifth game of the 1962 Eastern Conference playoffs.]* Sam drove on Wilt, made a shot and said something. Wilt got pissed off and he started chasing Sam. Being a wise man, Sam backed away and ended up off the court. He saw Wilt still coming after him, so Sam picked up one of the photographer's chairs and held it out at Wilt as if Sam were a lion tamer.

JOHN HAVLICEK: Sam held the chair up and said, "Wilt, I'm not gonna fight you fair." Those words changed the mood. Wilt stopped, Sam put down the chair and that was the end of it.

WILT CHAMBERLAIN: Sam just ran away from me. He had that chair and he was shaking. He was about ready to go up into the stands—he didn't want to fight, so I said, "Ah, forget it."

FRANK RAMSEY: Sam had a very quirky personality. One day, he was on the floor, obviously in pain. I said, "Sam, what's wrong?"

He said, "Oh, my mortgage."

I said, "What?"

He said, "My knee hurts and I just bought a new house. Who's gonna pay the mortgage?"

JOHN HAVLICEK: One night, Sam just wouldn't shoot the ball, even when he was wide open.

Red said, "Sam, you've got to take the shots."

Sam said, "I'm not shooting."

Red said, "Why not?"

Sam said, "I'm just not shooting the ball."

Red said, "You've got to have a reason."

Sam said, "I can't shoot the ball when my feet are cold."

Red just shook his head and went back to the bench. It was rare that Sam got into one of those moods, but when he did all you could do was wait for it to pass.

WAYNE EMBRY: When I was with the Celtics and Russell was the coach, he called a meeting and complained to the guards, "I don't have a leader out there. I need someone to take charge. Sam, I want you to be the leader. You control the game."

Sam said, "Russ, I can't do that."

Russ said, "Why not?"

Sam said, "Russ, I've got no authority to call the plays."
Russ said, "Well, I'm giving you the authority."
Sam said, "I just can't do it."
Like Red did before him, Russell just shook his head.

BOB RYAN: Sam was the guy everyone wanted to take the last shot in the game. Sam didn't want to do it, but Red and the guys just made him take it. He was the reluctant hero. He was one of the first great modern players—the quick 6-foot-4 guard, and his prime years were few because he was close to 30 before he became a starter. That's the thing about K.C. and Sam, they waited their turns—it would never happen in today's game. Not with all the money at stake and agents pushing guys to play. Also, there is no team with the mystique of those Celtics teams, where players were just content to be a part of it.

Havlicek Stole the Ball

Most fans assume that when John Havlicek "stole the ball" he stole the 1965 title for Boston at the same time. Not exactly, but close enough. It was the seventh game of the 1965 Eastern Conference Finals, the winner to meet the L.A. Lakers. The assumption was that the winner of the East would also beat whatever team came out of the West. That assumption was correct, as the Celtics would defeat the Lakers in five games.

The 1964–65 season was an emotional one for the Celtics. Usually they tried to find some new reason to win a championship. In 1963, it was because Bob Cousy retired. In 1964, it was Frank Ramsey who was quitting.

On September 7, 1964, owner Walter Brown died. Brown loved his players and paid them well, if the players could manage to get past Red Auerbach and corner the owner. Suddenly, the 1964–65 season became dedicated to the family of Walter Brown. But from a business standpoint, Brown's family told Auerbach to find a buyer for the team, and the man who came up with a $3 million offer was Marvin Kratter and his partner, Jack Waldron.

The first big sale of an NBA team had been in the summer of 1962, when Eddie Gottlieb took $850,000 to send his Philadelphia Warriors

to San Francisco. That left Philadelphia without an NBA team in 1962–
63. The NBA did not like that situation, and convinced Syracuse to
move to Philadelphia for the 1963–64 season. Danny Biasone sold the
Nats to a group led by Irv Kosloff and Ike Richman, and they renamed
the team the 76ers. This switch was much to the relief of Knicks owner
Ned Irish; instead of suffering the indignity of losing to Syracuse, Irish
could at least say he got beat by Philadelphia.

Continuing to stabilize in major markets, the NBA and ABC signed
a three-year contract to broadcast a Sunday Game of the Week. The
deal began with the 1964–65 season, ABC paying the NBA $650,000.
In the third year, the deal was worth over $1 million to the league. TV
was crucial to the league and the contract was a tribute to Walter
Kennedy, who had replaced Maurice Podoloff as commissioner in 1964.
Podoloff was the NBA's first commissioner, but was 73 and had lost the
league's contract with NBC. The league had no network deal from
1962–64 before Kennedy came to the rescue.

Another area of progress was the officiating. In 1951, the home team
won 75 percent of the games. In 1957, it was still 70 percent. By the
middle 1960s, it was close to 60 percent as the league's core group of
officials was experienced and not likely to be intimidated by the fans.

But on the court, it was business as usual in the 1964–65 season.
Boston roared in front, winning its first 11 games. Auerbach had slowly
revamped his team. The starting backcourt was K.C. and Sam Jones,
Bill Russell still ruled the middle, and Satch Sanders and Tom Heinsohn
were the forwards. Auerbach also breathed new life into his bench,
drafting Havlicek in 1962 and signing Larry Siegfried as a free agent
in 1963. In the West, the Lakers started the season at 15-6, and a Boston-
L.A. Finals was already looming by midseason.

Then it was time to reconsider. At the 1965 All-Star Game, San
Francisco traded Wilt Chamberlain back to Philadelphia for Connie
Dierking, Paul Neumann, Lee Shaffer and a bucket of bucks. All that
mattered was the bucket of bucks; the other guys were just bodies. (In
fact, Shaffer never even reported to the West Coast.) The amount was
$150,000, which doesn't sound like much now, but you could pay an
entire starting team for $150,000 in 1965. Also, the Warriors deducted
Chamberlain's $200,000 salary from their roster. They had a young
Nate Thurmond in the middle, and they didn't believe Thurmond and
Chamberlain could survive on the same team. Certainly their payroll
couldn't survive them, as the Warriors' attendance was disappointing
despite the obvious gate attractions they had in their two centers.

The Sixers were a .500 team when they obtained Chamberlain, but *they were a team on the rise. The backcourt featured Hal Greer and Larry Costello. The forwards were Luke Jackson, Chet Walker and defensive specialist Dave Gambee. The starting center was veteran Johnny Kerr.*

"I had been a center my entire career until we got Wilt," said Kerr. "On that day, I started calling myself a forward."

The coach was Dolph Schayes, the great forward. A man who believed in moving your feet and moving the ball. A nicer man never coached in the NBA, but Schayes was never comfortable with Chamberlain's desire to post up near the basket and stand there, arm up, awaiting a pass. Nor did he like Chamberlain's infatuation with the fallaway jumper, which took him out of offensive rebounding position. Finally, he realized that with Chamberlain, some people expected him to beat Boston.

The inevitable matchup came in the Eastern Conference Finals, and the Sixers were ready. In this seven-game series, the homecourt meant everything. The Sixers couldn't win at Boston Garden, though they defended their home turf with fangs bared. But in the regular season, Boston was 62-18, this Sixers team in transition was 40-40, and a team with a 40-40 record does not have homecourt advantage in the seventh game.

Boston roared off to a 30–12 lead. It was the seventh game, the Celtics were on their home court and they were ahead by 18 points before many of the sellout crowd of 13,909 settled into their seats. Many Celtics fans expressed absolute disdain for Chamberlain—"the loser" is how he was known in Boston—and the rout appeared to be on.

But the crowd didn't reckon with the full force of Chamberlain's Celtics frustration.

In the 1960 playoffs—Wilt's rookie season—his Philadelphia Warriors had lost to Boston in six games in the Eastern Conference Finals.

In 1962, they lost to Boston again in the Eastern Conference Finals, only it took all seven games.

In 1964, Chamberlain's San Francisco Warriors lost to the Celtics in five games in the NBA Finals.

In fact, a Chamberlain team had never beaten Boston in a playoff series.

Now it was 1965 and it was down to a seventh game. The fact that Boston had rushed to an early 18-point lead did not deter Chamberlain. By the third quarter, the Sixers had a 66–61 lead. Boston came back, and appeared in control as it led 110–103 with two minutes left. But

Chamberlain scored six straight points, and Boston's lead was down to 110–109 with five seconds left. The Celtics had the ball and all they had to do was get it in-bounds.

Later, no one would talk about how Bill Russell messed up the in-bounds pass, or how the Celtics couldn't score in the last two minutes of the game—a home game.

They would not remember that Wilt had outrebounded Russell, 32–29. Or that Wilt scored 30 and had carried the Sixers back into the game with his clutch play. Some fans would insist that Chamberlain "choked," incorrectly saying that Wilt threw away the in-bounds pass to Havlicek.

Instead, they'd talk about Sam Jones's 37 points and Havlicek's 26. And naturally, like Boston announcer Johnny Most, what they remember is that Havlicek stole the ball and Boston won, 110–109.

EARL STROM: There were five seconds left. Wilt had just scored. Boston had the ball and the lead. The game was at the Garden and Russell was in-bounding the ball under his own basket. Bill went to pass the ball, and he banged it off one of the wires that held up the basket— those wires don't exist anymore. I blew the whistle. Hitting the wire was a turnover and I gave the ball to Philadelphia.

Red went crazy. He was screaming at me. He didn't deny that Russell's pass hit the wire, but he claimed that Chet Walker was guarding Russell too closely and that Chet had jumped over the out-of-bounds line, and that caused Russell to make the bad pass.

I wasn't buying any of it.

Also, Russell never said a word to me. He just hung his head and left the court when Boston called a time-out.

JOHN HAVLICEK: Russell came into the huddle and said, "Man, somebody bail me out. I don't want to be wearing these horns."

DOLPH SCHAYES: Wilt was dominating Russell. Wilt had just dunked on him and we had a last chance to win. In the huddle, guys were saying, let's get the ball to Wilt.

EARL STROM: I can't remember if I actually heard it or was told Wilt said it, but I understand that Wilt didn't want the ball on the last play. He was afraid Boston would foul him and he knew he was a terrible free throw shooter. If Philly got the ball near the basket to Wilt, the

Celtics would never let him get a decent shot off. They'd clobber him and put Wilt at the line.

DOLPH SCHAYES: Wilt's problems at the foul line weighed on my mind. So I set up a play where Hal Greer would pass the ball to Chet Walker, and Johnny Kerr would set a pick to free Walker for a shot.

JOHN HAVLICEK: I looked down at the Philly huddle and they were all crowded around Dolph, who was drawing up a play. Red wasn't even in our huddle. He was out on the court, yelling at the officials for the whole time-out. The horn sounded and right before we stepped on the court, Red said, "Okay, don't foul anyone."

That was the extent of our strategy.

Philly came out with three guys at least 6-foot-10—Wilt, Kerr and Luke Jackson. Their other two players were Walker and Greer.

We had Sam and K.C. Jones, Satch Sanders, Russell and myself.

I said to Sam Jones, "I'll take Kerr."

Sam said, "No, I got him. I'll keep him off the boards."

I asked if he was sure, but Sam wanted Kerr. Had we played it my way, the steal might never have happened.

So I took Chet Walker.

Greer was in-bounding the ball under our basket. I stayed close to Walker, and at the same time I was counting in my head "one thousand one, one thousand two, one thousand three . . ."

Everyone knows that you have five seconds to get the ball in-bounds, and often the guy passing the ball in would count to himself. But I'd do it on defense, too. It gave me a better feel for what was going on.

When I got to one thousand four and the ball still hadn't been passed in, I took a peek over my shoulder and saw that Greer was about to lob a pass to Walker. As I said "one thousand four" to myself, I saw the flight of the ball.

DOLPH SCHAYES: Walker and Havlicek went for the pass like an end and a defensive back.

JOHN HAVLICEK: I realized that Greer's pass was going to be a little short. Had I not looked back, it would have been perfect because it would have gone right over my shoulder. But since I saw the ball leave his hand, I got a great jump on it. I was able to tip the pass away from Walker and the ball went right to Sam Jones, who dribbled it a few times, then threw the ball back to me and the game was over.

DOLPH SCHAYES: I saw Havlicek bump Walker. It wasn't a hard foul, but it was a foul. But the officials let the players decide the game. There was no whistle.

EARL STROM: It was a clean play. John never touched Walker.

JOHN HAVLICEK: Russell was the first to grab me and hug me. He kept thanking me.

WILT CHAMBERLAIN: There never was a time when I didn't want the ball, and I wanted it at the end of that game. I find it ironic that no one remembers that Russell almost blew the game for Boston. He hit that wire, which had been on the Garden's baskets forever. Was it a choke, or just a bad play? No one needed to answer that question, because Havlicek stole the ball.

JOHN HAVLICEK: As I was leaving the floor, it was hysteria and euphoria. Fans were grabbing me and a couple of fans ripped off my jersey. They tore it right across the collarbone where the shoulder straps are. I ended up with a couple of abrasions across my shoulders from that. Years later, I went to a party and a woman came up to me and showed me this brooch she had. She asked me if I recognized the material. I didn't. She told me it was a piece of my uniform that someone had gotten that night.

[The Celtics went on to win the 1965 title, beating the Lakers—playing without the injured Elgin Baylor—in five games. That was no surprise. They knew their real challenge was Philadelphia and the Sixers. After those 1965 Eastern Conference finals, Russell's record against Chamberlain was 56–28.]

RED AUERBACH: Havlicek is an example of what the Celtics were all about. He played on those great Ohio State teams of the early 1960s. Jerry Lucas was the star and the guy everyone went to see. When the draft came, I had been hearing good things about Havlicek, especially his defense. Also, Frank Ramsey was getting ready to retire and I needed someone to replace him, to come off the bench and play guard or forward. At 6-foot-5, Havlicek could do that. In that draft, I felt I had three choices—Terry Dischinger, Chet Walker or Havlicek, and I went with John because of his versatility.

JOHN HAVLICEK: Curt Gowdy takes credit for scouting me in what is called the Final Four today. Scouting was so primitive, no more than word of mouth between friends. Gowdy told Red, "There's this guy Havlicek who runs around like he's got a motor up his ass. He looks like a pretty good player to me." Bones McKinney had played for Red and he was the one who told Red to draft Sam Jones. Bones was coaching at Wake Forest, and he had seen me play a few times, so he also told Red about me. From what I understand, Red never saw me play in college.

At Ohio State, I didn't have to do much on offense—that was built around Jerry Lucas. I was there to guard people, to hustle. I got points off the fast break or in garbage time.

Before the NBA draft, I had a tryout with the Cleveland Browns. They gave me a contract for $15,000 and a Chevy Impala as a bonus. But the Browns cut me, and then Red wanted to sign me.

At the time, there was a new basketball team starting—the Cleveland Pipers [in the short-lived American Basketball League]. George Steinbrenner owned it and he offered me $15,000 in cash and $10,000 worth of his American Shipbuilding stock along with a free apartment.

The Celtics offered $15,000. I already had the new car from the Browns and I figured that with the Celtics' running game, I'd fit right in. So I signed with them. After being in training camp with the Browns, I was in great shape and I wasn't about to be intimidated by any basketball players. This was 1962 and the Celtics had just won four straight championships, so I was just another rookie. There was no hype whatsoever.

JERRY LUCAS: When John went to camp with the Celtics, people asked me if he'd make the team—sportswriters and people who were supposed to be knowledgeable.

I said, "Make the team? He can be a star. He averaged close to 20 points a game in the second half of his senior year. You should see the guy in practice. He's coming into his own."

SATCH SANDERS: John wasn't heralded when he came to the Celtics, but my first impression was that he was a guy who could run like a deer and he never got tired. That was what surprised us—how John was never tired.

RED AUERBACH: There was no better team player than Frank Ramsey and he knew he was coming to the end and he knew that Havlicek was there to eventually take his role. So Frank took Havlicek under his wing and trained him. I never even had to tell Frank to do it.

FRANK RAMSEY: John joined the team for Cousy's last year. He could run all day, he loved to play defense and he had a conservative personality that fit in well with the team. I showed him some of the little things I did. When you come off the bench, you know that you won't play for the first 6–7 minutes of a game. But when the call came from Red, I'd have the snaps and buttons on my warmup jacket and pants open so I could just rip them off and run into the game. It was a psychological ploy. When you come in, the other team is a little tired and there is a natural tendency to relax against a substitute. That man you're facing is vulnerable, so come right at him fast with a lot of energy. I did that, and so did John. But as a rookie, he wouldn't shoot the ball. I'd tell him to shoot. Red would tell him. Finally, he'd have an open shot and a bunch of us would scream, "Shoot it!" He needed to believe in his offense as much as we did. It took him about a year, but then he realized he could score big numbers. *[Havlicek averaged 14.3 points as a rookie, 19.9 in his second season.]*

JOHN HAVLICEK: I think there is an art to reporting into a basketball game. I never wore my warmup pants and I wore my warmup jacket loose on my shoulders, not even with my hands through the sleeves. That way, I could just throw off my jacket and run into the game. I saw too many guys unsnapping their jackets and pants, and they'd lose two minutes of playing time because they weren't ready to go in the game. There were times when Red would look at me, then I'd jump up and run to the scorer's table. Red would have to bring me back, saying, "It's not time yet."

I sat next to him on the bench so I could feel his pulse and the heartbeat of the game. That was why all he had to do was look at me and I knew he wanted me to go in.

When he did tell me something, he usually said, "I don't care what else you do out there, but make that guy covering you run. Make him chase you, and by the end of the game he'll feel it and we'll have him where we want him."

No matter what Red said, I'd say, "You've got it."

I didn't care if he wanted me to press from endline to endline. As a young player, I ran around like crazy. I had Cousy to give me the ball, and as a rookie I just made layups on passes from him. What impressed me the most about coming to the Celtics was how they made me feel welcome. One of the first guys to talk to me was Frank Ramsey. He knew I was going to take his sixth-man job, but instead of being threatened he said, "John, you're going to prolong my career for a few more years. By having you here, I won't have to do as much and I can watch you play and maybe help you with a few things." Well, Frank helped me a lot, but that was how they did things on the Celtics.

To Red Auerbach

who can be
indifferent?
not that
mad man
over there—
an owl's
scream away
from death.

—Tom Meschery

Auerbach's Signature on the Celtics

Red Auerbach won nine titles in his last 10 years as the Celtics coach, ending in 1965–66. That 1966 title was also Boston's eighth in a row, an NBA record that most basketball experts insist will never be duplicated. In that 10-year span, the Celtics also won nine regular-season division titles, an impressive achievement because many teams tend to coast until playoff time. Also, a regular season title ensures a team of the crucial homecourt advantage in the playoffs.

RED AUERBACH: I wanted a certain type of player on the Celtics, a player with no questions about his character or his work habits. It takes more than talent, and I've turned down deals for talented players because I didn't believe they would fit in with the Celtics. When it came to drafting, I took into consideration where a kid played in college. Frank Ramsey and Cliff Hagan played for Adolph Rupp at Kentucky, and Rupp's teams were always well disciplined and fundamentally sound. I knew these guys were more than good players. I knew they'd be coachable. I was friendly with a lot of college coaches and spoke at a number of their clinics. I made a lot of contacts that way and coaches were honest with me when it came to assessing talent and character.

The other thing I did was keep my team together. After the Russell trade, I didn't make a major trade for 13 years. I'd pick up a guy like Wayne Embry or Carl Braun at the end of their careers, but my top 7–8 players, they knew they weren't going anywhere. They could play out their careers with the Celtics. Too many teams think the grass is always greener; they overrate players on other teams and underrate their own players and that leads to stupid trades. If you want to be sure to lose, have constant turnover. If you want to win, pick your team carefully and give it time.

ZELMO BEATY: Players on other teams admired Red for keeping his players. He didn't get mad and trade a couple of guys during a losing streak. He made his players believe they could win a title every year and that he was behind them. I wish I could have played in that atmosphere.

TOM HEINSOHN: There was a bonding between the players and the organization because you knew you'd play your career in one town. You could buy a house, put your kids in school and settle down. You also knew that Red would give a veteran player an extra year when most other teams would have told him to retire or traded him off. But you also trained your replacement—which was unique in basketball. Ramsey worked with Havlicek. I worked with Satch Sanders. When we had Mel Counts, Red said to me, "What's wrong with him?"

I said, "He doesn't rebound and he doesn't catch the ball right. They knock it out of his hands."

Red said, "Take him aside, talk to him, teach him."

BILL SHARMAN: The key to Red's success was training camp. When he coached, there were no rules about when you could start training camp, so he started earlier than most teams and he played a lot of exhibition games. By opening night, we were the best-conditioned team in the league and Red believed that we'd steal 3–4 games early—especially on the road—because we were in better shape than anyone else. Even today, some coaches and players believe that you come to training camp and "play yourself into shape." That was the prevailing attitude years ago, but not with Red. So every year, he'd get us off to a great start, and that would bolster our confidence.

JOHN HAVLICEK: Red's camps were grueling, two-a-day practices. He wanted you irritable and a little angry. He created these Vince Lombardi–type grass drills—drills where you put your hands behind your head and then jumped and reached out at the same time. You kept jumping and reaching until you got to one end of the court, then he made us do it again—only we had to jump backward. The first guy who dropped out had to do sprints. Some days, it was pure torture.

FRANK RAMSEY: Most guys did not touch a basketball during the summer, and Red decided that he was immediately going to drive the demons out of everyone's body. There were two awful weeks of drills, then a schedule of 14 exhibition games in 15 days across New England.

JOHN HAVLICEK: Red had these long passing drills where he'd make you kill yourself to run down a full-court pass. We had 2-on-2 fast-break drills where you never had a second to catch your breath. We did situps, pushups, all kinds of exercises. At the end of practice, we ran sprints and the winner got to sit out while the other guys ran again. You should have seen Russell—he and Sam Jones were our fastest guys and they'd win the first two races. The rest of us would let them fight it out and then watch the field, figuring when we could really pour it on and win one.

RED AUERBACH: I played under Bill Reinhardt at George Washington and he was 25 years ahead of his time when it came to conditioning and running the fast break. He taught me to run an organized fast break. We ran more than any other team and we had certain players who ran to certain spots. Also, Reinhardt taught me to have my team in top shape for the opener so we could just run and hide from the rest of the NBA.

[Some of the fast Celtics starts by January 1 were 34-4 in 1960, 29-5 in 1962, 25-5 in 1964 and 31-7 in 1965. They also won their first seven games in 1963.]

JIM LOSCUTOFF: Red loved hard scrimmages—90 straight minutes— and fast breaks. He yelled at us to run and run some more. Sometimes, he'd put me in there for the entire 90 minutes and start talking to a friend on the sidelines. He'd forget to take me out and I about dropped.

JOHN HAVLICEK: We picked up Willie Naulls from the Knicks [in 1963] and he couldn't believe what Red put us through. Willie actually passed out in midstride during one of the drills. I'd always heard that if you push your body too hard, it would shut down and you'd pass out but I had never seen it happen until Willie went down. Later, he told me, "Man, with the Knicks, we spent the first two weeks getting acquainted and patting each other on the rear end."

FRANK RAMSEY: Poor Willie Naulls. There was another practice where we were doing pushups after lunch and Willie threw up. Russell thought it was hilarious, and he grabbed Willie's feet and pulled Willie off the court. Unfortunately for Willie, Russell dragged Willie's face through the vomit. We laughed about that story for years.

BILL SHARMAN: Red gave us speeches during camp, about how we were the champs, the greatest basketball team assembled. Then he'd say how everyone would be gunning for us and he'd say, "Is this the year you're going to let down? Is this the year you're going to loaf?"

TOM HEINSOHN: One day after camp Carl Braun said to me, "You guys have been doing this for years, right? No wonder you always win."

BOB COUSY: Arnold was never any exceptional Xs and Os guy. We had seven plays. We knew them. The league knew what we were going to run, but so what? Arnold believed if you did a couple of things well, no one could stop you.

TOM HEINSOHN: Red was the ultimate sports management person. He had a way of listening to players and being honest with them. It wasn't uncommon during a time-out for him to ask, "Anybody got anything?"

    If we had an idea, we knew he really wanted to hear it. Sometimes he took our advice, and sometimes he didn't. But he really listened.

In the dressing room, I sat between Cousy and Russell. If a lesser man were the coach, this could have been a difficult situation. The fans and press loved Cousy. He was great, he was flashy and he was white.

Meanwhile, we had a great player in Russell, who was black, and the people in Boston didn't understand what the hell he was doing. They thought basketball was scoring and they didn't appreciate that Russell was the greatest defensive player who ever lived. Red became Russell's John the Baptist. He spread the word about Russell to anyone who would listen, because he knew that Cousy's publicity would take care of itself. In that way, he balanced the egos, and Russell also understood and appreciated what Red was doing.

BOB COUSY: Like a lot of us, Arnold was a gutter rat out of the ghetto. His strength was motivation. During a game, he was demonstrative and emotional, up and down on the bench, yelling, wearing your ass out. I'm sure that modern coaches would laugh at him because he didn't use a big playbook, the videos and everything else that teams have today. But he understood people, and that is crucial at the pro level.

FRANK RAMSEY: Red knew there were times to take the pressure off, so he'd have scrimmages where all the little men played the big men. Cousy always wanted to play the pivot, so this was his chance. The five little men were Sam and K.C. Jones, Sharman, Cousy and me. The big men were Russell, Loscutoff, Heinsohn, Satch Sanders and Gene Conley. Sometimes, another player filled in for Russell and he was the official.

[Auerbach was also No. 1 on virtually every official's hit list, and he worked very hard to attain that distinction. In 1954, he was fined $100 for telling writers that official Arnie Heft was "stupid and incompetent, and I told the son of a bitch that to his face." In 1958, he ran onto the court screaming "Choker" and grabbing his neck as he approached official Richie Powers. That cost Auerbach $150. He was fined $300 for punching Ben Kerner, another $350 for calling officials Norm Drucker and Mendy Rudolph "a couple of chokers." These fines sound like pennies today, but the standard fine in the 1950s was $25, with a major offense costing $50. Auerbach was in such constant trouble that most seasons he paid more in fines than all the other coaches combined.]

NORM DRUCKER: Red would be on you from the opening tap. You'd throw up the jump ball and hear him scream, "Throw the damn ball straight, will ya?"

One night, I was working with a young official and I told him to be ready for Red.

The kid threw up the jump ball and Red screamed. The kid stopped the game, turned and banged Red with a T. It was the only time I ever saw Red speechless because he didn't know what hit him.

JOE GUSHUE: My biggest tormentor was Red. Every night he put me to the test. In my first year in the league, Red was suspended for three games for pushing me. Red's excuse was that I tried to make a name for myself by throwing him out of the game, and he wasn't going to be intimidated by any rookie ref, so he shoved me. But the truth was that I didn't even eject him until he wandered out on the court, went chest-to-chest with me and spit all over me with that foul mouth of his.

JOHN VANAK: Red loved to get as close as he could to you, and while he was screaming at you, he was spitting, too.

His usual attack was, "You don't know what the hell you're talking about. You'll never work another game in this goddamn league, you bush league punk."

With every word, he'd spit in your face.

There were nights when I closed my eyes and I thought, "I'm a mature adult. What am I doing here listening to this guy?"

Red drooled when he saw young officials. He ate them up like hamburger.

CHARLEY ECKMAN: Piss and moan, scream and yell, then piss and moan some more—that was all an official heard from Auerbach. Then he'd get in your face with that awful garlic breath of his . . . it was just awful. A lot of people are afraid to tell the truth about Auerbach because he's been a big shot in the NBA for so long, but he has bullied too many people and he was the luckiest man alive to end up with Bill Russell.

NORM DRUCKER: There were some games where Red and I just ended up screaming at each other. To this day, Auerbach claims I was hired by the league to get him. One season, the commissioner said if Red got thrown from another game he'd get suspended. Well, the next night he was all over me from the opening whistle, stomping, screaming, swearing. I had no choice. I threw him but as I tried to explain to Red, "You threw yourself." The next day, he was suspended for a couple of games and he blamed me for the whole thing.

JOE GUSHUE: Even when the game was over, you couldn't get rid of Auerbach. He would come to the officials' room, bang and try to kick down the door. Today a coach would get fined 10 grand and suspended forever if he tried some of Red's stunts. Back then, it cost him 50 bucks. That was supposed to stop him?

TOM MESCHERY: Every coach got on the officials, but Auerbach, he was in a league of his own because he had a strategy. Red would get into a screaming match with an official, then the five Celtics on the court would immediately show up and surround the official. Even if the players didn't say a word, to see those five tall guys looking down on you . . . it had to be intimidating. And it happened every time, so you know that it was no accident.

BOB COUSY: Arnold wore out officials. His game plan was to sound off from the first call of the night. It didn't matter if his complaint was justified or not, Arnold believed that you just started bitching right away. He believed that he could intimidate 80 percent of the officials. The guys were human and they got sick of listening to him, so they'd give his team a break just to shut Arnold up. With guys such as Sid Borgia or Earl Strom, this was counterproductive. They were gunslingers with chips on their shoulders and the minute you put pressure on them, they gave it right back to you in spades. But for over 80 percent of the guys who have to run by the bench and listen to the coach jabbering every time . . . I don't care who you are, that has to wear your ass out. Arnold not only intimidated officials, he nearly suffocated them with his barrage. By the fourth quarter, it had taken its toll and some officials just wouldn't make a call against us.

EARL STROM: Red and I had our moments, but they weren't nearly as bad as he had with other guys. Norm Drucker and Red . . . Joe Gushue and Red . . . they were oil and water. I threw Red out, but most of the time I knew that he wanted to get technical fouls—even get ejected—just to fire up his team. There were a lot of games where the Celtics went on 10–12–point runs after Red was ejected, so he did it intentionally.

One night, he was all over me. The team was playing poorly and I knew he wanted to be tossed. I told him, "Red, you've already got one technical, but that's the last one you're getting."

Red said, "What do you mean?"

I said, "If I have to stay and watch this shit, so do you."

Then . . . The Cigar

BOB COUSY: The one thing that bothered me was the cigar. Everybody thought we liked it when Arnold lit up the cigar. But just the opposite. The Boston players hated it. We'd be on the road and Red would sit on the bench and light up. There he was, puffing away, surrounded by two policemen. On the road, all the cigar did was piss off the fans for no reason, and we on the floor heard about it.

The cigar started as a lark. Arnold loves cigars and one day he just did it on the bench when we were beating a team. He never imagined that it would have an effect on the crowd, but the writers and fans started talking about Red's victory cigar. Never one to pass up an opportunity, Arnold made the cigar his trademark. If we cringed when he lit up, so what? And the thing was he never got burned—not once did we blow a game after he fired up that cigar.

JOHN HAVLICEK: In the early days of the NBA, it was common for coaches to smoke cigarettes on the bench. I was told that there was a game early in Red's career where the Celtics were way ahead; Red took out all the starters, leaned back in his chair and pulled out the cigar.

The next day, he got a call from the commissioner who wanted to fine him for smoking a cigar on the bench.

Red said, "What do you mean, smoking on the bench? Everyone smokes on the bench."

The commissioner said, "Yeah, but not cigars."

The last thing you want to do is tell Red that he can't do something, and the league never did fine him.

RED AUERBACH: I used to smoke a pipe in college, then I switched to cigars. There was a game where we were ahead of Philly by 30–40 points. I just took out the cigar because it seemed like the natural thing to do.

FRANK RAMSEY: I'd see Red take out the cigar and I'd say, "Red, it's not time yet."

He'd say, "We've got this one."

I'd say, "Red, not yet."

He'd light up.

I'd say, "Red, what if we lose?" Because I knew it infuriated everyone we played.

He'd say, "We're not going to lose."

NATE THURMOND: Personally, I liked Red Auerbach. But that cigar . . . it just didn't show much class.

RICHIE GUERIN: When Red lit up the cigar, it was like he blew smoke in your face. It was almost as if he had to make himself the focal point of the game, stealing the spotlight from his players.

BOB COUSY: I once heard that Paul Seymour said as much as winning an NBA championship, he'd like to see the Celtics lose a game after Auerbach brought out the cigar so he could go up to Arnold and stuff the cigar in his face.

FRANK RAMSEY: Alex Hannum said one of his biggest wishes was to shove that cigar down Red's throat.

TOM MESCHERY: On one level, Red was like a vaudeville character and the cigar was his shtick. But the thing that really pissed me off was the ceremonies at Boston Garden. Before every game or at halftime, they always were retiring some damn number or honoring one of their former players or giving a check to cerebral palsy or something. The fans would get all riled up, you'd have to stand there and watch the whole thing. You'd get cold and mad. I'm convinced that Red and the Celtics did this on purpose, just like the cold water in the shower and not enough towels for the visiting team.

ED MACAULEY: Red used to think he was a pretty good basketball player. Well, he wasn't. He never played in the NBA and when he scrimmaged with us, we could see why. He was the worst shooter I'd ever seen. Then he'd get mad and he'd play dirty—as dirty as anyone in the league, grabbing your shorts, stepping on your foot, stuff like that.

JOHN HAVLICEK: Red would play point guard and we were supposed to press him. But when you got near Red as he dribbled the ball up the court, he'd just whack you with a forearm or an elbow. Naturally, you weren't allowed to call him for a foul. If you dribbled past him, he'd grab your pants from behind and pull them down.

I'll give Red this much—he could make a set shot.

They had a promotion at Boston Garden where they were giving away money to charity based upon how many free throws you made. Red was in his street clothes and hadn't warmed up. He took off his sport jacket, went to the line and made 28 in a row.

SLICK LEONARD: Red hated to lose at anything. One night we were in a bar and Jim Loscutoff was arm wrestling [the Lakers'] Dick Garmaker. Loscutoff had about 50 pounds on Garmaker, but Garmaker whipped him.

Red came over and said, "Gotta do it again. Garmaker's elbow was off the table."

Garmaker beat him again.

Then Red said, "Garmaker got out of his seat."

Over and over, he made Loscutoff arm wrestle and he kept losing. We told Red, "Hey, you're carrying this Celtics pride thing to extremes."

JIM LOSCUTOFF: Red was so damn competitive about everything. When he drove us to exhibition games, we played a game called Zit. If you saw a dog, it was one point. If you saw a dog taking a leak, it was five points. A dog taking a dump was 10 points. If you saw two dogs screwing, you won. Red would weave all over the road, nearly causing accidents as he looked for dogs.

ED MACAULEY: The only thing Red did worse than play basketball was drive. He had a blue convertible Chevy and he drove it like a madman, 80 miles an hour, through the White Mountains to get to these exhibition games he had set up in little towns. The players also rode in cars and no one wanted to go with Red.

Once he said, "I'll drive Cousy and Macauley."

We said, "No you don't. We have wives and kids. If you don't like it, you can trade us." He'd usually end up with one of the rookies in the car.

JIM LOSCUTOFF: Gene Conley and I were in Red's car on a trip to Bangor, Maine. It was dark and foggy and tough to see, but Red still drove like hell, 85–90 miles an hour. Suddenly, the road went to the right, but Red missed it and drove straight. He went right on the little road that separated a Howard Johnson's from some gas pumps, and he was telling a story the whole time. He loved to talk when he drove, and he'd look at you when he drove instead of the road.

I said, "Red, didn't you see those gas pumps?"

Red said, "Nah, don't worry about it."

TOM HEINSOHN: Red always scheduled a million exhibition games and we must have dedicated every high school gym in New England for a 10-year period from the middle 1950s to 1960s. It was not uncommon to drive a 400-mile round-trip for a game. We traveled in a caravan and we were going up and down the mountain roads through the Berkshires. We had some apples and started an apple fight, throwing apples out of our car at the guys in another car. We were driving side-by-side, throwing apples at each other. We got pulled over by the cops because Red was driving on the wrong side of the road so his guys could get a good shot at us with the apples. The cops took him to a justice of the peace in one of those little mountain towns and they fined him 25 bucks.

JIM LOSCUTOFF: The cop pulled Red over and he said, "I'm Red Auerbach, coach of the Boston Celtics."

The cop said, "I don't care who you are, you're going to the justice of the peace."

Red said, "We have an exhibition game tonight in—"

The cop said, "I don't care, you're going to the justice of the peace."

We followed him about five miles down some dirt road into the woods and stopped at a log cabin. The justice of the peace was an old man in a rocking chair on the front porch.

The cop said Red was arrested for reckless driving.

The JP said, "Who are you?"

Red said, "I'm the coach of the Boston Celtics."

Then the old guy said, "Who are the Boston Celtics?"

Red started to explain, when the old guy interrupted him and said, "It's 25 bucks or you spend the night in jail."

This was in 1957 and 25 bucks was a lot of money. Red bitched as he dug into his wallet.

FRANK RAMSEY: The other time Red got into trouble with the law was when we were walking off the court in Cincinnati and a fan took a swing at him. Red swung back and punched the guy. We went back to the hotel, and a cop showed up at Red's door. He said, "Red, you better go down to the station with us. This guy is swearing out a warrant on you."

JIM LOSCUTOFF: Cousy saw the cops taking Red away and he said, "If you lock him up, make sure you have Chinese food and Coke." Red drinks Coca-Cola for breakfast and he has Chinese food at least once a day.

FRANK RAMSEY: Cousy and [trainer] Buddy Leroux went down to the station and Red had to post bond. Red didn't have enough money and he asked Buddy for it.

Cousy thought it was hilarious. He told the desk sergeant, "You can't put that man in jail because you don't have Chinese food."

Red was upset and yelled, "Cooz, will you just shut up already?"

Buddy was saying that he didn't have the $100 to cover the bond. It took a couple of hours, but Red finally talked his way out of that.

JIM LOSCUTOFF: The fan dropped the charges, and after that Red left the guy tickets every time we played in Cincinnati. They became buddies, which shows you how times have changed. Instead of making up, today a fan punched by a coach would get a lawyer and sue the coach's ass off. But fights were considered part of our game.

FRANK RAMSEY: Red had a lot of superstitions. He wanted the shirt of your jersey tucked into your pants. He did not want the strap of your jersey to be crooked. After warmups, the last person had to make a basket. If you missed the last shot and came over to the bench, Red would yell, "Get back out there—you missed the last one." That was exactly what he said, the words never changed.

BOB COUSY: Red did not want you to talk to a player on the other team, although Russell was an exception.

[The Celtics always wore black Converse tennis shoes. Auerbach told friends that he liked them because they didn't show the dirt.]

FRANK RAMSEY: Red never wanted us to sit down during time-outs, no matter how tired we were. If you sat down, he went crazy.

RED AUERBACH: It was a pure psych job. We ran more than any other team, and we knew that they were tired. I wanted the other team to see us and think, "Those guys have been running their asses off and look, they don't even sit down." A lot of the things people call superstitions were done for a reason. Even though I never met the man, I was influenced by [former baseball manager] Joe McCarthy. He said if you wanted to be a champion, then you had to look like one. So, on the road I required the players to wear shirts and ties. I had a fetish about a neat uniform: no T-shirts in practice and no jersey out of your pants during games. So before we went back on the court after a time-out, I'd look the guys over and make sure that they had their uniforms right. I wanted them to look sharp, not tired.

JOHN HAVLICEK: We were playing Philadelphia in a seventh game and about 10 minutes before the start, Red called us off the court and into the dressing room—something he never did. Everyone assumed that Red had some great pep talk prepared.

But in the dressing room, Red said, "Everybody, sit down."

Then he turned to Russell. "Hey, Russell, did you throw up?"

Russell said, "No, Red, I didn't."

Russell had a nervous stomach and threw up before every big game. Red believed that Russell had to throw up for us to win.

Red said, "I don't care if there's 15,000 people out there, a national television audience and everyone else waiting, we're not going back on the court until Russell throws up."

So Russell went into the bathroom. We heard these guttural sounds, and everyone was closing their eyes and trying not to listen because it's not real pleasant. But there was Red, smiling because his last superstition had been covered.

After the game, all the reporters were asking us what Red said before the game. We said he told Russell to throw up. They laughed and didn't believe us, as if we were hiding some secret.

CARL BRAUN: The thing that surprised me was after a bad loss, Red would just grab his coat and hat and leave. He didn't believe in screaming at the team after a defeat. Now, the next day at practice, it was a different story. But by waiting, Red gave the players time to think about the game, and he also gave himself time to decide exactly what he wanted to say. It's a good way to avoid saying something stupid, as coaches often do after a bad loss.

GENE CONLEY: Red was forever looking for an angle. There was a game in Philadelphia where Red was convinced that he was being cheated by the guy running the clock. He got into an argument with the timekeeper, then with [Philadelphia coach] Neil Johnston, who was a foot taller than Red. Suddenly, Red threw a punch at Johnston, the cops grabbed Red and took him off the court. As the cops dragged him past the bench, Red said, "Russ, Cooz, you guys take over. Don't let them do this to us." We were behind at that time and we came back to blow them out. After the game, we walked in the dressing room and there was Red puffing on a cigar and wearing a huge grin. He had planned the whole thing.

JOHN HAVLICEK: While Red didn't say much after games, it was a different story before and at halftime. He would pick on you about anything. He'd see a guy drinking tea and he'd say, "Oh, you must have your tea just like a little old lady. Maybe instead of drinking that damn tea, you should think about who you're guarding tonight."

Some guys ate a candy bar for energy and Red would say, "We must have our candy bar because if we don't eat our candy, then we can't play." He didn't nag at us all the time, but he did it when he believed a player wasn't focused.

GENE CONLEY: He was continually yelling at Heinsohn and Loscutoff, usually to hit the boards. There was one game where Red came into the dressing room at the half and before he could even yell at Heinsohn, Tommy said, "I didn't rebound, I didn't play defense and I took bad shots. Anything I missed, Red?"

That broke everyone up, even Red.

JIM LOSCUTOFF: Red blamed Tommy and me for everything. It was how he got across his message to Cousy, Russell, Sharman and the rest of the guys without directly insulting them. I didn't care. I had a tough hide, so if he wanted to chew my ass out, that was fine with me.

TOM HEINSOHN: Loscutoff and I were the whipping boys. Since I played a lot more than he did, I had to take a lot more from

Red. I knew what was going on, but once in a while I got tired of it.

I'd ask Red, "Do I deserve to start on this team?"

He'd say, "Sure you do."

I said, "Well, geez, you've been on my case all damn month so bad that the rookies are stealing my socks."

Red asked, "The rookies are what?"

I said, "They figure you've got so little respect for me, they're stealing my socks."

Red said, "Oh, I'll take care of that."

Then he'd back off for a while. That was Red's secret, he knew when to apply the needle and then when to pull back.

RED AUERBACH: I had very few discipline problems. In all my years coaching the Celtics, I fined only four guys. Three were caught after curfew and the fourth was Sam Jones, who was eating pancakes on the day of a game.

SAM JONES: Don't ask me why, but Red was convinced that the worst thing you could eat were pancakes before a game. We had gotten into Syracuse on a late-night flight and it was early in the morning. Rather than go right to bed, most of the players went to a diner for something to eat. I ordered pancakes. Red saw me and went crazy. "That will be five bucks."

I asked, "For what?"

Red said, "How can you eat pancakes on a game day?"

I said, "Red, the game isn't until tomorrow night."

He said, "It's after midnight, so this is a game day and those pancakes will cost you five bucks."

RED AUERBACH: How dumb can you be? Everyone knows that pancakes just lie in your stomach for hours.

FRANK RAMSEY: Sam tried to get out of it by saying, "If it's going to cost me five bucks, then I'll just finish these."

Red yelled, "That's five bucks a bite."

Sam put down his fork and pushed away the plate.

SAM JONES: Red stayed on me about little things. I bought a motorcycle. Red read about it in the newspaper and called me, "Sam, you better get your ass off that thing."

I said, "Red, you don't own my life."

Red said, "As long as you play for me, I do."

So I kept it in the garage and those few times when I did take it out, I made sure to ride it where Red would never see or hear about it.

Red was a little dictator. If you did things his way, everything was great. He really had few rules. He had one curfew when I was on the team. We had won something like 10 in a row and he said, "I want everyone in by midnight." He did a bed check and didn't catch anyone, but the next game we lost by 20 to Detroit, which was the worst team in the league. He never said another word about a curfew after that.

ED MACAULEY: Red wanted you to know he was in charge, and he did it with money. In the early 1950s, meal money was about $5 a day, but salaries were so low that five bucks was a lot of money.

On one trip, Red didn't give Bob Brannum his meal money. Brannum asked Red about it, and Red said, "The way you're playing, you don't deserve any."

After a few days, Brannum was about broke. He told Cousy and myself what happened and we said, "Next time Red says something about meal money, tell him to keep it."

Brannum asked Red for the money again and Red went on about not being deserving of the money.

Brannum said, "Fine, Red, just keep it."

Red said, "Listen, I don't want to keep your money." He had the cash out in a flash.

FRANK RAMSEY: There were no team buses back then, so we took cabs from the airport to our hotel. It was four guys in a cab, and the rookie had to pay the tab. The rookie then had to get the money back from Red, and if Red decided that you tipped the driver too much or if the fare should have been cheaper, he'd give you a hard time. Usually, he gave you what you paid, but he liked to harass you before he handed over the money.

RON GRINKER: They talk about Red's talent—and he had great players. But he also acquired those great players through trades and drafts. He was so far ahead of the rest of the NBA. It was like he was playing chess while they played checkers.

JIM LOSCUTOFF: Red had no assistants, no scouts. He was our coach, our traveling secretary, and on days off on the road he'd have practice in the morning and that night he'd rent a car and go watch a college game. It burned him out, that was why he quit coaching.

WAYNE EMBRY: I remember the last time Red lit up the victory cigar as a coach. It came the year after he left the bench and put Russell in charge of the team. There was a massive snowstorm in Boston and Russell was the only Celtic who didn't get to the Garden for the game. We were playing Golden State with Nate Thurmond. Red took over on the bench. With no Russell, I had to play 45 minutes instead of my usual 10–15. We beat them in a close game and Red made some moves at the end that made a difference. In the final minute, he got to sit back on the bench, smile and fire up that cigar one more time because he had come down out of the stands to coach the team and win one last game.

Red's Last Banner

In Red Auerbach's last year coaching the Celtics, he turned what could have been a trip into schmaltzy nostalgia into a challenge—to himself, his team and the entire NBA.

"Before the start of the [1965–66] season, I said I was quitting," said Auerbach. "I told the Lakers, the Sixers and anyone else, this was their last shot at me. I didn't want to be accused of going out while I was still ahead. They had one more chance to knock me off."

Auerbach was 47 years old. He had filled the roles of coach, president, general manager, player personnel director and resident bean counter. "Today, they have three assistant coaches," said Auerbach. "I never needed one. I did the work of six people."

He also paid the price. One day he saw his picture in the newspaper and wondered, "Who is that guy?" He went to a mirror and saw a man losing his hair, a man whose remaining hair was turning gray. Mostly, he saw a man getting old fast, getting old before his time. He had been coaching in the NBA since before it was the NBA, dating back to 1946 and the Washington Capitols of the Basketball Association of America.

Auerbach wasn't planning to just pick up some of his favorite Chinese food to go and then head down to Miami Beach. He'd still be a part of the Celtics. As president, he'd still be the Celtics, making sure that the Celtics stayed the Celtics by drafting and trading for players. But it was someone else's turn to coach the team.

The rest of the NBA was glad to see Auerbach go. They were sick of his cigar, sick of his egotism, sick of losing to Boston.

His Celtics also were getting old. Tommy Heinsohn joined Bob Cousy and Bill Sharman in retirement. Auerbach signed L.A. Lakers castoff Don Nelson to help the bench. The average age of the Boston starters was slightly over 30.

Even though they had lost to Boston in seven games in the 1965 Eastern Conference Finals, the Philadelphia 76ers were now convinced that they could beat Boston. The Celtics were aging, vulnerable and a John Havlicek steal away from sitting out the NBA Finals the year before.

Philadelphia would have Wilt Chamberlain for a full season. The Sixers had a terrific draft, adding Billy Cunningham out of North Carolina. With a starting lineup of Hal Greer and Wally Jones in the backcourt, Luke Jackson and Chet Walker at the forwards, Wilt in the middle and Cunningham as the sixth man, this figured to be their year. The Sixers were deep and balanced. They didn't need as much offense from Chamberlain, who led the league with a 33.5-point average, the lowest of his seven-year career. NBA players recognized that Chamberlain was making a commitment to team basketball and he was voted the MVP. From 1960–68, Chamberlain and Russell took turns winning the award, Chamberlain earning five, Russell receiving four.

The 1965–66 Sixers were convinced they—not Boston—had the best team. Then they went out and proved it, at least during the regular season.

For the first time in nine years, Boston did not win the Eastern Division. The Sixers won their last 11 regular-season games—beating Boston twice—to rack up a 55-25 record compared to 54-26 for the Celtics.

Since 1955, the NBA had employed a playoff system in which the division winners drew a first-round bye. What that usually meant was Boston practiced for 7–10 days while the other playoff teams took care of the first round, which was a best-of-5 series in 1966.

But now Boston had to play, and had to play a strong Cincinnati team led by Oscar Robertson. The Royals had a 45-35 record in the East, good for third place. Had they been in the West, they would have tied the Lakers for first.

This was a bizarre series. The home team lost each of the first four games. Robertson was battering the Celtics backcourt, regularly posting triple-doubles, although no one had a name for them yet. Auerbach's bald head showed more than the usual collection of beads of sweat and he was even more cantankerous with officials. He was thinking the unthinkable, asking himself, "Is this how I go out? In the first round? To Cincinnati?"

In Game 5, Robertson scored 37. But the Celtics received 34 from Sam Jones and pulled out a 112–103 victory.

Next up, Philadelphia.

The Sixers' regular season ended on March 20. They didn't play the Celtics until April 3, going 13 days without a game. The old debates were hashed and rehashed. How much rest is too much? Is it better to come off a tough playoff series and then move right into the next round, or would the physical and emotional price paid to beat Robertson and the Royals catch up with Boston against Philadelphia?

This much was certain—the Sixers were favored.

But in Game 1, Boston crushed the Sixers, 115–96, and they did it in Philly.

"There was a lot of whining about the layoff hurting them," said Auerbach. "Well, we went through that for years. It's no big deal, you just practice. You just stay ready to play whenever they tell you to play."

Auerbach was relishing his new role as the underdog.

In Game 2, Boston dumped the Sixers again, 114–93. The only notable thing about this game was that Billy Cunningham and Larry Siegfried traded punches in the final period. Russell and Chamberlain came to break it up and ended up screaming at each other—something that had never happened to them.

It took Boston only five games to dispose of Philadelphia. In Game 5, Chamberlain scored 46 points, but it was an ugly 46 as he was 8-of-25—from the foul line!

Dolph Schayes was the regular-season Coach of the Year, but being reduced to playoff ashes cost him his job. Alex Hannum would be hired to coach the Sixers for the 1966–67 season.

That put Boston in the Finals again, against the Lakers—again. It was the fourth time in five years that a Fred Schaus–coached Lakers team faced Boston in the Finals.

This also was not one of Schaus's better teams. With a 45-35 record, the Lakers were the only Western team to play .500 basketball.

At the start of the season, Bob Short had sold the Lakers to Jack Kent Cooke for over $5 million. It was still a centerless team, unless the name Leroy Ellis excites you. Jerry West averaged 31, but Elgin Baylor's knees were wearing down and he averaged only 16.6 points, sitting out 15 games.

Schaus was hoping that he could catch Boston flat, that the Celtics would believe they had won the title by beating Philadelphia. Furthermore, Schaus's Lakers had a knack of stealing an early game in Boston, and they did it again, beating the Celtics, 133–129, in overtime with West and Baylor combining for 77 points.

But Auerbach stole the spotlight before Game 2, saying that the new Celtics coach would be Bill Russell. Not only would Russell be the league's only player-coach, he would be the league's first black coach, the first "Negro coach" of any major league franchise. That led to serious discussions about a black man's ability to lead, to tell white men what to do, and what did this all mean to the future of the Republic?

Auerbach simply said that the best coach for the Celtics and Russell was Russell, end of discussion.

Then the Celtics won the next three games, and the series seemed about over with Game 5 at Boston Garden.

But the Lakers won, 121–117, as Baylor scored 41.

In Game 6 at L.A., the Lakers won again as rookie Gail Goodrich scored 28.

Suddenly, this was a seven-game series, and Auerbach found his shirt sweat-soaked again. Before the game, his last game, Auerbach gave one of his favorite pep talks. He discussed how the difference between winning and losing was $700 to each player, and then asked the players to consider where else they could earn $700 for a couple of hours of work. He brought up the topic of losing, of what a lousy summer it would be as everyone would want to know why they lost, to the Lakers, after being up 3–1.

The Celtics left the dressing room and received a standing ovation from their sellout crowd. They jumped out to a 10–0 lead and seemed to have the game under control, leading by 19 points in the third quarter.

With 16 seconds left in the game, Boston was ahead by six points and had the ball. Auerbach figured it was over. Massachusetts Governor John Volpe lit Auerbach's victory cigar, and then Red almost ended up eating it. The Celtics kept throwing the ball away. With four seconds left, it was 95–93 and the Lakers were pressing all over the court. Boston got the ball to K.C. Jones, who killed the clock.

Finally, it was over.

Russell had played all 48 minutes, scoring 25 and tearing down 32 rebounds. Sam Jones scored 22 on 10-of-21 shooting, which meant a lot since the rest of the Celtics shot only 33 percent. Havlicek had a nightmare from the field with 6-of-21, but he played all 48 minutes and hustled his way to 16 rebounds. Boston owned the boards 77–60.

In the Lakers' dressing room, Schaus and West were distraught. Schaus could not believe that Auerbach would light up a cigar in such a close game. Even for Auerbach, it was an absolutely appalling display of arrogance, or so it seemed to the Lakers.

"How I would have loved to have come back and won that game with Red puffing on that cigar," Schaus said years later.

West was brilliant. He played his guts out, 48 minutes, 36 points and 10 rebounds from the guard position. He was so drained that he could only speak in a whisper when it was over.

But West had little help. Baylor's body was breaking down and he scored 18 on 6-of-22 shooting. No other Laker scored more than 12.

For the fourth time in five years, Schaus, West and Baylor had no choice but to breathe Auerbach's smoke.

The Definition of Greatness

TOM MESCHERY: The winning atmosphere in Boston started with the Garden. The place would smell of old cigars. The floor looked great on television, but that checkerboard was a disgrace because of loose screws, dead spots and everything else. Nonetheless, that floor became a symbol of winning. Red Auerbach was the perfect coach for that building. He was brilliant, abrasive, and he smoked smelly cigars. He intimidated officials and other players, threatening to kick everyone's ass. The fans were the same way, yelling things about your mother, combative before the opening tip.

JOHN HAVLICEK: The visiting teams complained about the Garden, but it wasn't any better for us. The dressing rooms were some wooden benches located under the bleachers. That meant the taller guys had to dress in the front of the room where the ceiling was higher. As you went deeper into the room, the ceiling sloped down and that was where the smaller guys were. To call it a locker room is a misnomer, because there were no lockers. Just a strip on the wall with nails pounded into it. You hung your clothes on the nails and hooks. There was a six-foot area that had four showers and there was only one toilet, so guys would line up before the game. After playing at Ohio State where we had nice facilities, I couldn't believe this was really Boston Garden, home of the greatest team in the NBA.

SAM JONES: The rookies had to shower last, and since they had only one shower, I'd have to wait 45 minutes after a game to get cleaned up. Later, they expanded the dressing room to give us six showers and I thought I'd gone to heaven.

BOB COUSY: I talked to Walter Brown about the dressing room and he said that even though we were winning championships, we were barely breaking even financially. I suppose that could have been propaganda, but I don't think it was.

WAYNE EMBRY: Boston was a hockey town and the Bruins had the most fans and made the most money, so they had the best dressing room.

FRANK RAMSEY: We all had our pregame routines in the dressing room. It began when we arrived in our suits and ties and then had to hang our best clothes up on those lousy nails. Each player had two nails. Then we sometimes had our children in the dressing room, and about 40 minutes before the game we'd go out into the arena with them and take them to their seats. Then we'd warm up and come back into the dressing room. We had a little hot plate and a coffee pot to boil water. Everyone had a cup with their number on it. As the game grew near, Red would have a cigar, Heinsohn would smoke his cigarette. Sharman would do his stretching exercises and then he'd have tea. The rest of us usually had coffee. If it was a big game, we waited for Russell to throw up, then we were ready.

TOM MESCHERY: The Celtics wore those old, terrible black Converse shoes and bandages. God, the bandages, pads and tape those guys wore. When you arrived in Boston, there always were newspaper stories saying, "Russell is out with a broken neck. He may not live beyond tomorrow." He'd limp onto the court, death warmed over. Then he'd get 25 rebounds, block 10 shots and throw down three dunks in a crucial part of the game.

BARRY CLEMENS: During warmups, they looked like the walking wounded. They always started their layup line on the left side of the basket—everyone else did it on the right. One guy would be wearing a warmup top but no bottom. Another would have on the sweat pants but no warmup top. A third would be sitting on the bench while the trainer wrapped his leg in an Ace bandage. During the game, they never said much. If you tried to talk trash to them, you got nowhere. They wouldn't respond. It was as if you didn't exist.

WAYNE EMBRY: For all their injuries, the Celtics always had their big guns ready for the playoffs. I can't think of an example where they lost one of their key players for a long period, say half a season.

SATCH SANDERS: On the Celtics, guys played hurt for two reasons. First, we all wanted to be a part of the winning. Second, we were a deep team, 8–9 talented players. Cousy and Sharman knew that if they were out for long, Sam and K.C. Jones were good enough to take their jobs. Our practices were fierce because the guys on the bench wanted to play—they knew they were good enough to start on other teams— and the starters wanted to tell the bench guys, "You're good, but we can still kick your ass." We had a lot of fights in practice, and to us the games were usually a relief.

BARRY CLEMENS: I was told by some Boston players that they'd each put 10 bucks into a pot, then they'd divide up the team and play 5-on-5 with the winners getting the $100 pot. Those pickup games were supposed to be like the playoffs, because $20 bucks a man was a couple of days' meal money.

LENNY WILKENS: In my rookie year, Red would go to his bench and here would come Frank Ramsey, K.C. and Sam Jones—three Hall of Famers who didn't even start.

TOM GOLA: Part of the Celtics' success was that they could break in players such as the Joneses and Havlicek gradually. The guys who played with Russell should go down on their knees every night and thank the good Lord that they were in a system that accented their strengths and hid their weaknesses. They were groomed to be winners, not thrown into the sea and told to swim with the sharks like rookies on other teams.

RICHIE GUERIN: People forget that there were only eight teams, so when it came time to draft, the worst the Celtics would pick was eighth.

That's a lottery pick today. The last pick in the third round was No. 24, which is a low first-rounder today. So they had access to good college talent and the luxury of slowly developing their players.

JOHN HAVLICEK: We won so much and guys were willing to come off the bench because of Red's attitude. He convinced us that we would be paid on our value to the team, not on statistics. He'd say, Russell is my best player, he has the most to do with winning, so he'll be paid the most. But Russell did not score the most points. Cousy was the second-best player, so he was paid right after Russell on the salary scale. No one dared bring up stats. No one would say, "Hey, I got my 30. I can't help it that the other guys . . . " We were in double figures. Seldom did anyone average much over 20.

CARL BRAUN: I joined the Celtics in 1961 after a rough year and a half as coach of the Knicks. I was 20-59 one season, and I didn't want to go out of the game having been fired by New York. So Red asked me to play a year and I did. The first change I noticed was with the box scores. After a game in New York, there would be a wrestling match in the dressing room because guys wanted to see their stats. With the Celtics, the box scores sat on the table where they were left by the stat people. The Celtics only cared about the final score.

FRED SCHAUS: In the early 1960s, the Celtics had three of the greatest defensive players who ever lived: K.C. Jones, Satch Sanders and Russell. Russell shut down the middle. K.C. just bodied Jerry West and K.C. was so strong and quick that he was able to keep West off balance. Then there was Sanders with those long arms smothering Elgin Baylor. Our eyes would light up when Heinsohn came in for Sanders. Heinsohn could shoot, but we were grateful to get Sanders out of the game.

ELGIN BAYLOR: When I think of the Boston defense, I think of Satch Sanders. He was about my size [6-foot-6]. He was aggressive but not dirty, and he lived to play defense. He was totally unselfish and the toughest player I ever went against. And if you did beat him, then you had Russell to contend with.

JACK TWYMAN: To forwards, Sanders was a nightmare. He covered you like a blanket. I never faced a forward who played the defense Satch did.

SATCH SANDERS: When I came to the Celtics [in 1960], Loscutoff was coming off a back injury and there was a chance for me to play immediately if I could show I played very stern defense. I was there to guard people, to pass to my teammates and do only a minimum of shooting. If I stepped out of that role, I'd hear abuse from Red the likes of which I never heard before. In college, I was a scorer. I went into the NBA wanting to average 20 points, to make All-Star teams and make a lot of money. I would have preferred to shoot more, but we had other players to do that. I even went through a couple of weeks where I scored 20 a game, but we didn't play as well as a team. Then it dawned on me. I was shooting well, but I was messing up the team. So I went back to playing defense. At times, sacrificing my offense was frustrating. But I also knew that my teammates appreciated me, and I took tremendous satisfaction from the winning.

TOM MESCHERY: The Celtics won most of their games in the third quarter. You'd battle them even, maybe be ahead by a few points and you'd head into the dressing room. The third quarter would start, and all you could do was get one shot. They'd get every rebound, every loose ball, and then they'd fast break you to death. Auerbach gave his players a lot of freedom on offense, as long as they played good defense. You'd see Sam Jones or Heinsohn come down on a fast break 1-on-3, and they'd take—and make—a 17-footer. Most guys would say, "Wait a minute, they have three guys on defense, I better wait and set up my offense." Not the Celtics. Not guys like Ramsey and Havlicek. Of course, not everyone had the green light. Russell, Sanders and K.C. seldom looked to shoot. But the other guys, they would wear you out. Heinsohn was a great player. He introduced me to the NBA with a right cross that opened up a cut over my right eye. He had absolutely no conscience. We called him Ack-Ack, as in a machine gun.

BOB RYAN: Heinsohn was one of the most underrated players of his era. You remember him for the way he did things—his line-drive jump shot, his running hook shot, his knack of stealing rebounds, and he did it all with a crooked smile. A guy would get a defensive rebound and Tommy would sneak in from behind and take the ball away. Auerbach always accused him of not being in shape. Red once said Tommy was "an old 30." He carried too much weight and he should have quit smoking. But in the end, his knees got him; they were just bone on bone.

GENE CONLEY: When you have Ramsey, Heinsohn, the Joneses, Russell and all of our great players on one team, who are you going to double-team? Any one of those guys would step up and take the big shot. Red had so many options and so many players who wanted the ball in the clutch.

WAYNE EMBRY: My first year with the Celtics was Russell's first year as coach. We didn't win the title that year, Wilt and Philadelphia did. But how the Celtics acted in defeat showed me a lot. We dressed quietly and went on our way. No finger-pointing at each other or blaming the officials. If you lose with dignity, then you don't become a loser. We hated losing, but it was as if the entire team made a silent vow right then that we wouldn't lose again next year, and we came back to win the title.

BOB COUSY: What I point to with the most pride is that I was on six of the championship teams when the Celtics won 11 titles in 13 years. Because there were fewer teams, it was harder to win titles. The talent wasn't diluted as it is today. Rivalries, even hostilities, were more intense because there were fewer players and you saw them more often. To win 11 titles in 13 years will never be duplicated. While today's jock will fight to get to the top, he won't fight to stay there. He doesn't have the motivation, determination and dedication to repeat year after year as we did. That was the key to the Celtics' greatness—not getting on top, but making the sacrifices to stay there.

13

THEY BLEW THE
WHISTLES—AND THE CALLS

SID BORGIA: I started calling pro games in 1946, back in the old Basketball Association of America. I went straight from the Madison Square Garden Boys Club to what was the forerunner of the NBA. You couldn't get people to officiate pro games in the 1940s, 1950s and even into the 1960s. There was so much adverse publicity about officials. The money and travel were terrible. When I was supervisor of NBA officials in the early 1960s, I had to run advertisements begging qualified officials to try out. The best wanted to work college games. They might take a few pro games if they could fit them into their schedules, but the last thing they wanted to be was a full-time NBA official.

JOHN VANAK: Sid Borgia hired me to work a few NBA games in 1959. I was a policeman in Lansford, Pennsylvania, making $4,200, and had worked some amateur games, but not a lot. Someone had seen me ref a benefit game and had given my name to Sid. On a Monday night, I got a call from Sid, asking if I was interested in officiating in the NBA.

It was not something that I had thought about seriously, but here was the supervisor of NBA officials asking me if I wanted to work. I was amazed, but I said sure.

Sid said, "Fine, be at the Convention Center in Philadelphia on Wednesday. You'll work the first game of the doubleheader with me—New York and Syracuse."

Then he hung up. That was it. In two days, I would be in the NBA.

Obviously, I wasn't even close to being ready. I had a terrible game. I was so nervous that I couldn't even call out the right number when I called a foul on someone.

After the game, Sid surprised me when he said, "You have a lot of potential."

Later, I found out that having potential meant that you were a big guy who was willing to work cheap. In the NBA of 1960, there was no security. You went month to month, no contract. You were paid $40 a game, but only $25 for exhibition games.

The best officials also had regular jobs. Mendy Rudolph worked for WGN in Chicago. Earl Strom worked for General Electric, Norm Drucker was with the New York public schools. Those guys had to work most of their games on Friday, Saturday and Sunday, or at arenas near their homes so they could get to their day jobs.

The full-time refs were Jim Duffy, Joe Gushue, Richie Powers and myself. Joe Gushue and I worked nearly all of the games out west, which was St. Louis and L.A. In my first year, I spent 68 nights at the Hacienda Hotel in L.A.

NORM DRUCKER: Back then, Sid would try out a guy for a game or two in the middle of the season, then he'd disappear. You never knew what happened, just that the guy didn't cut it.

JOE GUSHUE: Guys would work two games and then you'd never see their name in a box score again. You could get fired for a lot of reasons, not just because you had a bad game. One of the owners may not have liked you, and he'd call the league office in New York. If he made a good enough case against you, you were history. There were no tapes of the games. It was just your word against his. And who are they going to believe—the raw rookie or one of the owners? And the owners were convinced that their players never lost a game, the officials did.

JOHN VANAK: I know of an instance where Sid Borgia worked a game with a kid official. Eddie Gottlieb was upset because the kid blew a goaltending call that cost his team the game. Gotty called the league and the kid never worked again.

SID BORGIA: John Vanak was the only official I ever fired and then brought back. He was a pudgy cop when I hired him and he didn't impress me. I told him to lose some weight and I'd give him a second chance. He came back thinner and I rehired him. But he was the one exception. We didn't have time to work with guys back then. We were just trying to keep all the games covered. I had to decide if a guy could make it or not. It was a gut feeling. The best official, the most natural official I ever saw, was Joe Gushue, and he had absolutely no background. But he had the guts and the heart to be an official.

JOE GUSHUE: I was working summer league games in Wildwood, New Jersey, when Sid Borgia spotted me. I never even worked a high school or college game. I had three babies and was a union carpenter out of Philadelphia. I worked the playground games to pick up a few extra bucks. But Sid was on vacation in Wildwood and he saw me one night. He asked me if I wanted to go to the New York Knicks training camp for a week. Sid said that he and I would officiate their scrimmages. It would be my tryout. He hired me at $50 for a regular-season game, and I'd say I made about five grand that first year because Sid liked my work and gave me about 100 games. I was very cocky and I never thought I'd be fired for being a bad official. But the great ones—guys like Strom, Drucker and Rudolph—would tell you to keep a day job because you never knew if you'd be an official next month. You had no security and worked on the whim of your boss, who could get pressure from a lot of different directions.

JOHN VANAK: Since officials worked month to month, the way you knew you were working next month was when the league mailed your schedule to you. Guys would be on the road and one of them would hear from their wives that the schedule had arrived. Word got out and every official in the league would call his wife to see if his schedule was there so he'd know if he was still working.

NORM DRUCKER: In the 1950s, Maurice Podoloff would call you personally to give you your schedule. I started in 1953 at $40 a game. The next year, it was $45 a game. My third year, it was $50 a game. Over the next ten years, it went up about $10 a year. After 14 years in the NBA, I was only making $140 a game. I know that there was a time in the middle 1950s when cash was so tight that Podoloff borrowed money from Ned Irish so the league could pay us.

JOE GUSHUE: After nine years in the league, I was only making $115 a game. They just nickel-and-dimed you to death.

JOHN VANAK: Where officials made a few extra bucks was the playoffs. Again, you wanted as many games as possible. Hey, we pulled for every series to go the full seven. I'm not saying that officials threw games to keep the series alive, but I do think it was a good idea when they finally changed to paying guys a flat fee for the playoffs.

JOE GUSHUE: Podoloff watched the league's purse strings as if they were his own. He went over your expense accounts . . . I mean, he knew what every cab fare was from every hotel to every arena. He knew the rate at every hotel. If you put in $8 for a cab fare he thought was supposed to be $6, he questioned you. In St. Louis, the cab fare was $5 from the airport to downtown. But they offered a limo where you rode with several people, and each person paid a dollar. I took the cab and put in for the $5. He wrote me a letter that said, "When I'm in St. Louis, I take the limo for $1."

I wrote him back to say that the limos were on strike and I had to take a cab.

He wrote me back to apologize, but then he said, "Continue taking a cab, but as soon as the strike ends, make sure you take the limo."

JOHN VANAK: The league didn't give you a laundry allowance and I wasn't making enough money to pay for it out of my own pocket. So after every game I'd run the water in the tub, throw in some shampoo and throw my uniform in. Then I'd let it soak while I called my wife. When I hung up, I'd squeeze out my clothes and hang them up in the bathroom.

JOE GUSHUE: Guys like John Vanak and I would be on the road for three straight weeks, but they still wouldn't pay for us to get our uniforms dry-cleaned. One day, I put in for it anyway.

Mr. Podoloff questioned my receipt.

I explained that I was working the Boston–St. Louis series and the fans went nuts, throwing eggs at the floor. I got pelted with eggs and my uniform was full of yellow stains.

He replied by asking if I was sure that I got hit by the eggs, and could I prove it.

I had to show him a newspaper article that discussed the egg throwing before he'd reimburse me the couple of bucks to get my uniform cleaned.

I'm telling you, we all got pretty good at washing our own stuff in the sink and tub. I always took an extra uniform on the road. But after three weeks away from home, you just couldn't get rid of all the stench, and after a while, you really couldn't stand your own smell.

JOHN VANAK: What I would have given to be like the kids of today and get something like $125 per diem to pay for hotel, meals and other expenses. You don't have to turn in expense forms. It makes life so much easier.

JOE GUSHUE: What people don't realize is that officials usually travel alone because they seldom work together two nights in a row. You may work six games a week and have five different partners. You seldom spend more than 24 hours in a town. I had a stretch where I worked 24 games in 28 days, and all I did was get to a town, lie down, get up and have lunch, relax for a couple of hours, work the game, then do it all over again the next day. Back then, there was a flight early in the morning and one in the afternoon between most cities. If you missed the morning flight, you were in big trouble. You were always operating with only a few hours of sleep.

Once, I left St. Louis at six in the morning and hit a snowstorm trying to get to a game in Fort Wayne. They had 28 inches of snow and I didn't get to the gym until 45 minutes after game time, about 9 P.M. I ended up taking a bus through all the snow from St. Louis to Fort Wayne because there was no other way to get there. They held up the game for me. I felt like dog meat when that game started. But as an official, you're a performer. Even if you're sick and about ready to fall asleep on your feet, you fight through it. If you don't keep on top of things, you can end up with a riot out there.

NORM DRUCKER: The conditions we worked under . . . in places like Syracuse and Fort Wayne, you felt like a Christian being fed to the lions. The arenas were small, the fans were on top of you. In Philadelphia, a guy in the front row would put his legs out and his feet would be on the out-of-bounds line. It sure looked like he wanted to trip you. They threw eggs and all kinds of garbage. As an official, you learned right away that during a time-out, never stand by the visitors' huddle or you'll get pelted with something; always stand near the home team's bench. It was safer.

JOHN VANAK: The one advantage we had was that there was no videotape, so the league couldn't fire you for kicking a call. The coaches could complain all they wanted, but there was no record of what happened. But you had much better officials back then because there were only eight teams—or four games a night. Since we used only two officials per game, that meant just eight would work. The coaches really got to know your tendencies. Willie Smith was king of the three-second call. The coach of a home team would send a ballboy into the official room with a towel or something just to see if Willie was there. If the kid saw Smith, then the coach would tell his center to stay out of the lane.

If there is one thing people should know about officials, it's that we have feelings. On every call, we piss off 50 percent of the people we work with. And you like some off those people who want to kill you. An official also knows that his calls can be a factor in a guy losing his job, because if he loses a close game his owner may pull the plug on him. What I'm saying is that there are nights when even if you did your best, you can't sleep because you wonder if you made the right call, or you might have kicked a call that cost a team a game, or even a good person his job. You learn to live with that pressure, but I never could ignore it. Those are the things you'd sometimes think about when you were lying in bed, staring at the ceiling and wondering if you were ever going to fall asleep.

Sid Borgia: The Godfather of Officials

Sid Borgia was bald, 5-foot-7 and gave the game some of the best and most controversial elements of officiating. He came into pro ball in 1946 and worked for 20 years. He once knocked out the front teeth of an abusive fan in Syracuse.

EARL STROM: Sid Borgia was the godfather of officials. He broke me in. He broke in a lot of guys. He had strong opinions about how the game should be officiated, and an even stronger personality on the court. He set the tone for the rest of us who came after him.

SID BORGIA: When I started in 1946, there was little prestige in being a pro official. The money was terrible—maybe 40 bucks a game. One year, I tore cartilage in my knee and I had to pay for surgery myself.

Pat Kennedy was the first great official. He was so colorful that his name would appear on the marquee when he worked in certain cities. When he retired [in 1950], he went on tour with the Globetrotters. But other than Kennedy, there were very few other officials of note.

When I came into the league, they didn't have a rule book. They handed us a college rule book and said we'd follow these rules, with certain exceptions. When it came to zone defenses, the rule said, "No zone defenses allowed." It was up to us to decide what was a zone. We eventually decided that a zone meant that a defensive player could not stand in the lane for more than three seconds, unless he was guarding someone. The early officials were the pioneers of figuring out how this game should be called.

CHARLEY ECKMAN: Most of the officials in the 1940s were like Chuck Solodare. He had false teeth and he had to stop and take out his teeth before he blew the whistle. Because it was such a pain to mess with his teeth, he only blew the whistle about eight times a night—just enough to keep traffic moving.

Then came Sid Borgia. I worked with Sid as an official. Later, I saw him from the other side when I became coach at Fort Wayne. Sid told me two things: First, "Let the players decide the game." He didn't get caught up in all the details and rules. His idea was to keep play moving, that no one bought a ticket to watch free throws. The other thing he said was, "Make the tough call on the road."

Sid had a barrel of guts. He didn't care if he made a call that brought the house down on him. If that was what he thought was the right call, he made it and then he took the abuse.

SID BORGIA: In my first 10 years as an official, the stigma for officials was "homer." It was nearly impossible to win on the road. Officials were introduced as "Sidney Borgia from New York City." So I'd be working a Knicks game in Philadelphia, and before I even made a call against Philadelphia, the crowd would come down on me because they figured I favored the Knicks because I was from New York. If you called a technical, the public address announcer would say, "And that technical foul on Red Auerbach was called by Sid Borgia." Again, the fans were at your throat. Fans believed they had the right to come to a game and hang the officials on a cross. It took a lot of intestinal fortitude to stand up to all that pressure.

JOE GUSHUE: You could not intimidate Sid. He was a banty little rooster who never took a step back from anyone. The players knew that Sid worked a unique style of game. They'd see him and say, "Sid's here. That means we can really pound the boards. We can get away with this and that."

I felt there were nights when Sid went out to see how few fouls he could call. He still had control of the game, but players went over each other's backs for rebounds. If you drove down the middle, you were fair game. There were nights when he had fights in his game, but not as many as you'd think, given how loosely he called it.

It was as if Sid had a second sense, he knew when to step in and take control. He'd call a technical, maybe even throw a guy out if he had to, but he would bring order back to the court.

SID BORGIA: What I brought to the NBA was common sense. Fans want to see action, so I let things go. I'd let two centers beat the hell out of each other. I had games where Harry Gallatin and Vern Mikkelsen would say, "Let us go." Both guys spoke Polish, and they'd be swearing at each other and at me. Usually, I just ignored them and they settled things between themselves. But what I made sure to do was let all the players get away with the same things. I wanted to be consistent and be fair on the road. That was how you got respect from the players and coaches.

JOE GUSHUE: The philosophy was, "At the end of a game, don't make a call that can be blown out of proportion." So you gave the players more latitude in the final moments. It's a terrible thing to say, but it's how we were taught to call the games. The intent of the game was that the best team on that night would win, not that the game would be decided because an official made a ticky-tacky foul in the final seconds and put a guy on the foul line.

NORM DRUCKER: Our rules were: Don't call three seconds unless it affected a play. Don't call traveling unless a player gained an advantage from it. Don't blow the whistle just to blow it.

PETE D'AMBROSIO: Sid sometimes carried things to an extreme. The dribbler would trip and fall down. Then Sid would blow the whistle and say, "It's not a travel because you were tripped." Then Sid would say to the defender, "It's not a foul, because you didn't mean to trip him." Sid would then give the ball out-of-bounds back to the offense and continue the game as if nothing had happened. He kind of made up his own rules.

JOHN VANAK: Sid would yell, "Nah . . . nah . . . nah," before he made most calls. George Yardley heard him do that and said to me, "Sid makes all that noise first because he's still trying to make up his mind what he's going to call."

SLICK LEONARD: Sid called you by name. He'd say, "Nice shot, Bobby." Or he'd say, "Nah . . . nah . . . nah, Bobby, you can't grab his arm like that. Don't look at me, you know you did it."

RUDY LARUSSO: I'd never seen an official like Sid. The calls he made— "The ball went off you, but Jackie pushed you, so you get to keep possession." Wow. I respected Sid a lot, but he was the King of the Makeup Call. If he blew one, you knew he'd even it up at the other end. That was his way of trying to be fair.

ROD THORN: Remember that hardly any games were on TV, so the officials could do almost anything they wanted. There was no tape to check what really happened. Late in a quarter, some officials would look at the scoreboard and see that one team had five fouls, the other had none. Suddenly, there would be three quick calls on the team with no fouls to sort of even things up. Not very often did one team shoot remarkably more foul shots than the other. The idea was, "Let's make it fair for everybody." The good officials could take the law into their own hands and make it work. But with other guys, you got a lot of crazy calls and very bad games.

Earl Strom: The Spiritual Son of Sid Borgia

When Earl Strom retired in 1990, it ended a 33-year career as an NBA official. Most NBA people consider the four greatest officials to be Pat Kennedy, Sid Borgia, Mendy Rudolph and Strom. Like Borgia, Strom was colorful and he was known as an official who was a law unto himself, a man far more concerned with the spirit of the rules than the details.

EARL STROM: Because I broke into the NBA when there were only eight teams, I had the benefit of working with a veteran official every night. The guys who influenced me the most were Norm Drucker, Arnie Heft and Sid Borgia. Early in my career, I worked a Boston game at Detroit with Sid. I was terrible, and Sid had to keep picking me up, making the calls I missed. Everybody on both teams screamed at me, and I still wasn't reacting. I just wasn't with it. To keep order, Sid had to step in and throw out Bill Russell, Tom Heinsohn and a couple of the Detroit players. After the game, we went into the officials' dressing room. Sid was hot. He closed the door—boom, boom, boom—there were three bolt locks on the door and he locked them all. Then he turned and ripped into me, telling me there was no excuse for calling that kind of game. He said, "We all have bad nights, but to consistently miss calls and then not even react when the players jump all over your ass . . . all you did was wait for me to pick you up."

For one of the few times in my life, I didn't have anything to say.

Sid said, "Look, I know you'll probably tell Jocko about all this, but I hope you learn something from it."

Sid meant that I'd tell Jocko Collins, who was the supervisor of officials. Jocko had hired me, and he and Sid did not get along.

I said, "Sid, I'm not going to say anything to Jocko because everything you said about me was absolutely right."

The next night, we were working a game in Cincinnati. We went to the Detroit airport to catch a red-eye, but there was a snowstorm and it was closed. So we caught a train and went into a compartment.

Sid said, "You know how one of these things works" meaning the train compartment.

At that point of my life, I knew everything. I said, "No problem, I'll see you in the morning."

Sid left and I looked at the compartment, having no idea how to pull the bed down. I looked for a conductor, but he wasn't around. So I sat up, reading the rule book, feeling really stupid.

There was a knock on the door and it was Sid. He said, "Whaddaya doing?"

I said, "Just reading, trying to figure out what I did wrong tonight."

Sid said, "Don't give me that crap. You don't know how the compartment works, do ya? And you didn't have the balls to ask me to help you."

I started to laugh and told Sid that he was right.

He pulled down the compartment and said, "Get some sleep, will ya?"

NORM DRUCKER: Early in his career, we called Strom the Pied Piper, because he blew the whistle so much. If he worked with a weak official, he'd just take the game over and make every call. When I was with Earl, I'd tell him, "Hey, remember, I'm here, too."

EARL STROM: Sid's advice to me was, "In this league, you can't bend to the pressure of the fans, the players, and most of all you can't let coaches intimidate you. You call the plays the same way at both ends of the court because you never want anyone to accuse you of being a homer. You have to be strong and you can't back off."

JOE GUSHUE: Earl changed his style over the years. As a young official, he told me, "I don't care what Sid Borgia says, a foul is a foul. You don't just let plays go to keep the action moving." He really had the red ass as a kid and wouldn't take any lip from anyone without banging them with a technical. But later, Earl mellowed. He got along with people. One day, he even said to me, "Maybe I haven't been calling the game the way it should be called. I'm going to let things go a little more out there." It was exactly what Sid Borgia had told him, but Earl is stubborn and he had to come to that realization on his own.

KENNY HUDSON: In the first game I worked with Earl, a fan yelled something insulting at him. Earl screamed, "Come down here and say that." At the same time, Earl was taking off his belt and wrapping it around his fist. He was ready to literally belt the guy.

EARL STROM: In the old days, the league didn't supply security for the officials so you had to be ready in case someone attacked you. Even the ushers and police were fans of the hometown team, so they weren't about to stand up for you. There was a night in Madison Square Garden when someone threw a whiskey bottle at me from the upper deck. It exploded at my feet and there was glass everywhere.

The announcer said, "Please refrain from throwing objects on the floor because they might injure the players."

I said to my partner, "Injure the players? What are we, chopped liver?"

JOHNNY KERR: The great officials like Strom and Borgia would call you by name. They'd say, "Hey, Kerr and Embry, you guys just break it up in there. I want to see daylight." That means they wanted you to stop pounding on each other, but they warned you instead of calling a foul. They were able to control the game without blowing the whistle every two seconds. Those robots that work games today could learn a lot from them.

JOHN VANAK: Earl Strom may have been as good as any official—ever. Not because of his ability, but his attitude and the rapport he developed over the years with people. The players and coaches trusted Earl because they knew he never gave an inch to the home team. Once, we had a bloopers film at an NBA officials camp. Earl made some of the most outrageous calls—if a young official had made those same mistakes, they would have been looking for a rope and a tree. But Earl got away with it because he was respected and he knew how to defuse a tense situation.

I say this while knowing that Earl was not my favorite person to work with. He wanted to dominate the game. I've seen him totally embarrass young officials by overruling them on the court. He did that to me.

Hell, just ask poor Dick Bavetta about Earl. Just as Sid Borgia locked the door on him after a game one night, Earl did the same with Bavetta. Only he nearly strangled Dick.

But I still say he was the greatest official.

RUDY LARUSSO: Earl was the best official ever because of his innate feel for the game—how far to let players go when they were pushing each other, or even when they were bitching at him about a call. And courage, he was the one man I wanted when I was playing on the road. He would almost favor the road team just to show he would not be intimidated. In Boston Garden, they killed most officials, but not Earl. Auerbach would start up with his crap, and Earl was the one guy who could put Red in his place.

14
THE KNICKS

After the advent of the shot clock in 1954–55, the Knicks did not win a playoff game until 1967—when they won exactly one. From 1956–68, they went through six coaches, but had only one winning season. The losing meant high draft picks, but the Knicks' No. 1 choices from 1953–63 were, in order: Walter Dukes, Jack Turner, Kenny Sears, Ronnie Shavlik, Charles Tyra, Mike Farmer, Johnny Green, Darrall Imhoff, Tom Stith, Paul Hogue and Art Heyman. Despite owner Ned Irish's being one of the wealthiest men in the NBA, the Knicks were poorly run, made lousy trades and on the court were seldom a factor.

RICHIE GUERIN: Even in the lean years, the Knicks had a number of quality players like Carl Braun, Dick McGuire, Sweetwater Clifton and myself. But we never had the center to compete in the age when the NBA was a center-dominated league. We were forever rebuilding, and we continually drafted for size instead of the best player available.

TOM GOLA: The Knicks were always drafting these big kids who were supposed to be Moses and lead them to the Promised Land. In the early 1950s, they were a very good team with Carl Braun, Ernie Vandeweghe, Harry Gallatin, Sweetwater Clifton and Dickie McGuire. They played ball the way you should—very team-oriented. I loved to watch them pass. But as the team started to age, the front office did not replace those players. I believe the problem came from on top. The Knicks were owned by the Madison Square Garden Corporation, and Ned Irish had the corporate mentality. There was a chairman of the board, a board of directors, all kinds of people with titles, but who was in charge? The Knicks' decision-making process always seemed muddled to me.

RICK BARRY: The typical Knicks decision was the one they made on me. I wanted to be a Knick, but Ned Irish said he'd never take me because I was "skinny and flaky."

RICHIE GUERIN: The successful teams of this era had hands-on men running them, either as strong owners or general managers. There was Ben Kerner [St. Louis], Eddie Gottlieb [Philadelphia], Danny Biasone [Syracuse] and Red Auerbach [Boston]. But Ned Irish was not in the trenches. He pretty much stayed in his office.

CARL BRAUN: We always traveled and dressed first-class with the Knicks. But there was something missing. Guys like Gottlieb and Kerner ran their teams out of their wallets. It was their blood. Irish could be cold and distant. He started as a sportswriter before moving to the Garden, and he distanced himself from the people he knew before. To me, he always seemed more interested in booking events into the Garden—the rodeo, college games, the circus—than the basketball side of his operation.

MARV ALBERT: I grew up as a Knicks fan, and then became the team's ballboy. I loved the team, but I saw they could never compete with Boston, St. Louis, any of the good teams. After a while, you became accustomed to seeing them fail. So the crowd would entertain itself by betting the point spread.

I fell in love with the Knicks because I loved basketball and I was from Brooklyn. My favorite player was Jim Baechtold from Eastern Kentucky, who wore No. 10. He was not their best player, but he became my player. I started imitating his jump shot when I played on the playgrounds. Then I started the *Baechtold Bulletin*—ah, yes, even then I had a way with words. It was a paper about Baechtold and the Knicks. For 50 cents you got a Baechtold button, a Jim Baechtold autographed picture and, of course, the famed *Baechtold Bulletin* authored by yours truly. The Knicks' management was very receptive to it because they wanted all the publicity they could get. We had about 400 members at one point. The Knicks let us hold meetings at the Garden, and Baechtold would bring players like Sweetwater Clifton to meet us. By the time I was 14, the Knicks said I should just make it a fan club for the whole team. That was fine with me and I changed the name of the paper to *The Knick Knack*—yet another clever title from the wordsmith. The fan club grew to about 1,000. I was such a fanatic that I'd listen to games on the radio and keep score. Being around the Knicks as much as I was, it was easy to become a ballboy, which wasn't exactly the most demanding position in the building. It was while I was ballboy that I got to know [broadcaster] Marty Glickman, who would have me do stats with him while he called the games. That was really my entrée into broadcasting because of the contacts I made through Marty.

GEORGE YARDLEY: The Knicks had good guards in Carl Braun and Dick McGuire, but not much up front. I didn't realize what McGuire could do for a team until I played with him in Detroit. Because of Dick, I led the league in scoring. I always felt Dick was a better pure point guard than Cousy because all he thought about was setting up his teammates. Cousy was a better all-around basketball player because of his scoring, but I never would have led the league in scoring with Cousy. If Cousy played with a group of players and got 50 assists in a week, McGuire would get 70 assists with the same guys.

[Dick McGuire averaged 8.0 points and shot 39 percent in an 11-year career. He won the 1950 assists title and averaged 6.1 for his career. The only Knick with more career assists is Walt Frazier.]

LEONARD KOPPETT: Dick McGuire was the best playmaker I ever saw, and that includes Cousy. He couldn't score at all. He had a mental block about it. He would not shoot the ball. Back then, teams had a guy known as a setup man. He was there to pass, period. The concept doesn't exist today, because the point guard also is expected to score. On the playground, they used to call a guy like Dick a feeder, because he fed the ball to everyone else.

CARL BRAUN: I roomed with Dick for six years and he would make these thread-the-needle passes—he'd do it from inside the foul line in a crowd, exactly where you were not supposed to pass from. Even though the defense knew that Dick wouldn't shoot, he had a knack of drawing the defense to him, then dropping off the ball to a teammate for a layup.

LENNY WILKENS: A point guard often is dependent on his teammates, especially a guy like McGuire. I don't mean to disparage Cousy, but he was very fortunate to play with Russell and all the other Hall of Famers. You put Cousy with the Knicks and McGuire on all those great

Celtics teams and you would hear more about McGuire today than you would about Cousy.

HOT ROD HUNDLEY: Dick couldn't shoot, he couldn't jump and he couldn't run. He had a squatty body, a two-handed set shot that he didn't trust and he would have been perfect as Mumbles in Dick Tracy. But Dick was one of the great playmakers of his day.

MARV ALBERT: Dick's brother, Al, was strictly in the league to get into fights. I guess Dick figured that Al McGuire did enough talking for the both of them, because Dick was painfully shy. That is why he mumbles. Even on the court, he was embarrassed to shoot the ball. The crowd would yell at him to shoot it, but he'd look and look until he found someone open for a pass.

FRANK McGUIRE: Dick McGuire was the first player I ever saw dribble through his legs, and he did it several times with ease in a pickup game. I said, "Why don't you do that in a game?" But he was too shy to do it.

MARV ALBERT: It was just such a different era. When Dick came back to coach the Knicks, he got into pickup games with the players. The Knicks were second bananas in their own building. Their games would be farmed out to the 69th Street Regiment Armory. Even some playoff games were moved because the circus was booked into the Garden. The story that tells you what you need to know about those times was that I was serving as ballboy for the visiting team—in this case, it was Syracuse. It was right before a Knicks game at the 69th Street Armory. A fan walked into the Syracuse dressing room, went right to the urinals and relieved himself right between Dolph Schayes and Paul Seymour, who were standing in uniform at the urinals. The guy finished, zipped up and walked out and no one said a thing.

The Typical Knicks First-Rounder

Walter Dukes was New York's first-round draft pick in 1953, although he played for the Globetrotters for two years because the Knicks did not come up with the cash to sign him. A 7-footer from Seton Hall who led his team to an undefeated regular season, Dukes finally played with New York in 1955–56. Then he was traded to Minneapolis. Finally, he played for Detroit. One of the NBA's first 7-footers, Dukes was supposed to be a player who would change the game. He turned out to be a journeyman center, averaging 10.4 points, 12.1 rebounds and 37 percent shooting. He played in 553 games, fouling out of 121 of them.

EARL STROM: Walter was one of the nicest men in the game. But he also was maybe the clumsiest guy—or at least the clumsiest good player—I've ever seen. He was so foul-prone that he'd hurt people during warmups. We'd hear a whack, then look under the basket and there was Walter getting someone with an elbow—and this was during the layup drill.

GEORGE YARDLEY: I played with Walter in Detroit and we honestly feared him during layup drills. He wouldn't hurt a flea intentionally. But when he'd get excited about getting a rebound—even during warm-ups—he was liable to run you over. It got so bad that Chuck Noble got a cowbell and put it around Walter's neck so we'd hear him coming when we were shooting around.

JOHNNY KERR: Some guys have club feet. Well, Walter had club elbows. He always was bumping into you. He didn't mean to, but he'd swing his elbows and he'd hit you. He'd hit the guys on his team. Everyone just ducked when Walter went to the basket.

BOB FERRY: On an offensive rebound, Walter would nail you with an elbow in the throat and nearly crush your windpipe.

JERRY WEST: I caught an elbow from Walter and it cost me a couple of teeth.

TOM MESCHERY: There was not an ounce of meanness in Walter's body, but he had such sharp elbows and knees. You'd block him out and he'd climb your back with his elbows trying to get the rebound. Or you'd try to get around Walter, and he'd hit you with his bony knee and you'd have a charley horse for a week.

HOT ROD HUNDLEY: I was with the Lakers and Ray Felix was our center. He was playing against Dukes. Walter intentionally tripped Felix while he was running up the court, and Walter did it right in front of an official. The ref tossed Walter.

Felix screamed at the official, "Don't you throw Dukes out. I want a piece of him."

But Dukes was ejected. This was the second quarter.

When the half ended, Felix went right off the floor and directly to the Detroit dressing room. Dukes had his back turned toward the door when Felix went in. Felix tapped Walter on the shoulder. As Walter turned around, Felix punched him right in the chops. Walter never knew it was coming. Before Walter could react, Felix got out of there and came into our dressing room.

BOB FERRY: The other thing about Walter was that he had some kind of glandular problem, or some kind of problem where he never took a shower. For whatever reason, his body odor was unbelievable. One day, we had a two-hour practice and everyone was sweating oceans. Walter put on his best suit and headed right out the door without even stopping for a shower. He said he had to get to an important meeting.

JOHNNY KERR: The joke about Walter was that he couldn't set a blind screen on you because you could smell him coming.

JOHN VANAK: You'd hear guys talking about not wanting to cover poor Walter because of his body odor. I've never smelled anything like it before or since.

BOB PETTIT: Walter Dukes . . . oh, my . . . when I think about him . . . well, Walter would just beat you to death without even trying. I hated playing against him.

EARL STROM: You could see Pettit's nose curl up when he had to play Dukes. One day, I had the ball for the opening tip. Pettit was standing next to Dukes, and you could tell that Bobby hated it. I bounced the ball up and said, "Everybody ready?"

Then I held the ball for an extra second or two, just to make Pettit stand there a little longer next to Walter.

Finally, Pettit said, "Throw the goddamn ball up already, will you?" Which was totally out of character for Bob, who was the ultimate gentleman.

ALEX HANNUM: Bob always had great games against Dukes, even though Walter was a good defensive player and had great stamina. He could run all day. But Pettit just went crazy when he played Walter. We joked that Walter's odor inspired Bob.

EARL STROM: The Pistons had their own plane and occasionally they'd let the refs ride with them to the next city. But one of the conditions was that the official had to sit next to Walter.

BOB FERRY: Walter loved chocolate candy. On airplanes, he'd get a bag of the gooey stuff and put it between his legs as he played poker with us on flights. After a while, it would start to get warm in the plane. Walter would get caught up in the card game and forget about the candy, which would melt all over his crotch. Then he'd reach down to get rid of the candy and his hands would get sticky.

GEORGE YARDLEY: As bad as Walter smelled, he had a lot of girl-friends . . . I'm talking about beautiful women. Sweetwater Clifton was with the Pistons one year. Sweetwater took 2–3 showers a day, brushed his teeth at halftime and was the cleanest man I'd ever been around.

Some of the guys got together and we decided that maybe Sweetwater could talk to Walter. Sweets did, but to no avail. Sweets gave him some toothpaste and some Ban deodorant. Everyone in the dressing room was watching as Walter opened the Ban. He knew it was deodorant, but apparently the only people he had seen use it were women because poor Walter started putting the stuff on the inside of his thighs and on his chest. We all had to bite our tongues to keep from laughing.

BOB FERRY: By the time I joined the Pistons, Walter had lost his effectiveness as a player. But he was taller than me. Dick McGuire was our coach and Dick would start Walter for the opening jump ball, figuring Walter had a better shot at winning the tip than I did.

During the first break, I'd come in. After about six games, Walter figured out that he was going to come out right away, so he stopped jumping on the opening tip.

One day he complained to McGuire about it and Dick said, "Walter, you're getting paid $20,000 for jump balls, will you at least try to get one?"

When I Was a Rookie with the Knicks . . .

Barry Clemens was a fourth-round pick by New York in 1965. A 6-foot-7 forward from little Ohio Wesleyan College, Clemens joined a team that had not won a playoff game since 1955 and was coming off a 31-49 season under Harry Gallatin. Clemens played in the NBA for 11 seasons with five different teams. Known as a fine outside shooter, Clemens was a career 6.7 scorer. His rookie year, 1965–66, was his only season with the Knicks.

BARRY CLEMENS: The Knicks had the worst reputation in the NBA. They always lost a lot, and they drafted very high, but they continually messed up when it came to drafting and trades. No one knew it at the time, but in 1965 the Knicks were starting to put together what would become their great teams of the early 1970s. In 1964, they took Willis Reed in the second round. In 1965, Bill Bradley was their first pick, but he didn't play because he was studying in England on his Rhodes Scholarship. In 1965, they also drafted Dick Van Arsdale and Dave Stallworth in addition to myself.

I got a letter from the Knicks saying that I was invited to rookie camp in June. It was on a Knicks letterhead and I remember staring at the team logo, being very impressed by that. My father had a different opinion. He thought I should go to dental or optometry school—I had been accepted at both. But since it was June, he gave me permission to try out. He probably figured I could get basketball out of my system and then work on finding a career. The Knicks coach was Harry Gallatin, who was a great player. I didn't know that. I'd never heard of Harry Gallatin.

I'm a stutterer, and naturally it is worse when I am nervous. The only directions the Knicks gave me were to take a bus from the airport to a certain street, then get off and take a cab to Madison Square Garden. When I got to the Knicks' office, I stuttered my way through just saying hello and explaining who I was. Someone—just an office worker—told me to check in across the street at the Midtown Hotel. They put four of us in a room—two each to a bed—which didn't make people very comfortable.

The camp was a four-day thing at some armory on the Lower East Side. I don't remember the name, but when you went inside the floor was down in a wide-open area that was the size of at least two football fields. It took about 10 minutes to get to the locker rooms, which were the usual pits. They told us to bring our billfolds up to the floor with us, "because you don't want to leave anything valuable down there."

I stepped on the court and—Jesus Christ—there must have been 50 guys out there. I'd played at a small school and I was one of the tallest guys in my league. I saw all the 7-footers the Knicks had in camp—I didn't know there were that many 7-footers in the world. They had us line up for calisthenics and we filled the court. I kept wondering how they were ever going to tell if anyone could play with all these bodies. We did some drills and scrimmaged a little bit, then they loaded us into cabs and sent us back to the hotel.

The next day, I noticed there were fewer guys at practice. After an hour or so, I saw Gallatin talk to some other guys, then they disappeared. After practice, Gallatin got into a cab with about four guys. When they got out at the hotel, they said they had been cut. It was pretty scary because guys were dropping left and right.

They had two players from the year before: Willis Reed and Emmette Bryant. In the scrimmages, I was on Bryant's team and he kept making me run and then setting me up for open jump shots, which was my strength. Eddie Donovan was the GM, and he was cutting guys, too. By the fourth day, only Larry Lembo and I were in our hotel room. We were terrified that Gallatin or someone would speak to us, because that was the kiss of death. But we were still standing at the end of camp, and later I got word that I was invited to the veterans camp in the fall at Fairfield University. My college coach knew Eddie Donovan, and he negotiated a contract for me, convincing Eddie to give me $10,000—assuming I made the team. I convinced my father that $10,000 was a lot of money and I really wanted to go to camp. I thought I was good enough to play and my dad let me try out.

Harry Gallatin's training camps were grueling. They were scheduled for two hours in the morning, two more in the evening, but they invariably went longer. Harry was a very physical player, so he wanted his team to be the same way. He had something called a "buddy drill." You were paired off with a guy who was your size, and you'd hoist him on top of your shoulders and carry him around the court. It was insane. In this era, they didn't believe in players lifting weights, then they'd tell you to carry around a 225-pound teammate. Tom Gola was on our team and he was a 10-year veteran. He came up with excuses to dodge that drill. He told me, "I just don't understand the point of this stuff."

Art Heyman was in camp. He was the Knicks' No. 1 pick in 1963 and the typical Knicks choice—a guy with a big name in college, a *Sports Illustrated* cover boy from Duke who was really overrated and then didn't do much in the NBA. I roomed with Johnny Egan, who was a nice point guard from Providence. Johnny and I liked to play cards in between the morning and evening sessions. Heyman would break into our games and say to me, "Hey, rook. You're going to get cut tomorrow. I heard it from a guy who knows."

He said garbage like that to me a couple of times. I couldn't understand it back then, but now I realize he was a guy just trying to hang on and make the team, and he was trying to get any edge on me that he could. He used to make fun of Lenny Chappell, one of our forwards. Lenny was a nice guy and he called Heyman Superflake, which was a perfect nickname. During the exhibition season, we drove to the games by car and I was often with Lenny and Heyman. Lenny was a very careful driver, always worried about making the wrong turn. When we were on the road and there were several signs, he turned down the radio.

"Why do that?" I asked him.

"I need to concentrate," said Lenny.

I thought, "Here's a guy who can't read signs and listen to the radio at the same time." Lenny did things like that, which made him a perfect foil for Heyman. Man, Heyman just talked and talked.

One day, Heyman told us, "I'm not going to be here much longer. They're trading me to Cincinnati. Can you imagine me and Big O in the same backcourt?"

Heyman thought he was a great player, but he said the Knicks didn't appreciate him. He really couldn't shoot and wasn't very quick. He had an ego, but it was getting deflated by the day. The irony was that he was traded to Cincinnati, but didn't last very long there, either. The Knicks didn't get much for Heyman and they were just glad to get rid of him.

I could never tell if Gallatin liked me. Our rookies were Dick Van Ardsdale, Dave Stallworth and myself. Gallatin called Dick "Van," he called Stallworth "Stall," but all he ever called me was "Rook." I always knew I was the low man, even among the rookies.

I made the team and found out that pro ball was really nothing more than playing games. Even our practices were mostly scrimmages. We never had chalk talks, films or anything like that. We had a couple of basic plays, and that was it. Our locker rooms were terrible, nothing more than a small room with nails in the wall to hang your clothes and cold water in the showers.

After the season started, the Knicks put me up at the Paramount Hotel, which was on 44th Street between Seventh and Eighth Avenues. There was a burlesque theater next to our hotel, so the strippers stayed at the Paramount. To see them walking around the lobby . . . I knew that I was a long way from my dad's farm in Xenia, Ohio. Some of the guys used to hit on them, although I don't think they had much success.

I had a small room, maybe eight feet by 12 feet. It overlooked a courtyard that was owned by the pigeons. If you left your window open, the next day your room would be full of feathers.

I got my first paycheck and didn't know what to do with it. The Knicks were paying for my hotel room. I was saving as much of my meal money as I could.

Two months into the season, Eddie Donovan called me into his office and said, "Barry, we've given you four paychecks and you haven't cashed any of them."

I said, "I don't need the money. I don't know what to do with them."

I had been stashing the checks in my drawer under my underwear.

Donovan shook his head, then wrote something on a piece of paper and handed it to me.

"Here," he said. "Take your checks and go see this guy at the Chase Bank and open a checking account, will ya?"

We didn't have a very good team and Gallatin was fired 21 games into the season. Dick McGuire took over. He had played for the Knicks for seven years in the 1950s and he was just a terrific guy. He mumbled and was a chain-smoker. You had to listen close to hear what he had to say.

He was nice to me. He'd take me to lunch and say, "Gee, you really play well in practice. But when I put you in the game . . ."

I said, "I know, I get nervous."

He said, "I'm going to try to play you more, I really am."

Sometimes he did and sometimes he didn't. But I appreciate the fact that he paid attention to me.

Dick realized that our team wasn't going anywhere. He wasn't going to cause problems and ran a loose ship. We played a lot of bridge. Tom Gola and I were partners and we played against Emmette Bryant and Lenny Chappell. Dick loved cards and he'd watch our games. Sometimes, we'd still be playing and it was time to go out for warmups. Dick would say, "Just finish the hand, then we'll go play." He wanted to see how it came out. The team would sit there until we finished our game, then we'd go out for warmups.

Dick just wanted to keep everybody happy.

Tom Gola still lived in Philadelphia and he'd drive to New York for every game. He usually had three friends with him. They came down with a case of beer in the trunk. After the game, they'd bring out the beer and drink it as they drove back to Philly.

One night, we had a game against the Royals in Dayton, which was only 12 miles from my father's farm in Xenia. My parents invited the team out and we got there about 10 in the morning. Willis Reed brought his shotgun and he was shooting my father's clay pigeons. Tom Gola and some other players rode horses. My father had built a cement half court and the guys took turns playing 2-on-2 games. My mother made a ton of food and we ate about 4:30, then piled into three cars and headed for the game. We got lost trying to find the Dayton Field House, and by the time we walked into the arena, the Royals were leaving the court because they had finished their pregame warmups. We just got dressed and stepped on the court for the game, no shooting around or anything. Dick McGuire played me all of the second and fourth quarters because he'd had such a great time at the farm and he knew that my parents were at the game.

I only lasted one year with the Knicks. I went to Chicago in the 1966 expansion draft. In 1966, the Knicks drafted Cazzie Russell. The next year, it was Walt Frazier and Phil Jackson. Red Holzman replaced Dick McGuire as coach. The pieces of their great teams were falling into place, but few of us who were at my parents' farm were around to see it happen.

15
SEASON OF THE SIXERS

In his first seven NBA seasons, Wilt Chamberlain did everything but beat Boston. He led the league in scoring in all seven of those seasons. He was an All-Star every year, led the league in rebounding five times and was the MVP three times. As the 1966–67 season began, Chamberlain also was 30 years old and had never won a championship. That made him a "loser" in the eyes of many fans and players. The fact that no one but Boston had won a title since Wilt came into the league in 1959 was beside the point. Wilt was the first to tell you he was "bigger than the game." He also was bigger than anyone in the game, a statistical giant. But he was continually dwarfed by Boston and Bill Russell.

In the summer of 1966, it was announced that Chamberlain signed a $100,000 contract with the Sixers. Red Auerbach immediately said he'd pay Russell $100,001. Chamberlain laughed at this with friends. "I was actually making about $250,000," he said.

In the summer of 1966, the Sixers made changes. Haunted by their disappointing loss to Boston in five games in the 1966 Eastern Conference Finals, Dolph Schayes took the fall and was replaced by Alex Hannum as coach. Sportswriter Leonard Koppett recalled that word around the league was that "Wilt got Schayes fired." Actually, not beating Boston after winning the regular season title was why Schayes was dumped. The Sixers' ownership was convinced that they had the best team in the league, and now they wanted the best coach.

In that same summer of 1966, Alex Hannum was canned by the San Francisco Warriors. Hannum took the rap because the Warriors had failed to make the playoffs the previous two seasons, even though they had a young Nate Thurmond in the middle and the 1966 Rookie of the Year, Rick Barry. Of course, the Warriors did things like trading Wilt Chamberlain for Connie Dierking, so it wasn't like Hannum had a lot of support from the front office.

As the Sixers looked for a coach, their eyes immediately turned to Hannum. He had made his reputation as a coach with St. Louis. Hannum also had coached Chamberlain before, getting to the 1964 Finals. Hannum liked Wilt, wanted to coach Wilt and believed he could win with Wilt.

Those were the words the Sixers wanted to hear. Hannum was hired.

Hannum and Chamberlain had a couple of long talks before the season. They both were big men, men of ego, yet men who lusted after the same thing—beating Boston.

"I told Wilt that things had changed for him," said Hannum. "He had a great team around him. It was not necessary for him to lead the league—or even his team—in scoring for us to win."

Chamberlain was a bit leery. He was the greatest scorer in history. While he wouldn't admit it, much of his identity was tied up in the fact that he was unstoppable, unguardable, unlike any player the NBA had ever seen. Hannum was asking him to give up a lot.

Chamberlain considered that, but he also told Hannum, "I want to win. I'll give it a try."

The 1966–67 season is known for two things:

1. For the first time since he came into the league in 1959–60, Chamberlain was not the NBA's leading scorer.

2. For the first time in his career, Chamberlain was a champion.

The two were related, but many historians have incorrectly leapt to the conclusion that Chamberlain would have won more titles earlier in his career if he had just passed the ball once in a while.

"That's unfair to Wilt," says Hannum. "He was never on a team with as much talent as we had on the 1967 Sixers. If we weren't that deep, I would have needed Wilt to score more."

Hannum had the most physically imposing front line in NBA history: Chet Walker, Luke Jackson and Chamberlain were tall, wide and rippled with muscles. They formed a wall in front of the basket that no team could penetrate, unless a player wanted to eat the ball or count his bruises.

Consider that this front line was so strong that Hannum had the luxury of bringing future Hall of Fame forward Billy Cunningham off the bench as super-scorer.

The backcourt had future Hall of Famer Hal Greer, solid veteran Larry Costello and the underrated Wally Jones (or Wali, as he later spelled it).

With Chamberlain fixed on rebounding (24.2), blocking shots and even setting picks and passing (his 7.8 assists ranked third in the league), Hannum had everything he wanted. Six players averaged double figures. Wilt still scored 24 per game, but he only shot when he knew he'd make it; he led the league in field goal percentage at .683. Consider that New York's Walt Bellamy was second at .521, and you can put Wilt's marksmanship into context. Chamberlain's critics were speechless. They raised Hannum to new heights as a coach, saying he was the only man who could convince Chamberlain to play with such a team attitude. That was partly true. But anyone who had ever dealt with Chamberlain knew this much—if Wilt didn't want to do it, he wouldn't do it and it didn't matter if the Almighty came down from on high to coach his team.

Wilt wanted a title and when he saw that Hannum's strategy was successful, he grasped it with both hands, often carrying it to such extremes that Hannum had to tell Wilt to shoot the ball.

The Sixers opened the season by winning 15 of 16, the one loss at Boston. At various stages of the season their record was 26-2, 37-3 and 46-4.

Their final record was 68-13, the best in NBA history.

Back in Boston, the Celtics were waiting for the playoffs. They didn't care how many games the Sixers won or what Wilt was doing in the middle. As long as they had Russell, they owned Wilt.

The Celtics were still the Celtics. They may have finished eight games in back of the Sixers, but their 60 victories was still the second-highest total in league history.

This was a strange season for the NBA. Only three teams had winning records: Philadelphia, Boston and San Francisco. The league had added an expansion team, the Chicago Bulls, so each division had five teams, and eight of the 10 teams made the playoffs. This also eliminated the first-round bye system.

In the first round of the playoffs, Boston knocked off New York and the Sixers took care of Cincinnati, setting up a rematch in the Eastern Conference Finals.

Both teams carried the burden of history with them. Boston had defeated Chamberlain and the Sixers in the last two Eastern Conference Finals, but Boston was not coached by Auerbach this time. There had been some questions about Russell as a coach, although none were expressed too loudly because the Celtics did win 60 games. But could he win in the playoffs? There also was the racial undercurrent: could a black man coach a team to a championship?

As the 1967 Eastern Conference Finals opened, much was made of the fact that although the Sixers were 68-13 they had only a 4-5 regular-season record against Boston.

Then there was the matter of Russell vs. Chamberlain. Before the series, Russell's teams had a 70-38 record vs. Wilt's. Boston fans expected that trend to continue, even if Philadelphia owned the homecourt advantage for the playoffs.

In Game 1, the Sixers raced off to a 36–14 lead and had no need to look back. The final was 127–113. Hal Greer scored 39. Wilt scored 24 and outrebounded Russell 32–15. Neither was a big factor scoring, but Wilt also passed off for 13 assists.

The Sixers also won Game 2, 107–102.

By halftime of Game 3, Philly was in front 59–52 and Chamberlain had set a playoff record for rebounds in a half—25. In the second half, Boston came close but never could take the lead and Philly won again, 115–104. Chamberlain had 20 points, 41 rebounds and 9 assists.

With a 3–0 lead, the Sixers could have swept the series in Boston, but the Celtics avoided that indignity with a victory, 121–117. Chamberlain struggled, shooting 8-of-18 from the field, 4-of-11 from the foul line. That would be Boston's last victory of the season.

Game 5 was pure fast-break basketball. At the half, Philly had sprinted to a 70–65 lead, Wilt outscoring Russell 22–2. Boston was never a real threat down the stretch, and the Sixers were 140–116 winners.

Consider these numbers: 36 rebounds, 29 points and 13 assists. That is a triple-double, and when have you ever seen a triple-double like that? Probably no man in basketball history would be capable of such staggering statistics, except Wilton Norman Chamberlain. That's what Wilt did to Russell in Game 5, and it was why Boston's run of eight consecutive titles was over.

In their matchup, Chamberlain averaged 22 points, 32 rebounds and 10 assists—he averaged a triple-double for a five-game series against Russell (11 points, 23 rebounds and 6 assists).

There was champagne and celebration in the Sixers' dressing room. Technically, the championship was still to be decided. The Sixers still had to beat the best from the West, which was San Francisco. But taking care of the Warriors would be nothing more than a formality for the Sixers.

San Francisco was led by Rick Barry, who took over the scoring title Chamberlain had relinquished. The Warriors were coached by ex-Celtic Bill Sharman, who let Barry loose to throw in 35 points a night. It

would take six games, and Barry would average 41 points in the series,
but the inevitable occurred—Chamberlain, Hannum and Philadelphia
were the champions.

WILT CHAMBERLAIN: Why did we finally beat Boston? Because we had
Alex Hannum as our coach.

ALEX HANNUM: Wilt and I had a history when I was hired to coach
the Sixers in 1966–67. I was surprised when they fired Dolph Schayes
at the end of the 1965–66 season; the Sixers had won 55 games and I
told Irv Kosloff that they already had a good coach in Schayes. Irv said,
"Listen, he's gone. Either you're going to coach this team or someone
else will." Irv felt that his team was good enough to beat Boston and
he said he thought I could get them a championship. So I went into
the job knowing that anything less than a championship would be un-
acceptable, but I also liked that kind of challenge when I had super
talent on the roster.

BILLY CUNNINGHAM: Dolph Schayes was a great guy, maybe even too
nice to be a coach. He had been a teammate of many of the guys he
was later coaching, and that's a tough situation. There has to be some
kind of wall between the coach and the players, and it's hard for the
players to look at a guy as a coach when he used to room and have
some beers with them.

Alex Hannum demanded and received immediate respect. He had
coached St. Louis to a title [in 1958] and had coached Syracuse and
Golden State. He had coached Wilt with the Warriors and word was
that Alex had challenged Wilt in the Warriors' dressing room. I don't
know all the details because I wasn't on the team, but everyone knew
that Alex was a big man and he would fight you.

ALEX HANNUM: I'll just say that Wilt and I always had an understanding
and mutual respect. When I got the Sixers job, we had lost Guy Rodgers
in the expansion draft to Chicago. Guy was Wilt's favorite point guard
and he made getting the ball to Wilt an art form. Costello was not the
fancy ballhandler and passer that Guy was, but I knew that Costello
and Hal Greer could be one of the best backcourt combinations that
ever lived. My idea was to talk Larry Costello out of retirement, but
before I did that, I called Wilt. I could tell that Wilt wasn't that fired
up about it, but he said, "Coach, if you think Costello will help us win,

then it's your decision." It was only after that conversation with Wilt that I called Costello.

LARRY COSTELLO: I was labeled the last of the two-handed set shooters. I could go to basketball camps, close my eyes and make 40 straight free throws. But I also had played 10 years in the NBA and had retired in 1965 and spent a season as a high school coach. I had no idea of playing again until Alex called. He said he had great scorers, but he needed a guard to pass the ball, play defense and keep everybody happy. He said I could help him win a title, and I said I'd like to give it a try.

BILLY CUNNINGHAM: Since Costello had sat out a year, he worked extra hard to get in shape. We had grueling two-a-days under Alex, but Costello was the first one to arrive and the last one to leave the gym after each of those sessions. It was like he was putting himself through three-a-day practices. To see a guy who had been in the league 10 years do that rubbed off on the other guys.

ALEX HANNUM: I talked to Wilt about everything, not just Costello. One of the big things was that Wilt wanted to play all 48 minutes. Yes, he could play every minute, but to do that he had to pace himself.

I said, "This is a different team from the ones earlier in your career. We have more talent and I need to play more guys. I don't give a damn who you are, you can't go at full speed for 48 minutes. I also don't think it's a bad idea to rest you for a few minutes, put someone else in there and give our team a different look." As was the case with Costello, he didn't necessarily agree with me, but he went along with the idea.

WILT CHAMBERLAIN: I just never understood how I could help my team while sitting on the bench. I felt that even if I was a little tired for a few minutes, I was still better than whoever took my place. It was my job to play 48 minutes.

MATT GUOKAS: Early in his career, Wilt dominated the game by scoring, which was what management wanted him to do. When I came into the league in 1966, Wilt wanted a ring. He had had so many heartbreaks in the playoffs. He knew we had a good team and that this could be the year we beat Boston, so he was very receptive to what Alex suggested.

TOM GOLA: Wilt's personal goals had all been achieved. He could score 50 points in any game, anytime he wanted. But he wanted more than statistics.

ALEX HANNUM: In one of our conversations, Wilt said, "You know, I can pass the ball as well as anyone in basketball."

I said, "Fine, let's see it."

This led to a decision made by both Wilt and myself to play him at the high post. Early in his career, Wilt was always near the basket so he could catch the ball in position to score. But he also clogged the middle so that it was hard for his teammates to drive. With all the talent we had, I wanted to give the other guys room to go to the basket. And Wilt wanted to get them the ball so they could score. That was our game plan, and we stuck to it.

BILLY CUNNINGHAM: Alex ran brutal training camps. Matty Guokas was a rookie and he committed the mortal sin of showing up for camp out of shape. Alex ran Matty until he literally fell down because he simply couldn't move. It was a tough camp, a lot of conditioning. Wilt had played for Alex before and Wilt never liked training camp much in the first place, and he especially didn't like Alex's camps. So what Wilt did was work out on his own and then sign his contract once the exhibition games started. *[Wilt actually joined the team at halftime of an exhibition game in Allentown, Pennsylvania.]*

LARRY COSTELLO: Many people didn't understand Wilt, but Alex Hannum knew that you didn't sweat the small stuff with Wilt, who was a man of great pride and intelligence. He also wanted to be known for being an all-around player, not just a scorer. Alex recognized that, and treated Wilt accordingly.

[Chamberlain's 24.1 scoring average that year was more than 15 points per game below his career average at that time. Remarkably, he reached that average on only 13 shots per game; his .683 shooting percentage was a league record. His 7.8 assists per game topped his previous average by more than four. He also set an NBA record with 35 consecutive field goals, and was 15-for-15 in a game against Baltimore.]

WILT CHAMBERLAIN: A center getting eight assists a game was absolutely unheard of in the NBA. The next year, I led the league in assists [8.6] and no center had ever done that before or has come close to it since. The way I passed the ball in those years may have been the thing of which I am most proud, because people said Wilt Chamberlain was selfish, Wilt Chamberlain was one-dimensional, when the truth was that Wilt Chamberlain was finally with a team where he was allowed to show that he could pass the ball, and I give Alex Hannum credit for that. Now all they talk about is triple-doubles. It was never mentioned back then, but I bet I had 40–50 of them that season. I averaged close to 10 assists, 24 points and 24 rebounds, so common sense tells you that I was near a trible-double every night.

BILLY CUNNINGHAM: Wilt is very goal-oriented, and under Alex he wanted to win a title and become the first center to lead the league in assists. He liked to pass the ball to Hal Greer or myself, because we just caught it and shot it. Chet Walker usually caught the ball, took a dribble or two and then shot it—no assist for Wilt. So Wilt preferred to give the ball to us. He played at high post. We'd pass the ball to him and cut past him. Some of the plays were like the old Globetrotters routines where Wilt would stick the ball in your stomach and you were convinced he had given it to you, but then he'd pull the ball away and pass it to an open man under the basket. He did it all with his one huge hand.

ALEX HANNUM: Wilt handled the basketball like you or I would a grapefruit. He had tremendous court vision and timing with his passes. When he made a good pass to a guy and the player missed the shot, Wilt also had a way of expressing his unhappiness to the guy who blew the shot.

We had such a great team. Hal Greer had the best medium-range jump shot ever. He had tremendous quickness and the ability to stop on a dime and go straight up with the shot. His jump shot was so accurate that he even took it from the foul line, the only player I've ever seen do that successfully.

AL BIANCHI: We called Greer Bulldog, because he had that kind of expression on his face, and it never changed. He had that jump shot . . . no one ever could stop and take a jumper faster than Greer.

ALEX HANNUM: Costello was the perfect complement to Greer because Larry was a tough SOB. When he got hurt, we had lost only four games. *[Costello ripped his Achilles tendon on January 6 when the Sixers were 38-4.]*

LARRY COSTELLO: I caught a pass from Matty Guokas, dribbled up the court and fell down. No one was around me and I had no idea what had happened. I never had Achilles problems before, but I needed surgery.

BILLY CUNNINGHAM: After Larry got hurt, he sat in the back of the bus from Baltimore to Philly, trying to hold back the tears. Not from the pain, but because he knew that we were destined to be a championship team and he wanted to be a part of it. Finally, he broke down and cried and you could see tears in the eyes of a lot of the other guys, too. We had become a very close team.

[The depth of the Sixers was demonstrated by the fact that they won eight in a row immediately after Costello's injury when Wali Jones moved into the lineup and were 46-4 on January 23.]

ALEX HANNUM: We had such power that Wilt could just pass. If we were 8–10 points behind early in the game, we never worried. We knew that we would wear teams down. We owned the fourth quarter.

Our front line was so deep and so physically overwhelming. Other than Wilt, Luke Jackson may have been the strongest man in the league. Chet Walker was a classy guy, a 20-point scorer who caught the ball on the baseline and could drive in either direction to get a jump shot, and he had a slight hesitation before he released the ball that got him open. Off the court, he was so easygoing. But on defense, he would be so aggressive. You never would have believed it was the same guy.

I had the luxury of bringing Cunningham off the bench. This was only his second year, and he was always a bit of an "I guy." By that, I mean he believed he had the best chance of scoring of anyone on the court, so when he came into the game, he immediately wanted the ball and that usually meant instant points. We had Dave Gambee on the bench and I'd use him to stir things up. When Gambee guarded you, you usually got so sick of him hanging on to you that you wanted to fight him.

BILLY CUNNINGHAM: My favorite on that team was Luke Jackson. He was so intense every day, at practice, in the games, setting picks to get Greer and myself open. He sacrificed more of his personal game than anyone.

Our team was so good that we shouldn't have lost 13 games.

We lost three in a row on a West Coast road trip. We started in

Detroit, then had a few days off and headed to Las Vegas before ending up on the West Coast. Alex would take the team to Vegas for two days to unwind. We unwound a little too much, and when we arrived on the West Coast we lost those three games.

I respect those great Celtics teams tremendously, and maybe they are even overlooked a bit. But for one year, our team was the best ever to play this game.

ALEX HANNUM: We won 68 games in a 10-team league, meaning we had to play Boston nine times in the regular season. Chicago was the only expansion team and they were good enough to make the playoffs. Now there are 27 teams—all those expansion teams—and it's a big difference. We rolled through the playoffs.

WILT CHAMBERLAIN: The greatest team ever to grace a basketball court was the 1966–67 Philadelphia 76ers. We were the consummate pro team, from how we acted off the court to how we performed on it. We had reached a stage of harmony where none of the players resented each other—a unique situation in the NBA. I look at the Celtics. What made them great was that all Bill Russell had to do was the blue-collar work— rebound and play defense. He had other great players around him to score the points. When Wilt Chamberlain was given that same luxury, the result was that the Sixers were the greatest team of all time.

ALEX HANNUM: I was so happy for Wilt when we won the title, because it eliminated the stigma that he couldn't win the big one. I got the ball from the championship game, had all the players sign it, and then I presented it to Wilt—that's how strongly I felt about what he did for us.

HARVEY POLLACK: The night after Wilt won his first title, I had a hotel room down the hall from him. The ladies were lined up outside his door from after the game and some were still there in the morning. Wilt had to set some kind of record that night.

BILLY CUNNINGHAM: For winning the title, we got $7,100 each, a ring, and there were a couple hundred people waiting for us at the airport.

RED AUERBACH: It's nice to let Philadelphia talk about being the greatest team. Hey, they were a great team—for one year. But what did they win? One championship. We won eight in a row, 11 in 13 years. The Boston Celtics were the greatest team, there's nothing to talk about.

John Havlicek: When Philadelphia eliminated us, their fans were chanting, "The Celtics are dead, the Celtics are dead." That made a lasting impression on me. The reporters asked me about the chant and I said, "Right now, we are dead for only one year." Then we came back to win two more titles in a row, so you tell me, who was the greatest team?

To Wilt Chamberlain

He appears from afar
A giant Cimmerian statue
Contested for a goal
He shivers strong ebony beads
Of sweat from his body
Turns suddenly
From inanimate to animal
Coils and springs
Sending men like ripples
Into inevitable nonexistence.

Off the court
He is enigma
Tropical and dense
As the jungle
Of his forebears
White men fear
Black men genuflect
And once long ago
We argued
Over a fallen tear.

—Tom Meschery

Is Wilt *Under*rated?

In his rookie season of 1959–60, Chamberlain broke nine league records. With 20 games left in the season, he had scored over 2,000 points—which had been done just twice before in a full season. For his career, he averaged 30 points, 22 rebounds, 4.5 assists and shot 54 percent. In 1968, he became the only center in history to lead the league in assists and proclaimed, "It's like Babe Ruth leading the league in sacrifice bunts."

TOM MESCHERY: I maintain that Wilt Chamberlain is underrated. Because of his size, it was always assumed that he would be the best. When he was, people said, "What else do you expect?" But when he fell a bit short, such as at the foul line or when his team lost to the Celtics, he took the criticism. Rather than looking at his accomplishments, people dwelled on the negative because he was so great.

KEVIN LOUGHERY: We'd go into a dressing room and see a box score from the night before where Wilt had 55 or 60 points. No one would think twice about it. Getting 50-some points, or even 60-some, wasn't news when Wilt did it.

JACK TWYMAN: In 1959–60, I was becoming the first NBA player to average 30 points. But no one noticed because it was Wilt's rookie year, and he averaged 37. He dwarfed us all, and not just physically.

LEONARD KOPPETT: Before Wilt, most fans and writers looked at a game in terms of who was the high scorer. The guy who scored 25 was the star. But Wilt shattered virtually every scoring record in his first few years in the league. In the process of doing that, he rendered statistics irrelevant. So when Wilt scored 70 points in a game, no one paid attention. That was Wilt being Wilt. He had so many records that they began to lose meaning.

LARRY STAVERMAN: Before the first time we played Wilt in Cincinnati, we had a practice where I took a broom and was swatting Wayne Embry's shots, pretending I was Wilt. We knew that we had never seen a physical specimen like him before.

BOB FERRY: The first time I guarded Wilt, I stood behind him and he was so wide that I couldn't see the rest of the game. Then I saw him dunk a ball so hard that it hit the court and bounced straight up back through the rim again.

CARL BRAUN: I never saw it, but I know guys who were there when Wilt was a kid and he'd win bets by jumping up and taking dollars off the top of the backboard.

ALEX HANNUM: When I coached the San Francisco Warriors, I thought Al Attles was the fastest guy on our team—by far. We used to gamble a lot—which player could jump the highest and run the fastest. So I set up a series of races, baseline to baseline. In the finals, it was Wilt and Attles and Wilt just blew past him. I'm convinced that Wilt Chamberlain is one of the greatest all-around athletes the world has ever seen.

WAYNE EMBRY: People lose sight of the fact that Wilt was a 440 champion, a guy with great coordination. He also was so strong that the double-teaming defenses used today wouldn't bother him.

FRED SCHAUS: They used to talk about George Mikan being a great center, and he was for his time. But Mikan played when the lane was only six feet. With a six-foot lane, Wilt would have *averaged* 70 a game.

WAYNE EMBRY: Early in his career, Wilt so dominated the game that it hurt his teammates. They just passed him the ball and watched and his passing skills weren't developed. But he worked on that part of his game and went from being a poor passer to a very good one.

WILT CHAMBERLAIN: The assumption was that I scored more than anyone else because I was bigger than everyone else. But I wasn't that much bigger. Centers such as Charlie Share and Clyde Lovellette weighed more than I did. Walter Dukes was just as tall as I am. But everyone said my success was due to my size, and that's a real kick in the ass. When I was a kid, I worked at the game 5–6–7 hours a day. I studied the game, learned how to pass, to rebound, to play defense. I was a great track man, a shot-putter, and I developed my own weight program before any other basketball player even thought about it. I was stronger than everyone else because I made myself stronger. I built up my body.

MARTY BLAKE: I was working the clock in an exhibition game in Omaha between St. Louis and Philadelphia. Neil Johnston was the Philly coach and he sent in a sub for Wilt, but Wilt wouldn't leave. Johnston and Wilt started arguing on the court. Neil said he wanted to give Wilt a rest, it was just an exhibition game. Wilt said he wasn't moving. Finally, Johnston gave up and Wilt stayed in.

WILT CHAMBERLAIN: Modern players put too many limits on themselves. They think that they can only play so many minutes or score so many points. They forget that one of the key things an athlete can have is endurance. To me, it was the sign of a great player to be able to wage battle through the course of an entire game. To do that, you not only must be strong but smart. You can't commit stupid fouls. You can't get thrown out or goaded into a fight. I take pride in never having fouled out of a game. I knew that grabbing some guy from behind after he stole the ball from me was not helping my team. Modern players forget that. In a sense, I was too big for the game—my talent, that is. In my rookie year, they didn't have the offensive goaltending rule so I was able to catch my teammates' shots and guide them into the basket. Then they put in a rule against that and people said that would hurt my game. Instead, my scoring average went up. I just found other ways to score. As the years went on, my scoring went down only because I wanted it to, because it was what was best for my team. I could always score 50–60 points if it was needed, but I knew that my team was more effective if I sacrificed my scoring and passed and played defense.

ALEX HANNUM: In 1967–68, Wilt wanted to lead the league in assists. We had a couple of our starters hurt and I mentioned to a Philadelphia reporter named Jack Kiser that I wanted Wilt to score more.

The headline of the story came out, "Hannum Says Wilt Can't Score."

That wasn't exactly what I said, but I figured I'd get what I wanted out of it. Wilt asked me, "Did you say this?"

I said, "If it's in print, then I said it."

He shook his head and sort of growled at me. We were starting a three-game road trip and I really didn't know how he'd respond.

WILT CHAMBERLAIN: Kiser kept dwelling on the fact that I wasn't scoring. I said the team was winning, so what did it matter? Then there was an article in *Sports Illustrated* about me not being able to score. So I went out and got 50-something the first game, then 60-something. After three games averaging over 50, I went back to my regular game. I saw Kiser and said, "Still think I can't score?"

[The three games were 68, 47, and 53 points. He also had a game where he was chastised in print for not taking a shot. In the next game, Wilt had 52 points and 37 rebounds.]

HARVEY POLLACK: The night Wilt set the record [February 2, 1968, vs. Detroit] with 21 assists—the most ever by a center—he also had over 20 points and 20 rebounds. That was a triple-double-double and I don't believe anyone else has ever done that.

LEONARD KOPPETT: I call Wilt Chamberlain a very honest workman. By that, I mean he always did what his employer wanted. No star athlete has ever given his boss more for the money than Wilt did during his career. Eddie Gottlieb wanted Wilt to score like no man ever had, so Wilt did. Hannum and some of his other coaches wanted him to pass and play defense, so he did that and he played 48 minutes a night. Those who criticized Wilt—first for his scoring, then for not scoring more—really should have criticized his employer.

16
CHAMBERLAIN VS. RUSSELL

According to Sixers stat man Harvey Pollack, the two squared off in 142 games, Russell holding an 88–74 advantage. Chamberlain averaged 28.7 points and 28.7 rebounds in those games, compared to 23.7 points and 14.5 rebounds for Russell. Wilt had a 62-point game on January 14, 1962, in Boston, and had six other games of at least 50 points against Russell. The most Russell ever scored against Wilt was 37, and he had only two other 30-point games. Chamberlain grabbed an NBA-record 55 rebounds against Russell on November 24, 1960, and had six other games of at least 40 rebounds against Russell. Russell's best rebounding night against Chamberlain was 40 on February 12, 1961. Chamberlain's teams lost all four seventh games they played against Russell's Celtics; the margins of defeat in those games totaled nine points. But there was more to the contrast between these two dominant figures than the results on the court.

Those Who Knew Wilt . . .

ALEX HANNUM: Wilt Chamberlain could never hide because the whole world always knew he was Wilt Chamberlain. Even people who weren't basketball fans would see all 7-foot-2, 300 pounds of Wilt in an airport or a restaurant and they'd say, "There's Wilt Chamberlain." He was the most recognizable athlete of his era, because there were so few men who were his size. For that reason, he was forever hounded by jerks who'd say, "Wilt, I don't want your autograph for me, but my kid is a great fan of yours . . . of course, I'm a big fan, too . . . so would you . . ."

On and on it would go. The temptation for Wilt would be to build a wall around himself, maybe go into isolation. But Wilt also was very warm, very patient with fans. Far more patient than most of us would be if we were in his situation.

BILLY CUNNINGHAM: I'm 6-foot-6 and I hate it when someone says, "How's the weather up there?" It doesn't happen that often, but when it does, it really annoys me. Wilt goes through life having people ask, "How's the weather up there?" I don't know how he takes it, but he does. I have seen fans be vulgar and insulting with him. If possible, he just ignores it. With regular people, he is invariably gracious and takes most things with good humor. Wilt wants to get along with people and he wants people to like him.

AL ATTLES: When we played in New York, the kids would stand right near the court as we warmed up. The NBA rule is that you can't sign autographs during warmups. One young man politely asked Wilt if he would sign. Wilt explained that the league wouldn't let him. Then he said, "Stay around after the game, and I'll sign whatever you want."

That's a line players give to fans just to get rid of them.

Well, the game was over. Wilt went into the dressing room, dried off and then headed back into Madison Square Garden. He was still in his uniform. The boy was not outside our dressing room. Then Wilt started walking through the dark arena, calling the boy.

He came from the other end of the arena. Wilt signed his stuff and talked to the young man.

How many guys would remember that they had made a promise like that to a kid? And with Wilt, this was far from an isolated incident.

TOM MESCHERY: One of Wilt's most notable traits is his generosity. One summer, I worked for the Seattle department of recreation and we were putting together an inner-city basketball league. Since he lived in the area, I called Bill Russell to come out and help us kick off the program. Russ wanted to be paid. I didn't want to spend the city's money. I thought of Wilt and how he traveled a lot in the summer; I thought maybe he might be in the area, so I called him.

Wilt said he was spending some time in L.A., but why not? He'd come to Seattle to help an old teammate.

He got on his motorcycle and drove from L.A. to Seattle. He talked to the kids, officiated a game and spent the day. Then he refused to take a dime, even for expenses.

AL ATTLES: A lot of people got the wrong impression of Wilt because he was outspoken. He was a black man who understood his worth and expressed his opinions, something that black men were not supposed to do in the 1950s and 1960s. Wilt drove big cars, had a lot of girlfriends and was very opinionated. This bothered some people, especially the establishment types and some of the older people in the media. So he was portrayed in a negative light, as if he were a troublemaker. Yet he was always there for practice. He'd play every minute of every game and he was good with the fans, teammates and coaches. But he also knew basketball was a business and he was not about to let people take advantage of him when it came to his contracts.

HOT ROD HUNDLEY: What puts some people off when they first meet Wilt is that he comes off as an expert on everything. He thinks he is smarter than he is, but really, most of it is his humor.

JOHNNY KERR: Around strangers, Wilt had this bravado. He would say something crazy like, "Tomorrow night, the stars won't come up." Then he'd wait to see if anyone would dare to disagree with him.

AL ATTLES: We'd be in a plane and the pilot would say, "We're flying over Omaha."
   Wilt would say to me, "How many people live in Omaha?"
   I'd say, "How do I know? I'm not a census taker."
   Wilt would say, "Take a guess."
   I'd say, "I don't know . . . 325,000."
   Wilt would say, "377,888."
   I'd say, "Come off it, Wilt, you don't know."
   Wilt would say, "I'll bet you."
   To keep him happy, I'd say, "All right, two bucks says I'm right."
   He'd say, "No, the bet is $2,000."
   I'd say, "Wilt, I can't bet $2,000 on how many people live in Omaha."
   He'd say, "Then you don't know."
   I'd say, "No, I don't want to bet."
   He'd say, "Well, if you won't bet, then I must be right."
   On and on it would go.

TOM MESCHERY: Wilt loved poker and he had his own style. He would never fold. It was impossible to bluff him. If you were in a game with Wilt, then you knew you had to play every hand to the end, because no matter how bad his cards, he would try to win with them.

BARRY CLEMENS: He dominated poker games like he did basketball. His personality was so strong that he almost ruined the game. He made you meet him on his own terms.

AL ATTLES: When we were teammates in Golden State, there was a guy on our team named Bud Koper. He wasn't much of a player, but shooting around in the gym, Bud Koper was sensational. I watched him go around the horn, making 32 in a row from 25 feet out. Wilt was watching this with me.

Then Wilt said, "I'm the best shooter on this team."

I said, "Wilt, you're not the best shooter on the team. Koper is a better shooter than you."

Wilt repeated, "I said I was the best shooter on the team. I can shoot better than Koper."

I said, "No, Wilt. You can't."

Wilt said, "I'll show you. Hey, Koper, they say you can outshoot me, but I don't think so. Let's shoot."

Koper said it was fine with him.

Wilt said, "Since I'm the challenger, I get to pick the spot on the court."

Koper agreed.

Wilt took the ball, went to halfcourt, and said they would have a contest of two-handed set shots.

Koper was in real trouble, since he was a one-handed jump shooter. They each took 10 shots. There were a lot of airballs. It was awful. Finally, Wilt made one from halfcourt, then he said, "I told you I was the best shooter on this team."

TOM MESCHERY: After we won the Western Conference title, Wilt and I went out drinking. Wilt was not one to drink. Being Russian, I thought I was a great drinker. Well, Wilt said he would drink me under the table. We went to a bar in New York. He ordered about 10 Scotches and milk. That's right, he drank Scotch and then a milk. He hammered them down, one after another. I tried to match him drink for drink, but the last thing I remembered was being facedown on a curb on Broadway with a cab coming about an inch from running me over. From what I understand, the 10 drinks didn't even touch Wilt.

ALEX HANNUM: Wilt had his rituals. He wore No. 13 because no one else would. He wore a rubber band on his right wrist. He sweated so much that he changed his jersey at halftime. And eating and drinking, boy would he consume the liquids—not booze, he wasn't a drinker or smoker, but Wilt loved milk and 7-Up.

TOM MESCHERY: I saw him eat a whole apple pie and drink two gallons of milk in one sitting. He'd drink a half gallon of milk at halftime and probably a gallon after the game.

MATT GUOKAS: At halftime, I saw him eat half an apple pie and drink a half gallon of 7-Up. Then he went out and played all of the second half.

MARV ALBERT: When I was a ballboy for the Knicks, Wilt sent me out right before the game to buy him a couple of hot dogs, then he ate them right on the bench while in uniform.

BARRY CLEMENS: When I was with Chicago in 1967, I shared an apartment with Gerry Ward and Don Kojis. Ward was Wilt's friend, and after games in Chicago Wilt would come over. We'd eat steaks. Basketball players have big appetites, so we bought the biggest steaks we could. One was enough for each of us, but Wilt would eat two. Once, Wilt sat on a chair and broke it, he was so huge. But we all laughed about it. Wilt was so nice, we figured it was an honor to have him break our chair.

CHICK HEARN: When he was with the Lakers, Wilt would come to the games and eat a whole chicken in the dressing room. This bothered one of his coaches—I won't say who. The coach called Fred Schaus, who was the GM. Fred joined the team on the road and asked Wilt not to eat a chicken in the dressing room. So the next game, Wilt showed up with a dozen hot dogs.

FRED SCHAUS: I have great respect for Wilt. When I was with the Lakers, he never missed a practice or a game, or was late for a plane. If I asked him to make an appearance, he did it. This man has gone through life with a bad rap. We are talking about a very good person.

FRANK McGUIRE: One night, we were on the road. We had lost, it was about two in the morning. I had gotten a terrible hotel room and I was standing in the hall. Wilt saw me and asked what was wrong.

I said, "Look at this room, it's like a shoebox."

Wilt grabbed my key, then gave me his key. "I got a room twice this size at the end of the hall, Coach. It's all yours."

Then he shut the door to my old room in my face, the point being that he didn't want any argument, he wanted me to take his room.

MATT GUOKAS: In restaurants, Wilt would quietly pick up the tab because he knew that he was making 10 times what we were. But he was very discreet, most of us not realizing what had happened until later. Or else he'd invite us to his room and he'd have a huge spread of room service food for us.

NATE THURMOND: When I was a rookie with the San Francisco Warriors, Wilt took me under his wing. He bought me meals, took me to Kim Novak's house for a party. Believe me, going with Wilt Chamberlain to Kim Novak's for a party was a real eye-opener for this young man from Akron. Wilt also took me to the San Francisco Jazz Festival. He was a legend, the man who scored 100 points in a game—the only man in basketball who literally could look down on me. I was in awe of him.

When the Warriors traded him and I was going to take his place at center, I was at his house. He asked me to walk around the block with him.

He said, "They aren't trading me because they think you're better than I am. So don't try to do what I do, do what you do best. Play your game. They're trading me because they don't want to pay me. This is business. I make more money than you and one of us has to go. Never forget, Nate, you may love this game, but it's also a business."

FRANK MCGUIRE: Whatever Wilt did, he wanted to do it best and he understood the value of a dollar. People from Kutsher's Country Club tell me that he was the best bellhop they ever had, back when Wilt worked there while he was in school.

HASKELL COHEN: At Kutsher's, they had several two-story units. Wilt worked with another bellhop, a small kid. Wilt would pile all the bags on his back. Then he'd send the small kid up to the second floor. The kid would open the window and Wilt would put the bags above his head and hand them to the kid. Bellhops worked for tips and no one had ever seen a guy carry more bags than Wilt, so he cleaned up.

TOM MESCHERY: Wilt would brag about his women, or how strong he was or whatever came into his head. He was a night person, staying up almost until dawn and then sleeping until early afternoon. He wanted life on his own terms, but he also was a sensitive guy. He cared about other people. For all his talking about Wilt, he also would listen and try to help when you had a problem. What Wilt happens to be is a very good friend to a lot of people.

TO BILL RUSSELL

I have never seen
an eagle with a beard
but if there is
in some strange
corner of the world
and the Hindu
belief is true,
you will return
and beat your wings
violently
over my grave.

—TOM MESCHERY

Those Who Knew Russell . . .

SATCH SANDERS: Bill Russell was never one to conform to what people wanted from him. He hung around with people he wanted to, and stayed away from those he didn't like. He didn't care what anyone else thought about it. He also was a guy who withheld judgment. He did not immediately become your friend once you were on the Celtics. It took him a month or two to learn my name. He was like that with all the rookies until they showed they belonged.

JOHN HAVLICEK: Bill's natural instinct was to keep up his guard. When new players came to the team, he seldom used their names. For first- or second-round draft choices, he'd just call them "Hey, No. 1," or "Hey, No. 2." If the guy was a free agent trying out for the team in training camp, he'd call the guy, "Hey, F.A." One of my theories was that he didn't want to get too close to you until he knew that you were going to be around—because he had lost so many things in his young life. Bill was very, very close to his mother and she died at a young age. I know that had a very profound effect on him.

But as thick-skinned as Bill is, he was one of the first players to become my friend when I joined the Celtics. I had just gotten a new car as a bonus from when I signed with the Cleveland Browns. I mentioned that I wanted to get a stereo for it but I didn't know where to go in Boston. Bill overheard me and said he'd take care of it. He picked me up and we went from place to place, I bet we went to eight places, until Bill was satisfied that we got the right equipment and the right deal. As a rookie, I couldn't believe that a great player like Bill Russell would take that much time with me. Russell is a very emotional guy, as any of his friends will tell you. But he also is a product of his mother dying young and of the racial climate of the country.

[Russell was 12 and his mother was 32 when she died. In Second Wind, *Russell wrote, "My mother was the best parts of a man and a woman, without the bad parts of either. . . . She was rich, tender and strong all at once. If I'd have run into a king or a queen, I would have been proud to show my mother off to them. . . . She made me feel so secure that I thought nothing could hurt me."]*

TOM HEINSOHN: Russell has never acknowledged the racial incidents that happened to him in Boston—he doesn't want those bigots to know they hurt him. The one I remember was when Bill bought a new home in Reading, Massachusetts. The town even had a night for him. It touched Bill deeply that he'd be accepted in a white town like Reading, and he broke down and cried. He said, "I'm going to spend the rest of my life here."

As the years passed, Bill started shopping for another house in a different neighborhood in Reading—a nicer neighborhood because he could afford it. And then some of those people who had honored him began circulating a petition against him. People broke into his home and put shit all over everything and wrote obscenities on the walls. He began to wonder, who can I trust? But for him to tell the world what happened—he felt that would just egg the people on to do it again. But you better believe that colored his outlook on Boston.

JOHN HAVLICEK: Bill spent much of his early life in Louisiana, where blacks went to the back of the bus and drank from separate fountains.

We played an exhibition game in Louisiana and his grandfather was there. Bill often said what an important influence his grandfather was. Anyway, the grandfather was in our dressing room after the game and he was crying. Bill asked him what was wrong. His grandfather said, "Nothing. I'm happy. I never thought I'd see a black man and a white man using the same shower."

That is strong, emotional stuff.

Bill did a lot of thinking about racial matters and how the world was changing in the 1960s, yet how some things never changed. He would pile his kids in the car and drive from Boston to Louisiana to see his grandfather, but once they got south of Washington, D.C., Bill said he had to be careful where he stopped to eat. His kids didn't understand why they couldn't go certain places. Here was Bill Russell, the greatest basketball player ever, and he couldn't take his family to some greasy spoon.

BOB COUSY: I want to preface my feelings about Russell by saying that if I had been born black, I probably would have been a bomb-thrower. I have a hunch I'd have been tougher on the world than Russ. He is a proud man who has been offended by a racist society and he won't give in an inch to it. So it is obvious that Russ always had a very strong chip on his shoulder and he demonstrated that to the outside world at every opportunity. His public persona was to thumb his nose at whitey. And whitey keeps giving him big contracts to sign. He signs, takes the money and then doesn't function as they expect and then laughs at whitey all the way to the bank. In his mind, he thinks he has gotten back at white society for all they have put him through. Can you imagine someone reaching the lofty status that Bill did and not being allowed to play at a country club in Boston? Or having some waiter be rude to you because you're black? It's fine to say "Turn the other cheek" if the other cheek doesn't belong to you.

Russell was not one to turn the other cheek, and I don't blame him even when he says outrageous things like, "I'd rather be in jail in Sacramento than mayor of Boston."

But the Russell we knew within the team, he was tremendous.

Part of it is due to Auerbach, who treated everyone more or less the same dating back to when he broke the color barrier in the league by drafting Chuck Cooper. Auerbach treated a minority like anyone else, thereby telling the person that he isn't a minority. Race was a very open subject on the Celtics. We could say things to each other that the outside world probably would find offensive, because we knew and trusted each other. We used to kid Russell about that goddamn laugh of his, which could pierce walls and break glass.

JIM LOSCUTOFF: God, that laugh. When Bill got a good hand in poker, he'd let out with his cackle and it was infectious. It also was a tip-off that he had a good hand and we'd just fold. Bill never had a classic poker face.

JOHN HAVLICEK: Bill was comfortable on the Celtics because he knew that Red was the first coach to draft a black player and that the Celtics were the first team to consistently start five black players. Our roommates were integrated. I roomed sometimes with K.C. Jones, other times with Satch Sanders. Bill had Christmas parties where all the players went—black and white. And he bought gifts for everyone. When it comes to his teammates, he doesn't shake your hand, he hugs you. He's very sentimental.

JIM LOSCUTOFF: On a lot of teams, the black players went one way, the whites another. On our team, we made a point of everyone hanging around together. We had parties where the wives came. Russell was a big part of this.

BOB COUSY: When Russell got outside of the team, he was a different guy. Some white guy would come up to him in a hotel lobby and say, "Mr. Russell, I've followed your career and I admire you. Would you please sign my . . ." Russell wouldn't even look at the guy. He could have a Jekyll and Hyde personality.

MARV ALBERT: I always thought Russell's attitude was wrong, especially when it came to signing autographs. He says that a kid should ask his teacher for an autograph, which is just a nonsense remark. He tried to make his refusal to sign autographs something deep and socially relevant, but the truth is that he just didn't want to take a minute to sign.

TOM HEINSOHN: If anyone does have a basketball with Bill's autograph, I signed it. I was the greatest Bill Russell forger of them all. I'm right-handed, but I made his signature even look left-handed. The guys on the team would give me something and say, "Hey Tommy, do your Russell on this one."

Russell could get away with it because he knew his place in the game, what he was worth and exactly what he was doing. Red Auerbach knew just how to deal with Russell. They say all men on the team are equal. Well, that's bullshit. A coach has to deal with every player as an individual. You can yell at some guys, but not at others. You pat some guys on the back, you boot others in the butt. So did Russell get special treatment from Red? Of course, but no one resented it because we knew what Red was doing and why he did it.

FRANK RAMSEY: Once the season began, Russ was never a good practice player. He was playing 45 minutes a night, all 48 minutes in a big game. We usually had 11 men on the roster, so if we really wanted to work up a sweat, we found it was better to tell Russell just to sit out. Sometimes, he'd practice and we could see he was tired so we'd tell Red, "Hey, get Russell out of here." Then Russell would just laugh. Or Red might tell Russell that he didn't have to practice, but he had to officiate our scrimmage.

CARL BRAUN: When I came to the Celtics, I was surprised at how little Russell practiced. He usually had some kind of minor injury—a sprained finger or whatever—that he was resting. I did detect a bit of an undercurrent of dissatisfaction from some of the players who were driving 50 miles round-trip to practice, and then they would see Russ sitting out. But no one ever said anything. The team was winning. Russell put his body on the line every game and the feeling was, why rock the boat?

WAYNE EMBRY: Russell would practice early in the year until he got into shape. Then he'd do just enough to stay in shape. When he was player-coach, he didn't practice, either. He'd sit on the sidelines drinking coffee and reading a newspaper while we practiced, while we were busting our asses. Listen, superstars get special treatment because they've earned it. It has always been that way in basketball, and the rest of us understood that.

SATCH SANDERS: Once in a while, Red would say, "Russ is practicing today." Then Bill would really practice—blocking so many shots that he just about ruined it for everyone.

TOM HEINSOHN: When Russell went into one of those things where he was blocking every shot, Red would say, "Russ, just sit down for Christ's sake." Russ wasn't the only one who sat out practices. Cousy did once in a while, but the difference was that Cousy liked to practice. We knew what we had in Russell and so did Red. If he didn't like practice, none of us were going to say anything.

GENE CONLEY: I was always amused when I read that I was Russell's backup. No one was Russell's backup—he often played every minute. A normal game, he went at least 40. An important game, he was a 48-minute man. So I played center in practice and Russ rested. How could we criticize the guy, even among ourselves? None of us had ever seen a more dominant player, a guy who wouldn't let us lose.

CLIFF HAGAN: A lot of coaches would have had problems with Russell's practice habits, but not Red. That was a key to the Celtics' success, the relationship between Auerbach and Russell.

RED AUERBACH: In training camp, Bill worked as hard as anyone in practice. During the season, I was using him 45–48 minutes a night. Why kill him in practice the next day? What was there to gain? Russell knew what he had to do to be ready for the games and the last thing I wanted out of him was for him to leave his game on the practice court. The idea is to win games, not to make Russell tired in practice.

SATCH SANDERS: We all knew that the Celtics revolved around Russell. He never had a serious injury. We knew he made us better—that he brought out the best in all of our individual skills. Also, Bill had no interest in scoring. He was totally unselfish. He was always there for us, getting the clutch rebound, making the big blocks. He was the reason we won and why all those championship banners hang at the Garden. He was the reason Red could keep us together, why there was no reason for trades. So we paid him the respect he deserved.

The Debate Lives On

BILLY CUNNINGHAM: Wilt and Russell were to basketball what Arnold Palmer was to golf. Turn on the television on Sunday and there they were: Wilt vs. Russell. They brought their sport into the living rooms of America, just as Palmer did with golf. They were individually bigger than the game. It was never Boston vs. Philly or Boston vs. L.A.; it was Wilt vs. Russell. You have to realize that the dunk as we know it— the scary power play it can be—started with Chamberlain. And the great defensive player, the man capable of stopping the dunk—that was Russell. They are the two greatest talents to ever play the game. When you were on the court with them, they so dominated that you'd find yourself stopping just to watch them. I've never had that feeling with any two other players.

TOM MESCHERY: We're talking about classic duels, like two huge dinosaurs going at each other. It was almost cataclysmic, as if they were about to fight to the death. Not that they were dirty. They never actually *fought* each other, but it was a basketball war between two great gladiators. You can talk about Larry Bird vs. Magic Johnson or Magic vs. Michael Jordan, but the difference is that those guys never actually covered each other. But Wilt vs. Russell, both centers, both went at it hammer and tongs.

WAYNE EMBRY: What made it fun to watch those guys was that everyone knew there was no love between them. Off the court, they got along back then, but they wanted to beat each other more than anything in the world.

NORM DRUCKER: I worked 25 Russell-Chamberlain matchups and I never saw one cheap shot between them, and neither ever said a word to the officials.

WILT CHAMBERLAIN: I loved those games, but somehow they were never viewed in the right perspective. It was not Chamberlain vs. Russell, it was Chamberlain vs. the Celtics. I didn't just play Russell, I played his entire team because basketball is not a one-man game and Russell was blessed because he played on the best *team* in basketball. I scored 40 or more points against Russell 26 times, but he never did it to me. Yet Red Auerbach was crafty enough to make Russell into some kind of defensive genius and I was supposed to be the offensive genius.

The Celtics never used Russell against me on offense, but I went against Russell all the time. Russell had all those great players—Heinsohn, Cousy, the Joneses, Havlicek—one of those Celtics teams had seven Hall of Famers on the roster. When I got Russell in foul trouble,

Red would change the defensive matchups and Gene Conley would guard me and Russell would guard one of my forwards.

I always wondered if Russell realized that during his career he was relegated to being a role player. Like most of the early black players, he was a blue-collar worker who was there to rebound and play defense—letting the other guys score. They didn't want any black player to steal the scoring thunder from the white stars, until yours truly did it.

Wilt Chamberlain made Bill Russell a star because Bill Russell was used to try and curb my offense. And also to prick me a little, saying I scored 40-some points, but Russell's team won. They never said Bob Pettit scored 35 points, but his team lost. The winning and losing only became personal when it was applied to me—I was the loser and Russell was the winner.

BOB COUSY: If Wilt thinks that with all the Hall of Famers on our team we'd have waited for him to get his ass down on offense the way Philadelphia did, forget it. We wouldn't watch anyone shoot it every time he got it, like he did the year he scored 50 a game. Nor would we have wanted to watch all the garbage he did in the pivot with the ball. He used to think he was a great passer because he led the league in assists. Hell, he couldn't shoot, he couldn't pass and he couldn't dribble, but he was the strongest man ever to play this game and he was a great athlete. He could have averaged those 50 points for us, but we never would have won a championship. It also would have produced a lot of disharmony. Russ didn't care about scoring. Listen, on the Celtics all the players were round pegs and we fit into round holes after Russell came. I don't mean to criticize Wilt. We probably would have won a couple of titles with him. He'd block shots and do a helluva job on the defensive boards. But Russ remains the most productive center ever to play this game, because the ultimate production is winning titles.

WILT CHAMBERLAIN: I give the Celtics and Russell credit. I think they had a great coach in Auerbach. They had great talent and Russell was the best clutch rebounder this game has ever seen. But they also seemed to be lucky. They'd beat us in the most amazing ways—Havlicek steals the ball, I got called for a dubious goaltending, on and on it went.

TOM MESCHERY: Wilt has had a bad rap for his whole career, and it's solely because he has been compared to Russell. Bill won because his team was always a little better, because his coach was a little better and because his team played together better than most of Wilt's teams.

But Wilt really finished second all the time. Does that make him a loser? That makes him second-best—at the worst.

JOHN HAVLICEK: When you played with Russell, you knew exactly what to expect from him each night. But Wilt, he was liable to decide, "Tonight, I'm going to score 60 . . . or tonight, I'm getting 40 rebounds . . . or 20 assists." He was preoccupied with answering people who said he couldn't do things—that he couldn't pass or that his rebounding was down. He'd have a great stat game, but his team would lose. It was as if he had an ax to grind with the press, whereas Russell never let himself get caught up in that.

CHARLEY ECKMAN: Wilt was the strongest man ever to play basketball, but he always took a fallaway jumper. It was the damnedest thing. He played basketball the hard way. For that reason alone, he couldn't carry Russell's jock. If Wilt had consistently driven to the basket, he'd have scored 200 in a game.

BOB COUSY: Wilt can say what he wants, but the fallaway bank is a result of playing against Russell. Wilt could overpower every other center, but Russell took away his drive. So Wilt countered with his outside shot, and Russell countered by pushing Wilt farther and farther from the basket—often, out of range of his jump shot. If he tried to dribble it, we could swarm Wilt and steal his dribble. The one area where he could push Russell aside was when Wilt went after an offensive rebound. That was when he was the strongest.

ROD THORN: Wilt looked at the game as an individual. He'd think, "I got my 50 points and my 25 rebounds, and if that's not enough, it's not my fault. You can blame those SOBs over there."

JERRY LUCAS: Wilt was too consumed with records: being the first center to lead the league in assists, or to set a record for field goal percentage. He'd accomplish one individual goal, and then go on to another. Russell only asked himself one question: "What can I do to make us win?"

HOT ROD HUNDLEY: The comparisons with Russell got to Wilt. He told me, "We win a game and I never hear anyone say, 'Old Wilty won it.' "
   Wilt called himself Wilty.
   Then Wilt said, "But when we lost, all I ever heard was how Wilty lost it. And when the Celtics lose, Russell didn't lose, the Celtics did. That's not fair."
   Wilt would go home at night, knowing he had outscored and out-rebounded Russell, but the Celtics won. It was as if he'd won the battle, but Russell won the war.

NATE THURMOND: You just can't say that because Bill won 11 championships, he was far superior to the rest of us centers in that era. He was a great player, but also in a great situation. Teams that had Wilt always viewed him as the savior. The whole thing was on his shoulders. Often, ownership would pay Wilt big money, but skimp on everyone else and he'd be surrounded by inferior talent. He was supposed to win games by himself, draw fans and do things no man had ever done before—he did that, but it still wasn't enough for some people.

AL ATTLES: An example of the difference between Wilt's teams and the Celtics was one night in the playoffs. Boston had the last shot to win the game. Who took it? Not Russell. It was Sam Jones who beat us. They had five guys on the court who could have taken that shot.

BOB COUSY: If we needed him to, Russ could have averaged 20 points for us. For God's sake, he got 15 a game and we only had one play for him to shoot the ball. When we were clicking, he'd get a half dozen slams a game on lob passes off the fast break. So that's 12 points there, it wouldn't have been that hard to get him another eight. Even though he didn't have a shooting touch, he arranged his game so that he never had to take a bad shot.

JACK TWYMAN: Russell was the greatest impact player in any sport. He couldn't throw the ball in the ocean, but he allowed his teammates to press and gamble. You knew that if you got by Cousy or Heinsohn, that SOB Russell was back there waiting to block your shot. No one ever dominated a sport the way Russell did with the Celtics.

SLATER MARTIN: Boston just wasn't much of a team until Russell showed up. They couldn't guard anybody. Take Cousy, who never was a good defensive player. With Russell, he never had to worry about guarding anyone, and he never did. If his man drove by Cousy, he'd just run down to the other end of the court knowing that Russell would get the rebound and throw one of those great outlet passes for him. Russell would play with your head. After a while, you just stopped driving on the guy.

ZELMO BEATY: Russell made shot blocking an art form, because he didn't whack the ball into the seats. A lot of guys blocked shots that way because they liked to hear the fans cheer. But Russell never cared what the fans thought. He was so good that he could almost gently tap it out to his teammates, and they'd turn it into a fast-break layup. So a blocked shot was worth four points to the Celtics—two that the opposition didn't get and two more on the fast break.

CHARLEY ECKMAN: Russell ended the careers of guys like Larry Foust and Neil Johnston. They'd take those slow, sweeping hook shots and Russell would time his jump so that he'd take the ball right out of their hands. I saw Foust get a couple of shots blocked, so he nailed Russell in the forehead with an elbow and then made one. All that did was piss Russell off and he blanketed Foust to the point where we couldn't even get a pass in to him.

WILT CHAMBERLAIN: They didn't keep blocked shots back then, but I'm convinced that I blocked twice as many as Russell and I know we both blocked more than anyone ever has before or since.

EARL STROM: Wilt and Russell were getting 8–10 blocks a game for most of their careers.

TOM HEINSOHN: If you go strictly by the record book, then you've got to say that Chamberlain was the greatest player in basketball history. The 50-points-a-game average, the 100-point game, all the rebounds, even the assists. But as great as Wilt was, he couldn't beat us. That's because Russell was the fulcrum of a team effort—he covered for us and we covered for him.

I've heard Wilt say, "If I had all those guys around me like Russell did, then I'd have won all those championships."

I don't buy that.

First, it is difficult to measure Russell's value in statistics. I believe he was worth 50–60 points a game for us. There was the 15 or so he scored. Then all the blocked shots, the intimidation on defense in the form of shots missed because they thought Bill would block it. He changed entire teams' offenses, and he was the starting point of our fast-break offense.

How can you put a number on what that's worth to a team?

As for Wilt, Russell used different tactics on him. Sometimes, he played Wilt tight, other times he gave Wilt room. But we helped Russell on Wilt. We respected Wilt and we were quick to double-team. Wilt also had two major weaknesses.

First, he didn't want to be known as some tall, freaky player, so he used the fallaway jumper. But when he missed, he was in no position to rebound. We'd get the ball off the boards and beat him down to the other end of the court for a fast-break layup.

Second, Wilt was a poor foul shooter. Our rule was that if Wilt got by Russell, we should just clobber him and put him at the line. Missing the free throws would frustrate Wilt.

Wilt was a great player. But he was there to be an individual, to draw fans and be the center of attention. I believe he liked that role, while Russell was more comfortable blending in and winning.

DOLPH SCHAYES: It's not fair how people use Russell as a way to criticize Wilt. Because of his size and his enormous physical ability, Wilt was such an easy target for the sportswriters. He took the criticism to heart. He was a much more sensitive person than Russell.

JACK TWYMAN: Bill Russell is a great player, but I've seen him send children away crying because of his personality and his refusal to sign autographs. Wilt is a much better person to be around than Russell.

TOM GOLA: Wilt was always patient with fans, signed autographs and did a lot of charity work—unlike another great center who never got any bad press.

HASKELL COHEN: Wilt went along with the publicity that his team and the league needed. Russell invariably gave you a hard time and he could be a very cold person.

BOB RYAN: You'd talk to Wilt and listen to all his bravado, but underneath you'd realize that what he wanted more than anything else was to be your friend. Russell, he never cared what anyone else thought about him except his teammates.

RED AUERBACH: I'm not going to knock Wilt. I will say that when he played in Philadelphia, Wilt lived in New York and he'd come and go his own way with the team. He wasn't at the heart of his team or as close to the players as Russell was with us.

FRANK RAMSEY: Wilt was very gracious. Even his critics will admit that. When he was playing in San Francisco, he had just built a new home and he invited the entire Celtics team over along with his team. He did a lot of things like that. What people don't realize is that when they played, Wilt and Russell were very close.

FRANK MCGUIRE: I used to get on Wilt to be more aggressive on the court with Russell. But Wilt, he liked Russell. They would go to dinner together after the game. One day, I saw Bill and Wilt together in a hotel elevator the afternoon before they were to play that night. A few hours later, I ran into Wilt alone and I asked him what he was doing with Russell.

"We always eat together before the game," said Wilt. "Sometimes I even go to his house."

I tried to tell him that Russell did that just to soften him up, but Wilt was too nice a guy to believe that.

WILT CHAMBERLAIN: On Thanksgiving, we took turns eating at each other's homes. One year, I'd eat with Bill and his wife. The next, he'd come to my mother's home in Philadelphia. He'd even sleep over at my house before a game. My friends told me that Bill was a con man and that he was being nice to me so I'd take it easy on him. They said that instead of eating dinner with the guy, I should have picked him up and stuffed him through the basket. He was my friend because it worked to his advantage. I didn't see it back then, but considering the shots Bill has taken at me over the years, they may have been right.

I think Bill has become very jealous of me.

If you were Bill Russell and you had won all those world titles and you were walking through airports and people came up to you and asked, "Are you Wilt Chamberlain?" how would you feel?

No one has ever asked me if I was Bill Russell.

When people see a big man of color who is about my age, the only name they think of is Wilt Chamberlain, and that has to gnaw at him. We have walked down the street together and people have yelled, "Hey, Wilt!" at me and acted as though Bill wasn't there because they didn't recognize him. Year after year of that would cut to the heart of any person.

Look, Bill was a married guy. I was single. I drove fast cars, had my share of women, and in the off season I had the lifestyle of a jet-setter. Later in life, Bill started driving fast cars and doing some of the things that would be considered out of synch with being a married man. I owned a nightclub, so he bought a nightclub in Boston and his failed. As I've gotten older, I've learned to understand where Bill and his supporters are coming from when they criticize me. A lot of it is envy.

BOB COUSY: I like and respect Wilt for how he has always graciously handled himself with fans. But maybe as we get older, we get a little insecure. That's what I sense in some of his statements about Russell over the last few years. Or when he says these outrageous things about still being able to play at the age of 50-some, or his taking shots at other players. He doesn't have to say anything. My God, he rewrote the record book. I feel bad that he has been caught up in this "I did this . . . I did that . . . ." That wasn't his style when he played because he never had a chip on his shoulder, as Russell did. Wilt was a great player and everyone knows it. I just wish Wilt would sit back and enjoy it instead of refighting the old wars.

LEONARD KOPPETT: I always believed that Wilt was more of a basketball player than Russell, and that would irritate Russell. If you ask yourself, "Imagine Wilt with Russell's Celtics teams, then how much would they have won?"

Or more revealing, "Put Russell on Wilt's teams, how many titles would they have won?"

The reason Wilt's teams were taking Russell's teams to seventh games in the playoffs was because of Wilt and his incredible ability. It is absolute nonsense to say that Wilt dragged his teams down.

BOB PETTIT: I've thought a lot about Russell vs. Chamberlain and it almost comes down to a matter of taste. No one has ever scored like Wilt, no one has ever played defense like Russell. They weren't just giants of their time, but of all time. I look at the guys today . . . nothing comes close to the battles they had.

17

TWO FOR THE ROAD

Two years after the 1966–67 Philadelphia 76ers were supposed to be the greatest team ever assembled, they had been dismantled.

So much for a dynasty.

After winning the 1967 title, the Sixers remained the best in the 1967–68 regular season with a 62-20 record. It wasn't 68-13, but it was eight games better than the Celtics.

Furthermore, Wilt Chamberlain did exactly what he promised—he led the NBA in assists. Chamberlain had 702 for an average of 8.6 assists. Lenny Wilkens of the St. Louis Hawks was second at 8.3. Actually, Oscar Robertson averaged 9.7 assists, but the Big O missed 17 games to injury and had fewer total assists than Wilt. So Wilt could lay claim to being the best passing big man the league had ever seen— at least in terms of sheer numbers, which was the ultimate measuring stick to Chamberlain.

But he couldn't say he repeated as champion.

The 1968 playoffs opened with everyone awaiting a Boston-Philly rematch in the Eastern Conference Finals.

First, the Sixers had to get past New York in the opening round. That used to be no problem, but the Knicks under general manager Eddie Donovan had finally gotten a handle on how to put together a team and how to draft. At midseason, Donovan installed Red Holzman as coach and the Knicks went on to finish with a 43-39 record, their best since the shot clock. New York had a green but very promising team— Walt Bellamy in the middle, Willis Reed and Cazzie Russell at the forwards, and Dick Barnett and Walt Frazier in the backcourt. Off the bench? How does Bill Bradley, Phil Jackson and Dick Van Arsdale sound?

The league would hear a lot from this group in the 1970s, and they were good enough in 1968 to force the Sixers to six games before shutting down Madison Square Garden for the season.

Meanwhile, Boston also needed six games to dust off a decent Detroit

team led by young stars Dave Bing and Dave DeBusschere. In his second
NBA season, Bing led the NBA in scoring at 27 per game.

So it was Philly vs. Boston, Chamberlain vs. Russell in the second
round. The first game of the series was April 5, 1968. It was the day
after Martin Luther King was killed. The players agreed to play the
opener, won 127–118 by Boston. The two teams then took five days
off to honor King's memory.

When the series resumed, it was more what people expected—for a
while. The Sixers won the next three games. Boston looked old, weary
and wondering if this was indeed the end. The only negative for Philadelphia was that Billy Cunningham suffered a broken right wrist in
Game 4, and would be out for the rest of the playoffs.

Meanwhile, obituaries were being written in Boston.

"When we went to Philadelphia for Game 5, there were things in the
paper about our never seeing the parquet floor again that season," said
Celtics backup center Wayne Embry. "John Havlicek and I led a team
meeting. We talked about what the Celtics meant. I said that even
though this was only my second year in Boston, I had never been
prouder to be on a team."

As Embry spoke emotionally to the players, the word "Pride" was
on the blackboard behind him—written by Embry.

Be it Cunningham's injury, Celtics pride or the fact that Russell
found his second wind, Boston came back to beat the Sixers, winning
games 5 and 7 in Philadelphia, and ended the "Sixers dynasty" at one
year.

Game 7 was a bizarre one for Chamberlain. During the season, Wilt
had become obsessed with assists, checking at the scorer's table during
halftime to see how many he had and if the official total matched the
total Wilt carried in his head. But in the second half of Game 7, Wilt
carried this beyond reason. His teammates were cold, yet Wilt kept
passing, not even making a threatening fake to the basket. He took
only two shots in the final 24 minutes, both on offensive rebounds when
he had to shoot the ball.

The Sixers lost, 100–96.

Wilt outrebounded Russell 34–26 in that Game 7. He said he didn't
shoot "because Boston had half their team on me. The other guys were
open."

But the other guys were knocking the bolts out of the rim—Chet
Walker (8-for-22), Wally Jones (8-of-22) and Hal Greer (8-of-25) had
nightmarish games.

Obviously, something was wrong in Philadelphia. While Boston was beating the Lakers in six games to reclaim the title, the Sixers soap opera went public.

Coach Alex Hannum didn't like the fact that Jack Ramsay had been hired as general manager. Hannum had both jobs—though only one title—in the 1967 championship season. Hannum thought Ramsay really wanted to coach—and was ultimately correct.

During the 1967–68 season, the American Basketball Association was born. Few in the NBA thought much of it or its chances, even when Rick Barry jumped leagues. But the ABA was just what Hannum wanted. He was a West Coast guy, and they had a team in Oakland. He wanted complete control of the franchise, and he got it. He quit the Sixers and was in the Bay Area before the ink was dry on his resignation papers in Philadelphia.

Chamberlain suggested that the Sixers hire Bill Sharman or Frank McGuire as coach. McGuire was coaching at the University of South Carolina; Sharman had resigned from the Warriors and was headed to the Los Angeles franchise of the ABA. Instead, the Sixers job was obviously going to Ramsay.

Like Dolph Schayes, Ramsay wanted a motion offense and he wondered how Chamberlain would fit into his system. Meanwhile, Chamberlain wanted a big raise. Rather than try to pound what Ramsay considered a square peg into the round hole that was his share-the-wealth offense, the Sixers unloaded Chamberlain and his contract demands on the team that wanted him and could most afford him—the L.A. Lakers.

This would set up the sixth Boston vs. Lakers Finals in eight years—only now, the Lakers had Chamberlain instead of Jim Krebs or Leroy Ellis in the middle.

Putting Together the Big Three

In the summer of 1968, the Lakers traded Jerry Chambers, Archie Clark and Darrall Imhoff to Philadelphia for Wilt Chamberlain. The Lakers had just lost in six games to Boston in the 1968 Finals—the fifth time the Lakers had been defeated by Boston in the Finals. Laker owner Jack Kent Cooke wanted to make a dramatic move to beat Boston, and nothing seemed more profound than teaming his stars Jerry West and

Elgin Baylor with Chamberlain. These players were coached by Butch Van Breda Kolff, who lasted two seasons with the Lakers, 1967–69.

FRED SCHAUS: When I became the Lakers' general manager in 1967, we needed a coach to replace me. Jack Kent Cooke said he did not want to take part in the NBA's "musical chairs." He didn't want to recycle a coach who was fired or hire another pro assistant. One day, he saw a *Sports Illustrated* with Bill Bradley on the cover, and he asked me who was Bradley's coach at Princeton. I'd known Butch Van Breda Kolff and had a lot of respect for him. We contacted Butch and interviewed him. We liked his enthusiasm and his honesty, so we hired him.

BUTCH VAN BREDA KOLFF: I was told by the Lakers that they liked how my teams played at Princeton. Even though I had played for the Knicks [1946–50], I had no overwhelming desire to coach in the NBA. I was happy at Princeton, but the chance to coach in L.A. and to coach Jerry West and Elgin Baylor fascinated me.

My first season with the Lakers was great. West and Baylor did everything I asked. The guys would dribble the ball more than I liked— I'm talking about the whole team—but we played together and finished the regular season on a 30-8 run. *[The team improved from 36-45 in 1966–67 to 52-30.]* Everyone got along. We were like a college team. We beat Chicago in the first round, then swept the Warriors in the second round to reach the finals. But we had to wait eight days to play again because Wilt's Philadelphia team blew a 3–1 lead and lost to Boston. It's hard to stay sharp when you don't play for eight days, I don't care what kind of practices you run. In the first game, we were up by 15 points in the third quarter, then hit a wall and blew the game. We lost in six games, and I'm convinced we could have beaten them if we hadn't sat around for eight days.

FRED SCHAUS: We had been in the market for a big man for years. It was a problem when we faced Boston when I coached, and it was the same thing again in Butch's first year. Wilt was unhappy in Philadelphia and said he wanted to play on the West Coast. Jack Kent Cooke and I heard that and knew we had an excellent chance to get him, so we contacted Philadelphia.

WILT CHAMBERLAIN: After the 1968 playoffs, Alex Hannum was quitting as the Sixers' coach to jump to the ABA. I was having some contract problems with Philly, and they didn't seem to be negotiating seriously.

I loved the city of San Francisco when I played for the Warriors; I also liked L.A., with all the beaches. I told some people who knew Jack Kent Cooke that I'd like to play for the Lakers, and that got things rolling.

FRED SCHAUS: Everyone always says there was a lot of money in the Wilt deal with Philadelphia, but we never gave them a dime—at least as far as I know, and I was in the middle of the talks. Philadelphia felt they needed to change some faces to move on, and we gave them an All-Star in Archie Clark, a solid center in Darrall Imhoff, and Jerry Chambers had been our first-round pick in 1966. I'd always been a big Wilt fan and felt he had gotten a bad rap over the years. I wish I could have coached him.

BUTCH VAN BREDA KOLFF: I was excited when Fred Schaus told me that we had a chance to get Wilt. It seemed that once a week, some center was getting his career high against us, either in points or rebounds. I thought that at the worst, we'd get a lot more rebounds. But right after the deal, one of my veteran players told me, "We just broke up a great team. We'd been to the Finals, why make a deal like that?" I told the player, "Look, we'll build another great team."

Then I met Wilt during the summer at Kutsher's Country Club for the Maurice Stokes Game. I asked him to put on the Lakers T-shirt I had for him so we could take a picture, but he didn't want to do it. We went around and around for a minute, and Wilt was just being contrary. He just wanted to see how far he could push me. It just pissed me off, but I let it go.

LEIGH MONTVILLE: When the Lakers picked up Wilt, it was a precursor of things to come—it was as if the Lakers were trying to buy a title because they were one of the few teams who could afford to pay Wilt.

BUTCH VAN BREDA KOLFF: On our first day of practice, Wilt was great. He moved the ball, got every rebound, blocked shots. We were ready to win the title right there—that first day. The second day, Wilt practiced, but he hardly moved, just moped around the court. The third day, he told me that he wanted to rest his knees, but not to worry because he'd be ready for the games. He'd come to practice, but showed no interest. After a while, it reached the point where the other guys didn't want Wilt to practice, because we couldn't have a good workout with him on the court. So he'd run on the side and the rest of the guys would practice. It was like that all season.

WILT CHAMBERLAIN: After the trade, Butch was quoted as saying he "could handle Wilt." Well, you handle horses, not people. Then there was all this talk about there not being enough basketballs for West, Baylor and myself. That didn't bother me. I was willing to sacrifice my offense and to concentrate on defense and rebounding so West and Baylor could score and we could make a run for the title. But with Butch, he always wanted me to know he was the boss.

BUTCH VAN BREDA KOLFF: Not having enough basketballs wasn't the problem at all for us. The trade changed our chemistry. Wilt would set up on the low left block. Elgin's favorite move was the drive from the left wing into the middle. Now when he did that, he ran into Wilt and Wilt's man. Wilt took that move away from Elgin. Imhoff loved to pick-and-roll with Elgin, but that wasn't something Wilt did very well. So we were able to throw the ball down low to Wilt and he'd score, but it was an awful offense to watch. When the ball stops moving, then guys don't rebound or play defense as well as they normally would.

WILT CHAMBERLAIN: Butch wanted me to play the high post so Elgin could drive, but they got me for my rebounding. Why pull a guy away from the basket when you want him to rebound?

BUTCH VAN BREDA KOLFF: I tried to talk to Wilt, I really did. Once, I said that we'd be better if he didn't spike the ball out-of-bounds after he blocked a shot. Then I made the mistake of mentioning Russell's name, and how the Celtics would fast break off his blocked shots.

Wilt said, "Boston is coached to come up with Russell's blocks."

I said, "What do you want me to do, put guys halfway up the stands? Are the ushers supposed to get your blocks?"

EARL STROM: During games, you'd see Butch yell at Wilt and then Wilt would yell right back at him. Or else they would get into it when Butch took Wilt out of the game. Wilt said that he got along with most of his coaches, which was true. But once I heard him say, "Yeah, I liked all my coaches but Jackass."

I thought, "Who's Jackass?"

Then Wilt said, "Good old Jackass Van Breda Kolff."

FRED SCHAUS: I had a couple of meetings with Butch and Wilt, just the three of us. Both guys wanted to win and I think they wanted to smooth things out, but they were such strong-willed people . . . one of them would say something, and they'd start to argue. They would get stuck on little things. They just were two people who could look at each other and that was enough to aggravate the hell out of both of them.

BUTCH VAN BREDA KOLFF: As the season went on, I saw how we really missed Clark and Imhoff. Clark became an All-Pro guard in Philly, a real shake-and-bake guy who gave us speed in the backcourt. When Jerry West would sit out a game with an injury, Clark would step up and score 30–35, no problem. And Imhoff, did we miss him. He'd set a pick on anyone. The man lived to set picks and if you coach this game long enough, you understand the importance of that. He also stayed out of the way and kept the middle open for our guys to drive. Another thing was that we'd lost Gail Goodrich in the expansion draft to Phoenix. Without Clark and Goodrich, we were very thin in the backcourt behind West.

Sure, we were winning, but I didn't enjoy it. The college atmosphere we had the year before the Wilt deal was gone. I didn't like how we were playing and around midseason I knew in my own mind that I wasn't coming back to coach the Lakers [in 1969–70]. I didn't tell anyone, and no one said anything to me. I just wasn't having any fun. I still wanted to win a championship, especially for Jerry West and Elgin Baylor. Those guys deserved it. So I was going to coach my ass off to win, regardless of the situation.

FRED SCHAUS: It was a myth about the Big Three, because Elgin was 34. He had had a serious knee operation and was coming back from a torn Achilles and he just couldn't physically give us a vintage Elgin Baylor performance every night. Listen, with Wilt, Jerry and Elgin in their primes, we could have won a championship with two guys off the street. But our team had a little age, and it wasn't going to be easy. But we still won the West [with a 55-27 record] and took Boston to seven games. And later [1972] under Bill Sharman, we were able to win a title with Wilt and West, just like I always thought we could.

Coach Russell

When Russell was named player-coach in 1966, he was the only player left from Red Auerbach's first championship team in 1957. Auerbach was still GM and he had been slowly retooling the Celtics so they would remain champions in the late 1960s. He drafted John Havlicek in 1962. He signed free agents Larry Siegfried (1963), Don Nelson (1965) and Wayne Embry (1967), all veterans who had been discarded by other teams. The only trade he made in Russell's 13 years with the Celtics was Mel Counts for Bailey Howell in 1966.

TOM HEINSOHN: I had retired in the summer of 1965. At the start of the 1965–66 season, Red said it would be his last year as coach. It wasn't like today, where there would be a lot of speculation about who would take his place. The season went along like any other. Late in the year, I had lunch with Red in Philadelphia and he said he wanted me to coach the Celtics next year.

I said, "Red, I'm the wrong guy right now. I couldn't handle Russell. No one can handle Russell like you."

We started thinking about who would make a good coach, and I said, "Why don't you make Russell the player-coach? He's so proud. He'd be the first black coach. I don't think anyone could motivate Bill as well as Bill could do it for himself. He loves challenges, and this would be the ultimate for him."

RED AUERBACH: I talked to some people about who should be my successor. One day, Russell came to see me. He didn't want me to quit. I told him that I had made up my mind. We talked later in the season, and I told him I was still quitting. Then he asked me for the job, he really didn't want to play for anyone else. I thought about it and realized, who would get more out of Russell than Russell? It was a delicate situation. I didn't want to bring in someone from the outside who might not understand Russell. As the years went on, motivation was tough for Bill. But as a coach, he had to motivate himself and the team.

LARRY SIEGFRIED: When I heard Red had hired Russell, I was happy. We knew that Russell the coach would get the most out of Russell the center. I don't think there was any resentment from the players about the move at all.

WAYNE EMBRY: I had retired in the summer of 1966 after eight years with the Royals. I had made five All-Star teams, but all I ever heard was that the reason the Royals never went anywhere in the playoffs was that they needed a center. This began to erode my confidence, and after a while I said the hell with it and took a job with Pepsi Cola.

In the summer, I was at the Maurice Stokes Game and playing golf with Russell at Kutsher's Country Club. As we went around the course, Russell asked, "How would you like to play for me? When we get to the clubhouse, let's talk to Red about it."

Red was waiting for me, and it was obvious that Bill and Red had worked all of this out in advance. I was flattered that Russell wanted me on his team, but I told them I needed some time to think about it.

Red kept calling me. Finally, I said, "Okay, what will you pay?"

He said $20,000.

I said I could make that much outside of basketball.

He said, "All right, $21,000."

I said the money still wasn't very good. Red talked about getting playoff money. Then he said, "Wayne, you play for us, you get a championship ring. You're not going to get that anywhere else."

Red had hit the right button with me, and I agreed to go to Boston. Red worked a deal with Cincinnati to get my rights [for $6,000], and I was on my way to Boston.

JOHN HAVLICEK: In the middle 1960s, we were changing our team. We had to replace great players—Cousy, Sharman, Ramsey. When it became obvious that we needed some guard help, I pushed Red to give Larry Siegfried a chance because we had been roommates at Ohio State.

LARRY SIEGFRIED: I was the third player taken in the 1961 draft, but instead of signing with Cincinnati, I went with Cleveland of the old American Basketball League. That turned out to be a major mistake. Cleveland was total confusion, and I ended up getting cut. While I was with Cleveland, the Royals traded my rights to St. Louis. I went to training camp with them, and they had a million guards. It didn't matter how well I played, I had no chance.

MARTY BLAKE: We [St. Louis] cut Larry in the parking lot of Quincy College after an exhibition game. We were watching the pennies so much that we made him give back his basketball shoes. We just left him there, and he stood watching the bus pull away.

LARRY SIEGFRIED: After getting cut by Cleveland and the Hawks, I talked to Havlicek and I knew he was trying to convince Red to sign me. I was teaching school and waiting for something to happen. Cleveland and the Hawks were both crazy situations. Going from the third player in the draft to a guy who was out of work doesn't do much for your confidence. But then I went to the Celtics, and it reminded me of being back at Ohio State. This was a team totally consumed with winning.

EARL STROM: For years, the Celtics lived off other teams' castoffs. Larry Siegfried wasn't good enough for the Hawks, but ended up starting for Boston. Bailey Howell was supposed to be too old for Detroit. Wayne Embry was supposed to be washed up in Cincinnati. Don Nelson wasn't good enough for the Lakers, all they saw was a guy who couldn't dribble, who was slow and not much of a leaper. Red saw a guy who never missed an open shot from medium range, and he knew the Celtics could set things up to get Nelson that shot.

DON NELSON: I was with Chicago for a year [1962–63], then played two years with the Lakers. The Lakers thought I just didn't have enough natural ability to be a forward in the league, and they cut me [in training camp of 1966] for a guy named John Fairchild, who didn't make it through the season with them. Now I'd call myself an unrestricted free agent. Back then, I was out of work. Like most guys in the league, I dreamed of playing for the Celtics, but I was absolutely shocked when Red called me. All he said was that I could try out when the team got home. I went to Boston, and the Celtics were on a West Coast trip for a week. I figured out that the guy I had a chance to replace was a rookie named Ronnie Watts. I moved into a hotel in Boston, worked out at a YMCA and ran through the streets to get my wind and conditioning. At night, I listened to the games, hoping Watts would not get hot. He didn't play much. When the team returned home, I wasn't greeted with open arms. The guys knew I was there to take someone's job. I practiced a few days, showed I could play, and then they cut Watts to keep me. After that, everyone was very warm because I had become one of them.

JOHN HAVLICEK: Both Siegfried and I encouraged Red to sign Nelson. Larry was very strong about Nellie because they had played against each other in college for three years. I knew Don would follow orders and bear down on defense.

LEIGH MONTVILLE: Nelson was the master of the YMCA head fake. He'd fake once, the guy would go up and Nelson would draw the foul. If the defender didn't move, Nelson would fake again, again, and even again. I swear, there were times when Nelson faked Wilt 37 times. Finally, on the 38th time, he'd get Wilt to go for it. Then he'd step to the line and shoot his signature one-handed free throw, where he looked like he was waving at the basket when he released the ball.

EARL STROM: Nelson drove Wilt crazy because Nellie put globs of stickum on the ball to help his grip. One game, Wilt went in for his finger roll and the ball wouldn't leave his hand. It stuck there and Wilt banged the ball on the rim a couple of times to get it loose. He and Alex Hannum both complained to me about it, and they blamed Nelson because he was the biggest offender. I said there was no rule against stickum. A week later, we got a memo from the league outlawing it. Nelson still used the stuff, but he'd hide it under his arms or up near his jock. Wilt always wanted me to check Nelson, and I did, but I wasn't going to put my hand up his pants.

BOB RYAN: In Don Nelson and Bailey Howell, the Celtics had two guys who knew every dirty trick. Howell was a pure Southern gentleman. His pregame routine was to drink a cup of tea with his pinky finger extended. He was the ultimate family man. He memorized all the flight schedules so he could catch a red-eye after a game to get home to his wife and kids, rather than leave the next morning with the team. He was a sincere, Bible-quoting man who would grab a player's shorts, stick his finger in a shooter's chest . . .

WAYNE EMBRY: Bailey would step on your foot, elbow you in the throat. He was a great offensive rebounder, but he'd kick you to get the ball. I was glad to have him on my team.

JOHN HAVLICEK: With the core of our team being veterans, and then adding experienced players such as Nelson, Howell and Embry, Bill didn't have to do a lot of teaching. He made me the captain. We ran the same plays that Red did. Even though we had no assistant coaches, the veterans served that role for Russell. If Bill and I were both in the game, then one of the veterans would watch the time-outs and fouls. Bill always made the substitutions, but we were a team that ran itself.

WAYNE EMBRY: In Russell's first day as coach, he did want the guys to know that he wasn't just their teammate anymore. Supposedly, one of the players hid Russell's sneakers. This was before anyone had shoe contracts and most guys only had one pair of sneakers in their locker.

Russell walked into the gym on the first day of practice in his stocking feet. He said, "Some wise guy took my sneakers, and you'll all pay for that."

I had reported to camp a good 25 pounds overweight because I thought I had retired until Russell and Red talked me out of it. So I put on two layers of sweatsuits, then a rubber suit on top.

"Put the balls away," said Russell. "Now, we run."

And all we did was run—two hours of sprints, line drills and exercises. He was killing us because of the shoes.

Before that practice, I weighed 285. After, I weighed 257. I took off that rubber suit and there was a puddle of sweat at my feet. I was lucky I didn't dehydrate, and I got into the shower and stuck my mouth up to the nozzle to get some liquid back into my body.

In his second training camp, Russell called a team meeting and said, "I was stubborn last year and I didn't want to admit it. Now, I look at the team and I see that we have guys with as much experience as I have. I know you guys wanted to help me. Now, I want your help. If you see a player getting tired on the floor or something else is on your mind, tell me and I'll make the substitution. Sometimes, I'm so caught up in the game when I'm playing that I miss things you can see."

The other thing was that Russell started talking to Red more. You have to give Red credit. He was around, but Russell was the coach. Red was not one to interfere.

LEIGH MONTVILLE: Red was never one to smother Russell or his other coaches. But he was like the guy living next door who knows how to fix everything. Just ask him for help, and he was there. But then he'd know when things were fixed and it was time to butt out.

LARRY SIEGFRIED: Russell relaxed things a lot, compared to Red. When Red called your name during a game, it was like a jolt of electricity went down your spine. Red was in charge of everything, from game strategy to practices to how you wore your warmups. Bill just gave us a lot more freedom, especially when it came to speaking our minds.

WAYNE EMBRY: In Russell's second season, we had lost a couple of games and Bill had a team meeting. Russell said, "All right, we haven't been playing worth a damn, so what's wrong?"

There was a long silence.

Russell said, "I want to hear what's on your mind."

Siegfried stood up and started ripping all of us—by name. He said one guy was chasing too many broads. He looked at me and said, "And Wayne, the other night you were bitching behind Russell's back because you weren't getting enough minutes."

He looked at Russell and said, "And you, Russell, you could use some more sleep, too."

People were sitting there with their mouths open, including Russell. Finally Siegfried ran out of gas and sat down. Russell said, "Anybody have anything else?"

No one said a word.

Russell said, "End of meeting," and walked out the door.

An outsider would have wondered what the hell was going on, but we all knew that Siegfried was wound so tight that it seemed like at times he was about to snap. He'd just go off, but when he was done, it was over. Russell knew it was best just to let it die.

LEIGH MONTVILLE: Russell did have a tremendous understanding of the players. This was the era of leisure suits and scarves, and one day Havlicek said to Russell, "That's a great scarf."

Russell talked about his wardrobe for a while and told Havlicek where he bought the scarf.

Havlicek said, "Yeah, but you've got to be tall to wear a scarf like that, or it doesn't look good."

Then they both were nodding as if this were some profound truth. I was thinking, "Wait a minute, Havlicek is 6-foot-5. How tall do you have to be to wear a scarf? Does it start at 6-foot-8 or what?"

WAYNE EMBRY: Most people now say that Russell was only a great coach because he had Bill Russell as a center. But there was more to it. Russell had played under Phil Woolpert at San Francisco and then under Red. He was always given credit for being a smart player. Well, he was smart and he learned a lot from those coaches in terms of dealing with players and the game itself. He was man enough to put away some of his stubbornness and pride after his first year, and then ask for help. Not many coaches could do that. Then he was able to sort through the advice, pick what would help and ignore things that would mess up the team. I'm convinced that if Russell had not replaced Red as coach, Boston never would have won the title in 1968 and 1969.

Russell's Last Stand

Entering the 1968–69 season, Boston was mounting one last defense of its title. It wouldn't be easy. As the season opened, K.C. Jones had retired. Sam Jones was 36 and said it would be his last year. Bill Russell was 35, Bailey Howell 32, Satch Sanders 30. They had a 48-35 record for fourth place in the Eastern Conference—their lowest finish in 20 years. They were trying to become the first team in NBA history to win a title without having a homecourt advantage in any playoff round. They dumped Philadelphia 4-games-to-1 in the first round. In the second round, they faced New York, a team that had won 6-of-7 vs. the Celtics in the regular season. Boston eliminated New York in six games. Then came the L.A. Lakers with Elgin Baylor, Jerry West and Wilt Chamberlain, a team that was the best in the West at 55-27 and had little trouble reaching the Finals. The odds seemed overwhelmingly against Boston, but as Frank Deford wrote in Sports Illustrated, *"Never trust a team over 30."*

BOB RYAN: The story of the 1968–69 regular season was not the Celtics, not even the Big Three in L.A. It was a given that the Lakers would get to the Finals with Wilt; they had been there the year before without him. But in the East, Baltimore was the big surprise, going from last place to first place thanks to Gus Johnson, Earl Monroe and Wes Unseld, who not only was Rookie of the Year but MVP. New York behind Willis Reed was also emerging. The Celtics? In the opener, Russell had 36 rebounds at Detroit, as if to say, "Yes, boys and girls, I can still play." But then he basically took the rest of the regular season off, averaging a career-low 9.9 points. Teams still worried about the Celtics, but when they finished fourth, most figured age had finally caught up with them.

EARL STROM: That Celtics team was so old and beaten up, when it took the court it needed only a fife and drum to look like the Spirit of '76. Satch Sanders could hardly walk. Sam Jones was limping. Russell was hunched over and everyone was taped up like mummies.

JOHN HAVLICEK: It was a Celtics tradition to play hurt. In his last game as a Celtic, Bob Cousy's body just gave out and he fell over. He went out for a minute, but came back, hobbled along and still controlled the team down the stretch as we won the [1963] title in six games. If there was a seventh game, I doubt Cooz could have played. But he made sure there would be no Game 7. Russell played one year on what later was discovered to be a broken foot. In that last year, he had terrible tendinitis in his knees. There was that mentality of playing with pain, of taking the pain—even if it was only to give the team 45 seconds. Back then, all we had was ice and a whirlpool for treatment. You could only hope that the Celtics' mystic power would come into play.

LARRY SIEGFRIED: We were beat up and we were the oldest team in the league. We played a tight rotation, eight guys—Russ, Havlicek, Nelson, Sam Jones, Bailey Howell, Satch Sanders, Emmette Bryant and myself. But we also knew we could play defense when it mattered. Russell would say, "I don't care about a guy's age, I just care if he can get it done." We knew that as long as we had Russell, we could get it done against the Lakers, Wilt Chamberlain or anyone else. We had seen Russell do numbers on Wilt before. We never feared him because we knew in a big game down the stretch, Russell would own Wilt.

JOHN HAVLICEK: We sort of limped through the regular season. In the last couple of weeks, Russell took time off [four games]. We could see he was resting up for the playoffs. All we wanted to do was stay in position to make the playoffs, we didn't care about homecourt advantage. We knew we had the experience and the confidence to win a short series anywhere. We didn't have much trouble with Philadelphia in the first round. Darrall Imhoff was their center, and Russell had his way. We could see that Russell was rested, and a rested Russell even at 35 was still the greatest money player ever. That came true when we faced New York in the second round. The Knicks owned us in the regular season, and Willis Reed was a terrific young player, but Russell rose up and neutralized him.

At the time, no one said a word about it being Russell's last year. In the back of our minds, we may have wondered how long he would go on because there were days when he was in complete agony. But we also knew that if he watched his minutes, he could play another 2–3 years. So when we faced the Lakers and Wilt, we looked at it as trying for another championship. Certainly adding Wilt to the Lakers made them formidable, and we respected Wilt. But we were never in awe of him because we knew that we had beaten Wilt in big games before.

BOB RYAN: Russell played monster minutes in those playoffs. They had no backup center to speak of. They lost Wayne Embry before the season to Milwaukee in the expansion draft. Jim "Bad News" Barnes was supposed to be Russell's caddy, but during the season Barnes had gotten off a plane, and the plane's exhaust backfired, knocking Barnes on his butt. Barnes said that it hurt his neck. Russell was not sympathetic, and by playoff time he simply ignored Barnes. You can check, Barnes didn't play a single minute in the postseason. On those rare occasions when Russell came out, he put Satch Sanders in the middle.

[Russell averaged 46 minutes per game in the Celtics' 18 playoff games in 1969. Havlicek averaged 47 minutes. Chamberlain averaged 46 for the Lakers. Another sidelight as the Finals began was that the Lakers had hammered Boston, 108–73, on national television late in the regular season.]

JERRY WEST: When I think of those Celtics playoffs, there is so much frustration. There were so many years of giving everything we had, but coming up short because we weren't good enough. But '69 was different. There was no question, we were the better team.

LARRY SIEGFRIED: Jerry West . . . good Lord, guarding Jerry West. I spent many nights tossing and turning, knowing I had to guard West the next day. It was awful. Racing through my mind were all the things he could do, and what I could do to try to stop him. The thing that was so tough about West was that you could play great defense on him, force him to miss a couple of shots, but it didn't matter, they were going back to him again. They had so much confidence in Jerry. When he didn't have the ball, he was in constant motion, running into one pick after another, daring you to quit playing defense on him because you were taking such a pounding. And in the last three minutes of the game, you knew that West would end up with the ball about 15–18 feet from the basket. You'd be isolated and he'd still have his dribble. You were alone on the island, just you and Jerry West.

[Because of West, the Lakers won the first two games of the series, both in L.A. West had 53 points, shot 20-for-41 and passed off for 10 assists as the Lakers took the opener, 120–118. Havlicek had 37 for Boston. In Game 2, West scored 41 and Baylor had 32, including his team's last 12 points in the 118–112 victory. Chamberlain sacrificed his scoring to concentrate on rebounding and defense and scored only four

points. In Game 3 at Boston, West and Baylor shot a combined 1-for-14 in the fourth quarter, while Havlicek scored 34 to give the Celtics a 111–105 victory. Game 4 at Boston was an 89–88 Celtics win, a game where the two teams combined for 50 turnovers. West still scored 40.]

BOB RYAN: Game 4 was the turning point. With 15 seconds left, the Lakers were in front [88–87] and Johnny Egan had the ball. The Celtics just raped him. I mean, they fouled the hell out of him, but there was no call. They got the ball back [Emmette Bryant was credited with the steal], and then set up the Ohio Play.

JOHN HAVLICEK: Larry Siegfried and I put in an out-of-bounds play that Fred Taylor used when we were at Ohio State. Basically, we set several picks to set up Sam Jones for the final shot. That was the great thing about Russell as a coach: if the players had a good idea, he wasn't afraid to let us incorporate it. So Sam broke free, I hit him with the pass, and he made an 18-footer.

BUTCH VAN BREDA KOLFF: That Sam Jones shot . . . that's the stuff that drives you absolutely crazy about the Celtics. That shot was totally off line. There is no way it ever should have gone in. It hit the backboard, it hit the rim. It hit everywhere and the damn ball dropped in. Then afterward, Sam said he was just trying to get the ball up there so Russell could get the rebound and dunk it. Well, Russell wasn't even in the game. He put all his outside shooters in there!

BOB RYAN: As the ball went in, I can still see Wilt standing under the rim, whacking the basket support. You knew he was thinking, "Not again."

[The Lakers came back to win Game 5, 117–104. Chamberlain had 13 points and 31 rebounds, compared to 2 points and 7 rebounds for Russell. West scored 39 for the winners. In Game 6, Boston prevailed, 99–90. West was hobbled with a hamstring and scored 26. Chamberlain was not a part of the offense, and had a mere 2 points. That set up Game 7 in L.A.]

JOHN HAVLICEK: Several things happened before that last game in L.A. that were pretty interesting. First, we knew the Lakers had champagne on ice. Jack Kent Cooke had 10,000 balloons in nets on the ceiling, and they were supposed to come down when the Lakers finally won their title. At the same time, the Southern California band was going to play "Happy Days Are Here Again." Before the game, one of the players got ahold of the itinerary that outlined the Lakers victory celebration, and we passed it around the dressing room. A couple of the guys looked at it and shook their heads, saying something along the lines of, "Who do they think they're playing? Do they figure we're just not going to show up?" Russell didn't say much. He gave his usual speech of, "Well, we've got a game and we've got to play it, so we may as well win it."

NORM DRUCKER: Earl Strom and I were working the game. I remember looking at how dolled up the arena was and how the crowd was pouring in, and I said to Earl, "Imagine, this is the seventh game, it's a sellout [17,568, the largest crowd in Lakers history] and you and I are working it for only $170 each." Then I saw Marvin Kratter coming.

EARL STROM: Kratter was the owner of the Celtics and he liked to work the room before a game, talking and shaking hands with everyone. I knew that he wanted to shake hands with Norm Drucker and me, but the last thing I wanted was to be seen talking to the Celtics' owner right before the seventh game. I said to Drucker during warmups, "Let's go out to midcourt and get away from that guy." But I saw he was coming right onto the court. I said, "Norm, let's both spit on our hands and rub them together, then maybe he won't shake hands with us."

Kratter came up to us and said, "Guys, rub my lucky rock."

He had a little stone in his hand.

Van Breda Kolff saw that and was screaming at us for talking to Kratter.

"It's my lucky stone from Israel," Kratter said.

I told him that I didn't care where it was from, we couldn't rub his lucky rock. Finally, he left.

JOHN HAVLICEK: The stone was from the Wailing Wall and Marvin had brought it back with him from his trip to Israel. He used to stand under the basket during our pregame layup drills with his hand out and he wanted us to rub his stone as we went by. I did once, we lost the game, and I never did it again. Most of the guys just went along with it—he owned the team and if he wanted you to rub his stone, it was easier just to rub it.

Kratter liked to be very visible. He'd signal to Johnny Most, telling Johnny that he was available if Johnny wanted a halftime guest. He sat by the bench and got to know our plays. Sometimes, he'd yell out "2" or some other play he wanted us to run. We just ignored him when he decided to coach.

LEIGH MONTVILLE: Even though this was 1969 and it was the Lakers and Celtics playing for the title, it just wasn't the mega-event that it is today. *The Boston Globe* had a morning and afternoon edition. The guy that covered the Celtics for the PM *Globe* was Herb Ralby, whose real job was as public relations man for the Boston Bruins. Herb couldn't cover the Finals because the Bruins were in the NHL playoffs, so the *Globe* asked me to do it, and I was just a kid reporter right out of school. This would never happen today.

JOHN HAVLICEK: Our only strategy going into the game was to run them. I noticed that when we slowed down and got into a halfcourt game, the Lakers controlled the tempo. We jumped out early [to a 24–12 lead], but we started to walk the ball and it was close [59–56] at the half. I told Russell, "Just keep the ball in my hands, I'll push it." My adrenaline was such that even though we were all dead-tired, I knew I could keep running all day.

[Early in the fourth quarter, the Celtics pushed their lead to 17 points as the Lakers went through a span where they missed 15 consecutive shots. But L.A. came back and cut the Celtics' lead to 103–102 with 1:17 left and Boston had the ball.]

DON NELSON: We just hit a wall. We had them by 17 points, and suddenly we couldn't make a shot and we couldn't stop them on defense. The clock was taking an eternity.

JOHN HAVLICEK: I was dribbling the ball with my left hand toward the middle of the court. I had beaten Keith Erickson, but he came from behind, poked my dribble away and the ball rolled right to Nelson at the foul line.

DON NELSON: The shot clock was about to run out, so I just picked the ball up and shot it. It went right off the heel of my hand, it had lousy rotation—it was the luckiest shot in basketball history. It banged against the back of the rim, went high into the air and dropped right in. That put us up by three points, and we weren't in trouble after that.

JOHN HAVLICEK: When a rebound goes up in the air like that, it usually comes down right or left. You can only hold your breath and hope against hope.

BUTCH VAN BREDA KOLFF: That was another of those incredible things. First, there was Sam Jones's shot in Game 4. Then Erickson knocked the ball away from Havlicek. Why didn't it go to one of our guys? Why did it roll right to Nelson, who was at the foul line? It could just as easily have gone to West. And then Nelson threw this thing up there and it bounced a mile high off the rim and dropped in. Listen, it was like Boston was fated to win.

WILT CHAMBERLAIN: Because of a coaching move, people will always ask "What if?" about that series. We were down by 9 points [with 5:13 left] when I came down with a rebound and banged my knee. It was really painful. They helped me off the court, and I just needed a breather for a second. Butch put in Mel Counts for me, but after a minute I said I was ready to come back in. Butch ignored me.

JOHN HAVLICEK: We were aware that Wilt went out, but we didn't know what the story was until later. We all figured he'd come back into the game and we were surprised when he didn't.

FRED SCHAUS: I wasn't on the bench, so I didn't know all the details. But sitting in the stands, we all were dying because Wilt was not on the floor. Of course you want the big guy in at the end of a game like that, but it was Butch's decision.

BUTCH VAN BREDA KOLFF: Wilt was hurting and you could see him limping. I put in Counts, he hit a couple of shots and we made a comeback, as we often did when Counts played for Wilt during the regular season. Wilt told me that he was okay, but I said we'd keep things as they were. He told me a second time he wanted to go back in, but I told Wilt the truth. I said, "We're playing better without you." It was nothing personal against Wilt. I simply decided to go with the guys who got us back into the game, and if Nelson hadn't made that shot, who knows what would have happened?

WILT CHAMBERLAIN: He was just trying to show he was the boss and that he could win a title without Wilt Chamberlain.

EARL STROM: In a sense, I respect Butch for making one of the dumbest moves any coach has ever made. You just don't try to win a title with Mel Counts when you have Wilt Chamberlain, but they hated each other so much. Butch was never one to compromise. He always was his own man and he would coach his own way.

What I remember very distinctly was Jerry West taking the final shot of the game. Bill Russell got the rebound, cradled it in his arms and winked at me as the buzzer sounded. He knew he had the championship in his hands. Then I saw Red Auerbach walking off the court with that big victory cigar in his mouth, while all those balloons were still stuck up in the ceiling of the Forum.

[Boston won 108–106. West had a triple-double with 42 points, 13 rebounds and 12 assists. He was named the MVP, the first time a player on the losing team was so honored. In his 43 minutes, Chamberlain shot 7-for-8, scored 18 points and had 27 rebounds. Mel Counts shot 4-for-13 and was called for traveling in the final two minutes. As usual, Russell went all 48 minutes and had 21 rebounds. In his final pro game, Sam Jones scored 24. This was the sixth time the Celtics beat West and Baylor in the Finals, the fourth time in a seventh game. It also was the fourth time Boston beat a Chamberlain team in a seven-game series. As for the balloons, the Lakers donated them to a children's hospital.]

The Aftermath

The 1969 championship was the end of Bill Russell's career, and the end of the Celtics' dynasty. In 1969–70, Henry Finkel was the starting Celtics center, backed up by Jim Barnes. The Celtics' record was 34-48, and they failed to make the playoffs under new coach Tom Heinsohn. In 1972, the Lakers finally won their title, beating New York in the Finals. Jerry West was still there. Wilt Chamberlain was the center while ex-Celtic Bill Sharman was the coach. Elgin Baylor played only nine games that season as his knees were shot. After the 1969 Finals, Butch Van Breda Kolff left the Lakers and went to Detroit.

LEIGH MONTVILLE: As the reporters were making their way to the dressing room after Game 7, we already knew that Van Breda Kolff was gone. He never said it, but from Butch's demeanor you could tell that he knew he was through. The only way he could have survived benching Wilt was to win.

BUTCH VAN BREDA KOLFF: It wasn't long after the playoffs that I told the Lakers I was quitting. I knew they would still win a lot of games, maybe even get back to the Finals. I loved Jerry West, Elgin and some of the other guys, but the game just wasn't fun. I figured I'd land on my feet somewhere, so I walked away.

People still talk about me not playing Wilt at the end of that game. It's ancient history. I get tired of explaining. I say it wasn't anything personal against Wilt, I was just trying to find the best guys to win the game. Why don't people talk about the 1968 playoffs when Philly was up 3–1 on Boston and blew it? Wilt was the center on that team, too. Why always my seventh game? Boston broke the hearts of a lot of teams.

Ask yourself why Russell has 11 championship rings and Wilt has only two. Wilt will say that Russell had great players around him. He did. But the players would leave, new ones would come in and Boston would still win. The one constant was Russell. He would adjust to any situation.

The difference between Russell and Wilt was this:

Russell would ask, "What do I need to do to make my teammates better?" Then he'd do it.

Wilt honestly thought the best way for his team to win was for him to be in the best possible setting. He'd ask, "What's the best situation for me?"

WILT CHAMBERLAIN: Butch never appreciated it, but I did sacrifice for him. When I came to the Lakers, Jerry West's scoring average went up, Elgin Baylor's went up. I was the only guy who scored less, and I did it by choice to try and fit in. Everywhere I went, people would say that I should take less shots. So I took less shots. But I was shooting 60 percent from the field. Why didn't someone say I should take more shots? I could have pressed the issue—saying, I shoot 60 percent, let me be more involved in the offense—but I didn't. That's why it hurts when people like Van Breda Kolff say I'm selfish.

[Actually, West averaged 26 points before and after Wilt's first season. Baylor dropped from 26 to 25 points. Chamberlain went from 24.8 points in Philadelphia to 20.5 points with the Lakers, and he took only 12 shots per game.]

LEIGH MONTVILLE: As time goes on, Wilt has been reinventing himself. He has all the statistics down cold and he makes his case well in his matchups against Russell. In another 20 years, Wilt will probably have turned himself into the NBA's Babe Ruth because of the sheer weight of all his numbers. He has the statistical momentum going for him. But it still doesn't account for the huge disparity in the number of titles he won compared to Russell.

Wilt was always bigger than his team. The 1969 Finals was typical. He was the story because he didn't play, overshadowing what the Celtics and Russell did. While we in the press were all concentrating on the Wilt/Van Breda Kolff controversy, no one had any idea this was Russell's last game.

DON NELSON: We never had any signal that Bill was quitting, but I remember being in the dressing room after we won the title and I heard Bill telling reporters, "In a game like that, they would have had to carry me out to get me off the floor." He was talking about Wilt, and I wondered why he'd say something like that about the big guy. Wilt and Russell always got along when they played against each other. I guess that should have been a tip that Russell was retiring, but I didn't realize it at the time.

LEIGH MONTVILLE: Will McDonough was also covering the playoffs for the *Globe* and he said to me, "Wait until all the writers are gone and when you can get Russell alone, ask him if it's his last game." I couldn't tell if McDonough knew something, or it was just a hunch. I believe he wanted me to ask the question because he wasn't on good terms with Russell. So I waited and waited. I wasn't looking forward to it, because you never knew what to expect from Russell. One day, you'd talk to him and he'd tell you things that came from the deepest corners of his soul. The next day, he'd see you and look at you as if you were a fly who just landed on his breakfast.

Finally, Russell and Jimmy Brown—the retired football star—were the only ones left in the dressing room. You could not find two more intimidating guys for a young reporter who was getting ready to ask a tough question.

I sort of stuttered and said, "Bill . . . well . . . are you going to retire now?"

Brown yelled, "Retire? How can you ask the man about retiring?

He just won a championship. You think he's going to retire? Let the man enjoy the championship."

Russell said something that had nothing to do with the question, and I crept away. That was the end of the retirement talk until the *Sports Illustrated* article.

WAYNE EMBRY: I was with Milwaukee during the 1968–69 season, but I had gotten close to Russell in my two years with him. We went out for dinner after a game and he said, "I think this is my last year." He said he was tired. I thought he might change his mind, but once he decided on something, he usually stuck with it.

BOB RYAN: The Celtics went into the college draft thinking that Russell would be back. That was why they picked a guard—JoJo White—instead of a big man. They thought they'd have Russell for another year. Actually, that turned out to be another stroke of Celtics luck because the big man they would have taken was Luther Rackley. Then a *Sports Illustrated* article came out later that summer with Bill announcing his retirement. He had sold his story, telling the magazine before the Celtics. No one wants to say it, especially Red, but Russell screwed the team by handling his retirement like that.

RED AUERBACH: Russell was still a great player, but it was the mental part that wore him out. Even after he told the magazine he was quitting, I said, "Hey, you can sell them another story called 'Why I Changed My Mind.' "

LARRY SIEGFRIED: Bill just ran out of gas, physically and mentally. He had played under pressure his whole life—the only thing acceptable was a championship, and winning a title was expected rather than appreciated. When you were a member of those Celtics teams, you were not supposed to have an off night. With Russell being a coach, it was a double burden on him; he couldn't have a bad night on the court or with his coaching. He spent his whole career like the top gunfighter with all these guys gunning for him, wanting to knock him off. Bill wanted to leave on top, and to leave on his own terms.

JOHN HAVLICEK: The guy I felt sorry for in those playoffs was Jerry West. He was so great, and he was absolutely devastated. As we came off the court, I went up to Jerry and said, "I love you and I just hope you get a championship. You deserve it as much as anyone who has ever played this game." He was too emotionally spent to say anything, but you could feel his absolute and total dejection about losing, and I hurt for him.

[West's reward as the Finals MVP was a car—a green car.]

JERRY WEST: Even though basketball was a team game, I constantly blamed myself for my team's failure. That was especially true in those playoffs. It was very hard for me to accept that even though I gave everything I had, it still wasn't enough because the facts are that we lost when we were better and we should have won because we were the better team.

LEIGH MONTVILLE: It was after that playoffs when Jerry West emerged as this tragic figure, such a wonderful, emotionally torn player whose team kept coming up short. He is still haunted by Boston and still won't set foot into Boston Garden because of all the terrible memories it brings back to him.

LARRY SIEGFRIED: It's a shame that Jerry couldn't have played for us, even just one season. We played basketball how you were supposed to, how Jerry played it. Even though we ran a lot and could score, the heart of our team was Russell and defense. All Russell cared about was winning, and that was true of the rest of us. We were a team that knew we needed each other, and could count on each other. Jerry would have loved that environment.

FRED SCHAUS: What told me so much about Russell was his foul shooting. For most of the game, you wanted him at the line. He was lucky to hit 60 percent. He had terrible form, sort of flinging the ball instead of shooting it. But down the stretch, he never missed a clutch free throw. At least he never did against us. Foul shooting was the weakest part of his game, yet it wasn't something he'd let defeat him.

[In their 108–106 loss in Game 7 to the Celtics in 1969, the Lakers shot a miserable 28-of-47 from the line, Chamberlain having a 4-of-13 nightmare.]

LEIGH MONTVILLE: To understand the Celtics, you had to see them at their party after the 1969 playoffs. One of the players invited me in, and it wasn't some huge, gala celebration. It was just guys sitting around a big hotel room, passing a bottle, telling stories and getting pleasantly smashed. They were just enjoying each other's company and what they had accomplished together. The odd thing was that Havlicek was getting drunk. This was a guy who was so neat that he hung his socks and underwear up on a hanger in his locker at the Garden. He believed in everything in its place, and a place for everything—the world's tidiest man. He seldom drank, but that night he got sort of smashed. I remember seeing him on the plane back from L.A. to Boston. He was really feeling it and was sitting there with a towel over his head.

WAYNE EMBRY: The Celtics like to keep their celebrations quiet and private. When we won the 1968 title, it was the same thing. No party was planned, the guys just got together and drank all night. Hey, we had a good time. I ended up drinking so much that I passed out in the hallway and someone helped me to a bed. It turned out to be Red's bed, but he had caught an early flight and his room was empty. Maybe because I came from another team and joined the Celtics at the end of my career, I appreciate them more than most people. What struck me the most was how the guys talked about the old days. You had a real sense of purpose and history being on those teams. You knew you were a part of greatness, and in the back of your mind you had a feeling that something like this might never happen again.

AFTERWORD

When Danny Biasone's 24-second brainstorm ushered in the modern era of pro basketball in 1954, there were only eight teams in the league and Boston had never won a title. Fifteen years later, the Celtics had 11 championships, and only two of those eight teams were in the same cities—Boston and New York.

Taking up new locations were the Philadelphia Warriors (in San Francisco, now Golden State), the Syracuse Nats (in Philadelphia), the Minneapolis Lakers (in Los Angeles), the Fort Wayne Pistons (in Detroit), the St. Louis Hawks (in Atlanta) and the Rochester Royals (in Cincinnati, now in Sacramento by way of Kansas City–Omaha).

The NBA had grown up and outgrown many of its cities. Once largely restricted to the Northeast, the league had stretched and expanded; the four teams added in 1967–68 and 1968–69 were in San Diego, Seattle, Phoenix and Milwaukee. The westward shift that started with the Lakers' move to Los Angeles in 1960 was a clear success.

With Russell in retirement and Chamberlain no longer the scoring machine he had been, the question was, who would be the next great big man? Even as the Celtics hoisted the last banner of the Russell era, the first of the "next Russells" or "next Chamberlains" was starting a career with the second-year Milwaukee Bucks. Kareem Abdul-Jabbar (then Lew Alcindor) came out of UCLA with three straight NCAA championships; in just two years the Bucks were NBA champions, giving Oscar Robertson his only title. But unlike his two famed predecessors, Kareem had no natural foil, no matched rival to test him and enlarge him in the public eye. He would go on to break Chamberlain's career scoring record, but he never captured the public imagination in the same dominating way.

What the 1950s and 1960s did for the NBA was to set a standard and a context. All future champions would be measured against the fast-breaking dominance of the Boston Celtics, whose run of titles is unequaled in professional sports. All big men would be judged by the

*lofty accomplishments of Wilt Chamberlain, who could score 100 points
and play 48 minutes night after night, and Bill Russell, who could be
considered the greatest ever without impressive scoring credentials.
Smaller men like Oscar Robertson, Jerry West, Bob Cousy, Sam Jones
and Lenny Wilkens demonstrated that the game need not belong to the
oversized. And Elgin Baylor tested the flight patterns for the generations
of leapers to come. These men brought basketball from Dolph Schayes's
set shots in Syracuse to Jerry West's deadly jumper in the Fabulous
Forum in Los Angeles. They brought the game to prominence, and by
their sheer talent they made sports fans take notice.*

And they still found time for some beers with the guys.

WILT CHAMBERLAIN: I watch today's players and I see all these 360-
degree dunks and other hot-dog moves and I think, "We never did that
garbage." Not because we couldn't do it. Don't you think that Wilt
Chamberlain or Elgin Baylor could do some incredible dunks? All you
had to do was see us in practice. But there was a code of conduct about
the games. Yes, you dunked, but you didn't dunk to show up an opponent. I mean, I see a guy doing this crazy dunk and his team is down
by 20 points. What the hell is that? You try that when I played and
your ass was on the floor because we'd take your legs out from under
you. Now, it is as if the game has a Globetrotters mentality, the show
being the main thing. In our day, the game was what mattered most.

JOHN VANAK: The NBA of the 1950s and 1960s was a game of giant
talents. On my wall, I have a picture of Wilt jumping against Russell
while Billy Cunningham leaned on John Havlicek as I threw up the
ball.

WILT CHAMBERLAIN: With only eight teams, that meant Bill Russell
and I squared off 11 times during the regular season—then came the
playoffs. I went against Johnny Kerr, Wayne Embry, Walt Bellamy and
Nate Thurmond 11 times a year. There were no expansion teams, no
nights off.

HOT ROD HUNDLEY: Many of today's players have more raw athletic
talent and are stronger than we were. Certainly Magic, Michael, Bird,
Karl Malone—these guys would be great in any era. But so would
Russell, Wilt, Oscar, West and Baylor. Also, there are about 300 NBA
players today compared to 80. I'm telling you this, there are guys in

the NBA today who wouldn't have gotten a second look from a pro team 30 years ago.

AL BIANCHI: Because there were so few jobs, you played. You played hurt, you played hung-over, you played when you were sick. You were afraid that if you didn't play, they'd cut you—and it wouldn't cost them a cent because no one had long-term guaranteed contracts—and they'd find someone to take your place.

DOLPH SCHAYES: The one area where the modern player is clearly superior to us is shooting. I shot 40 percent and that was considered terrific. Today, 40 percent gets you run out of the league. The good players are over 50 percent. I don't know if it's because they get more breakaway layups than we did. Perhaps a one-handed jumper is more accurate than our two-handed set shots.

NATE THURMOND: Kids today shoot better because they work at it harder. I signed for $15,000 as a first-round draft choice in 1963. No one went into pro ball with the idea being that if you could play a few years, you'd be set for life. Today, my first contract would have been worth $10 million. Kids in junior high and high school see the money paid to players. They realize the stakes are higher and they invest more of their time.

JERRY LUCAS: Coaching today is so much better than what we had. Between all the summer camps and clinics, kids are taught the proper shooting techniques right from the start. We taught ourselves to shoot, and a lot of us picked up bad habits. I also believe that weight training helps shooters. It makes them stronger and gives them more endurance. A tired shooter is a shooter who misses. But when we played, they told us that if we lifted weights, we'd mess up our shots. Coaches ordered us to stay out of the weight room.

CARL BRAUN: My biggest gripe about today's basketball is the total disregard for the rule book. They let players blatantly palm the ball and take that extra step on a drive. If they had let Elgin Baylor and Oscar Robertson have that advantage, you couldn't have guarded them with 20 guys. The old officials would not allow the palming and traveling we see today.

LARRY STAVERMAN: Pro coaching is so much better today. In our era, the best coaches were Red Auerbach, Fred Schaus and Alex Hannum. Most of the other guys were drinking buddies of the general manager and they never taught you a thing.

WILT CHAMBERLAIN: The debate about our era vs. today's players can go on and on, but the one thing that can't be disputed is that we built the game. Yet these players today don't know it. They don't know that Johnny Kerr and Wayne Embry were great centers, or that Guy Rodgers and Al Attles were super guards. They don't know what the first black players went through so they can experience the success, money and accolades they receive today. They should be aware of these things, but they're not. And worst of all, they don't care that we paid the dues so that the game could reach the level it has today.

BIBLIOGRAPHY

The following authors and books provided valuable background material:

- *On and Off the Court* by Red Auerbach and Joe Fitzgerald
- *Red Auerbach: An Autobiography* with Joe Fitzgerald
- *Heroes of Pro Basketball* by Phil Berger
- *Oscar Robertson* by Ira Berkow
- *Great Moments in Pro Basketball* by Bill Burns and Dave Wolf
- *Wilt* by Wilt Chamberlain and David Shaw
- *Basketball Is My Life* by Bob Cousy and Al Hirshberg
- *Cousy on the Celtic Mystique* by Bob Cousy and Bob Ryan
- *Hondo* by John Havlicek and Bob Ryan
- *Give 'Em the Hook* by Tom Heinsohn and Joe Fitzgerald
- *Tommy, Don't You Ever Smile?* by Tom Heinsohn
- *Red on Red* by Red Holzman and Harvey Frommer
- *Clown* by Hot Rod Hundley and Bill Libby
- *Bull Session* by Johnny Kerr
- *The NBA Finals* by Leonard Koppett
- *Twenty-four Seconds to Shoot* by Leonard Koppett
- *Strange but True Basketball Stories* by Howard Liss
- *Winnin' Times* by Scott Ostler and Steve Springer
- *From Cages to Jump Shots* by Robert Peterson
- *The Drive Within Me* by Bob Pettit and Bob Wolff
- *Go Up for Glory* by Bill Russell and William McSweeny
- *Second Wind* by Bill Russell and Taylor Branch
- *From Set Shot to Slam Dunk* by Charles Salzberg
- *Ever Green* by Dan Shaughnessy
- *Calling the Shots* by Earl Strom and Blaine Johnson
- *Mr. Clutch* by Jerry West and Bill Libby

INDEX

Fund Raising

by Alan R. Blackburn

I've written more than a million words—and every word was printed. I've retired early with a comfortable income, and still keep my hand in. Yet you have never heard of me—nor are you likely to in the popular press. I write for a lucrative hidden market: fund raising.

Nonprofit organizations—charities, hospitals, museums, colleges, community causes, and churches—constantly solicit money. These groups rely on professional writers—freelancers like yourself—to reach their prospective donors. Fund raising is a highly respectable pursuit approved by chambers of commerce and better business bureaus.

Here's how to find this market, write for it, and sell yourself to it.

First, make a list of philanthropic agencies and institutions in your city. You'll find them in the Yellow Pages under their categories, such as Social Service Organizations, Hospitals, Colleges and Schools, etc. Your best prospects are the smaller ones. Big ones use their own staffs or hire out-of-town fund-raising firms. But try them all.

Walk into the top person's office, be it the president of a college or the director of an agency. *Don't telephone in advance.* What? you ask. Isn't it better to make an appointment? Not when you're *selling* yourself. There are good reasons for walking in on your prospect unannounced: *You're there,* in person, right now—not waiting another month to suit the prospect's convenience. Telephoning in advance telegraphs your punch—your prospect ducks. Fortune favors the bold.

Tell the secretary you'd like to talk to the boss about fund raising and that you don't mind waiting. Chances are fifty-fifty you'll get in. If you don't, *then* make an appointment. At least the secretary knows you. Secretaries are important people. They open doors. Make friends with them.

I've called on scores of top executives this way. Fund raising is a continuing concern for the nonprofit executive. The agency *always* needs more money. Executives will shoehorn you in between appointments long enough to hear what you have to offer.

Once I walked into a natural history museum on the hunch they might be interested in a color-slide presentation of their work. The director himself saw me, and I left with a contract to run their annual fund-raising drive!

Walking in cold works. Try it and keep score.

Getting Experience

But before making such calls, you must have some experience in fund-raising writing. Here's a choice of ways to take the plunge:

Apprentice yourself to a local professional fund raiser. Usually there's a need for a part-time writer, and you'll earn while you learn. Look in the Yellow Pages under Fund Raising Organizations.

Take a crack at working for a nationwide fund-raising firm. To obtain a list of the big firms write to American Association of Fund-Raising Counsel, Inc., 25 W. 43rd St., New York NY 10036. These are top-of-the-line, and you'll get their fair-practice code. It will pay you to observe it. For cities outside your own, your library has the phone books.

Don't neglect your United Fund. It's your best source for data about the local fund-raising scene. It may even need a writer.

Volunteer for fund raising at a local church. There's hardly a church that doesn't raise money every year by letter appeal or personal canvass. Many use tested routines. Offer your services free. They'll be grateful, and you'll be paid many times over in experience.

Once I was asked to do a citywide cerebral palsy campaign, but they didn't have any money to pay me. That year I put out my best for them and charged them nothing. The campaign was a success; they became my paying clients for the next eight years.

I got my start as an apprentice. I was packing my bags on graduation from college when my former headmaster offered me a job as development secretary raising money for my prep school. It turned out that one of the school's board members was a top executive of one of the leading fund-raising firms in the US. I learned the basics from scratch and liked it. I stuck with fund raising and later set up my own firm, which ran successfully for twenty-five years. I estimate that 80 percent of the work I did was writing!

Fund raising is divided into two activities: organizing and writing. In a professional campaign, the key staff members are the campaign director (organization) and the publicity director (that's the writer).

The campaign director tangles with people and rarely has time for writing. This is where you come in. You write the campaign literature and publicity. But you don't *just* write, you research by reading reports, talking with staff, and saturating yourself with your client's work.

Limits of Sentimentality

To get the hang of this kind of writing, visit institutions in your city. Pick up their fund-raising publications. Study each piece—it will tell you a lot about the way to write for a campaign. Ask yourself if you can do as well or better.

Now, what's special about writing for this market? It is *appeal* writing—a mixture of facts and emotion. Your words must persuade people to volunteer their services or write out a check.

Make no mistake about it: Fund raising demands quality writing. It will test all the skill you've acquired in nonfiction *and* fiction techniques.

When I wrote a brochure for the Society for Crippled Children to raise money for a new building, I burrowed through piles of technical material and talked with staff. I was searching for an angle. Suddenly there it was! Building specifications called for an entrance door that would open automatically as crippled children wheeled up to it (this was back when such doors were not common). The architect referred to it casually as a ''magic door.'' I had my lead.

Here's what I wrote for the first page under a picture of the door:

Help them open the magic door* to a brighter day

This is the magic door—entrance to the new Heman Rehabilitation Institute on Cleveland's East Side.

Across this threshold thousands of handicapped children will step into a world of hope.

We ask you to help us raise $500,000 to complete and equip this vitally needed rehabilitation center.

This is the first and only capital campaign for the Society for Crippled Children since its founding in 1940.

*There actually is a magic door. It swings open by itself when a child approaches.

(Incidentally, this campaign went over its goal by $200,000.)

Put human beings at the center of your fund-raising writing. Be absolutely honest and sincere. But keep emotion under control. Sentimentality turns people off if you are approaching them for money. Your sober handling of human distress will touch the heart and release that inner urge to help others in trouble.

Here's an example from my brochure for a psychiatric clinic for emotionally disturbed children:

A six-year-old boy is unable to sleep the night through. Often his distraught parents find him wandering through the dark rooms of his home, unable to tell where he is. Shy with other children, he keeps on the fringe of their groups, prefers to play alone. For long periods he will rock in a chair, silent. Neighbors call him the "strange one." Secretly his parents fear that he may be "crazy." This child is *not* crazy; he's emotionally disturbed. The Guidance Center is bringing him back to normal through therapy.

Campaign Materials

You'll do the *campaign brochure* first because it contains all the data and appeal themes. It's the sourcebook for the rest of the campaign literature.

Use lots of photographs. Twenty is not too many for a sixteen-page brochure. You must have pix that shout the story out loud. To show just how one client agency helped children and adults handicapped by cerebral palsy I spent a day snapping pictures of children turning doorknobs, putting on their coats, playing drums, trying to hold a pencil, walking in bright sunshine, smiling—workers in the background. Out of sixty candid snaps, I got twenty that told it all.

You can hire a talented pro to do this work for you. But why not become your own top-notch photographer? It's legitimate to charge your client the going rate. If you are already a camera buff, the opportunities are limitless. But it isn't all that hard to learn photography. Don't sweat trying for texture—just get the focus, light, and composition right. Go for close-ups—freckles and eyelashes. Invest in a quality camera. Buy a how-to pamphlet (Eastman Kodak's are grade-A). In six months of picture taking, my camera paid for itself.

Photos need captions—short word gems. Tell the readers what they can't know. For example, "Jane stands proudly on her artificial leg."

You'll prepare *agendas*. Campaign directors love you when you take this burden off their backs. Meetings must produce action; otherwise